T0331162

Generation Z

No other generation in history has received as much coverage as the Millennial generation. Yet, Generation Z is comprised of our youth and young adults today and has received very little attention comparatively. Those in Generation Z are among our youngest consumers, students, colleagues, constituents, voters, and neighbors. Being able to better understand who they are and how they see the world can be helpful in effectively working with, teaching, supervising, and leading them.

Generation Z: A Century in the Making offers insight into nearly every aspect of the lives of those in Generation Z, including a focus on their career aspirations, religious beliefs and practices, entertainment and hobbies, social concerns, relationships with friends and family, health and wellness, money management, civic engagement, communication styles, political ideologies, technology use, and educational preferences.

Drawing from an unprecedented number of research studies, this is the authoritative defining work on Generation Z that market researchers, consumer behavior specialists, and employers sorely need – and it is a fascinating read for anyone interested in the sociology of generations.

Corey Seemiller is a faculty member in the Department of Leadership Studies in Education and Organizations at Wright State University. She is the author of numerous articles and books, including *The Student Leadership Competencies Guidebook*, *Generation Z Goes to College*, and *Generation Z Leads*.

Meghan Grace is a researcher, consultant, and speaker. She is the co-author of *Generation Z Goes to College* and *Generation Z Leads*.

Generation Z

A Century in the Making

Corey Seemiller and
Meghan Grace

Routledge
Taylor & Francis Group

LONDON AND NEW YORK

First published 2019
by Routledge
2 Park Square, Milton Park, Abingdon, Oxon OX14 4RN

and by Routledge
52 Vanderbilt Avenue, New York, NY 10017

Routledge is an imprint of the Taylor & Francis Group, an informa business

British Library Cataloguing-in-Publication Data
A catalog record for this book has been requested

Library of Congress Cataloging-in-Publication Data
A catalog record for this book has been requested

ISBN: 978-1-138-33731-2 (hbk)

Typeset in Goudy
by Apex CoVantage, LLC

Visit the eResources: www.routledge.com/9781138337312

Corey: I dedicate this book to my Generation Z daughter who is the most remarkable and amazing person I know. Thank you for inspiring me to write about your generation.

Meghan: To The Well Coffeehouse in Nashville, TN – Thank you for being a wonderful place to write this book, but even more for making a difference by providing clean drinking water to people around the world with the proceeds of each cup of coffee you sell. www.wellcoffeehouse.com

Contents

Authors   xii

Preface   xiii

Introduction   xviii

Understanding generations   **1**

1   Who came before Z?   3
    The G.I. Generation: Black Thursday, battlefields, and the suburbs
    The Silent Generation: Crisis to caution
    Baby Boomers: Economic prosperity, protests, and "peace and love"
    Generation X: I want my MTV and family time
    Millennials: The socially connected industry disruptors

2   Reflection on a century   16
    Why look at the G.I. Generation and Generation Z?
    The political climate of G.I. and Z
    The economic landscape of G.I. and Z
    Social issues influencing G.I. and Z
    Uniquely Generation Z
    Catalyst for change

3   Who is Generation Z?   28
    Characteristics of the cohort
    Values
    Motivations

Navigating the digital and physical world 37

4 Technology 39
Technology today
Navigating life – physically and digitally
Information and entertainment
Social connection
Online all the time

5 Communication 56
Many micro-conversations
Visual communication
Evolving communication etiquette
How Generation Z communicates

6 Entertainment 67
Hobbies
Popular culture

7 Money 81
The economic landscape
The "American Dream"
Generation Z's relationship with money
Banks
Saving and spending

Relationships 99

8 Family 101
Parenting trends
The new normal is nuclear no more
X raising Z
From Millennials to Alphas: Sibling relationships
Generation Z's perspective on family

9 Friends and peers 113
World Wide Web of friends
Making friends
Maintaining friendships
Foes, fallouts, and feeling alone

10 Romance 123
Sliding into the DMs: How Generation Z starts relationships
#BAE: Generation Z in a relationship
It's complicated: Ending relationships
"Hanging out" and hooking up

Mind, body, and spirit

Mind, body, and spirit   **133**

11   Physical well-being   135
Illnesses and diseases
Healthy eating and sustainable foods
Getting that kick: Soda, coffee, and energy drinks
Calories and portion sizes
Sedentary lifestyles and getting to 10,000 steps
Lack of sleep
Future of medicine

12   Mental health   145
A worried generation
Realism over optimism
Happy?
All stressed out
High rates of anxiety and depression
Factors contributing to mental health
Counseling and support services

13   Risky behaviors   157
Smoking
Drugs
Booze and binging
Sexual activity

14   Religion and spirituality   166
The religious
Christianity
Catholicism
The Church of Jesus Christ of Latter-day Saints
Other world religions
Interfaith
The unaffiliated
Importance of religion
The future of organized religion

Life and career preparation   **187**

15   Education   189
The K–12 experience
Higher education landscape

16   Learning   203
Information literacy in the digital world
Applied and practical learning

Moving from group to self-learning
Learning in an era of curated identities
Show me first and then let me try
Video-based learning
Digital distractions or learning aids?
Learning environments
Passionate and caring educators

17 Career aspirations   213
Future landscape of work
What Generation Z wants
Try it before you buy it

18 In the workplace   227
The ideal job candidate: Is it Generation Z?
Landing the job
Creating careers, not seeking jobs
Generation Z's career identities
Working with other generations

Making a difference   **247**

19 Societal concerns   249
Affordable, quality education
Breaking down walls, not building them
Inclusion and equality
Getting a J.O.B.
Affording life
A thriving and sustainable planet
Feeling safe and secure
Affordable and comprehensive healthcare

20 Politics   262
Political ideologies and Generation Z
Voter turnout
Candidate of choice in 2016
Why aren't they voting?

21 Civic engagement and social change   274
Trends in Generation Z civic engagement
Getting informed and forming opinions
Changing hearts and minds
Volunteerism
Community leadership roles
Military service

Litigation
Activism
Raising and spending money
Social innovation

22 The future and legacy of Generation Z   297
What lies ahead
Issues of the future
Generation Z's legacy

Additional resources   313
Afterword: The challenge of generational research
(available at www.routledge.com/9781138337312)
Appendix: Study methodologies
References
Website

Index   314

Authors

· ·

Corey Seemiller is the co-author of *Generation Z Goes to College*, which aims to prepare college administrators and educators for a new generation of college students. She is also the co-author of *Generation Z Leads*, a practical implementation guide for educators in designing meaningful leadership development experiences for Generation Z college students. Her TED Talk on Generation Z at TEDxDayton showcased how Generation Z plans to make a difference in the world. Dr. Seemiller received a bachelor's degree in Communication, a master's degree in Educational Leadership, and a Ph.D. in Higher Education. She has worked in higher education for more than 20 years – and for the last several, directly with Generation Z students. She serves as a faculty member in the Department of Leadership Studies in Education and Organizations at Wright State University teaching undergraduate courses in organizational leadership and graduate courses in leadership development. Dr. Seemiller is also the author of *The Student Leadership Competencies Guidebook* and associated measurements and tools to help educators develop intentional curriculum that enhances leadership competency development.

Meghan Grace is the co-author of *Generation Z Goes to College* and *Generation Z Leads*. She is an associate with Plaid, LLC where she delivers presentations on Generation Z research and works with clients to develop individual and organizational strategies to effectively educate, engage, and work with members of Generation Z. Meghan has diverse experience working in higher education and student affairs with a background in program design and management, Greek organizations, leadership development, event planning, curriculum design, and research and assessment. Meghan holds her undergraduate degree in communication studies from Chapman University and completed her master's degree in higher education at the University of Arizona.

Preface

· ·

Our Generation Z journey began during the summer of 2013 as we witnessed yet another incoming first-year class attend our university's summer orientation program. But, 2013 was different – well the students were different. While recruiting for our student leadership programs, as we did each year, we noticed that this cohort of students seemed more engaged in talking with us about involvement, even without their parents encouraging them to do so. And they asked questions about how their participation in our programs could help them engage in social change work, quite different from the resume building and making friends questions we had during previous summers. Knowing that the students seemed different, we needed to figure out what might be going on. What we came across was remarkable – with a little online investigation, we learned that the post-Millennial generation, Generation Z, was entering into young adulthood, with the oldest coming to college that very year. In order to learn more about this generation completely unfamiliar to us, we spent that school year reading every market research report we could get our hands on about this emerging generation of young adults. After a year of attempting to translate these reports to a higher education context, we decided to conduct our own study, which launched in the fall semester in 2014. The data we got back was fascinating, especially responses to the open-ended questions. We then decided to write our first book, *Generation Z Goes to College*.

Since then, we have written two more books, *Generation Z Leads* and this book, along with several scholarly articles. Our more recent publications have incorporated findings from our latest research, the Generation Z Stories Study, which included an analysis of responses to seven open-ended questions from Generation Z college students from 50 colleges and universities. We have also read, read, and read even more – including findings from numerous other studies, market research reports, books, and scholarly articles from other generational authors, and even online pop culture articles. To have a solid grasp of Generation Z, we needed to expand beyond our own research and perspectives to get a more holistic view of this generation.

This journey into better understanding Generation Z has been a fascinating one. What started as a simple interest in a new cohort of college students has turned into a quest for more knowledge to answer the question, "Who is

Generation Z?" This book is our effort to include what we know thus far about this generation. But, before we delve into writing about Generation Z, we wanted to take a moment to share a little about us – the Gen Xer and Millennial who wrote this book.

Corey, the Gen Xer

The year was 1973 when I was born – a Gen Xer through and through. My parents tell me that they named me Corey to help me better navigate a male-dominated world. Even then, they knew that my name might offer me opportunities that others with more female-associated names might not have.

During my birth year of 1973, while my parents were dancing to the Rolling Stones and Diana Ross, the U.S. ended participation in the Vietnam War, the Supreme Court ruled on *Roe v. Wade*, the Watergate scandal was in full force, and Billie Jean King took on Bobby Riggs to win the epic tennis match, the Battle of the Sexes.[1] My early childhood was situated in the 1970s where *Scooby-Doo* and *Little House on the Prairie* were staples on the TV set. While this era was in the middle of the Cold War, it was another war that captured the attention of many people during that time – Star Wars. We loved our space themes and drank our orange Tang. The 70s were a time when car seats were rare, houses were filled with our parents' cigarette smoke, and anyone could walk up to the gate at the airport to greet incoming passengers from their Pan Am flight.

Although I was born in the 70s, I consider myself an 80s kid – you couldn't have enough fluorescent jelly bracelets or banana clips. Michael Jackson and Madonna were icons, and we looked to Molly Ringwald and John Cusack to help us find our way. But, growing up in the 80s was a paradox. In one sense, I felt safe and comforted at school and at home as the Smurfs kept me company on the weekends, and the Girl Scouts kept me busy selling cookies door-to-door. There were no metal detectors in schools, and kids could play outside without an adult as long as they remembered to be home in time for dinner.

While we Gen Xers enjoyed our independence and felt fairly safe from the world's woes, we were not oblivious. I remember not being allowed to take Tylenol or other medicines for a while until the poisonings stopped, breaking Halloween candy into tiny pieces to make sure there were no blades or needles inside, and never talking to strangers . . . especially ones in vans. Even at my young age, I knew who Adam Walsh was, a young boy around my age who went missing from a mall and later found dead. Although we still played outside and enjoyed our freedoms, we were always looking over our shoulders to make sure we were safe.

Of everything I remember from the 80s, there is one moment that stands out to me and likely for many in Generation X – the explosion of the Challenger Space Shuttle. I was living in Florida at the time where following space shuttle launches was like following the NFL game schedule. The day of the Challenger explosion, I was at school. We watched the event on television, over and over again. I can still see the images in my head. As a kid, I wasn't sure how to process such a devastating tragedy and am not sure that I ever really did. More than 25 years later, when the space shuttle, Endeavour, was retired in California, I stood outside to watch as it passed through Tucson, Arizona, where I was living. I gathered around with my younger students and colleagues as they cheered and celebrated the space program. But for me, that moment brought back memories of the Challenger tragedy and the many who had sacrificed for scientific discovery.

By the time the 90s came around, I was in high school. I remember watching Channel 1 (the national school news channel) and learning about the Gulf War. As I was preparing to go off to college, I had male friends turning 18 that feared they were going to be sent to war. Thankfully, there was never a draft. But, many in my generation did end up serving during the Gulf War and continued their military service through 9/11. While we weren't a war generation, we certainly did have Gen Xers who served in combat.

During the early 90s, I was in college listening to grunge music and going to the actual library to do homework. I was among the majority of my friends to earn a four-year degree in four years and left college with zero debt because tuition was so low. During college, I voted in my first election – Clinton vs. Bush in 1992. I was thrilled to be able to vote but was deeply saddened when I was issued a provisional ballot because I couldn't get to my assigned precinct. I actually cried that day after I voted, worried that my provisional ballot wouldn't count.

As I graduated college in 1995, a lot was happening. Amazon, eBay, Match. com, and Craigslist were launched.[2] But, 1995 wasn't only about technology. That was the year of the Oklahoma City Bombing and OJ Simpson trial. But, it was also the first year of the birth of Generation Z.

While I can reminisce about all the fun childhood memories I had like playing in my clubhouse, riding my bike, sleepovers with friends, and school dances, it is many of these larger historical moments that have shaped my life . . . and thus shape the way I parent my Generation Z daughter. I have learned to carry on the legacy my parents intended with my name to address injustice. I have tried to provide my daughter the autonomy to live and learn while keeping a watchful eye out for danger. And I try to balance informing her of the realities of the world while protecting her for just a little while longer.

As my childhood and young adulthood have come and gone, I play an important role with Generation Z. First, I must leave the world better off than when I arrived, working toward making the Earth sustainable for the future, eliminating injustice, contributing to a stable economy, and helping our society guarantee that all people are healthy, safe, and secure. I know that I alone will not be able to do these things . . . yet I can do my part and I should do my part. Finally, though, I must give everything I have to parenting my Generation Z daughter. I need to support her, guide her, challenge her, and love her so she is prepared to make the world an even better place for generations to come.

Meghan, the Millennial

Born in 1990, I can proudly say that I'm a 90s kid. Back-to-school shopping was not complete without picking out my JanSport backpack and filling it with Lisa Frank folders and every color gel pen. In school, I lived for computer class where we raced to finish the Oregon Trail (if our wagon didn't sink crossing a river), and Microsoft Office became second nature. We also had plenty of time set aside for recess to play Red Rover, P.E. to play capture the flag, music class to learn Hot Cross Buns on the recorder, and art class to make paper mâché. The highlight of my Friday night was going with my dad to Blockbuster Video to pick out a movie for the weekend. And I had heated debates with friends over hard-hitting topics of Backstreet Boys vs. N*SYNC and if Disney Channel was better than Nickelodeon. Making sure my Walkman CD player had a new set of batteries was essential before going on any family road trip to make sure I could listen to the burned CD I thoughtfully curated.

My first Internet experiences included the sound of the AOL dial-up tone as I patiently waited to log into a world that allowed me to connect with my friends through Instant Messenger. My first experience learning HTML coding and using a social media site was on Myspace, where I spent hours making sure the fonts and colors were just right and I wasn't offending anyone with my Top 8 friend selections. As I prepared to graduate from high school, my older friends in college clued me into this new site called Facebook, and I couldn't wait to get my college-associated email address so I could set up my profile.

Growing up, I had no shortage of after-school activities to fill my time. My parents were very involved and beyond supportive of my extracurricular activities and academic pursuits. They kept me focused on my future and made sure I was prepared for college. When I started college in 2008, I knew I was going to have to take out student loans to pay for school but didn't understand how much and just how long it would take to actually pay back those loans. I also wasn't completely sure of my career plans but assumed I had time to figure that out later. Under my young Millennial optimism, I was hopeful that paying off my student loans would be easy after I started my career but found that my debt would be with me much longer than I anticipated. I was fortunate to go to graduate school and find employment in my field, but many of my peers experienced having to work jobs for which they were overeducated and underpaid. While generations before mine saw buying a home or car as a first major financial milestone, getting out of personal or educational debt is something many in my generation pine after even today.

There are a few moments from my childhood and adolescence that I'll never forget. I was in third grade when the Columbine shooting occurred. I'll never forget my teacher explaining to us what happened and trying to understand at the age of nine why someone would do that to other students or let that happen in their school. A place I had always felt was fun and safe suddenly made me feel a little uneasy. A few years later, I was in the 6th grade when 9/11 happened. I vividly remember waking up and knowing something was wrong as I heard my mom speaking on the phone in a concerned voice. We lived on the West Coast and my oldest brother had been driving near the Pentagon that morning. My mom let me turn on the television to watch the news and see what had happened, which we never did before school. When I got to school that day, the news was still being played. Usually having the TV on in class meant we were watching a movie for a lesson or because it was raining. The TV stayed on all day, and my teacher tried to help his class of 11 year-olds grapple with what happened as the news came out. These events stand out to me as being pivotal to many in my generation in how we reflect on the era in which we grew up.

Today, I joke that I was a 90s kid and grew up to be a walking, talking Millennial stereotype. My "helicopter" parents have become some of my closest friends. I care far more about investing in an experience, like traveling or going to a concert, rather than buying more stuff. I identify as a digital "nomad" and feel comfortable learning new technology and social media platforms. As a young adult and professional, I've experienced a fair share of discussion and criticism about my own generation. It sometimes feels like people's gut reaction to the word "Millennial" is to roll their eyes. But I never understood the reason until I started researching generations. It's easy to see a group of people doing something different from you and automatically write that off as wrong and eye-roll worthy. My reaction to Generation Z is exactly the opposite of eye rolling. I work to better understand Generation Z and learn what makes them unique. I'm not afraid of what makes them different from me, my Millennial peers, and those in older generations. Instead, I'm fascinated with learning more about who they are. I've been a researcher, interviewer, instructor, facilitator, supervisor, advisor, mentor, friend, babysitter, and aunt to members of this generational cohort. And, in every one of these settings in which I get to hang out with Generation Z, I witness something that makes this generation awesomely unique and makes me hopeful for the future.

Notes

1 The People History. (2018). *What happened in 1973: Important news and events, key technology and popular culture*. Retrieved from www.thepeoplehistory.com/1973.html
2 Pew Research Center. (2018b). *World wide web timeline*. Retrieved from www.pewinternet.org/2014/03/11/world-wide-web-timeline/

Introduction

••

It was 1995. Michael Jordan came back from retirement. The OJ Simpson case was at its peak. More than 150 people were killed during the Oklahoma City Bombing. Mary-Kate and Ashley Olsen played Michelle Tanner for last time as *Full House* aired its final episode. The Grateful Dead played their last show together. We said goodbye to the singer Selena far too soon. Alicia Silverstone played Cher Horowitz in *Clueless*, popularizing the iconic term "As If!" Microsoft released Windows 95. The Internet was commercialized. Companies like Amazon, Craigslist, eBay, Match.com, and MSN were created.

Among the many things that happened in 1995, the first members of Generation Z were born. While the events happening at the time of their birth are important, this book focuses on how both historical and contemporary societal events have been critical in shaping who Generation Z is today and who they will be tomorrow. In the Ernst & Young report titled *The Rise of Gen Z: New Challenges for Retailers*, Marcie Merriman points out that "Gen Z, like all generations, was borne from disruption. Today, the very goal of businesses and political groups – not just technology companies – is to disrupt the status quo, to change how people think and live."[1] This book offers insight into what we know about Generation Z and how we might expect this generation, as Merriman puts it, to disrupt the status quo and make a difference.

Birth Years

A generation can be defined as "the entire body of individuals born and living at about the same time."[2] Typically, generations span between 14 and 20 years, enough time to move from one life stage to the next. Generational researchers, William Strauss and Neil Howe, have traced back generations in the U.S. all the way to 1734 with the Awakening Generation.[3] In using their framework, Generation Z would be the fifteenth documented generation in U.S. history.[4] While Strauss and Howe have defined specific generational birth ranges, many other researchers, marketers, and polling agencies use others. In many cases, though, the start and/or end dates put forth by different entities are usually only off from each other by 1 to 2 years, leaving the remaining years in the middle the same. The dates selected for generational ranges usually reflect important societal and cultural issues of the time, thus there appears to be far more agreement in general on the overall birth year ranges even if the specifics may be slightly different.

In this book, we have used the birth years of 1995 to 2010 to frame Generation Z. We use the start date of 1995 for two reasons. First, in looking at significant societal events, those born in 1995 were only in Kindergarten when 9/11 happened. This doesn't mean that first-grade Millennials remember the details of the event, but somewhere around that time period, a post-9/11 generation began. The other reason we begin with 1995 is that during our initial investigation into Generation Z in 2013 and 2014, 1995 was a commonly referenced start year in many market research reports.

By the time we decided to conduct our own study and write our first book, we confirmed the start date of 1995 with the one put forth by Sparks & Honey in *Meet Generation Z: Forget Everything You Learned About Millennials* in 2014.[5] The Sparks & Honey report was one of the first comprehensive works available on Generation Z at the time and offered a meaningful starting place for engaging in generational research. We recognize, however, that researchers have put Generation Z's birth year range anywhere from starting at 1995, 1996, or 1997 and ending at 2010, 2012, and even with no end date. A small number have even put the start date after 2000. For example, the Pew Research Center designated 1997 as their start year for Generation Z due to the context of society around that time, advancement of technology, and presentation of differences with the Millennial generation.[6] However, those at Pew recognize the variance in the birth year range in saying, "Pew Research Center is not the first to draw an analytical line between Millennials and the generation to follow them, and many have offered well-reasoned arguments for drawing that line a few years earlier or later than where we have."[7] And, with no official group of researchers who gather to determine the start and end of generations, generational birth ranges end up being somewhat elastic.

On the cusp and micro-generations

Along with elasticity between generational cohorts, there is also some variance within generations. With generational birth ranges spanning 15 to 20 years, the experiences of the oldest and youngest members of a generation can be very different. In addition, the oldest may look a bit like the generation that came before them and the youngest may exhibit similarities to the following generation. The individuals who are born towards the beginning or end of a generational birth range are called cuspers, as they are on the cusp of two adjacent generations. The oldest members of Generation Z may exhibit some Millennial characteristics and behaviors just as the very youngest of Generation Z may pass on some of their traits to the oldest in the generation following them – Generation Alpha. And, even young Millennials may have some similarities with Generation Z.

Micro-generations can either be smaller groupings within a larger generation, typically either the older or younger segment, or a group comprised of those at the end of one generation and those at the beginning of the next. For example, Merriam-Webster uses the term "Xennial" to refer to the group of cuspers of younger Gen Xers and older Millennials who may share some similarities with each other.[8] In the case of Generation Z, the term "Big Z" refers to the oldest in Generation Z (born 1995 through 2002) and "Little Z" refers to the youngest members (born 2003 through 2010). Big Zs and Little Zs may have slightly different perspectives and behaviors based on when they were born. Big Zs might remember a time before smartphones and mobile devices, but Little Z's have likely only known them to be available and widely used. Because Little Zs are still quite young, there is less research on their perspectives and behaviors in relation to many of the topics covered in this book. Thus, we have chosen to focus primarily on Big Zs as they enter into young adulthood.

The quest for a name

Similar to identifying an agreed-upon birth year range, there is no group that officially designates the name of each generation. For our work, we utilize the name Generation Z for a few reasons. First, this cohort follows Generation Y (better known as Millennials) and before them, Generation X. It makes sense alphabetically that this generation assumed the name Generation Z. However, this generation has also been referred to by a variety of other names[9] including iGen, Digital Natives, the Homeland generation, Post-Millennials, Plurals, Founders, and the list could go on.[10] iGen and Digital Natives allude to the integration of technology in seemingly all aspects of their lives. The Homeland generation speaks to the events of 9/11 and its influence in shaping this generation. The Founders was put forth by MTV with the prediction that Generation Z will rebuild our society following in the footsteps of the labeled-as-disruptive Millennials.[11]

The New York Times also attempted to name this cohort by digitally crowdsourcing ideas through Facebook, Twitter, and email from more than 3,000 people, including members of both Generation Z and other generations.[12] While crowdsourcing might not offer the most scientifically sound methodology, it produced interesting results for consideration. Some suggested not using a name at all, which isn't surprising coming from a generation that challenges labels. Others suggested the Hopeful Generation, the Anxious Generation, or the Meme Generation. One promising name that was suggested by several people was the Delta Generation, a reference to the math term for change. This fits nicely with the characteristics of this generation in seeing themselves as change agents. Even in their attempts to generate alternate names, *The New York Times* reported that a significant minority of members of this generational cohort had grown comfortable with the name Generation Z.[13] In addition, a study by Stillman and Stillman found that 77 percent of Generation Z respondents either liked the name, Generation Z, or simply didn't have a preference.[14] Because of the overwhelming prominence and use of the name Generation Z both by others as well as members of Generation Z themselves, we refer to the generational cohort born from 1995 through 2010 as Generation Z.

Understanding generational research

Let's face it: People love talking about generations.[15] Doing so helps us better understand our reality and make sense of those who are different from us. Simply through observations, conversations, and experiences, it's easy to see that each generation is marked by its members' own unique set of characteristics and perspectives, otherwise known as peer personality. Political, social, economic, and technological events, circumstances, and advances can have a profound effect on a generation's peer personality as individuals respond and react to the world around them. So, by understanding historical and contemporary contexts, we can better comprehend and appreciate why individuals in a generational cohort may act and think in specific ways.

Lifecycle, cohort, and period effects

In concert with looking at the political, social, economic, and technological landscape, we must also pay attention to lifecycle, cohort, and period effects of societal events and the influence they have on generational cohorts. Lifecycle, or age, effect refers to the difference of perspectives of an event based on age or where a group is at during their lifecycle.[16] How young adults react to a situation will likely be very different to the reactions of middle-aged adults based on life stage. The Pew Research Center highlights voting as an example of lifecycle effect, pointing out that older generations are more likely to vote than younger generations.[17] However, younger generations grow into voting. Findings from the General Social Survey show that only 38 percent of the population of 18 to 34 year-olds voted in the 1996 election.[18] In the 2012 election when this same group was between the ages of 34 and 50, voting participation rose to 61 percent. These trends go back even further, though. In 1968, 33 percent of the population of 18 to 34 year-olds voted. In 2012, by the time this age group was between 62 and 78, 83 percent voted in the election.

Experiencing an event, circumstance, or societal force regardless of age is referred to as a period effect.[19] Wars, economic shifts, and social movements often serve as examples of period effects and tend to have a long-lasting influence regardless of age or generational cohort. Consider the stock market crash, the attack on Pearl Harbor, or the shooting of JFK. Those too young to remember or who were born after these events only know the details from their history books. Pop culture can also reflect period effects. For example, when the first *Star Wars* movie was released in the 1970s, it was a blockbuster sensation. The generations alive during that period of time had a cinema experience on the big screen that could not be captured with video rentals or re-releases. And seeing thousands of kids dressed like their favorite *Star Wars* characters for Halloween served as both a testament to the impact of the film and a rite of passage for many young people at the time.

The cohort effect explains how generational cohort differences develop as a result of a group's unique place in time in witnessing a historical or societal event.[20] When analyzing a generation through the lens of the cohort effect, it is important to pay attention to the events taking place in the formative years of adolescence and young adulthood. What occurs during those years is likely to influence the perspectives and attitudes of that cohort because members are developing a deeper and wider worldview. Consider the impact that experiencing the Great Depression had on adolescents at the time and how that experience influenced the definition of success and stability as those children entered adulthood. After the Depression and World War II, that generation valued financial stability and security as young adults raising families.[21] With looking at cohorts, we can analyze generations at specific times in their lives – for example, comparing Millennials when they were 18 to 21 year-old college students to those in Generation Z when they were the same age.

Cultural context

Cultural context plays a significant role in the shaping of perspectives and experiences of the people being studied. With so many diverse countries having such rich histories, the characteristics and perspectives of those in Generation Z may be different based on where they live. A global experience or event likely holds different significance depending on the country. Consider that the Great Recession, while global in nature, likely affected those in the U.S. who lost their homes due to the subprime mortgage crisis[22] differently than it affected those in Greece whose government engaged in a financial bailout.[23] And the Brexit vote, while critical across the world, has likely had a different impact on those in the UK whose ways of life are directly affected than on those in China who are thousands of miles from the day-to-day impact. In addition, culturally specific events and situations, such as the implementation of particular laws and policies, governmental structures, cultural norms, and demographic makeup of the population, offer vastly diverse contexts in which our Generation Z youth are being raised. For example, growing up in Pakistan, Bolivia, Switzerland, or Vietnam likely all provide incredibly different experiences and cultural contexts that affect the characteristics and perspectives of members of Generation Z in each of those countries. In the case of this book, it is critical to note that much of the research is from the U.S. and the context of the writing is situated in U.S. history and contemporary culture. Thus, while there may be applicability in understanding Generation Z in a global context, this book is highly reflective of the U.S.

Influence of older generations

We must also pay attention to the influence of prior generations in shaping the society in which younger generations come of age. Parental generations can pass down thoughts, characteristics, and perspectives that play a role in how younger generations come to understand the world around them. Similar to the passing down of biological DNA from parent to offspring, older generations can pass down their social DNA to their younger counterparts. For example, parents often tend to raise their kids with the same belief systems as their own; beliefs that are based on the parent's worldview and serve as a factor in the child's development of their own worldview.[24] We will go further in depth about Generation Z's parents later in the book, but understanding their parents can help us make more sense of the perspectives and behaviors of Generation Z.

Beyond parents, older generations have played a role in shaping the context of future generations in that they have been the ones to make political decisions that have had long-lasting effects. They have also been the ones to invent the technology that has impacted societal functioning as well as laid the groundwork for further innovation today. And their perspectives have created the social issues younger generations need to grapple with. Consider the iPhone. This powerful piece of technology was created by a Baby Boomer, but completely changed the way younger generations communicate and navigate life today. We can also look at this in terms of how current actions by older generations can impact future generations. For example, the way the U.S. government approaches issues related to climate change today will impact how younger generations will need to respond in the future. We cannot underestimate the impact that older generations have in creating the environment in which younger generations make sense of the world, develop beliefs, and behave in response to that environment.

Looking at themes

Finally, as we seek to understand generations, we have to recognize that generational research often focuses on themes that align with a group of people based on age demographics. Like race, gender, religion, and other groups, groupings by age can aid in our overall understanding of why people who share a particular demographic grouping might behave in certain ways. But, we cannot forget that generational themes are just that: Themes. There will always be outliers whose perspectives or behaviors do not align with emergent themes. Because of this, it is important to keep in mind that generational research is more informative than prescriptive, meaning that we research generations to help us gain insight on the views, preferences, and perspectives that many of them hold rather than tell us what we should do in every situation. This is especially important to remember in studying this generation. As more data on Generation Z emerges, our understanding of them will become richer and deeper.

Conclusion

Understanding generations allows us to gain insight on one of the many demographic variables of human beings. And, like any research, it comes with its shortcomings. But, we believe that even if we only uncovered a shred of information about how this generation sees and navigates the world, we have provided an opportunity for all of us to leverage their strengths, mitigate their weaknesses, and support them in their journey to make a difference.

Notes

1 Mackman, M. (2015). *Rise of Gen Z: New challenges for retailers*. Retrieved from www.ey.com/gl/en/industries/consumer-products/ey-rise-of-gen-znew-challenge-for-retailers
2 Dictionary.com. (n.d.a). *Generation*. Retrieved from www.dictionary.com/browse/generation
3 Strauss, W. & Howe, N. (1997). *The fourth turning: What the cycles of history tell us about America's next rendezvous with destiny*. New York: Broadway Books.
4 Strauss, W. & Howe, N. (1997).
5 Sparks & Honey. (2014). *Meet Generation Z: Forget everything you learned about Millennials*. Retrieved from www.slideshare.net/sparksandhoney/generation-z-final-june-17
6 Dimock, M. (2018). *Defining generations: Where Millennials end and post-Millennials begin*. Retrieved from www.pewresearch.org/fact-tank/2018/03/01/defining-generations-where-millennials-end-and-post-millennials-begin/
7 Dimock, M. (2018), para. 13.
8 Merriam-Webster.com. (2018). *Words we're watching: "Xennial."* Retrieved from www.merriam-webster.com/words-at-play/words-were-watching-xennial
9 Team CGK. (2017). *What's in a name? Gen Z vs. iGen (and others names that didn't stick)*. Retrieved from http://genhq.com/whats-name-gen-z-vs-igen/
10 Sanburn, J. (2015b). *How every generation of the last century got its nickname*. Retrieved from http://time.com/4131982/generations-names-millennials-founders/
11 Sanburn, J. (2015b).
12 Bromwich, J. E. (2018). *We asked Generation Z to pick a name: It wasn't Generation Z*. Retrieved from www.nytimes.com/2018/01/31/style/generation-z-name.html
13 Bromwich, J. E. (2018).
14 Stillman, D. & Stillman, J. (2017). *Generation Z @ work*. New York: HarperCollins.
15 Woodman, D. (2017). *From Boomers to Xennials: We love talking about generations but must recognize their limits*. Retrieved from http://theconversation.com/from-boomers-to-xennials-we-love-talking-about-our-generations-but-must-recognise-their-limits-80679
16 Pew Research Center. (2015g). *The whys and hows of generations research*. Retrieved from www.people-press.org/2015/09/03/the-whys-and-hows-of-generations-research/
17 Pew Research Center. (2015g).
18 National Opinion Research Center. (2017). *General Social Survey [Voter participation by age]*. Retrieved from https://gssdataexplorer.norc.org/trends/Politics?measure=vote
19 Pew Research Center. (2015g).
20 Pew Research Center. (2015g).
21 Howe, N. (2014b). *The G.I. Generation and the "Triumph of the Squares."* Retrieved from www.forbes.com/sites/neilhowe/2014/07/30/the-g-i-generation-and-the-triumph-of-the-squares-part-2-of-7/#14b57a629c8e

22 Duca, J. V. (2013). *Subprime mortgage crisis*. Retrieved from www.federalreservehistory.org/essays/subprime_mortgage_crisis

23 Amaro, S. (2017). *Greece is on track to exit its bailout plan but doubts over its future remain*. Retrieved from www.cnbc.com/2017/10/26/greece-is-on-track-to-exit-its-bailout-plan-but-doubts-over-its-future-remain.html

24 Eisenberg, R. (2013). *Focus on passing down your values, not money*. Retrieved from www.forbes.com/sites/nextavenue/2013/05/31/focus-on-passing-down-your-values-not-money/2/#7c4f029035ec

Understanding
generations
••

1 Who came before Z?

Whether establishing societal values and norms, creating laws and infrastructure, or developing inventions that the world has come to rely on, each preceding generation significantly influences future cohorts. So, before we delve into discussing Generation Z, it's important to examine those generations that came before. While we could certainly go back to the Awakening Generation in 1734,[1] our focus is on the five living generations of the twentieth century – G.I., Silent, Baby Boomer, Generation X, and Millennial.

The G.I. Generation: Black Thursday, battlefields, and the suburbs

The first generation of the twentieth century, the G.I. Generation, also referred to as the Greatest Generation, was born from 1901 through 1924.[2] They are the oldest living generation, and today, there are less than 4 million Americans well into their 90s.[3]

Growing up G.I.

Most members of the G.I. Generation were born during the Progressive Era led by Theodore Roosevelt and Woodrow Wilson. During that time, there was a focus to keep children out of factories and instead in school. In 1904, the National Child Labor Committee was formed to advocate and promote the "well-being and education of children and youth as they relate to work and working."[4]

By 1920, most were old enough to witness, and some even vote for, the passing of the 19th Amendment granting women the right to vote. This era of independence for women was followed by the "Roaring Twenties," where flappers pushed "economic, political and sexual freedom for women."[5]

When the Great Depression started in 1929, while the oldest were already part of the workforce, the youngest of the G.I. Generation were still children. Many of these young people faced overcrowded schools, malnutrition from family poverty, and increases in child abuse from psychologically stressed parents.[6] Although times then were tough, kids still found a way to have fun. They played cards and dominoes as well as put together puzzles.[7] Some played baseball, and others used their ingenuity to make their own toys from objects they were able to find.[8]

The G.I. Generation in adulthood

The oldest of the G.I. Generation entered adulthood during the Prohibition era and were not able to have their first legal drink until 1933. At the time, though, many were busy assisting with post-Depression recovery efforts. Nearly 2.5 million young men from the G.I. Generation participated in full force in the rebuilding of America through the Civilian Conservation Corps.[9]

With the Selective Training and Service Act of 1940, nearly all men in the G.I. Generation were eligible and required to register for the draft.[10] The G.I. Generation vastly made up a majority of the 16.1 million U.S. soldiers who served in World War II and the 292,000 who died in battle.[11] While the men were off at war, women were filling roles left vacant by the male workforce. By 1945, it is estimated that one in four married women held a job, giving rise to the iconic symbol of Rosie the Riveter.[12]

After the war ended in 1945, those in the G.I. Generation returned home to a time of peace and economic prosperity. The gross national product more than doubled after the war, and unemployment and inflation rates were low.[13] Many took advantage of earning a college degree through the recently passed G.I. Bill, which provided financial assistance for veterans going back to school.[14] Entering a phase of stability, those in the G.I. Generation started families of their own, something that was put off due to the financial insecurity of the Depression and the war. Those in the G.I. Generation became parents to the 76.4 million babies born from 1946 through 1964, aptly named the Baby Boomers because they were the largest group of babies ever born in one time period in the U.S.[15] The financial well-being of the G.I. Generation during that time allowed for them to buy houses, cars, and move their families to the suburbs,[16] fulfilling their version of the American Dream.[17]

The Silent Generation: Crisis to caution

The Silent Generation was born from 1925 through 1945.[18] This generation experienced the highs and lows of the first half of the twentieth century, growing up in the Depression era but entering adulthood after World War II.

Growing up Silent

The Silent Generation experienced a childhood during some tough times bookmarked with the Great Depression and World War II. They grew up with the notion that children should be seen and not heard.[19] This probably contributed to the Silent Generation being characterized as being cautious and rule-following, while working within a system instead of trying to change it.[20] Unlike the Baby Boomers who followed, many in the Silent Generation did not protest or question authority and typically trusted the government.[21] They lived during the McCarthy era, which the scare of speaking out likely didn't help their reputation of being silent. A 1951 *TIME Magazine* article dubbed them the Silent Generation and depicted them as conventional, hardworking, and conforming because they weren't causing a stir.[22]

The older members of the Silent Generation went with Dorothy and Toto to Oz as *The Wizard of Oz* hit theaters in 1939. The Silent Generation grew up during what is considered the golden age of radio as they gathered around to listen with their families for entertainment and to get the news.[23] This generation saw the Grand Ole Opry grow from a radio broadcast to a national weekly segment in the 1930s and 1940s.[24] While home TVs gained more popularity after the war, the youngest of the Silent Generation grew up watching *Howdy Doody*, *The Lone Ranger*, and *The Ed Sullivan Show*. They listened to Buddy Holly and Elvis Presley, popularizing rock 'n' roll in the 1950s. The Silent Generation saw leading ladies like Shirley Temple, Elizabeth Taylor, and Marilyn Monroe grace the big screen.

The Silent Generation in adulthood

Despite growing up during the Great Depression and World War II, the Silent Generation joined a booming job market and economy right after school. Richard Easterlin described the Silent Generation as fortunate due to the timing of their entrance into the post-World War II workforce that was in need of young employees.[25] In addition, the small size of their generational cohort helped push up wages early in their careers.[26] While this generation established economic stability early in their adulthood, the same cannot be said about their political prominence. The Silent Generation never gained major political power in the White House, as there has never been a U.S. president from the Silent Generation. They have, however, had notable leaders such as Martin Luther King Jr., Bernie Sanders, and Robert F. Kennedy[27] as well as Supreme Court Justice, Ruth Bader Ginsberg.

Many in the Silent Generation went on to become the parents of Generation X, another smaller generation sandwiched between two large generations. And many are also the grandparents of Generation Z. Being able to gain financial stability early in adulthood helped the Silent Generation go on to become the wealthiest of all age groups in 2010, with a median net worth of $225,000.[28] Today, the Silent Generation includes roughly 28 million people, with the youngest in their 70s and the oldest in their 90s.[29]

Baby Boomers: Economic prosperity, protests, and "peace and love"

After World War II, those in the G.I. Generation returning from war felt ready to settle down, get married, and have children. So much so that America saw 3.4 million babies born in 1946 alone, more than any other year prior.[30]

Birthrates increased steadily until 1964 with a total of 76.4 million babies born from 1946 through 1964.[31] With the post–World War II boom, we got the large and in-charge generational cohort known as the Baby Boomers.

Growing up Boomer

As children of the G.I. Generation, Baby Boomers were raised by parents who did not want their children to ever go without or suffer.[32] This was understandable considering that the G.I. Generation experienced the Great Depression firsthand, and many fought in World War II. While pop culture today is keeping up with the Kardashians, the Boomer generation grew up keeping up with the Joneses and the traditional image of the American Dream.[33] The Baby Boomer childhood was intertwined with the economic stability of post–World War II America, and Baby Boomer children experienced the growth of suburban neighborhoods[34] highlighting the white picket fence household.

Despite television having beginnings earlier than World War II, commercial television boomed along with the birthrates starting in 1946.[35] Growing faster than any other technology before it, by 1962 more than 90 percent of all households had a television.[36] Baby Boomers grew up loving Lucy, leaving it to Beaver, and dancing along with Dick Clark's *American Bandstand*.

While many were raised in the sprawling and quickly expanding suburbs, Baby Boomers have ties to starting a counterculture in America as they began the fight for social, political, and economic rights.[37] The oldest Boomers were just 11 years-old when Rosa Parks boycotted the segregated bus system in Montgomery, Alabama, and were coming of age in the midst of the Civil Rights movement, as nearly all were alive to watch Reverend Martin Luther King Jr. lead the March on Washington and the passing of the Civil Rights Act of 1964. As they got older, student activism supporting the anti-war movement, women's rights, racial equality, and the environment became a common occurrence on college campuses.[38]

By the late 1960s, many went off to war in Vietnam. Over the course of the war, 40 percent of male Baby Boomers had served in the military.[39] Having to balance the responsibility instilled by their G.I. Generation parents to serve their country with the concern of the increasing death toll of the war, there was a division – some supporting the war and others protesting.[40]

And while this era is heavily marked by the war, other significant events were also occurring. Boomers were living through the height of the hippie movement of free love and flower children, Vietnam, the Beatles, and Woodstock.[41] And America's race to space against Russia had Boomers watching with great anticipation as Neil Armstrong took the first steps on the moon.

The Boomer Generation in adulthood

As the 1980s rolled around, some shed their hippie personas and took up professional lives in business, assuming the new title of "yuppies." Inheriting a "hard work leads to success" attitude from their G.I. Generation parents, Baby Boomers popularized the traditional nine to five routine and the workaholic mentality.[42] Through most of the 1980s and early 1990s, many Baby Boomers lived their adult lives in a comfortable booming economy similar to that of their childhood. And, by the 1980s, most Boomers had taken on a new identity: Being parents.

Baby Boomers are the parents of late Generation X and early Millennials. As parents, Boomers instilled a similar sentiment that their G.I. Generation parents gave them: I never want my child to go without. With an increase in dual-parent working households, Boomer parents could provide more for their children.[43] And that support has continued well into their adult lives as many Boomers still provide financial support to their adult children, even well after moving out of the family home.[44]

Today, most Baby Boomers are at or approaching traditional retirement age, but many appear to be prolonging retirement. This later retirement seems to be influenced by a few things. Seventy-two is the new 65 for Baby Boomers who feel old age actually starts at age 72 and feel younger than their age reflects.[45] Many Baby Boomers also feel unprepared financially for retirement as evidenced by a study by the Insured Retirement Institute that found that less than a quarter of Baby Boomers are confident they are adequately preparing for retired life and have saved enough for retirement.[46] Regardless of their choice to retire, by 2030, all living Baby Boomers will be eligible to take Social Security. With their large population size, there is concern about how solvent the Social Security system will be in terms of supporting them.[47]

As they have progressed through childhood to adulthood and now to retirement, the Baby Boomer generation has been characterized by their individualism, strong work ethic, and comfort in economic prosperity. From the time of their adolescence and young adulthood, Baby Boomers have shaken things up with the social movements of the 1960s and 70s, and their large size will continue to impact the economy as it has their entire lives.

Generation X: I want my MTV and family time

Following the huge cohort of Baby Boomers, Generation X was born from 1965 through 1980.[48] Generation X is often associated with cynicism, justified by being been painted as the smaller "middle child" generation of 65 million in between the massive and much larger Boomer and Millennial cohorts.[49]

Growing up Gen X

The oldest of Generation X were just kids in the 1970s but were able to witness a growing distrust of the government and politics as Watergate unfolded and President Richard Nixon resigned. Further, this generation came of age with the highest divorce rates in American history, rising from 33 percent in 1970 to

52 percent in 1980.[50] They grew into their adolescent years in the midst of the AIDS epidemic, much different than the free love movement of the Boomers who came before them. And many likely watched the Challenger explosion on TV while in school.

But, it was not all doom and gloom for Generation X. They also saw important societal and cultural events that propelled America and the world forward. They were the first cohort of students to attend integrated schools since kindergarten.[51] As children, they were the first group to watch *Sesame Street*, where they learned more than the alphabet, but that neighborhoods were made up of many different types of people including large yellow birds and dessert-loving monsters.[52] They likely developed their sense of personal responsibility, independence, and self-guided decision-making by having little involvement from adults or authority figures and their latchkey kid afternoons spent flipping through *Choose Your Own Adventure* books.[53] They saw the Cold War come to an end and the fall of the Berlin Wall. They went to detention with *The Breakfast Club* gang, blew out *Sixteen Candles*, and explored space in a galaxy far, far away with *Star Wars*. They didn't just want their MTV; they were singing along watching Michael Jackson's *Thriller*, Madonna's *Like A Prayer*, and Prince's *When Doves Cry*.

Generation X in adulthood

Generation X was the first generation to use personal computers and, to this day, the highest rate of desktop computer users.[54] In 1995, they were utilizing Windows 95, and many entered the job market with the World Wide Web. They were prepared and eager to use their skills to earn high wages. Their financial stability over the course of their careers, however, has experienced multiple hits with the stock market crash of 1987, government spending on national security after 9/11, and the Great Recession in which they were beginning to reach their peak earning years.

Beyond their careers, Generation X has a strong focus on their family lives. Today, Gen Xers comprise the majority of parents of Generation Z. Their experience as latchkey kids having had both parents away working has helped them develop their own philosophies about work-life balance different from those of their parents. Their desire to spend time with their families motivates their preference for flexible work environments and a work-from-home friendly culture.[55] While Boomers became known for their workaholic tendencies, Gen Xers don't believe that spending more hours at work equates to higher levels of productivity.[56] It's no surprise then that half of startups have been founded by members of Generation X.[57] Not only has this given them the opportunity to exact their ingenuity, running their own startups allows them a flexible workplace where they can take time in the middle of the day to watch their kid's soccer game. As much as they may have been labeled as the "slacker" generation growing up, their focus as adults has been on family and responsibility.

Generation X also strives for flexibility in their love lives. Their own experiences as children of divorce likely influenced their viewpoints on marriage. In a study of Gen Xers and Millennials, two-thirds reported that cohabitating before marriage would help prevent divorce.[58] Many in Generation X are also getting married later in life and indicating staying together longer than previous generations.[59] Right after Millennials, Generation X was one of the first generations to support same-sex marriage rights.[60] From their preference to wait to get married to their commitment to work-life balance to their inclusion of marriage rights for all, Generation X has served as a catalyst for redefining love, relationships, and family.

As adults, many in Generation X strive for balance, have a focus on their families, possess a hard work mentality, and maintain the same independence they learned as kids.[61,62] They've also developed a "roll with the punches" adaptability through economic hard times and the advancement of new technologies. Generation X might be cynical, but they're also savvy and self-reliant.[63]

Millennials: The socially connected industry disruptors

Before they were Millennials, their generation was often referred to as Generation Y, the placeholder name aptly given to them as they followed Generation X alphabetically. The range of their birth years vary depending on the source, but with Generation X ending in 1980 and Generation Z starting in 1995, it would make sense that the birth range for Millennials would be 1981 through 1994. Millennials are sometimes called the "echo boom" as many are children of the Baby Boomer generation and are currently the second largest generation as reported in the 2016 Census data, with Baby Boomers being the largest.[64] Millennials are expected to surpass their Boomer parents in population size by 2019 and have always eclipsed their Generation X predecessors.[65]

Growing up Millennial

Millennials are the kids of the 90s and 2000s who took notes with gel pens, chatted with their friends on AOL Instant Messenger, and learned about the world's phenomena with Bill Nye the Science Guy. Drastically different than Generation X before them, Millennials grew up with the close involvement of their predominantly Baby Boomer parents, whose parenting style was dubbed as "helicopter parenting."[66] With their parents hovering not far away, Millennials grew up accustomed to well-planned schedules and very structured extracurricular involvement. While helicopter parenting has gotten a bad rap, the parental involvement of Baby Boomers in the lives of their Millennial children has helped them become the most educated generation to date, with 40 percent of 25 to 29 year-olds entering the workforce with a bachelor's degree.[67]

Known for their digital savviness, Millennials grew up with computers being commonplace in the classroom and at home, and they welcomed the widespread use of cell phones. It's no surprise that their generational cohort is commonly associated with, and criticized for, their close relationship with the Internet, social media, and mobile phones. As they developed their identity as teens and young adults, they were also doing so online as most now have some type of social networking profile.[68] They not only welcomed user-generated Web 2.0 platforms and social media, but members of their generational cohort helped create them. Millennial Mark Zuckerberg created the largest social media platform, Facebook, in his Harvard residence hall room. Along with Facebook, sites and apps like Instagram, Tumblr, Spotify, Snapchat, Tinder, and Groupon were all created by Millennials.[69] The development of social media has been one of the defining contributions of the Millennial generation.[70] It has changed the way they, and other generations, communicate, connect, and get information.

The Great Recession occurred as many Millennials were in their early years of career attainment. Although their childhoods were marked by a strong economy, Millennials entered the workforce or higher education facing an economic downturn and rising unemployment rates.[71] Despite facing debt and unemployment, Millennials still report higher levels of optimism about their future, as well as America's. Findings from a 2014 Pew Research Center study showed that 49 percent of Millennials believed the country's best days were ahead.[72] And, that same study found that Millennials were confident in being financially secure in the future, more so than previous generations at their age.[73]

Millennials in adulthood

Millennials' close relationship with and support from their Boomer parents has not waned as they have entered adulthood. The Better Money Habits Millennial Report in 2015 indicated that more than 40 percent of Millennials are financially supported by their parents in some capacity.[74] It's important to recognize, though, that 35 percent of Millennials have student loan debt,[75] and it's a lot. In 2017, the average monthly student loan payment was $351 per month for a college graduate ages 20 to 30 years-old.[76] While this data does include some of the oldest members of Generation Z, it does showcase the enormous amount of monthly debt repayment each month considering the average Millennial salary is roughly $35,500 annually.[77] And their salaries are 20 percent less, in real terms, than what their Baby Boomer parents were making at the same age.[78] Not only has the enormous amount of student debt delayed Millennials from living independently from their parents, but it has also influenced their decision to put off getting married, having children, and buying homes.[79]

As the most educated, yet worst paid modern generation,[80] Millennials are finding ways to stretch their dollar. One such way is by reducing self-ownership of property and material items. Doing so eliminates their responsibility for paying the full costs and the need to provide maintenance and upkeep. It's no surprise then that they are drawn to the sharing economy, where they can use shared resources such as rides with Uber or lodging with Airbnb.[81] Because of their preference for sharing, rather than buying, their generation has been accused of "killing" many things including hand soap, napkins, and diamonds.[82] The industry disruption caused by Millennials can be at least partially attributed to how they spend the little disposable income they do have, which not surprisingly, is on experiences or social events, rather than material items.[83]

The Millennial Generation is the most researched generation to-date, eliciting a great deal of talk about them in the media.[84] They have been labeled the "Me Me Me" Generation,[85] which has been amplified through their possible over-sharing and selfie posting on social media. They've been criticized for their self-interest, entitlement, and overconfidence. We can't ignore, however, that despite the financial cards stacked against them, that they are optimistic, entrepreneurial, socially connected, and innovative.

Conclusion

The following table offers a brief summary of generations pre-dating Generation Z based on content discussed earlier in this chapter.

While each generation is marked by different events, situations, and characteristics, they all provide the foundation for understanding future generations. Whether by shaping societal norms, creating laws and policies, or exerting influence through familial roles, these generations have created and preserved the world in which Generation Z lives.

Table 1.1 Overview of the Generations

	G.I. Generation	Silent Generation	Baby Boomer Generation	Generation X	Millennial Generation
Birth Years	1901–1924	1925–1945	1946–1964	1964–1980	1981–1995
Societal Context & Historical Events During Childhood and Young Adulthood	• Progressive Movement • World War I • Great Depression • World War II	• World War II • Prosperous job market	• Civil Rights Movement • Vietnam War • Space Race	• High divorce rates • Watergate scandal • AIDS epidemic	• High loan debt • Declining job market • Raised by helicopter parents
Commonly Associated Characteristics	• Rebuild mindset • Dedicated to society's future	• Risk-averse • Conforming • Financial stability	• Individualistic • Strong work ethic • Competitive	• Cynical • Independent • Family focused	• Digitally connected • Optimistic • Focused on self

Notes

1 Strauss, W. & Howe, N. (1997). *The fourth turning: What the cycles of history tell us about America's next rendezvous with destiny.* New York: Broadway Books.
2 Strauss, W. & Howe, N. (1997).

3 Knoema. (2016). *US population by age and generation.* Retrieved from https://knoema. com/infographics/egyydzc/us-population-by-age-and-generation

4 Natanson, B. O. (n.d.). National Child Labor Committee collection. *Library of Congress.* Retrieved from www.loc.gov/pictures/collection/nclc/background.html, para. 1.

5 History.com Staff. (n.d.c). *Flappers.* Retrieved from www.history.com/topics/flappers, para. 1.

6 Encyclopedia.com. (2004). *Children and adolescents, impact of the Great Depression on.* Retrieved from www.encyclopedia.com/economics/encyclopedias-almanacs-transcripts-and-maps/children-and-adolescents-impact-great-depression

7 Reinhardt, C. & Ganzel, B. (2003). *Having fun-family time.* Retrieved from https://livinghistoryfarm.org/farminginthe30s/life_20.html

8 Reinhardt, C. & Ganzel, B. (2003).

9 Encyclopedia.com. (2004).

10 The National World War II Museum. (n.d.c). *Research starters: The draft and World War II.* Retrieved from www.nationalww2museum.org/students-teachers/student-resources/research-starters/draft-and-wwii

11 World War II Foundation. (n.d.). *WWII facts & figures.* Retrieved from www.wwiifoundation.org/students/wwii-facts-figures/

12 History.com Staff. (2010c). *Rosie the Riveter.* Retrieved from www.history.com/topics/world-war-ii/rosie-the-riveter

13 History.com Staff. (2010d). *The 1950s.* Retrieved from www.history.com/topics/1950s

14 History.com Staff. (2010b). *G.I. Bill.* Retrieved from www.history.com/topics/world-war-ii/gi-bill

15 History.com Staff. (2010a). *Baby Boomers.* Retrieved from www.history.com/topics/baby-boomers

16 History.com Staff. (2010d).

17 Howe, N. (2014a). *Generations in pursuit of the American Dream.* Retrieved from www.forbes.com/sites/neilhowe/2014/07/16/part-1-generations-in-pursuit-of-the-american-dream/#4f6b609f5db0

18 CNN. (2017). *American generation fast facts.* Retrieved from www.cnn.com/2013/11/06/us/baby-boomer-generation-fast-facts/index.html

19 BridgeWorks. (2017b). *Traditionalist 101.* Retrieved from www.generations.com/2017/06/02/traditionalist-101/

20 Howe, N. (2014c). *The Silent Generation, "The Lucky Few."* Retrieved from www.forbes.com/sites/neilhowe/2014/08/13/the-silent-generation-the-lucky-few-part-3-of-7/#44c834592c63

21 Choudhury, S. (2016). *Silent Generation: Characteristics and other important facts.* Retrieved from https://historyplex.com/silent-generation-characteristics-other-important-facts

22 TIME Magazine. (1951). *People: The younger generation.* Retrieved from http://content.time.com/time/subscriber/printout/0,8816,856950,00.html

23 Encyclopedia.com. (2002b). *1940s: TV and radio.* Retrieved from www.encyclopedia.com/history/culture-magazines/1940s-tv-and-radio

24 Grand Ole Opry. (n.d.). *History of the Opry.* Retrieved from www.opry.com/history

25 Howe, N. (2014c).

26 Nicklaus, D. (2013). *Financially speaking, the Silent Generation is the lucky generation.* Retrieved from www.stltoday.com/business/columns/david-nicklaus/financially-speaking-the-silent-generation-is-the-lucky-generation/article_10a81c5a-bbe3-59af-8618-6dca77b758a3.html

27 McLaughlin, D. (2016). *Closing the book on the Silent Generation.* Retrieved from www. nationalreview.com/corner/431388/silent-generation-it-over

28 Howe, N. (2014c).

29 Knoema. (2016).

30 History.com Staff. (2010a).

31 History.com Staff. (2010a).

32 Sinek, S. (2014). *How Baby Boomers screwed their kids: And created millennial impatience.* Retrieved from www.salon.com/2014/01/04/how_baby_boomers_screwed_their_kids_%E2%80%94_and_created_millennial_impatience/

33 ushistory.org. (n.d.). *Suburban growth.* Retrieved from www.ushistory.org/us/53b.asp

34 ushistory.org. (n.d.).

35 Edgerton, G. R. (2016). *Television in America.* Retrieved from http://americanhistory. oxfordre.com/view/10.1093/acrefore/9780199329175.001.0001/acrefore-9780199329175-e-291

36 Edgerton, G. R. (2016).

37 History.com Staff. (2010a).

38 Janowiecki, M. L. (n.d.). *Protesting in the 1960s and 1970s.* Retrieved from http:// americanarchive.org/exhibits/first-amendment/protests-60s-70s

39 Wright, J. (2017). *The Baby Boomer war.* Retrieved from www.nytimes.com/2017/04/11/ opinion/the-baby-boomer-war.html

40 Wright, J. (2017).

41 History.com Staff. (2010a).

42 Tolbize, A. (2008). *Generational differences in the workplace.* Retrieved from https://rtc3. umn.edu/docs/2_18_Gen_diff_workplace.pdf

43 Laham, M. T. S. (2015). *The milestones moments in every Boomer's Life.* Retrieved from www.huffingtonpost.com/martha-ts-laham-/boomers-milestone-moments_b_7678270. html

44 Malcolm, H. (2015). *Millennials lean more on parents (but please don't call it mooching).* Retrieved from www.usatoday.com/story/money/personalfinance/2015/04/21/millennials-getting-help-from-parents/25812211/

45 Laham, M. T. S. (2015).

46 Insured Retirement Institute. (2016). *Boomer expectations for retirement 2016.* Retrieved from www.myirionline.org/docs/default-source/research/boomer-expectations-for-retirement-2016.pdf

47 Reuteman, R. (2010). *Will Baby Boomers bankrupt social security?* Retrieved from www. cnbc.com/id/34941334

48 United Nations Joint Staff Pension Fund. (2007). *Overcoming generational gap in the workplace.* Retrieved from http://aspringer.weebly.com/uploads/1/3/6/4/1364481/ designing_recruitment_selection___talent_management_model_tailored_to_meet_ unjspfs_business_development_nee.pdf

49 Knoema. (2016).

50 Jones, A. M. (2017). *Historical divorce rate statistics.* Retrieved from http://divorce. lovetoknow.com/Historical_Divorce_Rate_Statistics

51 Ryan, A. (2016). *Solving for X: How 10 events shaped a generation.* Retrieved from https:// soapboxie.com/social-issues/Solving-For-X-How-10-Events-Shaped-a-Generation

52 Ryan, A. (2016).

53 BridgeWorks. (2017a). *Generation X 101.* Retrieved from www.generations.com/2017/ 02/21/generation-x-101/

54 Zickuhr, K. (2011). *Generations and their gadgets.* Retrieved from www.pewinternet. org/2011/02/03/generations-and-their-gadgets/

55 Tolbize, A. (2008).

56 BridgeWorks. (2017a).

57 Sage Solutions, Inc. (2015). *Survey report: 2015 state of the start-up.* Retrieved from www. sage.com/na/~/media/site/sagena/responsive/docs/startup/report

58 Eickmeyer, K. J. (2013). *Generation X and Millennials attitudes towards marriage & divorce.* Retrieved from www.bgsu.edu/content/dam/BGSU/college-of-arts-and-sciences/ NCFMR/documents/FP/eickmeyer-gen-x-millennials-fp-15-12.pdf

59 Dawson, A. (2011). *Study says Generation X is balanced and happy.* Retrieved from www. cnn.com/2011/10/26/living/gen-x-satisfied/index.html

60 Pew Research Center. (2017c). *Support for same-sex marriage grows, even among groups that had been skeptical.* Retrieved from www.people-press.org/2017/06/26/support-for-same-sex-marriage-grows-even-among-groups-that-had-been-skeptical/

61 Kane, S. (2017a). *Common characteristics of Generation X professionals.* Retrieved from www.thebalance.com/common-characteristics-of-generation-x-professionals-2164682

62 Schawbel, D. (2015). *44 of the most interesting facts about Generation X.* Retrieved from http://danschawbel.com/blog/44-of-the-most-interesting-facts-about-generation-x/

63 Taylor, P. & Gao, G. (2014). *Generation X: America's neglected "middle child."* Retrieved from www.pewresearch.org/fact-tank/2014/06/05/generation-x-americas-neglected-middle-child/

64 Fry, R. (2016). *Millennials overtake Baby Boomers as America's largest generation.* Retrieved from www.pewresearch.org/fact-tank/2016/04/25/millennials-overtake-baby-boomers/

65 Fry, R. (2016).

66 Kendzior, S. (2014). *Only Baby Boomers could afford to be helicopter parents.* Retrieved from www.theatlantic.com/business/archive/2014/11/only-baby-boomers-could-afford-to-be-helicopter-parents/382671/

67 Graf, N. (2017). *Today's young workers are more likely than ever to have a bachelor's degree.* Retrieved from www.pewresearch.org/fact-tank/2017/05/16/todays-young-workers-are-more-likely-than-ever-to-have-a-bachelors-degree/

68 PewResearchCenter.(2010).*Millennials:Confident,connected,opentochange.*Retrievedfrom www.pewsocialtrends.org/2010/02/24/millennials-confident-connected-open-to-change/

69 Varshneya, R. (2017). *Top 20 most influential Millennial entrepreneurs.* Retrieved from www.inc.com/rahul-varshneya/top-20-most-influential-millennial-entrepreneurs.html

70 Tanner, R. (2017). *15 influential events that shaped Generation Y.* Retrieved from https:// managementisajourney.com/15-influential-events-that-shaped-generation-y-infographic/

71 U.S. Bureau of Labor Statistics. (2012). *The recession of 2007–2009.* Retrieved from www.bls.gov/spotlight/2012/recession/pdf/recession_bls_spotlight.pdf

72 Pew Research Center. (2014). *Millennials in adulthood: Detached from institutions, net-worked with friends.* Retrieved from www.pewsocialtrends.org/files/2014/03/2014-03-07_ generations-report-version-for-web.pdf

73 Pew Research Center. (2014).

74 Malcolm, H. (2015).

75 Fleming, J. H. (2016). *Americans' big debt burden growing, not evenly distributed.* Retrieved from http://news.gallup.com/businessjournal/188984/americans-big-debt-burden-growing-not-evenly-distributed.aspx

76 Student Loan Hero. (2017). *A look at shocking student loan debt statistics for 2017.* Retrieved from https://studentloanhero.com/student-loan-debt-statistics/

77 Josephson, A. (2017). *The average salary of a Millennial.* Retrieved from https://smartasset. com/retirement/the-average-salary-of-a-millennial

78 Josephson, A. (2017).

79 Shell, A. (2017). *Parents: No empty nest for you: Student debt prompts many Millennials to move back home, survey finds.* Retrieved from www.usatoday.com/story/money/markets/2017/05/10/td-ameritrade-millennial-college-survey/101503580/

80 Rattner, S. (2015). *We're making life too hard for Millennials.* Retrieved from www.nytimes.com/2015/08/02/opinion/sunday/were-making-life-too-hard-for-millennials.html?smid=tw-share&_r=1

81 Arthursson, D. (2016). *How Millennials are defining the sharing economy.* Retrieved from www.entrepreneur.com/article/275802

82 Paul, K. (2017). *Here are all the things Millennials have been accused of killing-from wine corks to golf.* Retrieved from www.marketwatch.com/story/here-are-all-of-the-things-millennials-have-been-accused-of-killing-2017-05-22

83 Eventbrite. *Millennials: Fueling the experience economy.* Retrieved from http://eventbrite-s3.s3.amazonaws.com/marketing/Millennials_Research/Gen_PR_Final.pdf

84 National Chamber Foundation. (2012). *The Millennial Generation: Research review.* Retrieved from www.uschamberfoundation.org/sites/default/files/article/foundation/MillennialGeneration.pdf

85 Stein, J. (2013). *Millennials: The me me me generation.* Retrieved from http://time.com/247/millennials-the-me-me-me-generation/

2 Reflection on a century

· ·

Before exploring who Generation Z is, it is important to discuss the contextual factors that have shaped this generation. Economic downturn. War and violence. Redefinition of the family structure and gender roles. Tension regarding immigration. Reconstruction of societal infrastructure. Debate over universal healthcare. Extensive entrepreneurial spirit. Interestingly, there are some stark similarities between the issues of today and those from the G.I. Generation era. If history is any guide, examining the context of that historical era may be able to help us better understand who Generation Z is today.

Why look at the G.I. Generation and Generation Z?

Although we could look back as far as several centuries or as recent as a few decades in reflecting on how predecessor generations align with Generation Z today, we pay particular attention to the G.I. Generation for a few reasons. First, even though every generation has played a part in shaping Generation Z, the broader infrastructure and societal perspectives that emerged during the G.I. Generation era has provided a grounding for what the U.S. looks like today. In his book, *The Greatest Generation*, Tom Brokaw paints a picture of the G.I. Generation as having built the foundation for modern America. Many inventions and ways of life that are embedded into society today can be traced back to a time in history linked to the G.I. Generation.

In addition, both the G.I. Generation and Generation Z share a particular context – many were born and/or grew up around the turn of a century. This provides a unique timeframe to explore how much has happened over the last hundred years. As the G.I. Generation influenced the social fabric of society in the twentieth century, Generation Z is positioned to do the same in the twenty-first century. What is also interesting regarding these two generations is that there is still an opportunity for both to interact with each other. As the G.I. Generation is the oldest living generation in today's population, their ability to share their stories with their younger counterparts, bypassing history books, is remarkable.

But more important than any other factor, there are several similarities between the political, economic, and social contexts of both the G.I. Generation and Generation Z. Whereas issues and impacts of war, global conflicts, immigration, gender roles, and economy are not entirely identical, there are some commonalities. How the G.I. Generation responded to these issues may provide insight into the characteristics, perspectives, and behaviors of Generation Z today when faced with similar circumstances.

The political climate of G.I. and Z

Both the G.I. Generation and Generation Z are similar in regard to the political climate they experienced during their young adulthood. Generation Z's first presidential election was in 2016 between Democrat, Hillary Clinton, and Republican, Donald Trump. The U.S. had just come off of a two-term Democratic president. But, Donald Trump ended up winning the electoral vote on his platform of cutting taxes, limiting immigration, and his slogan, "Make America Great Again."[1]

If we go back in time nearly a century to the 1920 election, the first of which the oldest of the G.I. Generation could vote, we see some interesting parallels. In 1920, Democrat, Woodrow Wilson, was also just finishing two terms in office. So, for both the 1920 and 2016 elections, there was no incumbent running. Despite the fact that the outgoing presidents differed in their popularity ratings, Wilson's being quite low[2] and Obama's being considerably high,[3] both elections were more than a referendum on the outgoing president; they were both a call by the opposition party to shift to the better times of the past. Like Trump's, "Make America Great Again," mantra, Warren Harding, the pro-business Republican candidate who won the 1920 presidential bid, did so on a platform of a "return to normalcy."[4] During Harding's time in office, he reduced taxes, instituted high tariffs, and limited immigration.[5] While there are differences between these presidents, the first elections of both the G.I. Generation and Generation Z also offer some curious similarities in the platforms of the winning candidates and the context of what Americans were seeking in their presidents at the time.

Witnessing war

As the most uniformed generation per capita in U.S. history, the G.I. Generation was on the front lines and stormed the beaches of Normandy on D-Day.[6] Although it wasn't Generation Z on the battlefield in the Middle East after 9/11, technology has opened up a window to see and experience violence and conflict from afar with the ongoing War on Terror. For the G.I. Generation, witnessing a bombing or seeing the aftermath of war violence were things typically reserved for only those fighting on the front lines unless a photo appeared in the newspaper. Even with media coverage, the delay in getting the news through the radio or daily newspaper moved at a snail's pace in comparison to the almost instantaneous news coverage and ability to live stream events today.

Global relationships

The presence of war for both generations might also contribute to their perspectives on global relationships, tensions, and safety. Still feeling the impacts of the Great Depression and World War I, America was hesitant and opinions were split about whether to send troops to fight in World War II – that was until the attack on Pearl Harbor.[7] But, the rise and formation of Axis powers made it easier to recognize a global threat despite America's attempt to stay isolated and uninvolved in the conflicts in Europe and Asia.[8] Today, Generation Z lives in a world where ongoing global tensions are simply the way of life. The long-standing American involvement with conflicts in the Middle East since 9/11 has spanned the majority of Generation Z's lifetimes. They've grown up knowing that global unrest and enemies exist.

> ❛❛ *I am most concerned about war and terrorism because they are the things that not only affect our country, but the entire world. They are two things that could truly kill us all and to me that is frightening.* ❜❜
> – Member of Generation Z

Both generations experienced America entering a war after an attack on American soil – Pearl Harbor for the G.I. Generation and 9/11 for Generation Z. While the entire G.I. Generation had been born by the time the attacks on Pearl Harbor had occurred, half of those in Generation Z were not yet alive at the time of 9/11. But, after Pearl Harbor in 1941, World War II came to an end just 4 years later.[9] Arguably, nearly two decades after 9/11, the War on Terror has continued,[10] still occupying the spotlight for young members of Generation Z to see.

For both generations, messaging surrounding these conflicts perpetuated fear and fostered xenophobia in the name of terrorism.[11,12] Whether scapegoating Japanese during World War II or Muslim people during the War on Terror, the common feeling was that the world is a scary place, and there are enemies of America threatening our security. Everyone who has lived through these times has experienced both the global unrest and the surrounding sentiment, but the impact on adolescents and young adults may have a more lasting effect on their worldview as many lack the experience and perspective to realize that the world isn't always in a state of conflict.

Immigration

With global unrest, it is common for people to leave their war-torn homes to seek refuge in a new country. Beyond war, though, some simply seek a healthier, safer, and more stable life for themselves and their families and move to countries that offer better opportunities. Over the last century, various groups of people have immigrated to the U.S., making immigration an issue each generation in the twentieth century has had to grapple with. But, the young adulthood eras of both the G.I. Generation and Generation Z, specifically, share some unique parallels.

While immigration to the U.S. occurred long before the twentieth century, it was the Immigration Act of 1917 and subsequent acts in 1921 and 1924 that shaped immigration policy as we know it today. Restrictions on who could be admitted, the introduction of passports, and the creation of the Border Patrol were all taking effect during the time many in the G.I. Generation were growing up.[13,14] In 1933, the agency, Immigration and Naturalization Service, was created in an effort to streamline paperwork as well as enact a law enforcement approach to address illegal immigration.[15] In 1939, while many in the G.I. Generation were entering young adulthood, Congress rejected a bill that would welcome 20,000 Jewish immigrant children fleeing Nazi Germany.[16] After the attack on Pearl Harbor, the G.I. Generation immediately saw policy changes that impacted Italian, German, and Japanese immigrants in the U.S. These ranged from stricter naturalization processes to restrictions on curfew and the prohibition of owning certain items that could be utilized for sabotage like cameras or radios.[17] Some of the older members of the G.I. Generation even helped create these policies.

Today, Generation Z is growing up in a world where travel bans are proposed for citizens from Muslim countries and the talk of building a wall to regulate immigration from Mexico was a winning platform for President Trump. The focus during Generation Z's young adulthood has been on the restriction of groups from certain countries and deportation of residents who were already here. The Administration even put an end to the Deferred Action for Childhood Arrivals program giving Congress a chance to renew it, which they failed to do by the deadline.[18] The collection of policies and ideologies put forth since 2016 are reflective of "America First," tapping into a nativist sentiment,[19] liken to that of the early 1900s.[20]

The economic landscape of G.I. and Z

The Great Depression (1929 through 1939) and the Great Recession (2007 through 2009) are two of the most monumental economic downturns in American history.[21] The Great Depression began with the stock market crash on Black Thursday and was followed by years of cutbacks and rationing by many families as they struggled with high unemployment rates and unstable housing.[22] But, the New Deal was positioned as the solution to put America back on track financially.[23] By 1942, American involvement in World War II stimulated the economy and the New Deal came to an end.[24]

The Great Recession, on the other hand, didn't begin with a certain event. It was triggered by a culminating economic decline related to the subprime mortgage industry, after having granted loans to high-risk borrowers. While there was no New Deal for the Recession, the federal government still intervened to help the economy adjust.[25] Despite different means of government intervention during these two downturns, the effects of the Depression and Recession on the population were similar. People lost jobs and homes and had to find ways to make ends meet. Although both the Depression and Recession had widespread impact across all generations, the majority of children during the Depression were from the G.I. Generation and during the Recession were from Generation Z. As their parents tried to find work or places to live, these kids were taught to be conservative with their money as any day could be that rainy day.

Innovation

Innovation contributes to economic growth and development, and findings show that innovation accounts for roughly 50 percent of the U.S. GDP growth.[26] Innovation also drives perceptions of progress and increases life expectancy and standards of living.[27] Both the G.I. Generation and Generation Z are closely associated with innovation. Inventors born into the G.I. Generation can be credited for the creation of the turbojet, Polaroid camera, car radio, pacemaker, and even Toll House cookies.[28] Innovation seems to be in DNA of Generation Z as well. These young people have seen their Millennial predecessors develop social media and technology platforms, and Generation Z is following suit, but perhaps more in inventing gadgets, tools, and devices. Long gone could be the days of waiting for your cell phone to charge because, at 18 years-old, Eesha Khare of Generation Z invented a cell phone battery that charges in 30 seconds.[29] In 2012, at the age of 15, Jack Andraka invented a cost-efficient cancer detection tool that costs 3 cents and takes 5 minutes to run.[30] And we haven't even seen this entire generation grow into adulthood. Who knows what we can expect when these young innovators reach their 40s and 50s. But, as we can see today, it appears that Generation Z is taking a page from the G.I. Generation's playbook in utilizing innovation to create a better future.

Social issues influencing G.I. and Z

The social landscape of society at the time also provides a platform to draw a connection between the two generations. While there are differences, the presence, evolution, and resurgence of particular social issues have been at the forefront of both generations' young adulthoods. Three of these issues include racial equality, gender equality, and family structures.

Racial equality

Both the G.I. Generation and Generation Z have seen the overt presence of racism in society, whether exhibited in public policy or through societal attitudes. During World War II, most African-Americans were still living in the states that were formerly part of the Confederacy.[31] As the war called for more American soldiers, Black men left the South and were "drafted and placed into segregated military units."[32] In addition to the discrimination of African-Americans during this time, after Pearl Harbor, President Roosevelt signed the executive order that put 120,000 Japanese-Americans in internment camps.[33] As much as the G.I. Generation is credited with building the traditional notion of the American Dream, that American Dream was not entirely inclusive of everyone in America. The post-war development of suburban neighborhoods is also associated with the flight of White families from metropolitan cities to suburban single-family homes.[34] This occurred during the same time that there was a large migration of Black Americans from the rural South moving to larger cities in the North and Midwest.[35] Many of the suburban neighborhoods that were built during this time were restricted and banned African-American families from purchasing a home.[36]

In addition, although the G.I. Bill contributed to the educational attainment and future economic prosperity of many members of the G.I. Generation, African-American war veterans often ran into barriers in an attempt to take advantage of the G.I. Bill's benefits.[37] While the G.I. Generation is often associated and attributed with the positive aspects of winning the war and rebuilding America, it cannot be glossed over that the rebuilding did not equally benefit all American citizens, especially people of color.

The next two decades brought about landmark advances to dismantle racism by some G.I. Generation advocates. For example, the Civil Rights Act of 1964 was passed by a Congress in which, at the time, the average age of membership was mid-50s, right in the midst of the G.I. Generation age range.[38] In addition, Oliver Brown, *Brown v. Board of Education*'s lead plaintiff, was a member of the G.I. Generation as was his lawyer, Thurgood Marshall. And Rosa Parks, a member of the G.I. Generation, is often attributed to spurring a movement to end segregation.

And while those advances helped the U.S. make great strides, racial inequality still exists in America today. Generation Z is witness to pay inequality and employment gaps[39] as well as underrepresentation of African-Americans in elected political roles[40] and overrepresentation in prison.[41] With movements such as Black Lives Matter, those in Generation Z see people speaking out to address issues of racial discrimination and promote equality. And, while racism has been an ongoing issue across all generations in the twentieth century, a resurgence of White supremacy has emerged ever so strongly since the 2016

❝ [My generation will make the world a better place] by coming together as a whole to show oppressive institutions that there is no tolerance for such and respect and equality is demanded, not requested. ❞
– Member of Generation Z

election, heightened by the death of a protestor at a White nationalist rally in Charlottesville, Virginia, in 2017.[42] Whether integrated into the fabric of society or appearing as overt acts of discrimination, Generation Z is coming of age during a time when, like their G.I. predecessors, there is great racist sentiment. Only time will tell if those in Generation Z will make the same contributions their great-grandparents did in the 1960s to dismantle racism.

Gender equality

As America entered World War II, every adult needed to play a role. With Rosie the Riveter as an icon, many women entered the workforce to backfill for the men who went to war, changing the conversation about gender roles. Tom Brokaw, in *The Greatest Generation*, notes that as those in the G.I. Generation returned from the war, "women in what had been men's jobs were part of the new workaday world of a nation at war."[43] Despite their involvement in the workforce during the war, many women in the G.I. Generation went back to traditional roles in the home afterward,[44] some by choice and some because men were rehired to take those roles back.[45]

While there have been great strides toward gender equality in the U.S. since World War II, inequality still exists in the United States today. Of the many issues facing women, one is their low representation in leadership roles in government, business, and educational administration.[46] But, it is more than just numbers; how women are portrayed in leadership roles is also a significant indicator of gender inequality. For example, in 2016, Generation Z witnessed the nomination of the first female presidential candidate from a major political party. While Hillary Clinton's campaign was similar to that of her male counterparts over the years, one interesting tactic stands out – the "We Can Do It" Rosie the Riveter posters showing female strength. But these posters were reminiscent of images from World War II where Rosie encouraged women to take on men's jobs, as a placeholder of sorts, until the men returned from war.[47] Although a presidential nomination is progress for representation of women in leadership, the perception of women as placeholders for men will likely continue to make the election of a female President an uphill battle. World War II may have stirred conversations of women's rights and feminism, but Generation Z is still confronting the realities of gender inequality today.

Family structures

The structure of the family for the G.I. Generation and Generation Z also draws parallels. Many in the G.I. Generation waited to have children until after the war when finances and safety were stable and consistent. Similarly, Generation Z is already factoring in finances and security for the future in regard to starting a family.[48]

In addition, both generations have experienced the prominence of the multigenerational household, which includes one or more generations of adults living under one roof. Providing an economically efficient opportunity for all occupants, these households typically include grandparents or elder generations living with their middle-aged children and their grandchildren. Multigenerational households made economic sense during the Great Depression but saw a decline when the economy rebounded after World War II.[49] This move away from multigenerational households continues today for those in the G.I. Generation who opt to live on their own in senior citizen communities instead of moving in with their children.[50]

There has been a recent resurgence of multigenerational households, especially those led by Generation X parents, who were greatly impacted by the Recession.[51] Here we might see Silent Generation grandparents living with their Generation X children, who are raising their Generation Z kids. For those living in multigenerational households, that experience may play a role in the priority and value Generation Z puts on their family.[52] Only time will tell if Generation Z, like the G.I. Generation, moves away from the multigenerational household dynamic as their finances stabilize and they feel they can both afford their own living spaces while helping to pay the cost for their aging parents to live in retirement communities.

Uniquely Generation Z

While there are multiple connections and similarities between these two generations, there are also vast differences. First, technology, the Internet, and social media have created a different contextual layer for understanding Generation Z, one that cannot be similarly applied to the G.I. Generation. For example, those in the G.I. Generation as young people likely never thought of being able to send a message to a friend that wasn't written on a piece of paper. With the amount of technology available today, those in Generation Z might consider using paper, pen, envelope, and stamps to send a message, but only as a last resort after texting, messaging, posting, emailing, and calling.

Education has also played an important role in shaping the economic contexts for both generations. The G.I. Generation saw the largest gains in educational attainment in high school diploma achievement.[53] And, as they returned from the war, the G.I. Bill was introduced, making a college education more accessible and affordable for more people. But due to continuously increasing tuition rates,[54] higher education today has become more financially inaccessible than ever before, creating educational barriers for those in Generation Z. For one generation, education was seen as a window of opportunity for a brighter future that became more easily affordable after the war. For the other, education is a necessary and expensive means to an end for a brighter future, but one that some may need to forgo due to high cost.

While war and global issues play a part of the political context for both generations, the viewpoint on government and politicians provides a strong distinction between the two generations. Many in the G.I. Generation appeared to have trusted

> ❝ *Political corruption causes me the most concern. . . . Government in the hands of the wrong group of people can cause all other issues to become a bigger threat in our society.* ❞
> — *Member of Generation Z*

the government and elected leaders, as evidenced by the four-time reelection of Franklin Roosevelt as President in the 1930s and 1940s. Even after Roosevelt's death and the passing of the 22nd Amendment creating presidential term limits, many in the G.I. Generation voted to reelect Harry Truman who won in a landslide victory against the favored Thomas Dewey.[55] With a message of good citizenship, which resonated with the G.I. Generation's desire to further America's future, it's not surprising then that the first president from their cohort, John F. Kennedy, continues to have some of the highest approval ratings of any American president.[56] On the other hand, many in Generation Z are concerned about a dysfunctional government and distrust elected officials and politicians.[57] As they have seen government gridlock and shutdown along with hyper-partisanship, trust in the government in its current state is hard to come by.

Catalyst for change

As we look at Generation Z, being raised in a time of conflict, violence, racial injustice, political turmoil, and an economic downturn, you'd likely expect young people to be disengaged and pessimistic. But many in Generation Z are motivated to make the world a better place, like those in the G.I. Generation nearly a century ago who are often credited with laying the foundation for the success of future generations. The G.I.s have been idealized as catalysts for change and propelling our society forward through the twentieth century.[58] As

> ❝ *The wonderful thing about this generation is that we are both dreamers and doers. . . . More than just seeing it through, we work to achieve it.* ❞
> — *Member of Generation Z*

the twenty-first century began and the oldest in Generation Z were in preschool, it's almost as though the oldest members of our society, the G.I. Generation, were handing the reigns over to our youngest generation, Generation Z, to reinvigorate, rebuild, and reimagine modern American society.

Conclusion

Generation Z and the G.I. Generation, as unique as they are in some respects, are also very similar. As children, both cohorts experienced an economic downturn that took a toll on their families and loved ones. Throughout their lives, they have experienced war and global turmoil. And, where the G.I. Generation began to see that the female presence was not solely in the home, Generation Z will continue to witness and promote female leadership. We cannot fully predict Generation Z's future based on the similarities drawn to the G.I. Generation, but history can be informative in helping to understand human behavior and the impact that context could have on Generation Z.

Notes

1 Tumulty, K. (2017). *How Donald Trump came up with "make America great again."* Retrieved from www.washingtonpost.com/politics/how-donald-trump-came-up-with-make-america-great-again/2017/01/17/fb6acf5e-dbf7-11e6-ad42-f3375f271c9c_story.html?utm_term=.e3a32b551a1f

2 Cunningham, J. M. (2011). *United States presidential election of 1920.* Retrieved from www.britannica.com/event/United-States-presidential-election-of-1920

3 Gallup. (n.d.a). *Presidential approval ratings: Barack Obama.* Retrieved from http://news.gallup.com/poll/116479/barack-obama-presidential-job-approval.aspx

4 History.com Staff. (2009e). *Warren G. Harding.* Retrieved from www.history.com/topics/us-presidents/warren-g-harding

5 History.com Staff. (2009e).

6 Howe, N. (2014b). *The G.I. Generation and the "Triumph of the Squares."* Retrieved from www.forbes.com/sites/neilhowe/2014/07/30/the-g-i-generation-and-the-triumph-of-the-squares-part-2-of-7/#14b57a629c8e

7 The National World War II Museum. (n.d.a). *From arsenal to ally: The United States enters the war.* Retrieved from www.nationalww2museum.org/war/articles/arsenal-ally-united-states-enters-war

8 Office of the Historian. (n.d.). *American isolationism in the 1930s.* Retrieved from https://history.state.gov/milestones/1937-1945/american-isolationism

9 History.com Staff. (2009f). *World War II.* Retrieved from www.history.com/topics/world-war-ii/world-war-ii-history

10 Engelhardt, T. (2018). *A new map shows the alarming spread of the U.S. War on Terror.* Retrieved from www.thenation.com/article/a-new-map-shows-the-alarming-spread-of-the-us-war-on-terror/

11 Robinson, G. (2001). *The consequences of terror.* Retrieved from www.economist.com/node/788126

12 Committee on Hispanic Psychiatrists. (2010). *Resource document on xenophobia, immigration, and mental health.* American Psychiatric Association. Retrieved from www.psychiatry.org/File%20Library/Psychiatrists/.../rd2010_Xenophobia.pdf

13 U.S. Citizenship and Immigration Services. (n.d.b). *Mass immigration and WWI.* Retrieved from www.uscis.gov/history-and-genealogy/our-history/agency-history/mass-immigration-and-wwi

14 U.S. Citizenship and Immigration Services. (n.d.a). *Era of restriction.* Retrieved from www.uscis.gov/history-and-genealogy/our-history/agency-history/era-restriction

15 U.S. Citizenship and Immigration Services. (n.d.b).

16 Lind, D. (2017). *How America's rejection of Jews fleeing Nazi Germany haunts our refugee policy today.* Retrieved from www.vox.com/policy-and-politics/2017/1/27/14412082/refugees-history-holocaust

17 Mintz, S. (n.d.). *Immigration policy in World War II*. Retrieved from www.gilderlehrman. org/history-by-era/world-war-ii/resources/immigration-policy-world-war-ii

18 Kopan, T. & Fox, L. (2018). *Bipartisan DACA, border security deal fails in Senate, putting immigration bill's future in doubt*. Retrieved from www.cnn.com/2018/02/15/politics/ trump-immigration-veto/index.html

19 OpenStax College. (2015). *Transformation and backlash*. Retrieved from https://legacy. cnx.org/content/m50151/1.3/

20 Friedman, Y. (2017). *What is a nativist?* Retrieved from www.theatlantic.com/ international/archive/2017/04/what-is-nativist-trump/521355/

21 Mitchell, D. (2015). *These were the six major American economic crises of the last century*. Retrieved from time.com/3957499/american-economic-crises-history/

22 History.com Staff. (2009a). *Great depression*. Retrieved from www.history.com/topics/ great-depression

23 History.com Staff. (2009d). *New deal*. Retrieved from www.history.com/topics/new-deal

24 History.com Staff. (2009d).

25 History.com Staff. (2017a). *Great recession*. Retrieved from www.history.com/topics/ recession

26 U.S. Chamber Foundation. (2015). *Enterprising states: Executive summary*. Retrieved from www.uschamberfoundation.org/enterprisingstates/

27 Greenstone, M. & Looney, A. (2011). *A dozen facts about innovation*. Retrieved from www.brookings.edu/wp-content/uploads/2016/06/08_innovation_greenstone_looney. pdf

28 The Famous People. (n.d.). *Famous 20th century inventors and discoverers*. Retrieved from www.thefamouspeople.com/20th-century-inventors-discoverers.php, information from this site was used to look up individuals born in the G.I. Generation birth range.

29 Yandoli, K. (2013). *Eesha Khare, 18-year-old, invents device that changes cell phone battery in under 30 seconds*. Retrieved from www.huffingtonpost.com/2013/05/20/eesha-khare-18yearold-inv_n_3307519.html

30 Andraka, J. (2017). *About Jack Andraka*. Retrieved from www.jackandraka.com/about

31 Brokaw, T. (1998). *The greatest generation*. New York: Random House Trade Paperbacks.

32 Brokaw, T. (1998), p. 8.

33 History.com Staff. (2009b). *Japanese-American relocation*. Retrieved from www.history. com/topics/world-war-ii/japanese-american-relocation

34 Boustan, L. (2017). *The culprits behind white flight*. Retrieved from www.nytimes. com/2017/05/15/opinion/white-flight.html

35 Boustan, L. (2017).

36 Khan Academy. (n.d.). *African Americans, women, and the GI Bill*. Retrieved from www.khanacademy.org/humanities/ap-us-history/period-8/apush-postwar-era/a/ african-americans-women-and-the-gi-bill

37 Khan Academy. (n.d.).

38 Fehrenbach, D. N. (2017). *The capitol's age pyramid: A graying congress*. Retrieved from http://online.wsj.com/public/resources/documents/info-CONGRESS_AGES_1009. html

39 Irwin, N., Miller, C. C., & Sanger-Katz, M. (2014). *America's racial divide, charted*. Retrieved from www.nytimes.com/2014/08/20/upshot/americas-racial-divide-charted. html

40 Brown, A. (2016). *Blacks have made gains in political leadership, but gaps remain*. Retrieved from www.pewresearch.org/fact-tank/2016/06/28/blacks-have-made-gains-in-u-s-political-leadership-but-gaps-remain/

41 Gao, G. (2014). *Chart of the week: The black-white gap in incarceration rates.* Retrieved from www.pewresearch.org/fact-tank/2014/07/18/chart-of-the-week-the-black-white-gap-in-incarceration-rates/

42 Katz, A. (2017). *Unrest in Virginia.* Retrieved from http://time.com/charlottesville-white-nationalist-rally-clashes/

43 Brokaw, T. (1998), pp. 9 and 11.

44 The National World War II Museum. (n.d.b). *History at a glance: World in World War II.* Retrieved from www.nationalww2museum.org/students-teachers/student-resources/research-starters/women-wwii

45 Wallace, L. (2011). *The complex legacy of Rosie the Riveter.* Retrieved from www.theatlantic.com/national/archive/2011/01/the-complex-legacy-of-rosie-the-riveter/69268/

46 Brown, A. (2017). *The data on women leaders.* Retrieved from www.pewsocialtrends.org/2017/03/17/the-data-on-women-leaders/

47 Wallace, L. (2011).

48 Seemiller, C. & Grace, M. (2017). *Generation Z stories study.* Unpublished raw data.

49 Pew Research Center. (2010b). *The return of the multi-generational household.* Retrieved from www.pewsocialtrends.org/files/2010/10/752-multi-generational-families.pdf

50 Howe, N. (2014b).

51 Pew Research Center. (2010b).

52 Seemiller, C. & Grace, M. (2016). *Generation Z goes to college.* San Francisco: Jossey-Bass.

53 Howe, N. (2014b).

54 Seemiller, C. & Grace, M. (2016).

55 Hamby, A. L. (n.d.). *Harry S. Truman: Campaigns and elections.* Retrieved from https://millercenter.org/president/truman/campaigns-and-elections

56 Gallup. (2017). *Presidential approval ratings: Gallup historical statistics and trends.* Retrieved from http://news.gallup.com/poll/116677/presidential-approval-ratings-gallup-historical-statistics-trends.aspx

57 Seemiller, C. & Grace, M. (2016).

58 Brokaw, T. (1998).

3 Who is Generation Z?

Mikaila Ulmer started her entrepreneurial days at the age of four after having been stung by a bee . . . twice. Like other kids, she could have simply put on bandages and waited for the stings to subside, hoping to avoid bees in the future. But instead, Mikaila became fascinated with bees. She wanted to learn more about them, their role in pollination, and their path to potential extinction.[1] It seemed natural then that her passion for bees would lead her to develop her own brand of lemonade, which involved sweetening her grandmother's flaxseed lemonade recipe with honey from local beekeepers.[2] Mikaila went on to enter her lemonade into a business competition for children, and Me and the Bees Lemonade was born.[3] Mikaila's motivation isn't just serving up a refreshing glass of lemonade; her motto is "Buy a Bottle . . . Save a bee"[4] as a portion of the proceeds go back to supporting local and international organizations that work to save honeybees. Mikaila has since expanded her original lemonade stand as Me and Bees has been featured on Shark Tank and is now sold at Whole Foods across the U.S.[5]

Amandla Stenberg stole the hearts of many in her role as Rue in *The Hunger Games* but has since captured the attention of millions using her voice and platform as a social activist. In an assignment for her history class, Amandla and a classmate studied cultural appropriation. From this project, Amandla went on to create a Tumblr page on the subject and YouTube video, "Don't Cash Crop On My Cornrows,"[6] which has more than 2 million views.[7] At the age of 17, *Dazed* magazine called her "one of the most incendiary voices of her generation."[8] When Amandla uses her voice for activism, people hear it – including her 310,000 Twitter followers, 1.4 million Instagram followers, and even Oprah Winfrey.[9] In addition to speaking out against cultural appropriation, Amandla promotes acceptance of others across race, gender, and sexual orientation.

Mikaila and Amandla are just two members of Generation Z, but they share similarities with many of the nearly 70 million in their generational cohort.[10] They're smart, digitally infused, driven, and ready to bring about change in our world.

Characteristics of the cohort

Just as Millennials have been characterized as optimistic and self-interested[11] and Generation X as independent and cynical,[12] Generation Z has developed their own cohort identity and characteristics. In an effort to learn more about Generation Z, we thought no one would be better to look to for answers than members of Generation Z themselves. In our 2014 Generation Z Goes to College Study, we asked students to describe themselves utilizing a list of characteristics. More than 70 percent identified as loyal, thoughtful, determined, compassionate, open-minded, and responsible.[13] However, when asked to describe their peers of the same age, they instead chose words like competitive, spontaneous, adventuresome, and curious.[14] While our study offers one view on the characteristics associated with Generation Z, we are not alone in our pursuit to better understand this generation. Dr. Candace Steele Flippin, author of *Generation Z in the Workplace*, found that those in her study described themselves as eager, hardworking, creative, and motivated.[15] And findings from the College Senior Survey point to their self-identified characteristics of perspective-taking, tolerance for different beliefs, cooperation, and drive.[16]

> **❝** *'I think being kind to one another, looking on the bright side, and being an honest genuine person' can make the world a better place.* **❞**
> – Member of Generation Z

Another set of descriptors useful in understanding Generation Z centers on character strengths. The VIA Institute on Character is a nonprofit organization dedicated to helping individuals uncover and leverage their character strengths.[17] More than 150,000 members of Generation Z have taken the VIA Character Strengths Survey to better understand their core characteristics, qualities, and strengths. Findings from the data highlight Generation Z's top strengths, which include honesty, kindness, humor, fairness, and judgment.[18] As honesty focuses on having goals and actions that accurately reflect interests and intentions,[19] there is a link to their desire for authenticity – both in expressing it themselves and expecting it from others.[20] There is also a clear connection between those in Generation Z identifying with kindness[21] and fairness[22] as character strengths and their self-description of being compassionate and open-minded.[23] Another prominent strength for many in this generation is judgment, which does not allude to close-mindedness or being judgmental but rather the willingness to actively search for evidence from multiple sources to make a fair decision about a situation.[24] Their open-mindedness may help them look at situations and issues from multiple perspectives and in unconventional ways. Finally, as it sounds, the strength of humor is about making people laugh and finding a cheerful view on adversity.[25] Growing up alongside YouTube, the hub of entertaining videos, it makes sense that those in Generation Z would seek out and use humor as a way to balance the more serious concerns they have in life. Table 3.1 clusters the aforementioned characteristics into four main thematic categories.

Table 3.1 Major Characteristics of Generation Z

Integrity	Openness
Honesty	Creativity
Fairness	Open-Mindedness
Loyalty	Humor
Responsibility	Curiosity
Judgment	Sense of Adventure
	Spontaneity
	Perspective-Taking
	Tolerance

Tenacity	Care
Eagerness	Understanding Others
Hard work	Thoughtfulness
Motivation	Compassion
Determination	Kindness
Competition	
Drive	

Generations do not just haphazardly develop cohort identities and characteristics. There are many larger influences at play, including the impact of societal events during their upbringing, technological advancements, and relationships with parents, family, and peers, which will be explored further in this book.

Diversity

To say that Generation Z is diverse is an understatement. With 49 percent identifying as non-White, Generation Z is the most racially diverse generation to date.[26] While their diversity includes a growth in the makeup of people of different races, the number of multiracial youth has also been increasing, making it the fastest growing of all identity groups in the U.S.[27]

In addition to substantial racial diversity, this generation has high rates of non-heterosexual orientation and acceptance of gender fluid identification. A 2015 study by the J. Walter Thompson Intelligence Group found that only 48 percent of Generation Z identified as exclusively heterosexual.[28] This same study found that 81 percent feel that gender doesn't define a person as much as it used to, so much so that those in Generation Z are less likely to ascribe to traditional gender binaries and are more open to gender fluidity.[29] Further, more than half know someone who prefers non-traditional gender pronouns, such as "they/them."[30] Their openness and non-conforming identities have expanded the makeup industry, specifically, for men. In 2016, Cover Girl announced its first male makeup model, 17-year-old member of Generation Z, James Charles.[31] Cover

Girl is not alone as other companies such as Sephora and Giorgio Armani have created gender-neutral beauty lines to appeal to men.[32] While makeup may be moving towards being more gender-neutral, perhaps the clothing industry will be next as only 44 percent of those in Generation Z actually buy gender-specific clothing.[33]

Beyond the diverse makeup of their own generation, members of Generation Z have grown up in a world in which they see more diversity in leaders and high-profile individuals than perhaps even young people did a generation ago. President Barack Obama's presidency, followed by Hillary Clinton's 2016 Democratic nomination, showed Generation Z that people of color and women can serve in leadership roles at all levels, a sentiment many in older generations didn't experience when they were young. Growing up in an increasingly diverse world has set the stage for many in Generation Z to be accepting of people from backgrounds different from their own,[34] develop open-mindedness, and cultivate a strong desire for inclusion and equality,[35] all of which in their minds are fundamental to making the world a better place.[36]

*   I think inclusion will make our world a better place. We tend to push people aside that are different from what we know or consider 'normal,' but that shouldn't be the case. *
– Member of Generation Z

As more than 60 percent of members of Generation Z believe diversity is an asset that strengthens America,[37] it's not surprising then that the vast majority are making an effort to leverage that asset. The 2017 College Senior Survey found that 83 percent of members of Generation Z rated themselves as above average in their "ability to see the world from someone else's perspective"[38] and 87 percent in their "ability to work cooperatively with diverse people."[39] Between the diversity within their own cohort and their ability and ease in working with others who may be different from them, we may have a generation that doesn't see diversity as something to be managed, programmed on, or hired for – but instead, simply just a reflection of who they are.

Identity

Whether it is a profile picture, avatar, Twitter handle, or Bitmoji, members of Generation Z are easily able to showcase their individual identities in a world of digital customization. While those in older generations experienced their adolescent and young adult years predominantly live and in person, for those in Generation Z, many exist in two different places at the same time. Their "real life" identity and online identity can reflect two entirely different people, one for each setting. And, some may even be managing several different identities online. A report by design and innovation firm, Ziba Design, found that more than 75 percent of those in Generation Z are comfortable negotiating multiple identities online.[40]

David and Jonah Stillman, authors of *Gen Z@Work*, point out how Generation Z is able to manage their digital preferences as a way to control how they express their online identities.[41] Many have grown accustomed to privacy settings, in which they can monitor who they interact with and who sees particular content. In addition, these young people can carefully curate their identity with every Instagram post, Snapchat, and tweet, sharing only what they want others to know about them. It makes sense then that social media plays a role in how members of Generation Z see themselves, how they see others, and how others see them. GenHQ's iGen Tech Disruption study found that 42 percent of those in Generation Z believe that "social media has a direct impact on how they feel about themselves."[42] This is double that of Baby Boomers, almost 20 percent higher than their Gen X parents, and even 11 percent higher than tech-savvy Millennials.[43]

Values

Like any culture, generational cohorts have their own set of beliefs and values in what they deem important. For Generation Z, Dr. Steele Flippin found that happiness, relationships, financial security, and careers ranked among the most important.[44] Our 2017 Generation Z Stories Study elicited similar responses to the question, "What to you would be a good life?" More than half described financial stability, making it the most discussed of any response.[45] Family and relationships, meaningful work, and happiness were not far behind.[46]

Table 3.2 Generations Z Values[47]

Financial Security	Happiness	Family and Relationships	Meaningful Work
"A good life would be a life where I am happy and comfortable in my job which then allows me to provide for myself and/or my family to the point we can live comfortably and not be in need of basic necessities."	*"[A good life would be] one where I'm happy with the way I'm living and feel fulfilled. Including a stable income (not necessarily high income), supportive friends, family (spouse and kids ... maybe some dogs), a job I love to do."*	*"The idea of having meaningful conversations with people and making personal connections [gets me excited for the day]."*	*"I get excited knowing that one day I will have a career that impacts society in a positive way."*

Motivations

Members of Generation Z may describe themselves as motivated,[48] determined,[49] and driven.[50] But, what exactly drives and motivates them? First, as many greatly value relationships,[51] it makes sense that they are relationally

motivated. For example, 75 percent of respondents in our Generation Z Goes to College Study
indicated being motivated by
not wanting to let others down
and 75 percent by making a difference for others.[52] This generation is also highly motivated
by engaging with their passions,
specifically those related to
causes they care about; 74 per-

*❝ I am excited to get out
of bed each day because
it might be the day that I
change the world. There are
so many people who need help
in the world and I want to
help them. ❞*
– Member of Generation Z

cent of respondents in our study reported that advocating for something
they believe in can be motivating.

In addition, 74 percent of those in Generation Z find motivation through
achievement, especially in terms of knowing they could gain credit towards
the next milestone or an opportunity for advancement.[53] Where Millennials
got a reputation for being the "participation trophy" generation,[54] those in
Generation Z might prefer to earn credit in the form of a collection of gold
stars for a job well done or a designation on their transcript for developing a
new skill. Receiving credit for Generation Z can also involve earning badges
or tokens through gamified experiences. Growing up with more access to
video games, many in Generation Z may be accustomed to the instant feedback and individualized nature of progressing through an experience with
levels, lives, and unlocking new territory as a reward for their work. Regardless of method, awarding credit can both prepare those in Generation Z for
advancing to the next level and motivate them to keep moving forward in
their pursuits.

While there are a number of motivating factors for Generation Z, there are
several tactics that just don't appeal to this generation. For example, we found
that fewer than 30 percent are motivated by public recognition, acceptance by
others, competition with others, or the possibility that someone will return the
favor of a good deed.[55] It appears that they aren't motivated by the potential of
receiving accolades or acceptance, or for the opportunity to win, but instead
because doing good work and helping others is the right thing to do.

Conclusion

Generation Z can be characterized as an open-minded, caring, and diverse generation grounded in a sense of integrity and tenacity. These young people value
financial security, family and relationships, meaningful work, and happiness,
and are motivated through relationships, engaging with their passions, and
achievement. But, this generation is more than just a list of words; they are a
powerful force ready to leverage their capacities and tap deeply into what they
care about so they too can leave their legacy.

Notes

1 Me and the Bees. (2017a). *Our story*. Retrieved from https://meandthebees.com/pages/about-us

2 Me and the Bees. (2017a).

3 Me and the Bees. (2017a).

4 Me and the Bees. (2017a), para. 6.

5 Me and the Bees. (2017b). *Where to buy*. Retrieved from www.meandthebees.com/pages/where-to-buy

6 Workneh, L. (2015). *16-year-old Amandla Stenberg schools everyone on cultural appropriation in this powerful video*. Retrieved from www.huffingtonpost.com/2015/04/14/amandla-stenberg-cultural_n_7064420.html

7 YouTube. (2018a). *Don't cash crop on my cornrows*. Retrieved from www.youtube.com/watch?v=O1KJRRSB_XA

8 Amandlastenberg.com. (2018). *About*. Retrieved from www.amandlastenberg.com/about.html, para. 11.

9 Amandlastenberg.com. (2018). para. 11.

10 United States Census Bureau, Population Division. (2016). *Annual estimates of the resident population by single year of age and sex for the United States: April 1, 2010 to July 1, 2016*. Retrieved from www.census.gov/data/datasets/2016/demo/popest/nation-detail.html

11 Stein, J. (2013). *Millennials: The me me me generation*. Retrieved from http://time.com/247/millennials-the-me-me-me-generation/

12 BridgeWorks. (2017a). *Generation X 101*. Retrieved from www.generations.com/2017/02/21/generation-x-101/

13 Seemiller, C. & Grace, M. (2014). *Generation Z goes to college study*. Unpublished raw data.

14 Seemiller, C. & Grace, M. (2014).

15 Steele Flippin, C. (2017). *Generation Z in the workplace*. n.p.: Author.

16 Higher Education Research Institute. (2017). *College Senior Survey*. Data prepared by Higher Education Research Institute.

17 VIA Institute on Character. (2018b). *Home*. Retrieved from www.viacharacter.org/www

18 VIA Institute on Character. (2018g). *The VIA Survey of character strengths: United States Gen Z*. Data prepared by The VIA Institute on Character.

19 VIA Institute on Character. (2018c). *Honesty*. Retrieved from www.viacharacter.org/www/Character-Strengths/Honesty

20 Cheung, J., Davis, T., & Heukaeufer, E. (2017). *Gen Z brand relationships: Authenticity matters*. Retrieved from www-01.ibm.com/common/ssi/cgi-bin/ssialias?htmlfid=GBE03855USEN&

21 VIA Institute on Character. (2018f). *Kindness*. Retrieved from www.viacharacter.org/www/Character-Strengths/Kindness

22 VIA Institute on Character. (2018a). *Fairness*. Retrieved from www.viacharacter.org/www/Character-Strengths/Fairness

23 Seemiller, C. & Grace, M. (2016). *Generation Z goes to college*. San Francisco: Jossey-Bass.

24 VIA Institute on Character. (2018e). *Judgment*. Retrieved from www.viacharacter.org/www/Character-Strengths/Judgment

25 VIA Institute on Character. (2018d). *Humor*. Retrieved from www.viacharacter.org/www/Character-Strengths/Humor

26 Vespa, J., Armstrong, D. M., & Medina, L. (2018). *Demographic turning points for the United States: Population projections for 2020 to 2060.* Retrieved from www.census.gov/library/publications/2018/demo/p25-1144.html

27 Sparks & Honey. (2014). *Meet Generation Z: Forget everything you learned about Millennials.* Retrieved from www.slideshare.net/sparksandhoney/generation-z-final-june-17

28 Tsjeng, Z. (2016). *Teens these days are queer AF, new study says.* Retrieved from https://broadly.vice.com/en_us/article/kb4dvz/teens-these-days-are-queer-af-new-study-says

29 Tsjeng, Z. (2016).

30 Tsjeng, Z. (2016).

31 Thomas, E. (2016). *Makeup for men: Fad or future?* Retrieved from http://wwd.com/beauty-industry-news/beauty-features/beauty-brands-market-makeup-men-10678934/

32 Thomas, E. (2016).

33 Thomas, E. (2016).

34 Engelmeier, S. (2017). *Gen Z: The global generation.* Retrieved from www.inclusion-inc.com/single-post/2017/04/25/Gen-Z-The-Global-Generation?archive_page=60

35 Seemiller, C. & Grace, M. (2014).

36 Seemiller, C. & Grace, M. (2017). *Generation Z stories study.* Unpublished raw data.

37 The Associated Press-NORC Center for Public Affairs Research. (2017). *American teens are politically engaged but pessimistic about country's direction.* Retrieved from www.apnorc.org/projects/Pages/HTML%20Reports/american-teens-are-politically-engaged-but-pessimistic-about-countrys-direction.aspx

38 Higher Education Research Institute. (2017). DIVRATE 1.

39 Higher Education Research Institute. (2017). DIVRATE 5.

40 Suzuki, J. (2016). *Designing for the identity-fluid Gen Z.* Retrieved from https://medium.com/@zibadesign/designing-for-the-identity-fluid-gen-z-b80209e188fa

41 Stillman, D. & Stillman, J. (2017). *Gen Z @ work: How the next generation is transforming the workplace.* New York: HarperCollins, p. 107.

42 The Center for Generational Kinetics. (2016). *Is Gen Z's self-worth determined by social media?* Retrieved from http://genhq.com/igen-genz-social-media-trends-infographic/, para. 3.

43 The Center for Generational Kinetics. (2016).

44 Steele Flippin, C. (2017).

45 Seemiller, C. & Grace, M. (2017).

46 Seemiller, C. & Grace, M. (2017).

47 Seemiller, C. & Grace, M. (2017).

48 Steele Flippin, C. (2017).

49 Seemiller, C. & Grace, M. (2014).

50 Higher Education Research Institute. (2017).

51 Seemiller, C. & Grace, M. (2017).

52 Seemiller, C. & Grace, M. (2014).

53 Seemiller, C. & Grace, M. (2014).

54 Stein, J. (2013).

55 Seemiller, C. & Grace, M. (2014).

Navigating the digital and
physical world

···

4 Technology

••

Humans have been using technology in its most basic form since the earliest record of history.[1] Prehistoric people created technology with tools made of rocks, and Ancient Egyptians developed papyrus as the earliest form of paper.[2] And, until 1827, when the first modern version of a photograph was created, the only way to capture an image was through painting or sketching.[3] Today, many of our tools are completely digital. Writing on actual paper instead of typing on a device can feel archaic. And, if you want to capture a special moment, it only takes a few swipes to snap a photo and upload it to social media or the cloud.

Technological advances have unique impacts on generations. Both the G.I. and Silent Generations gathered around the radio for entertainment and news. But, that shifted drastically with Baby Boomers who grew up with television where they could actually see, rather than solely hear, what was happening. Generation X was the first to go to college with desktop computers. And, Millennials helped create and usher in the era of social media and user-generated content. The technology that shapes Generation Z builds on and evolves from prior generations but also sets the stage for what is to come in the future. So, what technology does Generation Z use and how do they use it?

*** The Internet is my generation's calling. We have the smarts and the determination to use that tool a hundred different ways to connect people, build friendships, and use it to make the world a better place. ***
- Member of Generation Z

Technology today

Technology today has changed the way we do just about everything – from shopping and researching to getting the news and accessing healthcare. Those born before 1995 might remember having to read a map for directions or having to wait to buy a newly released vinyl record, cassette tape, or CD. If you wanted to catch up with a friend, you had to write a letter or call on the phone. The world changed in 1995 when the Internet was commercialized,[4] as it has allowed everyday users access to new information and new ways of life. Today, there are over 3.5 billion Internet users worldwide[5] with 88 percent of Americans having utilized the Internet at least once in the last year.[6]

Generation Z has never known a world without the Internet. For most of their lives, this generation has lived life through not just one screen, but in some cases, up to five screens.[7] These young people have had access to smartphones, tablets, and laptops nearly their entire lives. Even older forms of media, such as radio and television, have since evolved into streaming services where nearly any show or movie can be accessed 24 hours a day. Wearable technology is now available, and monitoring steps and activity through a fitness tracker has become normal. Almost anything needed is just a swipe away.

Smartphones and the mobile movement

Today, those without cell phones are part of a very small minority as 95 percent of American adults now have some type of cellular phone.[8] In 2002, that number was only 62 percent.[9] Similarly, smartphone usage, specifically, has more than doubled since 2011 with 77 percent of American adults today owning a smartphone.[10] In addition, the time spent per day utilizing a smartphone has been on the rise. In 2017, the Nielsen Company reported that the average time spent by adults per day utilizing apps or the Internet on a smartphone has risen to nearly 3 hours a day, an increase of a full hour since 2015.[11]

In looking just at Generation Z teens, 78 percent use a smartphone.[12] The widespread use by those in Generation Z is not surprising in that the median age for this generation to receive their first cell phone is 12 years-old.[13] A study by Google found that getting a cell phone was among teens' top milestones in life, right after graduating school and getting a driver's license.[14] Not only do most of those in Generation Z own a smartphone, it is their preferred device over laptop computers, tablets, and gaming consoles.[15] Ninety-one percent use their smartphones to access the Internet.[16] But what they do most frequently is text and chat with friends and family.[17] Wondering if they are Android or Apple users? This generation is fairly evenly divided.[18]

Computers

The earliest versions of the modern computer were developed in the 1930s to assist in calculations and computation of equations,[19] meaning members of the G.I. Generation and Silent Generation were utilizing the earliest versions of a piece of technology that has become integral in modern life. While the initial versions of the computer were constructed in the 1930s, personal computers did not become a reality until the late 1970s and early 1980s.[20] Today, 78 percent of households in the U.S. have a computer, a tenfold growth since 1984.[21]

Desktop computers are more popular among older generations with 69 percent of Generation X and 64 percent of Boomers owning a desktop computer.[22] In a 2011 Pew Research Center study, only 57 percent of Millennials owned a desktop computer, but 70 percent actually owned laptops.[23] While Generation Z heavily uses mobile technology, they have not abandoned computers altogether. Eighty-eight percent of Generation Z teens own or have access to a computer of some sort.[24]

With the growth of the number of households with computers, it is not surprising that the age in which Generation Z started using computers was early in their childhood. Common Sense Media found that 88 percent of youth ages five to eight have used a computer. While this study included some members of Generation Z's successor generation, Generation Alpha, their key findings highlight that the youngest members of Generation Z have likely already used a computer by the time they have entered kindergarten.

Tablets

Even in the late 1990s, the term "tablet" was still associated either with a paper booklet used to take notes or a vitamin supplement. While Microsoft introduced the first modern-day tablet technology in 2000, Apple revolutionized it in 2010 with the iPad.[25] Since its release, global sales for the iPad have reached around 300 million.[26] With the popularity of the iPad, other technology companies have introduced their own version of the tablet including Amazon's Kindle and Fire, Microsoft's Surface, and Samsung's Galaxy Tab. Tablets give users the modified power of a computer with mobility similar to a smartphone. As of 2015, there were more than 1 billion tablet users worldwide, equivalent to 20 percent of the world's population.[27] And, this number is projected to grow.[28] In 2015, the Pew Research Center found that nearly half of adults in the U.S. owned a tablet of some kind.[29] While tablets can have similar functions to the smartphone or laptop computer, they are more often used for a very specific reason – entertainment. Whether watching videos, listening to music, reading, or gaming, 43 percent of the time that adults spend on a tablet is for entertainment purposes.[30]

Tablet use is not solely reserved for adults as the image of a small child watching videos or playing games on a tablet has become more common. In a study of parents of children under 4 years-old, more than a third of children had used a tablet or smartphone before their first birthday.[31] In a separate study of parents, Common Sense Media found that 42 percent of children under the age of 8 have their own tablet, with more than half of them getting their device between the ages of 5 and 8 years-old.[32] While those studies might be referring mostly to their Generation Alpha younger brothers and sisters, having a tablet in the home seems commonplace today. In looking specifically at Generation Z, though, their tablet use is also significant. It is projected that by 2020, 16.9 million 12- to 17-year-old Generation Z tweens and teens and 18.7 million 18- to 24-year-old Generation Z young adults will be tablet users.[33]

Television: From console to digital

Watching television has been a common leisure activity for generations. During the 2017–2018 television season, there were an estimated 119.6 million households in the U.S. with a television set.[34] Television technology has come a long way since the first T.V.s hit the market in 1928.[35] Think back to the big, bulky, black and white televisions that families would gather around to watch shows. Today, if the whole family doesn't want to watch the same program, everyone can view their favorites on their own devices in separate rooms.

Television content for early viewers in the 1940s and 1950s was limited to black and white content from a few networks transmitted over an antenna.[36] Cable television was made available in the 1980s allowing users to pay for a subscription to access hundreds of channels through direct cable.[37] Today, streaming television through an Internet connection has become a prominent way for viewers to tune in. More than half of households with televisions have at least one Internet-enabled device with streaming capabilities,[38] which is helpful to the 61 percent of those younger than 30 who indicate that online streaming is their primary way of watching T.V.[39]

Watching a television show, however, is no longer just an activity in which you have to use an actual television set. Streaming technology allows for viewers to tune in from wherever they choose through an Internet-enabled device, meaning catching up on your favorite show or tuning in for a news segment may take place on the go via a mobile device like a smartphone or tablet. Seventy percent of those in Generation Z actually refer to streaming content online as "watching television."[40] YouTube, Netflix, and Hulu are rated as the "coolest" streaming platforms by Generation Z teens to consume video content.[41]

With tuning in more flexible than ever before, it would be assumed that young people, who are likely the savviest with technology, would be watching more television than other generations. While the average time Americans over the age of 15 spend per day watching T.V. shows is 2.73 hours, the average time spent per week watching television by those ages 15 to 24 (which is mostly comprised of Generation Z) is considerably lower at 2.03 hours per week.[42] Interestingly, Millennials (ages 24 to 34) report watching the least amount of television per week at 1.95 hours.[43] Despite the dip for the Millennial age group, T.V. watching rates seem to increase with each age cohort peaking at 4 hours per week for those over 65.[44] While members of Generation Z watch less television than the average American across all age groups, it's hard to know now if that rate will increase over time following the path of older generations or decline in their mid-20s and 30s to be comparable with viewing patterns of their Millennial counterparts.

Wearable technology

Tracking your steps, sleep, location, and workout activity from a small device attached to your body would seem like a thing from a science fiction movie. Wearable technology, such as smartwatches, smart jewelry, health and fitness trackers, and smart glasses, combine both physical and online experiences through "smart" versions of everyday accessories. Wearable devices like the Apple Watch do not just track health and physical activities but can also connect to a smartphone through a Bluetooth connection, allowing for users to get notifications from their phones to their watches when they get a call or text message. Wearable technology has steadily grown in adoption since 2015, and nearly one in four adults utilize wearable technology of some sort.[45] While there is not much data specifically on Generation Z users, research indicates that younger adults, between the ages of 18 and 34 years-old, make up the largest share of wearable technology users.[46]

Navigating life – physically and digitally

There is no shortage of technology available in today's society, and there is no denying that technology has changed the way most of us live. But, how is Generation Z, specifically, using technology to navigate the world around them?

Payment apps

Today's technology allows us to navigate life and accomplish tasks differently and possibly more efficiently than ever before. Gone are the days of having to visit a bank teller in person to deposit or withdraw money. Almost all banks offer an online banking option, and more than half of smartphone users have done their banking on a mobile device.[47] Beyond just doing banking online, payment apps remove the need to write a check or withdraw cash and instead allow users to send people money or make purchases online, regardless of the user's bank. Payment apps really seem to resonate with young people. A study by Dealspotr found that more than 46 percent of those in Generation Z prefer payment apps over using a credit card when buying online. But, this generation doesn't use just any payment app. Nearly 22 percent of those in Generation Z prefer PayPal, and 12 percent prefer Apple Pay.[48]

From clothes to food: Online buying

While using platforms like Amazon might make it easy to purchase a book or pair of shoes, it's even easy to order food online to be delivered directly to your door. Whether getting groceries from the supermarket or having a courier bring your favorite dish fresh from a restaurant, we never seem to have to leave our homes. And food delivery apps are becoming quite popular. For example, in 2017, GrubHub, a dining delivery app, reported having more than 14 million diners worldwide.[49] But, those diners don't necessarily include everyone. In a study by Mintel, 53 percent of those 55 and older said, "nothing would motivate them to use these services," whereas that was only the case for 11 percent of 18 to 24 year-olds.[50]

eMedicine

Even managing our physical and mental health has evolved with technology. Sixty-two percent of those with smartphones have used their mobile devices to get information about a health condition.[51] We can do more than just check our symptoms before going to see a medical professional; we can even vet healthcare providers by searching online for background information, reviews, and ratings similar to how we would shop online for a product or find a good restaurant with Yelp. In addition, telemedicine has made it possible for providers to connect with their patients through online messaging and video chatting, possibly streamlining the wait time for an appointment and reducing overcrowded waiting rooms. And, while telemedicine might seem like something from the future, in 2017 alone, 70 percent of healthcare providers had utilized telemedicine.[52] While we don't yet know the details of Generation Z's use of eMedicine, having so many digital options in the palm of your hand can make managing health easier and more convenient, perhaps being quite the draw for this generation.

GPS meets social media

Mobile technology even serves as a literal navigation tool when users are behind the wheel and on the go. More than two-thirds of smartphone users utilize a GPS while driving.[53] While traditional navigation apps like Google Maps and Apple Maps offer turn-by-turn directions, the app, Waze, uses crowdsourcing and other integrated social features to provide navigation. By incorporating the option for users to earn points for reporting or editing a map, Waze integrates gamification,[54] which aligns with one of the primary ways many in Generation Z like to be motivated – by achieving milestones.[55] Waze has also forged a partnership with the music app, Spotify, to make listening to music and navigation seamlessly connected by integrating features across both apps while in use.[56] With 25 percent of those in Generation Z having used Spotify in the last month, it's no surprise that an app like Waze may be appealing.[57]

Information and entertainment

Along with using technology as a tool for daily tasks, many in Generation Z are using it for learning new information and for entertainment. Their devices provide a means for consuming content, and the countless platforms available make it easy to find nearly any information online.

Push notifications and breaking news

Technology today allows users to access seemingly limitless information and provide more ways to stay up to date on current events. For instance, more than two-thirds of smartphone users utilize their phones to follow along and stay informed of breaking news.[58] And more than half get news alerts sent directly to their phones through push notifications.[59] Even with the increasing access to mobile technologies, however, television is still the most preferred platform for getting the news on a global scale – at least for members of the Silent Generation, Baby Boomers, and Gen Xers.[60] Generation Z, on the other hand, is the least likely to utilize television for staying up to date on the news and current events.[61] Why would you wait to tune into the nightly news or watch a news show the next day when you can follow along with breaking news on a mobile device?

From DIY hacks to how-to videos

Searching for information online has come a long way since the days of Netscape. In fact, Generation Z has probably never even used Netscape as it was disbanded in the early 2000s.[62] Google now serves as a one-stop shop to find any information at any time. "Google It" is more than just a commonly known phrase used to look up something online; the word, Google, was officially added to the dictionary as a verb in 2006.[63] The Internet is the first place more than three-quarters of those in Generation Z look when in need of information.[64] But they are not just using a search engine to find what they need; many in Generation Z also turn to online videos. We found in our Generation Z Goes to College Study that video-based platforms offered the digital space of preference for this generation in gaining new knowledge.[65] Another study found that two in three members of Generation Z utilize YouTube as a way to learn and, further, half of those in Generation Z couldn't live without YouTube.[66]

For a good laugh

Where the G.I. Generation had the radio and Baby Boomers had the television for entertainment, those in Generation Z can use a variety of devices including smartphones, computers, and tablets. The Trifecta Research Group found that Generation Z teens spend an average of nearly 9 hours per day using technology for entertainment purposes, such as listening to music or watching television shows or videos.[67] In a study by Google, more than 70 percent of Generation Z teens (ages 13 to 17) reported watching three or more hours of videos a day for entertainment on their smartphones alone.[68] This is nearly three times the average amount of time adults spend using digital devices to watch videos.[69] And when those in Generation Z are not surfing YouTube or other online sites for videos, they are on social media doing so. According to the Global Web Index, nearly half of those in Generation Z report using social media to find funny or entertaining content.[70]

Social connection

We've come a long way since the Internet was only a collection of static web pages where a small group of select developers curated digital content. Now, the Internet has become synonymous with Web 2.0 user-generated content[71] where everyday people can develop and distribute information online. In Generation Z's lifetime alone, the number of websites has grown from 23,000 in 1995 to more than 1.7 billion as of 2017.[72] Not only has Web 2.0 ushered in the opportunity for more content creators, it has generated a space for digital social connection.

An account for every occasion

Ninety-four percent of Internet users have at least one account on a social media platform,[73] meaning nearly all contribute to the Web 2.0 format through consuming and/or creating content. While members of all living generations have access to social media, Generation Z was born and raised during the social media era. It's no surprise then that younger Internet users are more likely to have more social media accounts compared to older users,[74] with those under the age of 24 having an average of 8.7 accounts on different social media platforms.[75] Having many accounts to manage, it makes sense that more than half of Generation Z teens report using social media for three or more hours a day,[76] and young people ages 16 to 24 spend a third of their time online on social media.[77] But, they don't use each of these accounts and platforms uniformly; each has a specific purpose that reflects the diverse ways in which they use social media.

Snapchat and generational agency

Consider that the oldest in Generation Z were just 9 years-old when Facebook was created in 2004 and 11 years-old when Twitter emerged in 2006. Until Snapchat came out in 2011, Generation Z had primarily inherited social media platforms from older generations. While they are on these sites, it has been Snapchat that has been this generation's go-to for social media. With more than 178 million daily users,[78] Snapchat has become the most used and preferred social media platform among members of Generation Z in keeping in touch with friends.[79] As Grace Masback, author of *The Voice of Gen Z*, points out, Generation Z has a sense of ownership and agency in regard to Snapchat,[80] lending credence to the nearly half of Generation Z teens who believe Snapchat is the most important social network.[81]

> **❝ I use Snapchat the most, because it is a way to communicate with others quickly while getting to see their facial expressions. ❞**
> *- Member of Generation Z*

Instagram and managing multiple identities

With more than 90 million posts shared by users daily,[82] Instagram is also adored by Generation Z users. In a 2017 study, researchers found that 73 percent of 13 to 24 year-olds reported using Instagram, just slightly fewer than the number who use Snapchat.[83] Those in Generation Z prefer to use Instagram to share about themselves[84] as the platform allows users to carefully tailor their profile and audience to determine who sees their content. Being able to customize and restrict the information they share aligns with Generation Z's concerns for privacy.[85] It makes sense then that more than half of Generation Z teens have chosen to not post something online or on social media for fear of the impact doing so would have on their reputations.[86] Some members of Generation Z have taken their identity curation to new levels and operate multiple Instagram accounts dependent on the audience – their Rinsta and their Finsta. Rinsta refers to a "real Instagram" account, which typically has more followers and features content that is carefully crafted.[87] The Finsta account is a much more private account, shared with a small group of friends, where users may post silly content, memes, and screenshots.[88]

Facebook for family

While Generation Z favors Snapchat and Instagram, many are still using Facebook – but for a very specific purpose. Results from our Generation Z Goes to College Study indicate that 87 percent use Facebook to keep up with others, but only 53 percent use it to share information about themselves.[89] The disproportionate rate of seeking out information about others versus sharing content about themselves is not surprising as many older people have taken to Facebook making it less than ideal for young people to connect with their peers with a sense of privacy. In the early years, Facebook was a relatively "adult free" zone for college-aged and young adult Millennials to openly express themselves and gather with their friends. But now, just about everyone is on Facebook, including Generation Z's parents and grandparents. Seventy percent of Generation Z Facebook users are friends with their parents, and more than 90 percent are friends with extended family members.[90] But, they're not on Facebook sharing intimate details reserved for their friends; many use Facebook for the main purpose of staying connected to family.[91] With parents and family members being heavily present, Facebook is simply no longer the "adult-free" space it was at its inception. Given the many different options for social media, many in Generation Z have found digital spaces on other platforms, like Snapchat and Instagram, away from their parents and older family members.

Twitter and the fast-paced feed

While not as popular as Snapchat, Instagram, or Facebook, Twitter still engages more than a third of 13 to 24 year-olds.[92] In our Generation Z Goes to College Study, we found that those in Generation Z use Twitter far more so to keep up with others than to post content.[93] Many like to quickly access information and follow celebrities and other brands.[94] And the hashtag makes it easy for them to keep informed about certain topics, people, or even movements.

For those in Generation Z who do share content on Twitter, the platform allows them to post as often or as little as they would like. With the limited character count and fast-paced feed, Twitter is Generation Z's space to share quick snippets of themselves.[95] And, with customizable privacy functions, users can protect their tweets from public views should they so choose; doing so allows those in Generation Z to maintain the online privacy they desire.

Anonymity and avatars in a sharing world

With a high concern for privacy online, it is understandable that many in Generation Z gravitate toward platforms where they can share their opinion or expertise in an anonymous way.[96] For example, sites such as Tumblr allow users to blog under nicknames.[97] Therefore, Generation Z bloggers could share their opinions while staying anonymous and disassociated from their offline identities. It appears that Tumblr is quite the draw for many young people as 20 percent of all 18- to 29-year-old Internet users use Tumblr, a rate nearly double that of 30 to 49 year-olds.[98] And, with Generation Z specifically, a study by the Global Web Index found that 29 percent are on Tumblr.[99]

" I keep my Tumblr very private and use it mostly to re-blog relatable posts and pictures. "
- Member of Generation Z

Participating in an online community, such as Reddit, can also foster anonymity as users can share and rate content under their usernames and avatars.[100] By being able to comment or rate content without disclosing names or personal descriptors, users can share their thoughts and feelings without any consequences to their offline identities. And with 58 percent of Reddit users being between 18 and 29 years-old, it appears that this is a highly trafficked platform for young people.[101] It's not surprising then that 16 percent of those in Generation Z report having used Reddit.[102]

Table 4.1 Generation Z and Social Media Platforms

Social Media Platform	How Generation Z Uses It	Prevalence of Use Among Generation Z	What Generation Z Has to Say About It[103]
YouTube	Learn new information and for entertainment	84 percent of those in Generation Z have used YouTube in the last month.[104]	*"I use YouTube the most because I am able to listen to music and find videos that sometimes are related to school or just random facts."*
Snapchat	Connect with friends	67 percent of those in Generation Z use Snapchat and 1 in 3 use it to stay connected to friends.[105]	*"It's fast and more fun than texting."*

Social Media Platform	How Generation Z Uses It	Prevalence of Use Among Generation Z	What Generation Z Has to Say About It
Instagram	Share about themselves	73 percent of teens and young adults (13 to 24 year-olds) use Instagram.[106]	*"Instagram is the method I use most because I like to communicate through pictures."*
Facebook	Follow others' lives, especially family	46.2 million users between the ages of 13 and 24.[107]	*"More of my friends and family are on Facebook so I can talk to them much more than through another social media outlet."*
Twitter	Keep up with short updates and news posts	1 in 3 teens use Twitter.[108]	*"Twitter is a good way to get short concise information"*
Tumblr	Share opinion or expertise	1 in 6 teens and young adults (13 to 24 year-olds) use Tumblr.[109]	*"It's anonymous and I can express myself freely."*
Online Communities/ Reddit	Share opinion or expertise	1 in 6 Generation Z users are utilizing online communities/ Reddit.[110]	*"It gives me specific boards made to talk about the things I'm interested in with others who share my interests."*

Online all the time

With today's technology allowing users of all ages to be online at any time, logging on and engaging in the digital world has become an integral part of life. But, technology use has a delicate tipping point between the benefits of unlimited content/connection and overuse/dependency. Growing up in a constantly connected world has shaped Generation Z's perspectives and behaviors related to technology use – for better and for worse.

Digitally native and digitally dependent

With the widespread access and use of digital technology today, the potential for dependency and addiction is a real concern. Nearly half of American adult smartphone users indicate that they could not live without their phone.[111] In a study by LivePerson, researchers found that 70 percent of younger Millennials and older members of Generation Z have their phone within arm's reach when they sleep, and more than half check their phones if they happen to wake up sometime during the night.[112] Another study, conducted by Deloitte

> **❝** *[My generation can make the world a better place] by taking a step back from technology and knowing that there is a limit with certain things.* **❞**
>
> *- Member of Generation Z*

in 2017, found that 18 to 24 year-olds report checking their phones 86 times a day, which is higher than any other age group.[113] With 89 percent of Generation Z teens utilizing the Internet multiple times a day,[114] it's unlikely they will disconnect from the online world with ease. Even monetary rewards wouldn't likely sway them toward giving up their phones and online technology. LivePerson found that 43 percent of people under the age of 35 would give up their smartphone forever if they were paid to do so, but only to the tune of $5 million.[115]

Multitasking across multiple devices

With many having a vast array of digital devices at their fingertips, the ability to multi-task across these devices can be alluring. It's not surprising then that two-thirds of those in Generation Z frequently are on multiple devices at one time.[116] They can answer a text message on their smartphones while working on their schoolwork on their laptops as their favorite show is streaming in the background. While it might be obvious that dividing attention across so many devices and discrete tasks can be challenging, more than half of Generation Z teens report engaging in multitasking across devices while completing school-work and don't feel doing so negatively impacts the quality of their work.[117] Although these young people may not feel their multitasking has a downside, others argue that it can lead to decreases in the filtering of irrelevant or incorrect information.[118]

eMotional impact and support

There are many ways that digital technology can influence the lives of those in Generation Z, and its effect on emotional health is no exception. The Center for Generational Kinetics found that 39 percent of members of Generation Z reported social media having an impact on their self-esteem.[119] This is not only because the identities of many in Generation Z are intertwined with their online lives but also that technology offers a venue to connect with others for emotional support. In a study of Generation Z teens, the Pew Research Center found that nearly 70 percent had received support on social media while dealing with a challenge or going through a tough time.[120] It appears that if these young people can't find someone in real life that is going through a similar experience or they just don't want to talk in-person to somebody in their inner circle about an issue, they can use their digital technology to try to find that support and connection online.

Conclusion

Digital technology has become an essential part of everyday life for many, and thus, a defining contextual force shaping Generation Z. While this generation is not solely synonymous with technology and social media, we cannot ignore the profound impact it has had in how they communicate, build relationships, learn, lead, and work.

Notes

1 Woodford, C. (2018). *Technology timeline*. Retrieved from www.explainthatstuff.com/timeline.html
2 Woodford, C. (2018).
3 Woodford, C. (2018).
4 WebpageFX. (2009). *The history of the internet in a nutshell*. Retrieved from www.webpagefx.com/blog/web-design/the-history-of-the-internet-in-a-nutshell/
5 Smith, K. (2018). *Marketing: 116 amazing social media statistics and facts*. Retrieved from www.brandwatch.com/blog/96-amazing-social-media-statistics-and-facts-for-2016/
6 Smith, A. (2017). *Record shares of Americans now own smartphones, have home broadband*. Retrieved from www.pewresearch.org/fact-tank/2017/01/12/evolution-of-technology/
7 Sparks & Honey. (2014). *Meet Generation Z: Forget everything you learned about Millennials*. Retrieved from www.slideshare.net/sparksandhoney/generation-z-final-june-17
8 Pew Research Center. (2018a). *Mobile fact sheet*. Retrieved from www.pewinternet.org/fact-sheet/mobile/
9 Pew Research Center. (2018a).
10 Pew Research Center. (2018a).
11 Nielsen. (2017c). *The Nielsen total audience report: Q2 2017*. Retrieved from www.nielsen.com/us/en/insights/reports/2017/the-nielsen-total-audience-q2-2017.html
12 Google. (2017b). *It's lit: A guide to what teens think is cool*. Retrieved from https://storage.googleapis.com/think/docs/its-lit.pdf
13 Google. (2017a). *Generation Z: New insights into the mobile-first mindset of teens*. Retrieved from http://storage.googleapis.com/think/docs/GenZ_Insights_All_teens.pdf
14 Google. (2017a).
15 Cheug, J., Glass, S., McCarty, D., & Wong, C. K. (2016). *Uniquely Generation Z: What brands should know about today's youngest consumers*. Retrieved from www-01.ibm.com/common/ssi/cgi-bin/ssialias?htmlfid=GBE03799USEN&
16 Lenhart, A., Duggan, M., Perrin, A., Stepler, R., Rainie, L., & Parker, K. (2015). *Teens, social media, & technology over 2015: Smartphones facilitate shifts in communication landscape for teens*. Retrieved from www.pewinternet.org/2015/04/09/teens-social-media-technology-2015
17 Cheug, J., Glass, S., McCarty, D., & Wong, C. K. (2016).
18 Google. (2017b).
19 Encyclopedia Britannica. (2018). *Computer*. Retrieved from www.britannica.com/technology/computer/History-of-computing#ref235877
20 Encyclopedia Britannica. (2018).
21 United States Census Bureau. (2014). *Computer and Internet access in the United States: 2012*. Retrieved from www.census.gov/data/tables/2012/demo/computer-internet/computer-use-2012.html

22 Zickuhr, K. (2011). *Generations and their gadgets.* Retrieved from www.pewinternet. org/2011/02/03/generations-and-their-gadgets/

23 Zickuhr, K. (2011).

24 Anderson, M. & Jiang, J. (2018). *Teens, social media & technology 2018.* Retrieved from http://assets.pewresearch.org/wp-content/uploads/sites/14/2018/05/31102617/PI_ 2018.05.31_TeensTech_FINAL.pdf

25 Bort, J. (2013). *Microsoft invented a tablet a decade before Apple and totally blew it.* Retrieved from www.businessinsider.com/heres-visual-proof-of-just-how-badly-microsoft-blew-it-with-tablets-2013-5

26 Statista. (2017b). *Global Apple iPad sales from 3rd fiscal quarter of 2010 to 4th fiscal quarter of 2017 (in million units).* Retrieved from www.statista.com/statistics/269915/ global-apple-ipad-sales-since-q3-2010/

27 Statista. (2017e). *Number of tablet users worldwide from 2013–2020 (in billions).* Retrieved from www.statista.com/statistics/377977/tablet-users-worldwide-forecast/

28 Statista. (2017e).

29 Anderson, M. (2015d). *The demographics of device ownership.* Retrieved from www. pewinternet.org/2015/10/29/the-demographics-of-device-ownership/

30 Nielsen. (2017b). *The Nielsen total audience report: Q1 2017.* Retrieved from www.nielsen. com/us/en/insights/reports/2017/the-nielsen-total-audience-report-q1-2017.html

31 Sifferlin, A. (2015). *6-month-old babies are now using tablets and smartphones.* Retrieved from http://time.com/3834978/babies-use-devices/

32 Common Sense Media. (2017). *The Common Sense census: Media use by kids age zero to eight 2017.* Retrieved from www.commonsensemedia.org/research/the-common-sense-census-media-use-by-kids-age-zero-to-eight-2017

33 Statista. (2018c). *Number of tablet users in the United State by age group from 2014 to 2020 (in millions).* Retrieved from www.statista.com/statistics/805143/us-tablete-users-by-age-group/

34 Nielsen. (2017a). *Nielsen estimates 119.6 million TV homes in the U.S. for the 2017– 18 TV season.* Retrieved from www.nielsen.com/us/en/insights/news/2017/nielsen-estimates-119-6-million-us-tv-homes-2017-2018-tv-season.html

35 Television History. (n.d.). *Brief history of TV.* Retrieved from www.tvhistory.tv/ History%20of%20TV.htm

36 Encyclopedia Britannica. (2017). *Television in the United States.* Retrieved from www. britannica.com/art/television-in-the-United-States#ref283600

37 Encyclopedia Britannica. (2017).

38 Nielsen. (2017b).

39 Anderson, M. (2017). *Key trends shaping technology in 2017.* Retrieved from www. pewresearch.org/fact-tank/2017/12/28/key-trends-shaping-technology-in-2017/

40 Hulu. (2017). *Gen Z: The generation at the forefront of TV's evolution.* Retrieved from www.hulu.com/advertising/gen-z-the-generation-at-the-forefront-of-tvs-evolution/

41 Google. (2017b).

42 U.S. Bureau of Labor Statistics. (2016). *Average hours per day spent in selected leisure and sports activities by age.* Retrieved from www.bls.gov/charts/american-time-use/activity-leisure.htm

43 U.S. Bureau of Labor Statistics. (2016).

44 U.S. Bureau of Labor Statistics. (2016).

45 Adams, A., Shankar, M., & Tecco, H. (2016). *50 things we now know about digital health consumers.* Retrieved from https://rockhealth.com/reports/digital-health-consumer-adoption-2016/

46 GlobalWebIndex. (2016). *Trends 2016: Waiting for the wearable revolution.* Retrieved from https://pro.globalwebindex.net/cotds/137

47 Smith, A. (2015). *U.S. smartphone use in 2015.* Retrieved from www.pewinternet. org/2015/04/01/us-smartphone-use-in-2015/

48 Quoc, M. (2018). *Mobile payments survey: Apple Pay leads Google Pay in usage and interest among Millennials & GenZ in 2018.* Retrieved from https://dealspotr.com/article/ mobile-payments-survey-apple-pay-google-pay-millennials-generation-z

49 Statista. (2018b). *Number of active Grubhub diners worldwide from 2011 to 2017 (in millions).* Retrieved from www.statista.com/statistics/667937/number-diners-grubhub/

50 Mintel. (2016). *9 in 10 US food delivery service users say it makes their lives easier.* Retrieved from www.mintel.com/press-centre/food-and-drink/9-in-10-us-food-delivery-service-users-say-it-makes-their-lives-easier, para. 5.

51 Anderson, M. (2015c). *6 facts about Americans and their smartphones.* Retrieved from www. pewresearch.org/fact-tank/2015/04/01/6-facts-about-americans-and-their-smartphones/

52 Beaton, T. (2017). *71% of healthcare providers use telehealth, telemedicine tools.* Retrieved from https://mhealthintelligence.com/news/71-of-healthcare-providers-use-telehealth-telemedicine-tools

53 Smith, A. (2015).

54 Wazeopedia. (n.d.). *Your rank and points.* Retrieved from https://wazeopedia.waze.com/ wiki/Global/Your_Rank_and_Points

55 Seemiller, C. & Grace, M. (2016). *Generation Z goes to college.* San Francisco: Jossey-Bass.

56 Lunden, I. (2017). *Spotify and Waze partner to play music and navigate seamlessly.* Retrieved from https://techcrunch.com/2017/03/14/spotify-and-waze-partner-to-play-music-and-navigate-seamlessly/

57 GlobalWebIndex. (2018). *Generation Z.* Retrieved from https://cdn2.hubspot.net/ hubfs/304927/Downloads/Generation-Z-Infographic.pdf

58 Smith, A. (2015).

59 Lu, K. & Masta, K. E. (2016). *More than half of smartphone users get news alerts, but few get them often.* Retrieved from www.pewresearch.org/fact-tank/2016/09/08/more-than-half-of-smartphone-users-get-news-alerts-but-few-get-them-often/

60 Nielsen. (2015). *Global generational lifestyles: How we live, eat, play, work, and save for our futures.* Retrieved from www.nielsen.com/content/dam/nielsenglobal/eu/docs/pdf/ Global%20Generational%20Lifestyles%20Report%20FINAL.PDF

61 Nielsen. (2015).

62 Arrington, M. (2007). *A sad milestone: AOL to discontinue Netscape browser development.* Retrieved from https://techcrunch.com/2007/12/28/a-sad-milestone-aol-to-discontinue-netscape-browser-development/

63 Schwartz, B. (2006). *Google is now a verb in the Oxford dictionary.* Retrieved from https://searchenginewatch.com/sew/news/2058373/google-now-a-verb-in-the-oxford-english-dictionary

64 GlobalWebIndex. (2018).

65 Seemiller, C. & Grace, M. (2016).

66 Bazilian, E. (2017). *Infographic: 50% of Gen Z "can't live without YouTube" and other stats that will make you feel old.* Retrieved from www.adweek.com/digital/infographic-50-of-gen-z-cant-live-without-youtube-and-other-stats-that-will-make-you-feel-old/

67 Trifecta Research. (2015). *Generation Z media consumption habits: True digital natives.* Retrieved from trifectaresearch.com/wp-content/uploads/2015/09/Generation-Z-Sample-Trifecta-Research-Deliverable.pdf

68 Google. (2017a).

69 eMarketer.com. (2015a). *US adults spend 5.5 hours with video content each day.* Retrieved from www.emarketer.com/Article/US-Adults-Spend-55-Hours-with-Video-Content-Each-Day/1012362

70 Buckle, C. (2018). *Gen Z prefer fun content over friends on social.* Retrieved from https://blog.globalwebindex.com/chart-of-the-day/gen-z-social/

71 Nations, D. (2016). *What does "Web 2.0" even mean?* Retrieved from www.lifewire.com/what-is-web-2-0-p2-3486624

72 Internet Live Stats. (2018). *Total number of websites.* Retrieved from www.internet livestats.com/total-number-of-websites/

73 Radcliffe, D. (2017). *The media habits of Millennials, Generation Z, and the rest of us: In five key charts.* Retrieved from www.huffingtonpost.co.uk/entry/the-media-habits-of-millennials-generation-z-and-the-rest-of-us-in-five-key-charts_uk_5a149436e4b 0815d3ce65ac5

74 GlobalWebIndex. (2017). *GWI Social.* Retrieved from https://insight.globalwebindex. net/social

75 GlobalWebIndex. (2017).

76 Google. (2017a).

77 Radcliffe, D. (2017).

78 Statista. (2017d). *Number of daily active Snapchat users from 1st quarter 2014 to 3rd quarter 2017 (in millions).* Retrieved from www.statista.com/statistics/545967/snapchat-app-dau/

79 Bazilian, E. (2017).

80 Masback, G. (2016). *The voice of Gen Z.* (n.p.): Author.

81 Statista. (2017c). *Most popular social networks of teenagers in the United States from fall 2012 to fall 2017.* Retrieved from www.statista.com/statistics/250172/social-network-usage-of-us-teens-and-young-adults/

82 Social Pilot. (2017). *171 amazing social media statistics you should know in 2018.* Retrieved from www.socialpilot.co/blog/social-media-statistics

83 Statista. (2018e). *Reach of leading social media and networking sites used by teenagers and young adults in the United States as of February 2017.* Retrieved from www.statista.com/statistics/199242/social-media-and-networking-sites-used-by-us-teenagers/

84 Seemiller, C. & Grace, M. (2016).

85 Seemiller, C. & Grace, M. (2016).

86 Madden, M., Lenhart, A., Cortesi, S., Gasser, U., Duggan, M., Smith, A., & Beaton, M. (2013). *Teens, social media, and privacy.* Retrieved from www.pewinternet.org/2013/05/21/teens-social-media-and-privacy/

87 Lorenz, T. (2017). *The secret Instagram accounts teens use to share their realest, most intimate moments.* Retrieved from https://mic.com/articles/175936/the-secret-instagram-accounts-teens-use-to-share-their-realest-most-intimate-moments#.hSXS12uxZ

88 Lorenz, T. (2017).

89 Seemiller, C. & Grace, M. (2016).

90 Madden, M., Lenhart, A., Cortesi, S., Gasser, U., Duggan, M., Smith, A., & Beaton, M. (2013).

91 Seemiller, C. & Grace, M. (2016).

92 Statista. (2018e).

93 Seemiller, C. & Grace, M. (2016).

94 Seemiller, C. & Grace, M. (2016).

95 Seemiller, C. & Grace, M. (2016).

96 Seemiller, C. & Grace, M. (2016).

97   Ochs, J. (2017). *What is Tumblr? Parent and teacher guide (video)*. Retrieved from https://smartsocial.com/what-is-tumblr-parent-teacher-guide/

98   Pew Research Center. (2015b). *Demographics of Tumblr*. Retrieved from www.pewinternet.org/2015/08/19/mobile-messaging-and-social-media-2015/2015-08-19_social-media-update_05/

99   GlobalWebIndex. (2018).

100 Boyd, J. (2018). *What is Reddit?* Retrieved from www.brandwatch.com/blog/what-is-reddit-guide/

101 Statista. (2016). *Distribution of Reddit users in the United States as of February 2016, by age group*. Retrieved from www.statista.com/statistics/517218/reddit-user-distribution-usa-age/

102 GlobalWebIndex. (2018).

103 Seemiller, C. & Grace, M. (2014). *Generation Z goes to college study*. Unpublished raw data.

104 GlobalWebIndex. (2018).

105 Bazilian, E. (2017).

106 Statista.com. (2018). *Reach of leading social media and networking sites used by teenagers and young adults in the United States as of February 2017*. Retrieved from www.statista.com/statistics/199242/social-media-and-networking-sites-used-by-us-teenagers/

107 Statista.com. (2018). *Number of Facebook users in the United States as of January 2018, by age group (in millions)*. Retrieved from www.statista.com/statistics/398136/us-facebook-user-age-groups/

108 Lenhart, A., Duggan, M., Perrin, A., Stepler, R., Rainie, L., & Parker, K. (2015).

109 Statista.com. (2018).

110 Bazilian, E. (2017).

111 Anderson, M. (2015c).

112 Bradbury, R. (2017). *The digital lives of Millennials and Generation Z*. Retrieved from www.liveperson.com/resources/reports/digital-lives-of-millennials-genz/

113 Deloitte. (2017). *2017 global mobile consumer survey: US edition: The dawn of the next era in mobile*. Retrieved from www2.deloitte.com/us/en/pages/technology-media-and-telecommunications/articles/global-mobile-consumer-survey-us-edition.html

114 Anderson, M. & Jiang, J. (2018).

115 Bradbury, R. (2017).

116 Cheug, J., Glass, S., McCarty, D., & Wong, C. K. (2016).

117 Common Sense Media. (2015). *The Common Sense census: Media use by tweens and teens*. Retrieved from www.commonsensemedia.org/research/the-common-sense-census-media-use-by-tweens-and-teens.

118 Ophir, E., Naas, C., & Wagner, A. D. (2009). *Cognitive control in media multitaskers*. Retrieved from www.pnas.org/content/106/37/15583.full.pdf

119 The Center for Generational Kinetics. (2017). *The state of Gen Z 2017: Meet the throwback generation*. Retrieved from http://genhq.com/gen-z-2017/

120 Lenhart, A. (2015b). *Chapter 4: Social media and friendships*. Retrieved from www.pewinternet.org/2015/08/06/chapter-4-social-media-and-friendships/

5 Communication

••

During the 1920s and 30s, making a telephone call was a radical and innovative way to communicate, especially as only 41 percent of households in 1930 actually had a phone.[1] Today, phones aren't associated with a household but rather an individual. Not only can we simply dial a number on our phones to make a call but we can even use synced wearable technology to converse with someone through our watch, use Bluetooth to engage in hands-free calling while driving, see the faces of friends and family from around the world through video chat, and engage in digital messaging across a number of platforms and social media sites. And although we can do all of this with a device that fits in our pocket, we also have tablets and laptop technology, making it possible to be connected and communicate with others using a variety of devices.

Today, 73 percent of 18 to 34 year-olds communicate with people more in digital settings than in-person settings.[2] And while it might be common for people across all generations to use technology to stay connected with others, many older individuals know of a time when most, if not all, of these devices and platforms didn't even exist. It's important to recognize that the perspectives, preferences, and behaviors of Generation Z are likely informed by the digital era in which they are growing up. At the same time, though, the digital era is likely influencing their perspectives, preferences, and behaviors in how they navigate life.

Many micro-conversations

Prior to email, texting, and messaging apps, young people had to see each other in person or talk on the telephone to communicate with others. This meant conversations were continuous and synchronous, often having a clear start and stop all in a one-time period. While synchronous communication still occurs today, the opportunity to connect through digital messaging has changed the very nature of the meaning of conversation. Digital communication can occur in short, asynchronous spurts with a transfer back and forth between two or more people and over a span of multiple hours or days.

More frequent asynchronous conversations may take place in several smaller chunks as users may start a line of communication and pick it up later.

Conversations can also occur in multiple settings and across a variety of platforms, such as talking to the same friend throughout the day via text message, email thread, social media site, and Snapchat. These communication exchanges are not usually lengthy or even related to each other. For example, a user can send a popular meme from Instagram or Twitter, a text message about something going on in their day, and a Snapchat about what they are eating all to the same person resulting in three separate, smaller simultaneous conversations rather than one longer synchronous conversation in person, via video chat, or on the phone.

❝ I use text the most to communicate with others. It is quick, easy, and allows me to do two or three other things while carrying on a conversation. ❞
– Member of Generation Z

While it may be convenient or even helpful to segment conversations across multiple platforms, managing those conversations can be challenging. No more just checking email; now you have to check all of your social media accounts, texts, and messaging platforms. Having to frequently manage several different accounts could lead to missing a message or getting it too late. In addition, trying to respond to various conversations on one platform could result in miscommunication, as it might be easy to accidentally text a response in the wrong conversation feed. Doing so might be harmless, however, depending on what was said could result in disclosure of private information or hurt feelings.

Visual communication

Before the time of smartphones, you would have to find precisely the right words to express feelings in a letter or email. At least with phone calls, you can hear emotions to a certain extent. Even then, there was room for misinterpretation since you can't see a person's reaction. Today, there are more ways to digitally communicate emotion and feelings when in-person communication is not an option.

From emoticons to emojis

Emoticons were some of the first ways to express emotions in a text format. In 1982, Scott Fahlman, a computer scientist, noticed that his colleagues were often misinterpreting posts on their electronic message board and suggested using a colon, dash, and parentheses to indicate the post was intended to be funny.[3] By using a series of symbols on a keyboard,[4] emoticons now range from using the semi-colon followed by a dash and right parentheses to create a winking face or colon, dash, and capital O to indicate a big shock.[5]

Although emoticons can still be used today, their emergence paved the way for the creation of emojis. Different from emoticons, which are simple pictorial icons using alphanumeric characters,[6] emojis are cartoon-like pictures.[7] Emojis can be embedded within a text conversation or sending a string of them can serve as the conversation in its entirety. Although there is still room for interpretation with emojis, sending a mad face emoji to express anger, for example, can help paint a picture of what the sender might be feeling. And, it appears that emojis, in particular, really resonate with Generation Z as a study of 13- to 17-year-old teens found that 95 percent use emojis in their communication.[8]

GIFs and memes: Emotional expression and humor

GIFs, on the other hand, are short-looped motion pictures clips that are used on social media, in texts, and on email to show an expression or reaction. While similar to the intent behind emojis, GIFs offer more than a pictorial symbol of an emotion; the clip often displays the emotion. Need to react to a friend's email about an upcoming trip but don't feel like words completely summarize your excitement? A GIF of someone excitedly dancing should do the job. And, sites like Giphy have a GIF for every reaction and conversation.[9]

Similarly, Internet users may communicate using memes, which are pictures, GIFs, or quick videos that convey a commonly understood concept or idea, typically used in pop culture and spread quickly through social media between online users.[10] However, memes and GIFs are not one in the same. Memes connect to a topic or cultural reference,[11] whereas a GIF is simply the technical format of a looped video that can be used as a meme.[12]

There is a new form of meme taking hold with Generation Z, though. Rather than putting forth an image or GIF with a pop culture reference, many teen girls are actually creating personal and customized memes, specific to their own life experiences. These memes, referred to as niche memes, are collages of pictures with personal comments shared by the user.[13] Think of it as a combination of a diary and a scrapbook but posted online for the world to see. Niche meme accounts typically have a following of like-minded individuals who understand the user's posts, unlike that person's general followership on a named account.[14] For example, someone might create a niche meme entitled, *3 Things I Did Instead of Studying for My Test*. Then, that user would add personal pictures with captions and post on an anonymous social media account. Others would tune in to follow the storyline, awaiting the next day's meme to see how the test actually went.

While often just simple ways to spread viral humor, satire, or emotional expression, memes can also influence actual behavior. For example, there are countless memes online about eating liquid Tide Pods in the so-called Tide Pod Challenge.[15] While it's hard to imagine anyone taking this seriously, according to the American Association of Poison Control Centers, from 2016 through the first 2 weeks of January of 2018, there had been 131 cases of teens ingesting single-load laundry packets.[16] So, while memes can certainly be a fun form of expression, we are finding that there can be unintended results.

Using written communication in a digital format has become an easy and convenient way to communicate. But corresponding with others through written text can leave a lot of room for interpretation. Users today, however, now have more ways to visually share their reactions, emotions, and expressions when words cannot fully capture their thoughts in a digital conversation.

Evolving communication etiquette

As we spend more time in digital settings, social etiquette around communication is changing. It used to be considered rude to call a house landline during the evening as it would interrupt family time during dinner. Communicating digitally allows for asynchronous conversations to take place at all times of day and be put on pause if need be. Sending a text message to someone in the evening likely won't interrupt dinner, but the person receiving the text might not get back to you right away.

Considering the increasingly constant connection to smartphones and technology, certain types of communication are becoming more common and acceptable in settings that were considered off limits for those in other generations when they were young. We see people of all age groups communicating and chatting in settings that we would not have prior to mobile technology – walking down the street while chatting on the phone, texting while on a cardio machine at the gym, FaceTiming a friend from a store to get their opinion on an outfit before purchasing it, or sending Snapchat videos of a concert. However, there is a generational divide with what is considered acceptable in terms of appropriate times and settings for communication. For example, a higher number of those in Generation Z compared to those in other generations feel it's okay to use their phone while attending a religious service, eating dinner with family members, or meeting the family of the person they are dating.[17]

Online RSVPs and the digital no-show culture

Online communication has impacted aspects of written etiquette as well. Prior to sites like Evite and Punchbowl or even Facebook event pages, getting an actual physical event invitation was often the norm. Those invited needed to mail an RSVP card to the event host or call on the phone to confirm attendance. Today, the ability to send or post a digital invitation is not only cost-effective but also far less time-consuming than having to write out and mail actual invitations. Despite the convenience, digital invitations can create a challenge for an event host. Just as easy as it is for a person who is invited to an event to reply online with a "Yes" to attend an event, it's just as easy for that person to send a text to back out of an event, change an RSVP online at the last minute, or just no-show altogether. And, the "Maybe" feature can be a way for people to not fully commit to attending, sometimes even forgetting they had RSVP'd by the time the event comes around.

The informality and convenience of digital invitations are also present with the move from handwritten thank you cards to online ones. It's much easier and time efficient to send a thank you via email, text message, or even e-card platform to a friend or family member who sent a nice birthday gift. But, we all know that receiving an e-card ends up in the digital recycling bin seconds after it's read whereas an actual card might be placed on a shelf for a couple weeks as a reminder of someone's thoughts and wishes.

While it's hard to track specific behavior of young people around digital social etiquette with RSVPs and thank you cards, it's important to note that not sending an RSVP, canceling at the last minute, not showing up after confirming, indicating the placeholder "Maybe" response, and sending off a quick thank you text might be the new normal of digital communications. So, when those in Generation Z don't show up to an event or forget to send a thank you card, consider that they are growing up in a culture where those in older generations are exhibiting this exact behavior.

The new "public" sphere

Digital communication is also changing etiquette when it comes to topics we discuss with others. What is considered acceptable and taboo to talk about in larger settings has changed as the public sphere now extends to online environments, with a much larger reach. Before Facebook, expecting parents were likely to only share their sonogram photos with family and close friends as they announced their pregnancy. Parents can now share pregnancy news and reveal the sex of their babies through social media posts, engaging a much larger audience than simply their inner circles. In addition to sharing personal milestones on social media, we have the ability to post our opinions and thoughts on topics. While social media platforms might seem private, reserved for only our followers, that very feeling of intimacy may make it alluring to discuss topics online that we wouldn't normally discuss in person. But, in reality, social media posts can be accessible to others far beyond our own followers, leading some to have their opinions spread virally without the intention to do so. In other cases, people can use social media to push the envelope in sharing personal details of their lives or their opinions on topics purposely for all to see.

How Generation Z communicates

Today, there are many different ways in which people can communicate with each other. Between face-to-face communication, texting and messaging, emailing, and calling on the phone, it's not surprising that Generation Z moves between multiple communication methods, using each for different reasons and with differing frequencies.

Face-to-face first

Even with the multitude of technology available for communication, many in Generation Z place value on in-person connection. We found in our Generation Z Goes to College Study that of all communication methods, 83 percent of those in Generation Z reported that face-to-face communication was a preference for them, higher than any other method including texting.[18] And, only 2 percent indicated actually disliking face-to-face communication.[19] Similarly, in a study by Stillman and Stillman, 84 percent of members of Generation Z reported liking face-to-face communication.[20]

> *I usually prefer to talk in person with someone because you can better connect with whoever you are talking to. You can't read facial/body expressions through phone or email. Only with the human interaction.*
> *- Member of Generation Z*

Video chatting platforms are certainly a great alternative to chat with someone when face-to-face is not possible, allowing users to connect with people around the world in a more personal setting. But even then, users cannot hug a friend who needs consoling via FaceTime or shake the hand of an interviewer through Skype.

Texting and messaging frequently

A global study from IBM found that 73 percent of members of Generation Z engage in texting and chatting as the primary use of their smartphones.[21] We also found that just more than 60 percent of participants in our Generation Z Goes to College Study reported liking text messaging as a way to communicate.[22] And, with apps like GroupMe, users can text message groups of people all at the same time.[23]

> *It's so much easier to send someone a text than it is to contact them through any other form of communication.*
> *- Member of Generation Z*

While texting and instant messaging are similar, those in our Generation Z Goes to College Study in 2014 did not see them as one in the same. Only 27 percent indicated liking instant messaging, and only an additional 37 percent reported that they only somewhat liked instant messaging.[24] Actually, more than 36 percent reported not liking it at all.[25] This left us curious because Millennials, the predecessor generation to Generation Z, were raised on AOL Instant Messenger, making instant messaging revolutionary at the time. As the years went on, though, instant messaging had to compete with the plethora of other communication and social media sites that have since emerged, leaving platforms like AOL Instant Messenger by the wayside.[26]

But, in the time since our Generation Z Goes to College Study in 2014, many traditional desktop-based messaging platforms have gotten a mobile makeover and function similar to text messaging, making them more in line with Generation Z's preference for texting. Now more than half of Internet users utilize a messenger app such as Facebook Messenger or WhatsApp, with one in three members of Generation Z doing so.[27] In fact, messaging apps have become so popular that more than 50 percent of Generation Z teens report using them for 3 or more hours a day.[28]

Regardless of platform, one area of concern that has emerged involves sneaky messaging codes. Acronyms like LOL for Laughing Out Loud and L8R for Later have been around even before digital messaging[29] and are fairly harmless. However, IWSN means "I want sex now," and KMS means "kill myself."[30] These types of abbreviations give Generation Z teens a language to use away from their parents' periphery. And it's not just secret codes parents need to be worried about, teens are also engaging in sexting, which involves sending inappropriate pictures of themselves over text message or receiving those types of pictures from others.[31] Studies have found that anywhere between 7 percent and 25 percent of teens have engaged in sexting.[32]

So, while digital messaging might be highly utilized and offer great benefits for those in Generation Z, there are some concerns that digital spaces can create a haven for inappropriate and potentially dangerous interactions to occur.

Unsubscribing and disconnecting: Non-preferences for email and phone

While many in Generation Z like to communicate face-to-face and through text messaging, they aren't so keen on emailing and phone calls.[33] We, like many others working with Generation Z, have become frustrated when they wouldn't read or respond to emails or we would call them only to reach a voice-mail inbox that was not setup or was completely full. Considering all of the ways Generation Z can connect and communicate, this makes sense. If they want to hear someone's voice when they can't meet in person, they can use a video chat platform like Skype, FaceTime, or Google Hangouts, which also allows them to see nonverbal behavior and facial expressions. And, if they want to have a written conversation with someone, it might make more sense to text where messages can be exchanged quickly and on-the-go.

Email might be a go-to messaging platform for those in older generations who remember a time when emailing was the only real form of digital communication. But, email doesn't seem to have quite the same draw for those in Generation Z. Studies have shown that young people don't necessarily strongly dislike emailing but a large number don't prefer it. In our Generation Z Goes to College Study, we found that nearly half of Generation Z college students indicated that they only somewhat liked using email, with a solid quarter not liking to use it at all.[34] And, a study by the Pew Research Center found that only 64 percent of teens ages 13 to 17 use email with their friends, and only 6 percent use it daily.[35] That same study also found that far fewer teens engage in emailing than in text messaging, instant messaging, social media messaging, or even talking on the phone with their friends.[36] While they may need to use email for school or work or even to connect with a family member, the preference for those in Generation Z appears to be for other types of digital platforms that elicit quick and short bursts of communication.

But, Generation Z is just now entering the workforce where email is a common and necessary way to communicate within a variety of industries. Interestingly, a study by Adobe Systems Incorporated found that 48 percent of 18- to 24-year-old professionals check their work emails on their phones, whereas 50 percent report doing so on a desktop computer.[37] For those 35 and older, however, only 29 percent check their work emails on their smartphones with 66 percent doing so on a desktop computer.[38] Perhaps with the ease of being able to send and receive email from a smartphone rather than only from a desktop computer, those in Generation Z may end up not being as adverse to using email in the workplace.

Along similar lines, nearly two in three members of Generation Z do not like or only somewhat like talking on the phone.[39] What is interesting is that with growing rates of individual phone ownership (cell phones and smartphones),[40] more people now have the freedom to make a phone call when they want without waiting for someone else to hang up on the family landline. In 2005, 92 percent of U.S. households reported having a landline phone, whereas only 5 percent of households were using cell phones only.[41] Just 12 years later, the percentage of U.S. households with landlines dropped to 44 percent with "cell phone only" households rising to 53 percent.[42]

So, now that young people have their own phones, why aren't they talking on them all the time? For most of their lives, cell phones, and more recently smartphones, have been the dominant way to connect with someone. But that connection doesn't always mean engaging in a phone call. With social media, texting, and messaging apps, there are many other ways to communicate. Despite their choice in communication platform, though, there are some specific reasons they have for not talking on the phone. In a panel of teens conducted by Business Insider, young people shared that they believe texting is easier than calling, that it's harder to call someone during class than to text them, and that texting also allows a conversation to span multiple hours or even days which couldn't easily be done talking on the phone.[43] A study by the Pew Research Center found that 69 percent of teens noted that calling on the phone was one of their three most preferred ways of communicating with their closest friend, yet 80 percent reported a preference for texting.[44] It makes sense then that

> *I use email because it is the fastest way to communicate with my teachers.*
>
> – Member of Generation Z

if they had to make the choice between only having a messaging app or a voice calling app on their phone, 73 percent of Generation Z and Millennials in the U.S. would get rid of voice calling.[45]

Just because many in Generation Z do not readily prefer emailing or phone calling does not mean you won't ever get an email or phone call from them. They just likely won't be using these platforms to communicate as frequently as those in other generations do. Perhaps, though, they may develop a different mindset and affinity for emailing and phone calling as they grow older and engage in full-time employment in a workforce that is increasingly more mobile, technologically infused, and remote work friendly . . . and where their older colleagues will likely be using email and phone calls to communicate with them.

Conclusion

Workplaces, organizations, communities, and social settings are increasingly becoming inhabited by several different generations with a variety of preferences in communicating and connecting with others. This variety can create ample opportunity for frustration, friction, and miscommunication to occur. For those from different generations, communicating with members of Generation Z may require some level of compromise. It is unrealistic to stop using email just because it is not the most preferred or practiced method of communication for those in Generation Z. Instead, those in older generations can mentor and teach Generation Z members proper email etiquette. Similarly, those in older generations may benefit from learning from Generation Z's savvy when it comes to texting and messaging. And, by the time everyone has learned all of the platforms available, new ones will emerge challenging both Generation Z and older generations to overcome the learning curve together.

Notes

1 Statista. (2018d). *Percentage of housing units with telephones in the United States from 1920 to 2008.* Retrieved from www.statista.com/statistics/189959/housing-units-with-telephones-in-the-united-states-since-1920/
2 Bradbury, R. (2017). *The digital lives of Millennials and Generation Z.* Retrieved from www.liveperson.com/resources/reports/digital-lives-of-millennials-genz/
3 Steinmetz, K. (2014). *In praise of emoticons :-).* Retrieved from http://time.com/3341244/emoticon-birthday/
4 Grannan, C. (n.d.). *What's the difference between emoji and emoticons?* Retrieved from www.britannica.com/story/whats-the-difference-between-emoji-and-emoticons
5 Sieber, T. (2009). *15 popular codes for smiley faces & their meanings.* Retrieved from www.makeuseof.com/tag/15-popular-codes-for-smiley-faces-their-meanings/
6 Grannan, C. (n.d.).
7 Grannan, C. (n.d.).

8   Bank of America. (2017). *Trends in consumer mobility report 2017*. Retrieved from https://promo.bankofamerica.com/mobilityreport/assets/images/BOA_2017-Trends-in-Consumer-Mobility-Report_Wave2_FINAL_8_2.pdf

9   Hyatt, E. (2017). *What is a GIF, who invented the image format, how is it pronounced and what's an animated meme?* Retrieved from www.thesun.co.uk/tech/3800248/what-is-gif-how-pronounced-animated-memes/

10 Gil, P. (2017b). *What is a meme? The more you know about memes, the cooler you are*. Retrieved from www.lifewire.com/what-is-a-meme-2483702

11 Kachroo-Levine, M. (2015). *What is a meme? Here's what the thing is you always hear people talking about so you can stop smiling and nodding*. Retrieved from www.bustle.com/articles/86077-what-is-a-meme-heres-what-the-thing-is-you-always-hear-people-talking-about-so

12 Hyatt, E. (2017).

13 Lorenz, T. (2017a). *"Niche memes" are the secret clip art diaries teens are posting on Instagram*. Retrieved from www.thedailybeast.com/niche-memes-are-the-secret-clip-art-diaries-teens-are-posting-on-instagram

14 Lorenz, T. (2017a).

15 Golgowski, N. (2018). *There's a really dumb reason why some teens are eating Tide Pods*. Retrieved from www.huffingtonpost.com/entry/tide-pods-health-warning_us_5a5f478ae4b00a7f171c2926

16 American Association of Poison Control Centers. (2018). *ALERT: American Association of Poison Control Centers warn about potential poison exposure to single-load laundry packets*. Retrieved from www.aapcc.org/press/83/

17 The Center for Generational Kinetics & Dorsey, J. (2016). *iGen Tech Disruption: 2016 national study on technology and the generation after Millennials*. Retrieved from http://genhq.com/wp-content/uploads/2016/01/iGen-Gen-Z-Tech-Disruption-Research-White-Paper-c-2016-Center-for-Generational-Kinetics.pdf

18 Seemiller, C. & Grace, M. (2014). *Generation Z goes to college study*. Unpublished raw data.

19 Seemiller, C. & Grace, M. (2014).

20 Stillman, D. & Stillman, J. (2017). *Gen Z @ work: How the next generation is transforming the workplace*. New York: HarperCollins.

21 IBM. (2017). *Uniquely Generation Z: What brands should know about today's youngest consumers*. Retrieved from www-935.ibm.com/services/us/gbs/thoughtleadership/uniquelygenz/

22 Seemiller, C. & Grace, M. (2016). *Generation Z goes to college*. San Francisco: Jossey-Bass.

23 Gil, P. (2017a). *GroupMe: Text messaging for groups-a review*. Retrieved from www.lifewire.com/groupme-text-messaging-for-groups-2483568

24 Seemiller, C. & Grace, M. (2016).

25 Seemiller, C. & Grace, M. (2016).

26 Murphy, M. (2017). *AOL instant messenger is dead*. Retrieved from https://qz.com/1096546/aol-instant-messenger-is-shutting-down-after-20-years/

27 Manger, J. & McGrath, F. (2017). *GWI social: GlobalWebIndex's flagship report on the latest trends in social media*. Retrieved from https://insight.globalwebindex.net/social

28 Google. (2017a). *Generation Z: New insights into the mobile-first mindset of teens*. Retrieved from http://storage.googleapis.com/think/docs/GenZ_Insights_All_teens.pdf

29 Hiscott, R. (2017). *LOL, WTF? The origin stories of your favorite Internet acronyms*. Retrieved from www.huffingtonpost.com/2014/07/17/internet-acronyms_n_5585425.html

30 Jolly, J. (2017). *Sneaky teens texting codes: What they mean, when to worry.* Retrieved from www.usatoday.com/story/tech/columnist/2017/05/21/sneaky-teen-texting-codes-what-they-mean-when-worry/101844248/

31 Lohmann, R. C. (2017). *5 reasons teens sext.* Retrieved from https://health.usnews.com/wellness/for-parents/articles/2017-05-18/5-reasons-teens-sext

32 Lohmann, R. C. (2017).

33 Seemiller, C. & Grace, M. (2016).

34 Seemiller, C. & Grace, M. (2016).

35 Lenhart, A. (2015c). *Teens, technology, and friendships.* Retrieved from www.pewinternet.org/2015/08/06/teens-technology-and-friendships/

36 Lenhart, A. (2015c).

37 Adobe Systems Incorporated. (2017). *Adobe consumer email survey report 2017.* Retrieved from www.slideshare.net/adobe/adobe-consumer-email-survey-report-2017

38 Adobe Systems Incorporated. (2017).

39 Seemiller, C. & Grace, M. (2016).

40 Pew Research Center. (2018a). *Mobile fact sheet.* Retrieved from www.pewinternet.org/fact-sheet/mobile/

41 Richter, F. (2018). *Landline phones are a dying breed.* Retrieved from www.statista.com/chart/2072/landline-phones-in-the-united-states/

42 Richter, F. (2018).

43 D'Onfro, J. (2015). *A bunch of teens told us they have "never" called their friends on the phone.* Retrieved from www.businessinsider.com/teens-say-they-never-talk-on-the-phone-2015-12

44 Anderson, M. (2015b). *For teens, phone calls are reserved for closer relationships.* Retrieved from www.pewresearch.org/fact-tank/2015/08/17/for-teens-phone-calls-are-reserved-for-closer-relationships/

45 Bradbury, R. (2017).

6 Entertainment

· ·

While each generation entertained themselves with activities prevalent during the time period in which they grew up, playing with games and toys, gathering with friends, and going to the movies haven't seemed to have gone out of style over the years. But, in today's digital environment, how do classic forms of entertainment stack up to the high tech options available to Generation Z?

Hobbies

While some traditional hobbies may be popular with those in Generation Z, technology has opened a whole new array of opportunities for how these young people can spend their time. For some, the digital world offers a space for them to engage in old hobbies in new ways or in new activities altogether.

Sports and extracurricular activities: Changes in participation

In a 2015 Pew study of Generation Z's parents, 73 percent shared that their school-aged children had participated in a sporting or athletic activity in the last year.[1] According to Google's *It's Lit* report, researchers found that soccer, basketball, and running are the most popular among members of this generation.[2] But, a study by the Sports and Fitness Industry Association found that there was a 9 percent decrease in youth sports participation between 2009 and 2014.[3] The greatest declines were seen in wrestling, touch football, volleyball, and tackle football.[4] However, there were some increases – rugby, ice hockey, and lacrosse.[5] When comparing contact and non-contact sports as a whole, though, the story is a little more nuanced. Contact sports overall experienced an 11.6 percent decline, whereas non-contact sports only had a decrease of 8.1 percent.[6] This isn't surprising in that a research study on why members of Generation Z might have an aversion to physical activity found that a primary reason was out of fear of getting injured.[7] For them, avoiding contact sports is one way to avoid injury.

> **❝ I smile because I enjoy my life, I enjoy my extracurricular activities and the people I have met. ❞**
> — Member of Generation Z

When not on the court or the field, many are engaged in other extracurricular activities. For example, the 2015 Pew study also found that more than half of parents of Generation Z reported that their children were busy outside of school volunteering or taking lessons in art, music, or dance.[8]

Youth organizations: Shifting and shrinking

Membership in a youth organization continues to offer a great way for young people to have fun while connecting with their peers. According to a 2015 Pew study, 14 percent of Generation Z's parents from lower-income families and 28 percent from higher income families reported that their children had participated in an organization like the scouts sometime during the last year.[9] For generations, the Boy Scouts and Girl Scouts, specifically, have served as important organizations for youth to learn skills and make friends. From 1910 through 1971, the Boy Scouts saw consistent increases in membership, however, other than a slight bump around 1990, from 1971 through 2009, the rates of participation began a declining trajectory.[10] The Boy Scouts has changed since its emergence during the G.I. Generation era, even officially changing its name to Scouts BSA and accepting female, gay, and transgender youth into the program.[11,12] While these moves were implemented to address declining engagement,[13] only time will tell if the changes actually end up making a difference in participation rates. But, it isn't just Scouts BSA (Boy Scouts) that has seen a dip in membership; the Girl Scouts have too.[14] It's hard to know if these organizations are just not fitting with the interests of today's Generation Z youth or that young people are finding other things to do with their time.

Reading: Still fun but on the decline

Throughout history, great books have served as a reflection of events, norms, and concerns of various eras. For example, *The Great Gatsby* told the tale of the Roaring 20s and the Jazz Age.[15] *The Grapes of Wrath* highlighted the impacts of the Great Depression and the Dust Bowl.[16] *Fahrenheit 451* reflected the dangers of censorship in a futuristic society.[17] And readers in the 1960s were tuned in to war both through books like *Catch 22* and the debate in the U.S. on the actual Vietnam War.[18] Books give readers, of all ages and generations, an opportunity to delve deeper into a topic, look at the current context of society, and maybe even engage in a little escapism from daily life.

It's no surprise then that reading appeals to many in Generation Z, with a quarter ranking it as second on their list of top three leisure activities.[19] But, in looking more specifically at age groups within the generational cohort, different

Table 6.1 Youth Reading Rates Over Time[20]

	1985 (Generation X)	2004 (Millennials)*	2012 (Generation Z)
9 year-olds who read at least 1–2 times per week for fun	81%	80%	76%
13 year-olds who read at least 1–2 times per week for fun	70%	64%	53%
17 year-olds who read at least 1–2 times per week for fun	64%	52%	40%

*For 9 year-olds, this data may include some in Generation Z

patterns of reading behavior emerge. For example, a higher percentage of younger youth read more frequently.[21] But, the lower number of older youth readers does not likely stem solely from a growing disinterest in reading as one ages; the decline may also be attributed to the challenge for older youth in finding books that interest them. According to research from Scholastic, 41 percent of kids struggle to find books they like as they get older.[22]

It also appears that rates of reading have been decreasing over time for all age groups, lower in 2012 than for any preceding time periods.[23] But, findings from the Scholastic study indicate that 76 percent of youth know that they should read more for fun.[24] That's likely because 86 percent of them think being a good reader is important to their future.[25] And, when it comes to encouraging reading, 82 percent said their parents and families play a significant role, higher than the 67 percent who identified teachers doing so.[26]

Like the youth cohort where the youngest appear to have the highest readership rates, a similar pattern emerges in looking at adults. In a 2016 study by the Pew Research Center, 83 percent of the youngest group studied, 18 to 29 year-olds, reported having ever read for pleasure compared to 78 to 81 percent of those in older age brackets.[27] While this study combined younger Millennials with older members of Generation Z, the data does point to the fact that a higher number of younger adults have engaged in reading for fun. It's important to note, though, that 27 percent of 17 year-olds in 2012 reported either never or hardly ever reading for fun, up from 19 percent in 2004 and 9 percent in 1984.[28] Thus, as these teens move through their 20s, we may see a decline over time in aggregate rates of young adult readership.

With so many digital options for reading and the general rise in tablet and e-reader ownership,[29] it's easier than ever for those in Generation Z to pick up a good book. However, a global study of college students found that young readers

❝ What gets me excited about getting up every day is reading - the fact that sometime during the day I'm going to emerge myself in a story of someone else's, real or fiction, life. ❞
— Member of Generation Z

prefer to read a print copy over an electronic copy,[30] and a number of other studies also point to young people preferring printed versions.[31] So, it might be a long time before paperback and hardcover books are retired as this is a generation not quite ready to let them go.

Watching movies: Literary characters to on-screen heroes

Those in Generation Z aren't just reading to be entertained; characters in books actually serve as role models for them. More than half of Generation Z young people identify literary characters as having an influence on their values.[32] They want these characters to be smart, brave, and strong as well as have the ability to face challenges and overcome them.[33] And some of these literary heroes actually get to come to life on-screen where young people watch them take on the world and fight forces of evil. While the first *Harry Potter* book was released when the oldest in Generation Z were only toddlers, the phenomena that followed the series ignited readers and set the tone for movies, merchandise, and theme parks that have become popular across all ages.[34] Since Harry Potter, we've seen book series like *Twilight*, *The Hunger Games*, and *Divergent* take to the big screen where the main characters have somehow been entrusted to give up their own freedoms to save one's society. Even comic books have been adapted for the theater, such as Marvel's *Guardians of the Galaxy* and *The Avengers*[35] as well as *Wonder Woman* from DC Comics.[36] With five of the top ten grossing movies released in 2017 being those about comic-book superheroes,[37] it's no surprise that pop culture website, The Ringer, has dubbed this era the Superhero Movie Generation.[38]

Whether following their literary heroes to the theaters or simply watching a new release of original content, those in Generation Z go to the movies a lot. In 2017, 12 to 17 year-olds had the highest per capita movie attendance, with the rate of 18 to 24 year-olds second among all other age groups.[39] Interestingly, in 2015, 2016, and 2017, 12 to 17 year-olds and 18 to 24 year-olds represented much higher proportions of frequent movie-goers than the general population.[40,41,42]

High demand for on-demand: TV binging

Video content has come a long way from early motion picture movies the G.I. Generation and Silent Generation grew up watching. Baby Boomer children lived through what was considered the Golden Era of television between the later 1940s and 1950s with on-screen stars like Lucille Ball, Jackie Gleason, and Ed Sullivan.[43] Gen Xers hurried home to watch their favorite bands and musicians on MTV[44] and were the first teens and young adults to enjoy numerous channel offerings as cable television became available throughout the 1980s.[45] Millennials vividly remember picking out an entire TV series on DVD at Blockbuster but had to mourn the loss of the video rental chain in 2014.[46]

Today, those in Generation Z are growing up in a streaming video era where they can watch shows any time they want on any of their multiple Internet-ready devices. While 26 percent of households with a television have someone in Generation Z living there,[47] given streaming technology, it's not surprising that fewer than half of these young people consume video content by watching an actual television.[48]

With the seemingly limitless access to video, those in Generation Z have no reason to watch a scheduled episode when it airs on TV, especially if they can access it at their convenience another time. Some may wait to watch the newest episode the next day when it becomes available to stream online or wait until the entire season is released so they can binge-watch back-to-back episodes. But, they do have a preference. More than half would rather watch multiple episodes in a single sitting.[49] A consumer insights study by Hulu found that 20 percent more of those in Generation Z prefer to binge-watch television shows than their Generation X parents.[50] This fares well for them as some streaming channels are now creating their own content and only releasing the entire season of episodes at one time.[51]

Transitions from book to screen have also taken place with TV series. Netflix has adapted the classic, *A Series of Unfortunate Events*, and young adult novel, *13 Reasons Why*, into successful TV shows.[52,53] With the sheer number of cable channels and streaming services, there is a calling for interesting storylines leading networks and film companies to draw from older works for ideas. For example, Margaret Atwood's, *The Handmaid's Tale*, was turned into a television series more than 30 years after the book was originally published.[54] Since fans have tuned in to watch the on-screen adaptation, sales of the original book have skyrocketed.[55] While it's likely that those in Generation Z will see their favorite books made into shows or movies, they might also be inspired to read classic books after seeing the adaptation on-screen.

Staying up to date about trending television shows is important to many in this generation as it's a way to stay in the conversation. A study done by Hulu found that 43 percent of those in Generation Z watch shows so they can talk about it with their friends, 32 percent watch just to impress others, and 23 percent watch to look smart.[56] Video consumption has become such a form of social currency that one in five members of Generation Z have posted online about a show they haven't even seen yet.[57]

From records to recordings: New ways to listen to music

The G.I. Generation saw the rise of jazz and big band music in the 1920s and 30s,[58] and the Silent Generation had swing music.[59] Baby Boomers lived through Beatlemania and grew up listening to rock and roll, while Generation X later made hip-hop and grunge popular.[60] And Millennials had the pop sounds of boy bands and Britney Spears.[61] Generation Z is growing up with artists like Taylor Swift, Drake, Shawn Mendes, and Selena Gomez,[62] highlighting the vast diversity of their taste in music. In a study by Pandora, a 16-year-old user averages seven different genres, higher than five for 26 year-olds and four or less for those 50 and older.[63] So, it's hard to pinpoint an actual generational music genre that fully represents Generation Z.

Not only have musical genres and artists changed with each generation, so too have the ways people listen to music. Household radios were to the G.I. Generation what transistor radios were to the Silent Generation, vinyl records and 8-tracks were to Baby Boomers, cassettes were to Generation X, and CDs and MP3s were to Millennials. While some of these technologies are still around today, streaming is the musical technology of Generation Z. If they want to listen to their favorite song, they don't have to wait to hear it played on the radio. It's now possible to consolidate an entire album collection onto one device for unlimited listening capabilities. Streaming apps like Spotify, Pandora, and Apple Music have revolutionized the music experience. Instead of purchasing, owning, and downloading entire albums, streaming allows users to access and listen without physically owning an actual copy of the music. With the prominence of smartphones and Internet-based technology, it's not surprising that 80 percent of American adults use a streaming service to listen to music.[64] This number is even higher for younger generations as on-demand and always-accessible music typifies how Generation Z prefers to listen. Ninety-two percent of those in Generation Z use a streaming platform for music,[65] with 84 percent of them streaming music daily.[66] Their platforms of preference have one thing in common – they are free. Only 22 percent of music streamers ages 16 to 24 pay for a streaming service.[67] For those who do pay for an account, they are more likely to pay for a premium subscription through Spotify or Apple Music as opposed to a paid subscription with Pandora or YouTube Red.[68]

With the ease of being able to stream music from a personal device 24/7, it makes sense that Generation Z is always plugged in. The music site, Pandora, refers to this group as the "earbud generation" as these young people listen to music while doing just about everything.[69] Fifty-five percent listen while eating and 70 percent while on social media.[70] And 87 percent have music on in the background when doing homework.[71] Nearly half spend at least 4 hours a day wearing earbuds.[72] Although listening to music can be entertainment in and of itself, it appears that, for this generation, it is something they engage in while participating in other activities.

From games to gaming: The rise in popularity of video games

Games such as chess or Monopoly have been a form of entertainment for kids and adults for many decades. Pull out the pieces, setup the game board, and play. But, the world Generation Z is coming of age in is one where these very games can also be played in the digital world. Physical games like Yahtzee or Scrabble now have mobile versions such as New Yahtzee with Buddies[73] and Words with Friends.[74] Robust technology and high definition images, though, have led to the creation of new online games not associated with any physical game previously in existence. These games allow players to explore faraway lands and fantasy storylines or fulfill a professional sports aspiration all through their devices.

Although high-tech video games have emerged more recently, the technology and allure for playing is far from new. The earliest video games emerged in the 1950s and 1960s, with the first personal gaming console available in the 1970s.[75] Gen Xers were some of the first children to spend their time playing Pong on Atari as well as Super Mario Bros. on Nintendo.[76] While Minecraft, Call of Duty, and The Legend of Zelda top the lists of those in Generation Z today,[77] it is Fortnite that is most prominent due to the integration of cartoon-like figures, humor, and ability to dress players.[78] It also doesn't hurt that it's free.[79]

Twenty-eight percent of video gamers in the U.S. are under the age of 18.[80] And, while 90 percent of teens overall play video games, there are differences in rates of engagement by gender with 97 percent of teen boys and 83 percent of teen girls playing video games.[81] Video games are not just for older members of Generation Z, though. In 2014, two-thirds of Little Zs (ages 6 to 11 years-old) indicated that playing video games was a preferred form of entertainment.[82]

Video gaming has grown in popularity over recent years, reflective of the massive growth in the profit-generating gaming industry. At the tune of more than $30 billion in revenue in 2017, video gaming is not just literally fun and games – it's big business.[83] Gaming has become so prominent that nearly half of U.S. households have a dedicated video gaming device, such as an Xbox or PlayStation, with an additional 22 percent of households having a handheld gaming device.[84] And people are not just playing video games on consoles or devices either; they are also playing them on computers, tablets, and smartphones.[85] Generation Z teens use a variety of devices for gaming with the most common being the computer, console, and smartphone.[86] But, for those who play daily, their preference is for mobile devices over consoles.[87]

> ❝ I like to use social gaming the most because I can play with friends across long distances and have a conversation while having fun. ❞
>
> – Member of Generation Z

Virtual reality presents a new frontier for video gaming and entertainment. Whereas video games allow players to experience a story or fantasy in a two-dimension format, virtual reality creates an even more immersive gaming experience.[88] A 2015 study by Greenlight VR and Touchstone Research found that nearly 80 percent of Generation Z teens had an interest in virtual reality.[89] Being quick to adopt and integrate technology, we can expect Generation Z to be early virtual reality users.

Video games not only give players a way to escape into a storyline and virtual reality, but they also include social elements that allow people to connect with other players.[90] Forty-one percent of video gamers report playing multi-player video games with friends.[91] And, watching others play video games online has become a new industry for entertainment. In 2017, 181 million people in the U.S. tuned in for live stream viewing of video games.[92] Being able to watch others engage in gaming greatly appeals to those in Generation Z as 37 percent of video game viewers on Twitch and YouTube are in the 16- to 24-year-old age bracket.[93] Whether playing, engaging, or watching, a large share of those in Generation Z are being entertained through social gaming.

Popular culture

The throwback generation

Some are calling Generation Z a "throwback" generation.[94] If the re-emergence of popular media, movies, and shows is any indication, the name is actually quite fitting. Since Generation Z has become teens and young adults, we've seen reboots of classic 90s shows, like *Fuller House* with DJ, Kimmy, and Stephanie now raising kids in their old family home[95] or *Girl Meets World* centering on Cory and Topanga's daughter exploring her tween years in the modern age.[96] The trilogy saga, *Star Wars*, which originally debuted while older members of Generation X were entering their teenage years, has re-emerged with new episodes and anthology backstories.[97]

A number of Disney's animated classic films have also gotten live-action redesigns, including *The Jungle Book*, *Beauty and the Beast*, *Cinderella*, and *Alice and Wonderland*.[98] Instead of remaking the films, they are updated with computer-generated imagery and special effects that capitalize on the vast modern technology available to filmmakers today.

Even 90s games like Pokémon have found a way to find relevance among Generation Z. The Pokémon Go! phase of 2016 gave the original console-based video game and trading card game an app-based makeover through mobile integration. At the launch, 22 percent of users were 13 to 17 years-old, and 46 percent were 18 to 29, making this unsurprisingly a teen and young adult gaming experience.[99] It's not just Pokémon making a comeback, though, as classic SEGA games that Generation Z's parents grew up playing, like Sonic the Hedgehog, have also made the move to mobile.[100]

A different face of famous: Non-celebrity celebrities

With the sheer number of magazines and TV shows dedicated to celebrity news coverage, it seems as though fans have always been able to keep up with their favorite stars. But, as media delivery and consumption habits have changed, so has fan access. You don't have to follow the weekly tabloid headlines or be a member of the Paparazzi to get up close and personal with celebrities. There are more ways than ever to peek into their lives. By following celebrities on social media, it's easy to discover personal details about them like what they had for breakfast or see pictures of their newborn baby.

So, while celebrities have become more like everyday people, everyday people have become more like celebrities. For instance, we've been keeping up with the Kardashian-Jenner sisters since before the many of the Little Zs were even born.[101] Kim Kardashian, in particular, pioneered the way for gaining mega-fame without being a professional actor, singer, artist, or athlete – what some would consider "traditional" celebrity professions.[102] With more than 100 million Instagram followers and more than 50 million Twitter followers, she is a quintessential social media influencer that characterizes this new type of fame.[103] But, other non-celebrity celebrities have taken to the scene as well and are winning over Generation Z. One such person is Jazz Jennings who has risen to popularity by openly sharing her experience as a transgender teen.[104] She entered into the spotlight with an interview with Barbara Walters in 2007, followed by a documentary about her life, which aired on the Oprah Winfrey Network.[105] Jazz now has her own show on the TLC Network and an active YouTube channel.[106]

In addition to celebrities using YouTube as a platform, the platform itself has launched everyday people into stardom. YouTube stars range from makeup artists hosting tutorials, comedians putting out shorts or sketches, lifestyle video bloggers sharing tips, or just people documenting their lives via their YouTube channel. With millions of viewers, YouTube stars can generate a profit through advertisements played on their channels. In 2017, the highest-paid YouTube star, Daniel Middleton, who goes by the username DanTDM, made more than $16 million through his YouTube channel by reviewing video games and posting video gaming tips.[107] Finding fame and influence online is not reserved solely for YouTube, though. Instagram has opened another avenue for users to gain a high volume of followers. Instagram influencers come in all shapes, sizes, genres, and backgrounds from traditional celebrities, fitness coaches, and nutritionists to comedians, travelers, and photographers. Like YouTube stars, some influencers are turning a profit from their online reach through ads and sponsored posts, making Instagram their job. Although celebrity influencers, like Selena Gomez, any of the Kardashian-Jenner sisters, or LeBron James, can bring in six figures per sponsored post on Instagram,[108] prominent non-celebrity influencers, like makeup artist and beauty blogger, Huda Kattan, report making up to $18,000 per sponsored Instagram post.[109]

And who is tuning in to view these videos and posts? Generation Z. This generation is drawn to YouTube and Instagram celebrities because they seem more like normal, relatable people, whereas Hollywood stars seem distant and elusive.[110] Perhaps that is why a study by Google and Ipsos found that 70 percent of teens who subscribe to YouTube relate more to everyday YouTube content creators than traditional celebrities.[111]

Conclusion

Members of Generation Z enjoy spending time doing many of the same things that young people in older generations liked to do when they were young such as play sports, join organizations, read, and watch movies. While their rates of participation might be declining for some of these activities, this is a generation that has new forms of entertainment literally at their fingertips. With a swipe or tap, they can stream music, binge-watch a new TV series, play video games, or follow their favorite YouTube celebrities . . . all without even having to leave home.

Notes

1   Parker, K., Horowitz, J. M., & Rohal, M. (2015). *Parenting in America: Outlook, worries, aspirations are strongly linked to financial situation.* Retrieved from www.pewsocialtrends.org/2015/12/17/parenting-in-america/

2   Google. (2017b). *It's lit: A guide to what teens think is cool.* Retrieved from https://storage.googleapis.com/think/docs/its-lit.pdf

3   Langhorst, P. (2016). *Youth sports participation statistics and trends.* Retrieved from www.engagesports.com/blog/post/1488/youth-sports-participation-statistics-and-trends

4   Langhorst, P. (2016).

5   Langhorst, P. (2016).

6   Langhorst, P. (2016).

7   Biber, D. D., Czech, D. R., Harris, B. S., & Melton, B. F. (2013). Attraction to physical activity of generation Z: A mixed methodological approach. *Open Journal of Preventive Medicine, 3*(3), 310–319.

8   Parker, K., Horowitz, J. M., & Rohal, M. (2015).

9   Parker, K., Horowitz, J. M., & Rohal, M. (2015).

10 Hubbard, M. F. (2016). *A cartographic depiction and exploration of the Boy Scouts of America's historical membership patterns.* (Unpublished Master's thesis). University of Kansas, Lawrence, KS.

11 Pelletiere, N. (2018). *Boy Scouts of America will change an iconic name as girls enter older youth program.* Retrieved from https://abcnews.go.com/GMA/News/boy-scouts-america-change-iconic-girls-enter-older/story?id=54878120

12 Chokshi, N. (2017a). *Boy Scouts, reversing century-old stance, will allow transgender boys.* Retrieved from www.nytimes.com/2017/01/30/us/boy-scouts-reversing-century-old-stance-will-allow-transgender-boys.html

13 Kauffman, G. (2016). *Boy Scouts 100 years ago vs. now: What's changed?* Retrieved from www.csmonitor.com/USA/Society/2016/0615/Boy-Scouts-100-years-ago-vs.-now-What-s-changed

14 Miller, J. R. (2017). *Boy Scouts of America not just for boys anymore: Membership opening to girls.* Retrieved from www.marketwatch.com/story/cub-scouts-to-admit-girls-boy-scouts-of-america-announces-2017-10-11

15 The Literature Network. (n.d.). *The great gatsby.* Retrieved from www.online-literature.com/fitzgerald/greatgatsby/

16 CliffsNotes. (n.d.). *Grapes of Wrath at a glance.* Retrieved from www.cliffsnotes.com/literature/g/the-grapes-of-wrath/the-grapes-of-wrath-at-a-glance

17 Sparknotes. (n.d.). *Fahrenheit 451 plot overview*. Retrieved from www.sparknotes.com/lit/451/summary/

18 AARP.com. (2014). *Readers' picks: 10 books Boomers love*. Retrieved from www.aarp.org/entertainment/books/info-2014/baby-boomer-generation-best-books-photo.html#slide11

19 Nielsen. (2015). *Global generational lifestyles: How we live, eat, play, work, and save for our futures*. Retrieved from www.nielsen.com/us/en/insights/reports/2015/global-generational-lifestyles.html

20 Common Sense Media. (2014). *Children, teens, and reading*. Retrieved from www.commonsensemedia.org/file/csm-childrenteensandreading-2014pdf/download

21 Scholastic. (2016). *Kids and family reading report: 6th edition*. Retrieved from www.scholastic.com/readingreport/files/Scholastic-KFRR-6ed-2017.pdf

22 Common Sense Media. (2014).

23 Common Sense Media. (2014).

24 Scholastic. (2016).

25 Scholastic. (2016).

26 Scholastic. (2016).

27 Perrin, A. (2016). *Book reading 2016*. Retrieved from www.pewinternet.org/2016/09/01/book-reading-2016/

28 Common Sense Media. (2014).

29 Statista. (2017e). *Number of tablet users worldwide from 2013–2020 (in billions)*. Retrieved from www.statista.com/statistics/377977/tablet-users-worldwide-forecast/

30 Robb, A. (2015). *92 percent of college students prefer reading print books to e-readers*. Retrieved from https://newrepublic.com/article/120765/naomi-barons-words-onscreen-fate-reading-digital-world

31 Crum, M. (2015). *Sorry, ebooks: These 9 studies show why print is better*. Retrieved from www.huffingtonpost.com/2015/02/27/print-ebooks-studies_n_6762674.html

32 Varkey Foundation. (2017). *Generation Z: Global Citizenship Survey*. Retrieved from www.varkeyfoundation.org/what-we-do/policy-research/generation-z-global-citizenship-survey/

33 Scholastic. (2016).

34 Buzacott-Spear, E. (2017). *The "Harry Potter effect": How seven books changed the face of children's publishing*. Retrieved from www.abc.net.au/news/2017-06-26/harry-potter-effect-how-seven-books-changed-childrens-publishing/8630254

35 Abad-Santos, A. & VanDerWerff, T. (2018). *Avengers: Infinity War to Iron Man: Every Marvel movie definitively ranked*. Retrieved from www.vox.com/culture/2017/5/8/15559410/marvel-movies-ranked-avengers-black-panther-captain-america

36 Bunbury, S. (2017). *Wonder Woman: New movie tells the real story behind the comic-book creation*. Retrieved from www.stuff.co.nz/entertainment/film/98483672/Wonder-Woman-New-movie-tells-the-real-story-behind-the-comic-book-creation

37 IMDB. (n.d.d). *Top-US-grossing feature films released 2017-01-01 to 2017-12-31*. Retrieved from www.imdb.com/search/title?year=2017&title_type=feature&sort=boxoffice_gross_us,desc

38 Fennessey, S. (2017). *This superhero life*. Retrieved from www.theringer.com/movies/2017/11/13/16643172/superhero-movies-2017-box-office-future

39 Motion Picture Association of America. (2018). *2017 theme report*. Retrieved from www.mpaa.org/wp-content/uploads/2018/04/MPAA-THEME-Report-2017_Final.pdf

40 Motion Picture Association of America. (2016). *Theatrical market statistics 2015*. Retrieved from www.mpaa.org/wp-content/uploads/2016/04/MPAA-Theatrical-Market-Statistics-2015_Final.pdf

41 Motion Picture Association of America. (2017). *Theatrical market statistics 2016.* Retrieved from www.mpaa.org/wp-content/uploads/2017/03/MPAA-Theatrical-Market-Statistics-2016_Final.pdf

42 Motion Picture Association of America. (2018).

43 Encyclopedia Britannica. (2017). *Television in the United States.* Retrieved from www.britannica.com/art/television-in-the-United-States#ref283600

44 History.com Staff. (2009c). *MTV launches.* Retrieved from www.history.com/this-day-in-history/mtv-launches

45 Encyclopedia Britannica. (2017).

46 Stern, J. (2013). *Blockbuster to close 300 stores, killed by streaming video.* Retrieved from https://abcnews.go.com/Technology/blockbuster-close-300-stores-continues-offer-online-video/story?id=18285591

47 Nielsen. (2017b). *The Nielsen total audience report: Q1 2017.* Retrieved from www.nielsen.com/us/en/insights/reports/2017/the-nielsen-total-audience-report-q1-2017.html

48 Vision Critical. (2016). *The everything guide to Generation Z.* Retrieved from www.visioncritical.com/resources/gen-z-guide/

49 Hulu. (2017). *Gen Z: The generation at the forefront of TV's evolution.* Retrieved from www.hulu.com/advertising/gen-z-the-generation-at-the-forefront-of-tvs-evolution/

50 Hulu. (2017).

51 McAlone, N. (2016). *The 2 reasons Netflix refuses to release shows on a weekly schedule.* Retrieved from www.businessinsider.com/netflix-refuses-to-release-a-weekly-show-for-these-reasons-2016-1

52 Shamsian, J. (2018). *13 huge changes Netflix's "A Series of Unfortunate Events" TV show made from the book.* Retrieved from www.thisisinsider.com/a-series-of-unfortunate-events-book-show-changes-2017-1

53 Raftery, L. (2017). *13 ways 13 Reasons Why broke from the book.* Retrieved from www.tvguide.com/news/13-reasons-why-netflix-differences-book/

54 Armstrong, J. K. (2018). *Why the Handmaid's Tale is so relevant today.* Retrieved from www.bbc.com/culture/story/20180425-why-the-handmaids-tale-is-so-relevant-today

55 Schaub, M. (2017). *"The Handmaid's Tale" is the most-read Kindle book of the year, Amazon says.* Retrieved from www.latimes.com/books/jacketcopy/la-et-jc-handmaids-tale-20171213-story.html

56 Hulu. (2017).

57 Hulu. (2017).

58 Moore, D. (2013). *Big band in the barracks: Looking back at the music of WWII and the Greatest Generation.* Retrieved from www.veteransunited.com/network/big-band-in-the-barracks-looking-back-at-the-music-of-wwii-and-the-greatest-generation/

59 Hilton, R. (2008). *The sound of a generation.* Retrieved from www.npr.org/sections/all-songs/2008/06/the_sound_of_a_generation.html

60 Hilton, R. (2008).

61 Dangelo, J. (2000). *Nsync, Britney, Backstreet boys rule in 2000.* Retrieved from www.mtv.com/news/1435375/nsync-britney-backstreet-boys-ruled-in-2000/

62 YouTube. (2018b). *Teen party music 2018: Today's teen hits playlist.* Retrieved from www.youtube.com/playlist?list=PL5D7fjEEs5yd04bMgz6lWUVBNh2S1uRKG

63 Pandora. (2018). *Engineering for engagement: Generation Z is the earbud generation.* Retrieved from http://pandoraforbrands.com/insight/events_engineering-for-engagement-generation-z-is-the-earbud-generation/

64 Fluent, LLC. (2016). *Facing the music: The takeover of streaming services.* Retrieved from www.fluentco.com/insight/musicstreamingreport/

65 Fluent, LLC. (2016).

66 Fluent, LLC. (2016).

67 Beer, C. (2018a). *Chart of the day: Music streaming yet to prove premium worth.* Retrieved from https://blog.globalwebindex.com/chart-of-the-day/music-streaming-premium/?utm_campaign=Chart%20of%20the%20Day&utm_source=hs_email&utm_medium=email&utm_content=62158387&_hsenc=p2ANqtz-9R8hPlkm YbbipFpXmyyPaUAnUAOOa4X7IucNxPFZjv4i5Pq4ynivmXcbq58EV6T5D-PjhETnMqz7YfkUgwdcXpRXb4ZGw&_hsmi=62158387

68 Fluent, LLC. (2016).

69 Pandora. (2018).

70 Pandora. (2018).

71 Pandora. (2018).

72 Pandora. (2018).

73 Scopely. (2018). *New Yahtzee® with Buddies.* Retrieved from http://scopely.com/game/new-yahtzee-with-buddies/

74 Howard, B. C. (2012). *Words with friends beat scrabble at its own game.* Retrieved from www.fastcompany.com/1810607/how-words-friends-beat-scrabble-its-own-game

75 History.com Staff. (2017b). *Video game history.* Retrieved from www.history.com/topics/history-of-video-games

76 History.com Staff. (2017b).

77 Google. (2017b).

78 Stuart, K. (2018). *Fortnite shoots to the top of teenagers' most-wanted games list.* Retrieved from www.theguardian.com/games/2018/mar/23/fortnite-shoots-to-the-top-of-teenagers-most-wanted-games-list

79 Stuart, K. (2018).

80 Statista. (2018a). *Age breakdown of video game players in the United States in 2017.* Retrieved from www.statista.com/statistics/189582/age-of-us-video-game-players-since-2010/

81 Anderson, M. & Jiang, J. (2018). *Teens, social media & technology 2018.* Retrieved from http://assets.pewresearch.org/wp-content/uploads/sites/14/2018/05/31102617/PI_2018.05.31_TeensTech_FINAL.pdf

82 Sparks & Honey. (2014). *Meet Generation Z: Forget everything you learned about Millennials.* Retrieved from www.slideshare.net/sparksandhoney/generation-z-final-june-17

83 Entertainment Software Association. (2017). *2017 sales, demographics, and usage data: Essential facts about the computer and video game industry.* Retrieved from www.theesa.com/about-esa/essential-facts-computer-video-game-industry/

84 Entertainment Software Association. (2017).

85 Cleverism.com. (2015). *The gaming industry: An introduction.* Retrieved from www.cleverism.com/gaming-industry-introduction/

86 Lenhart, A. (2015c). *Teens, technology, and friendships.* Retrieved from www.pewinternet.org/2015/08/06/teens-technology-and-friendships/

87 Common Sense Media. (2015). *The Common Sense census: Media use by tweens and teens.* Retrieved from www.commonsensemedia.org/research/the-common-sense-census-media-use-by-tweens-and-teens

88 Sin, B. (2016). *Yes, a VR headset makes you look dumb, but the immersion is worth it.* Retrieved from www.forbes.com/sites/bensin/2016/02/14/yes-a-vr-headset-makes-you-look-dumb-but-the-immersion-is-worth-it/

89 eMarketer.com. (2015b). *Virtual reality interest highest among Gen Z.* Retrieved from www.emarketer.com/Article/Virtual-Reality-Interest-Highest-Among-Gen-Z/1013295
90 Google. (2017b).
91 Entertainment Software Association. (2017).
92 Statista. (n.d.). *Gaming video content market: Statistics and facts.* Retrieved from www.statista.com/topics/3147/gaming-video-content-market/
93 Statista. (n.d.).
94 The Center for Generational Kinetics. (2017). *The state of Gen Z 2017: Meet the throwback generation.* Retrieved from http://genhq.com/gen-z-2017/
95 IMDB. (n.d.a). *Fuller House plot.* Retrieved from www.imdb.com/title/tt3986586/plotsummary
96 IMDB. (n.d.b). *Girl Meets World plot summary.* Retrieved from www.imdb.com/title/tt2543796/plotsummary
97 IMDB. (2018). *Star Wars movie series in chronological order.* Retrieved from www.imdb.com/list/ls068055646/
98 Devoe, N. (2018). *A complete list of every Disney live-action remake we know about so far.* Retrieved from www.seventeen.com/celebrity/movies-tv/g2936/list-of-disney-live-action-remakes/
99 Skinner, H., Sarpong, D., & White, G. R. T. (2018). Meeting the needs of the Millennials and Generation Z: Gamification in tourism through geocaching. *Journal of Tourism Futures.* https://doi.org/10.1108/JTF-12-2017-0060
100 Etherington, D. (2017). *SEGA's new SEGA Forever collection brings classic games to mobile for free.* Retrieved from https://techcrunch.com/2017/06/21/segas-new-sega-forever-collection-brings-classic-games-to-mobile-for-free/
101 Rai, M. K. (2017). *How rich is Kim Kardashian and how did she make millions by "just being famous"?* Retrieved from www.ibtimes.co.uk/how-rich-kim-kardashian-how-did-she-make-millions-by-just-being-famous-1633207
102 Rai, M. K. (2017).
103 Rai, M. K. (2017).
104 Grinberg, E. (2015). *Why transgender teen Jazz Jennings is everywhere.* Retrieved from www.cnn.com/2015/03/16/living/feat-transgender-teen-jazz-jennings/index.html
105 Grinberg, E. (2015).
106 Grinberg, E. (2015).
107 McAlone, N. & Lynch, J. (2017). *Meet the YouTube millionaires: These are the top 10 highest-paid YouTube stars of 2017.* Retrieved from www.businessinsider.com/highest-paid-youtube-stars-2017-12/#no-10-lilly-singh-105-million-1
108 Hopper HQ. (2017). *Instagram rich list 2017: The platform's highest-earners revealed.* Retrieved from www.hopperhq.com/blog/instagram-rich-list-2017-platforms-highest-earners-revealed/
109 Hopper HQ. (2017).
110 Masback, G. (2016). *The voice of Gen Z.* (n.p.): Author.
111 O'Neil-Hart, C. & Blumenstein, H. (2016). *Why YouTube stars are more influential than traditional celebrities.* Retrieved from www.thinkwithgoogle.com/consumer-insights/youtube-stars-influence/

7 Money

· ·

Most of us in older generations can recall the famous line from the movie, *Jerry Maguire*, "Show me the money!" While this line might have been the mantra of the time, today, those in Generation Z have different thoughts about money – thoughts that harken back to an earlier time of craving financial security and abandoning notions of great wealth, like those in the G.I. Generation.

Perhaps that is what growing up during a recession can do. Or, maybe this socially conscious generation sees that money is necessary for survival and not for luxury. Regardless, Generation Z's financial views and behaviors will have a major impact on us all.

The economic landscape

Whether it's the implementation of the New Deal in the 1930s or the introduction of trickle-down economics in the 1980s, the economic landscape during one's lifetime can have both a physical impact on actual wealth as well as a cultural impact on one's view of money. How has the economic landscape of the late twentieth century and early twenty-first century affected how those in Generation Z view money? And, how will those views shape their financial behaviors and decisions they make as they age?

Recession kids

Like those in the G.I. Generation, Generation Z's youth has been marked by an economic setback that resulted in people losing jobs, homes, and even the money they set aside for retirement. As first-time homebuyers overpaid for houses only to have them foreclosed on shortly after and aging Baby Boomers saw the balances in

❝ *Growing up at one point, my family and I were in food stamps and free and reduced lunch. We all shared a car, and we got by with the bare minimal. I don't want to be in that situation when I have a family of my own.* ❞
– *Member of Generation Z*

their retirement accounts substantially drop, hardly anyone of any age group was immune to the Great Recession. Growing up during this era likely contributed to what might have felt like a sense of scarcity, whether real or perceived. When all you know is that mom lost her job or dad's hours got cut, or grandpa says that much of what he invested in his retirement for the last 20 years seemed to disappear, it's hard to imagine these young people not worrying about money.

For some Generation Z kids, growing up during the Recession might have meant forgoing allowances, whereas for others, it might have meant contributing to the family revenue stream by earning an income at a young age. Although many families are back on their feet, the work ethic instilled in their Generation Z children seems to have continued. A study by Generational Kinetics found that 77 percent of 14 to 21 year-old members of Generation Z make spending money through doing freelance work, working a part-time job, or earning an allowance.[1]

Despite the economy bouncing back to some extent, Generation Z is entering adulthood in a time of higher unemployment and underemployment for their age group than before the Recession.[2] And, they are still faced with a rising cost of living, stagnant wages, and the question of whether social security will be available when they retire.

College days and college debt

Twenty years ago, it was common for college students to work part-time and be able to cover their tuition. Now, even working full-time while in school barely makes a dent in college expenses. Between 2003 and 2013, college tuition has risen more than 80 percent.[3] It makes sense then that Generation Z college students are concerned about the cost of college more than any other issue.[4] With rising tuition comes rising debt as evidenced by the 8 percent increase between 2004 and 2014 in students taking out federal loans for college.[5] Results from a Sallie Mae study found that a third of students in 2017 took out student loans,[6] contributing to the total national student loan debt of $1.31 trillion.[7]

❝ My family has always had a constant worry about paying bills and getting by so naturally I developed that worry. My grants and loans have taken a lot of that worry away from me now but I still worry about after graduation. ❞

– Member of Generation Z

Researchers have found that the more debt a student takes on, the more likely it is that the student will drop out of college.[8] It's important to consider then that with higher college costs, we may see more Generation Z students leave college for financial reasons than ever before.

But, for those students who opt to stay in college, they are finding ways to increase income and reduce expenses. For one, the number of students who need to work while in college is growing.[9] A study by Sallie Mae found that, in 2017, 76 percent of students worked as a way to help pay for college expenses.[10] Some may work on campus, using their time staffing the information desk to do homework during slow times. But, those jobs are limited, leading some students to work off campus further from classes and in an environment that may be less conducive to students' class schedules and campus commitments. With needing to work so many hours, it is easy to understand why students might feel overwhelmed in managing their course loads. More than half of students indicate the number one reason for dropping out is trying to balance work and classes.[11] And, if a student does not pass a class or takes a reduced course load because of job demands, the time to graduation is then extended, ultimately increasing the total cost of a college degree.

In addition to working, many Generation Z college students receive federal grant money. Findings from Sallie Mae indicate that 47 percent of students in 2017 received grant money to attend college.[12] But, often that money only helps with some expenses as students are left to fill in the gaps with other funding sources (parental assistance, scholarships, or loans) or find a way to reduce costs.

We found in our Generation Z Goes to College Study that many in this generation are conservative spenders.[13] Given the nature of their frugal habits[14] along with the hesitance in taking out large student loans, some in Generation Z are simply making different choices about college attendance. For one, 69 percent of students and their families today are eliminating specific colleges from the list of possible schools to attend due to cost, a notable increase from the 58 percent who did so in 2008.[15] Second, nearly three-quarters are going to college in state, getting a reduced tuition rate.[16] Finally, while they still prefer physical print when reading,[17] many are renting textbooks or buying digital rather than print copies simply to save money.[18]

And while many do end up taking out loans for tuition and fees, the idea of spending borrowed money on a fancy residence hall can be unnerving and may seem unnecessary for some of them. Georgia State University recognized this concern and offered a scaled-back, modest residence hall with the notion that the experiment was likely not going to be all that popular. When the less expensive residence hall filled faster than other halls, the institution acquired two local hotels and converted them into cost-effective housing.[19] But, even the lowest cost residence hall on a college campus can be expensive, leaving many Generation Z students choosing to live with their parents as a way to save money.

Working years

For a generation highly concerned about money, it would be assumed that most are seeking high paying careers. But, as we discuss later in the book, many simply want to have a salary that pays enough to live off of without having to worry about money.[20] In one sense, that might be wishful thinking on their part. They may decide that money plays a far more crucial role in their happiness after spending time in the workforce, finding that the financially comfortable life they desire may also come with having to repay student loan debt, difficulty finding a job in their field, or being underemployed.

And, as discussed later in this book, many may turn to the gig economy as a way to blend their passions into their careers as well as be in control of their own financial destinies. We may see those in Generation Z entering and exiting the freelance world as they try to balance their desire for entrepreneurship with the reality of financial security. Tough times? "Maybe I should get a job with an established organization." Lots of business? "Maybe this whole working for myself thing will really work."

An important element to consider for Generation Z's working years is the high cost of healthcare. For fear of not having insurance or having high premiums and low coverage, those budding entrepreneurs in Generation Z may decide to take a job in an established organization that provides employer-sponsored healthcare. The anxiety of not being able to care for themselves or their families[21] may take precedent for these passionate, free-lancing spirits who want to make the world a better place through their own entrepreneurial initiatives.

Retirement

Although decades away, members of Generation Z are already thinking about retirement.[22] That's likely because they are watching their grandparents retire or prepare for retirement. Many of those in Generation Z know that social security will likely not be around for them like it is now for their eldest family members. And if by chance it is, the pool of money will likely be so depleted that they will be lucky to get any amount of money that will cover their expenses. It isn't just that Baby Boomer retirees are draining the coffers. Compared to previous generations, Millennials are having less children, resulting in a baby bust.[23] Fewer children being born means fewer future taxpayers whose social security and Medicare contributions are those that Generation Z would be dependent on for their retirement benefits. Considering these factors, it makes sense that only about one-quarter of those in Generation Z believe they will get some form of government assistance when they retire, lower than the one-third of Millennials who believe they will.[24]

❝ The biggest issue my generation will face in 30 years is 'never being able to retire.' ❞
– Member of Generation Z

Those in Generation Z know they need to be prepared if they plan to retire, and some are starting at a young age. Twelve percent of 14 to 21 year-olds are already saving for retirement, while 35 percent plan to start saving once they are in their 20s.[25] Although more than half of those in Generation Z are planning to tap into their own savings for retirement,[26] they know that those savings will run out quickly. With a lack of a nest egg taking them through their golden years, many may need to continue working well after retirement, even if simply freelancing in the gig economy.[27]

The "American Dream"

Writer James Truslow Adams was first credited in 1931 for the term "American Dream," describing it as "that dream of a land in which life should be better and richer and fuller for everyone, with opportunity for each according to ability and achievement."[28] While Adams points out that the American Dream is not about cars, homes, and material goods,[29] the vision of the American Dream has evolved with each generation, and, for some, those things have become tangible signals of achieving the American Dream.

With a childhood and adolescence stricken by war and economic downturn, it is understandable that the G.I. Generation sought out peace and prosperity in their adulthood – not just for themselves, but for others as well. They envisioned the better, richer, fuller life in which Adams described. More than envisioning this dream, they achieved it for the most part by fostering a healthy economy and building comfortable lives with houses in the suburbs,[30] setting the trajectory for American culture that pines for a better life.

Bridgeworks, a generational group, charted the evolution of the image of the American Dream for each modern generation. For the Silent Generation, the idea of the American Dream was the self-made man with icons such as Walt Disney, Henry Ford, or John D. Rockefeller.[31] With the benefit of a small cohort population size, increase in the job market, and passing of the Depression, the Silent Generation could achieve their version of their American Dream. The Silent Generation is the only modern American generation to think it was easier for them to a get a job than it was for their parents to do so at their age.[32]

As Baby Boomers were born into a time of prosperity and security their parents dreamed of, they developed a version of the American Dream associated with high wages and the ability to be a contributing consumer in the economy through buying homes, cars, and other goods to support a comfortable lifestyle.[33] A 2015 study by New America found Baby Boomers are the most likely, aside from the Silent Generation, to believe it is about the same or easier to afford raising a family than it was for their G.I. Generation parents.[34]

Children from the Silent Generation and Generation X, both sandwiched between two massive generational cohorts, grappled with their small size by redefining the American Dream by associating it with success, but not necessarily monetary or consumer assets.[35] As adults today, Generation X is the generation least likely to believe there are a good number of jobs not requiring a college degree.[36] Along with their Generation Z children, Generation X has the highest levels of skepticism about being able to find a well-paying job.[37] This likely stems from the competitive job markets they entered following the Baby Boomers or jobs they might have lost during the Recession. With the economic and job market cards somewhat stacked against them at times throughout their lives, it is not surprising that Generation X's version of the American Dream is linked to overcoming adversity to find success in their career.

Millennials have further refined the American Dream by extending the pursuit of living richer and fuller lives through focusing on experiences and seeking happiness in both their work and personal lives.[38] Their redefinition of the concept of success involves seeking out a life that is abundant in experiences and promotes health and wellness, both which can be costly but still supported by stable employment.[39] Success in life for Millennials is not an end goal or monetary milestone but more so the enjoyment of the experience or journey.[40]

Generation Z's version of the American Dream, however, is a blend of the dreams of each of their predecessor generations, as those generations laid the groundwork for the world that Generation Z was born into and lives in today. Their version of the American Dream is quite similar to the American Dream of many in the G.I. Generation who strived for a comfortable life after the war, where they could buy a home and move their family to the suburbs.[41] They recognize that dream is not attainable without the hard work, financial security, and self-reliance similar to what was modeled by the Silent Generation. Like Baby Boomers, those in Generation Z are powerful and influential consumers with the goal of being able to support their future families. However, they know that spending power and financial security are achieved through determination, something they've inherited from their Generation X parents. Finally, Millennials modeled the way, showing that all the money and material items in the world wouldn't be fulfilling without happiness and meaningful experiences.

> **❝ The good life to me would be 'The American Dream.' ❞**
> *- Member of Generation Z*

While much has changed in the last century when it comes to the American Dream, 95 percent of those in Generation Z still believe in it,[42] and 78 percent believe it is attainable.[43] And, those in Generation Z are confident in being able to achieve that dream . . . even more confident than Millennials.[44]

Generation Z's relationship with money

The economic landscape of the last few decades, along with the personal financial experiences and beliefs of those in Generation Z, have laid the groundwork for how members of this generation learn about, view, and spend money today.

Families, friends, and financial literacy

With so much to know about money, though, where are those in Generation Z getting their information to be financially literate? Two-thirds indicated that they have learned about money from their family and friends, a higher number than the 54 percent of Millennials who indicated doing so.[45] This isn't surprising in that Baby Boomers, the parental generation of many Millennials, tend to get information about finances from the bank or financial advisors and not from their parents or friends, whereas the Gen Xer parents of Generation Z get most of their information about money from family and friends,[46] likely emphasizing the importance of sharing financial insight with their own kids. With 65 percent of those in Generation Z having had discussions with their parents about money,[47] and more than half having had them in just in the last 6 months,[48] it is clear the large role that parents play in their Generation Z children's financial literacy. And while parents are likely sharing money tips with their kids during these discussions, many are also filling them in on their family's finances. Sixty-two percent of those in Generation Z claim to know a great deal about their family's financial situation.[49]

In addition to learning about money from their parents, TD Ameritrade reported that nearly four in ten have taken a class about saving or investing money,[50] and a study by Better Homes and Gardens found that 41 percent have learned about the Recession in school.[51] All of these factors likely explain why more than half of those in Generation Z think they are more knowledgeable about saving money than their parents were when at their age.[52]

Financial security and basic necessities

The old saying goes, "money can keep you up at night." And, as much as we don't want our youth to be worrying about money, many Generation Z children have been worrying about money from a young age. Whether learning about the Recession at school, seeing the impact of it at home, or having conversations with family members about the realities of money, they worry. In our Generation Z Goes to College Study, we found that nearly three-quarters indicated being concerned about

" A good life to me would be one where I can minimize any financial anxieties. I don't want a huge house, a super fancy car, or a lot of stuff. I think it would be great to have completely average things without having to worry about how I'm going to afford the most basic necessities. "
– Member of Generation Z

financial security,[53] with 14 percent of students in our Generation Z Stories Study indicating that what they worry about most is their current financial situation. Interestingly, 11 percent also indicated that they worry about their future financial situation[54] and not having enough money to provide for themselves or their families.[55]

Forces of the sharing economy

Uber, Airbnb, and the hundreds of other sharing apps have transformed the way we do business today. Millennials seem to have been the driving force behind the sharing economy[56] with their desire to share living spaces, rides, services, and items. Why not make money on the guest room that always sits empty or rent out your skis on a weekend you won't be hitting the slopes? But, as much as many Millennials may like the notion of sharing for a profit, those in Generation Z have some criteria that must be met in order to see the sharing economy as one that meets their needs. They need these experiences to be convenient, efficient, and economical, all at the same time.[57] While they might not want to pile into a tiny house with three of their friends for a more permanent living situation, renting out their couch on a weekend they are out of town seems to align better. Take, for example, a student from Emerson College who rented out his residence hall room on Airbnb to make a little cash. He wasn't looking for a permanent roommate or even someone to share his space while he was home. But, with a vacant living space in the heart of Boston, it seemed obvious to him that he could help tourists with low-cost lodging while engaging in a lucrative venture for himself.[58]

The identity footprint

In addition, we found in our Generation Z Goes to College Study that 60 percent of Generation Z college students indicated being concerned about having their money stolen through identity theft.[59] This may be a contributing factor to their private online nature as discussed in the technology chapter. By securing their privacy the best they can, they then protect their identities, money, and reputation. But, this isn't a generation that grew up with their social security numbers on every ID card like those in older generations. So, where did those in Generation Z get their overwhelming need for protecting their privacy? Likely from stories of hacking and tech breaches of banks, credit card companies, and businesses that resulted in compromising personal information as well as conversations with their parents warning them of identity theft. When older generations were younger, it wasn't uncommon to share social security numbers as they provided an identifying number used for applications and memberships. This didn't seem like a risky practice at the time, as most people had never even heard of identity theft. Today, however, businesses store an overwhelming amount of people's personal data in the cloud or on servers, creating an identity footprint far bigger than any paperwork with a social security number. And by being able to use credit card numbers online without an actual card, it seems easier than ever for online purchases to be made with a stolen credit card. Taking caution from the tales of older generations' financial experiences with privacy breaches, Generation Z worries about identity theft, maybe even more than the rest of us do.

Banks

Although some people stock their money away in safety deposit boxes or even under mattresses, it has become a standard practice to keep our money in the bank. With direct deposit and credit being tied specifically to banking institutions, it has become quite difficult to navigate the world without using a bank. But, banking hasn't always been a low-risk place to keep money. During the Great Depression, many in the G.I. Generation watched as stocks tumbled and banks failed. In 1929, somewhere around 650 banks closed their doors with that number rising to more than 1,300 in 1930.[60] During the time, people's confidence in banks was eroding.[61] The events of the 1920s and 1930s ushered in new laws, policies, agencies, and ways of doing business to ensure that banks could stay open for business.[62]

Fast-forward to the Great Recession of the late 2000s where the government stepped in with the Troubled Asset Relief Program along with other initiatives, otherwise known as the bank bailout, to keep banks from closing.[63] In 2012, the marketing firm, Edelman, conducted a global study on trust in banks and found that, at the time, only 41 percent of Americans trusted banks.[64] That number sunk to just 27 percent by 2016.[65] However, Generation Z's trust in financial institutions is much higher with 74 percent being very or somewhat trusting of financial institutions.[66] This may stem from simply being too young to really understand how banking works, especially as many likely don't use banks in such a comprehensive manner yet (home loans, investments, credit lines, etc.) as their older counterparts do. While they may lack experience with banks, they also appear to lack the negative perception that older generations harbor when it comes to financial institutions, creating a somewhat clean slate for building trust between banks and Generation Z.

A study by Raddon Research Insights found that Generation Z is comprised of three very distinct types of consumers when it comes to banking.[67] The Digitals, who make up 38 percent of those in Generation Z, like banking with traditional providers such as banks and credit unions but prefer to do their banking with those providers through digital means.[68] Thirty-four percent are considered the Conventionals, who have a distrust of technology being infused in traditional banking and prefer face-to-face interactions.[69] The Pioneers makeup the smallest group of Generation Z bankers at 28 percent and are comprised of those who are comfortable with the idea that technology will impact banking, possibly eliminating the need to rely on traditional providers altogether.[70]

Saving and spending

Many market researchers have studied the spending and saving patterns of this generation as a way to gauge what they buy and how to sell to them. The beliefs, aspirations, and motivations of members of Generation Z might offer a more telling story as they embark on not only saving and spending, but investing, borrowing, and donating their money.

Saving for a rainy day

Of all of Generation Z's financial behaviors, one of the most predominant is saving money. Fifty-seven percent prefer to save their money than immediately spend it.[71] This isn't all that unexpected given their concern about not having enough money to live off of in the future. According to a study by the credit agency, TransUnion, although 52 percent of Generation Z teens are saving their money for something specific, 35 percent are saving money without having a particular purpose in mind.[72]

What do they do with all that money they are saving? With their favorable attitudes about banks, it makes sense that they would put it in the bank, which is exactly what some of them have done. Twenty-one percent of those in Generation Z had opened a savings account before they were 10 years-old.[73] This is not necessarily the norm for all generations. Only 15 percent of Millennials had a savings account before the age of 10.[74] Despite opening them at a young age, those in Generation Z use these bank accounts as more than just practice labs to help them develop financial literacy; they are able to put money away for important expenses like college. Results from a Sallie Mae study found that 11 percent of the money that goes towards higher education expenses for Generation Z students comes from their own income and savings.[75]

Coupons and discounts

Despite the financial concerns of many in Generation Z, along with their saving mentality, it is interesting then that many do not capitalize on trying to get discounts on purchases. Compared to Millennials, those in Generation Z are less likely to use coupons, discounts, and loyalty programs[76] and less likely to change products or services if offered better rewards.[77] But, when they do use discounts, they don't want to be clipping coupons; they want to receive and use these promotions through digital apps.[78]

Buying and spending

While they are financially cautious and possess a strong mentality for saving, those in Generation Z still spend money. But, their spending habits are quite different from those in previous generations. For example, a study by investment bank and asset firm, Piper Jaffray, found that the number one purchase for those in Generation Z is food.[79] It's not surprising then that they love to spend money on their coffee and their lunches, frequenting Starbucks and Chick-Fil-A more than any other food establishment.[80]

When they do buy products and merchandise, however, they prefer to do so online and make more purchases using their mobile devices than any other generation.[81] They don't just shop anywhere online, though. Findings from the Piper Jaffray study indicate that 44 percent of those in Generation Z prefer shopping on Amazon, nearly eight times higher than the next retailer on the list.[82] But, other than Amazon, an earlier study by Piper Jaffray found that members of Generation Z believe it is important for their online retailers to also have a physical location.[83] And a substantially higher number of them prefer to shop at an actual store than online.[84] So, before shutting the storefront doors, it's important to consider the legitimacy that having an actual location might provide to Generation Z online shoppers, even if they never step foot inside.

Those in Generation Z also have preferences for how they want to pay, which is mostly through online payment portals and card-branded digital wallet payments like Visa Checkout and device-specific mobile payments like Apple Pay.[85] This is a shift from how Millennials like to pay, which is through third party services like Venmo or PayPal.[86]

Loans and debt

While not everyone in Generation Z has attended or will attend college, those who opted to enroll and took out loans to pay for it will start their careers saddled with enormous debt that they have to account for in their personal budgets. In trying to cover basic living expenses along with debt repayment, many in Generation Z may teeter on the edge of making ends meet. Whether attributed to their tight-belt upbringing or their conservative purchasing habits (other than coffee), 29 percent of those in Generation Z think that only a few select items warrant accumulating personal debt, and 23 percent believe that personal debt should be avoided no matter the circumstances.[87]

❝ I worry about money a lot. Whether it's paying bills, buying food, or repairing my vehicle, it seems as if I never have enough of it. I know that if I become sick or injured I will not be able to pay my hospital bills even with insurance, and I will either live in massive debt or not be fiscally able to obtain treatment. ❞
– Member of Generation Z

Despite their feelings about accruing personal debt, many feel a sense of responsibility for paying off their debts. For those who have taken out student loans, 84 percent expect to pay them back on their own, and 21 percent plan to pay back loans taken out by their parents for their school expenses.[88] Historically, more than one in five young college graduates with student loan debt got a second job to pay expenses.[89] This is a trend that may continue with Generation Z as they couple debt with their overwhelming sense of responsibility to pay it off. Their feeling of personal accountability may contribute to why 84 percent said they feel confident they could repay their loans.[90]

Credit: Buy now, pay later

The irony is that while many in Generation Z may try to avoid personal debt, they will also be limiting their opportunities to establish a solid credit history. Despite that nearly one in five Generation Z teens are authorized users on a parent's credit card,[91] a study by Experian found that those in Generation Z have fewer credit cards of their own than any other generation.[92] This is not totally unexpected given their age. But, there may be a few other factors at play that can help explain why they may have fewer credit cards. First, as a generation literally fearful of debt, it makes sense that as teens they would be fine spending money on mom's credit card without wanting the responsibility and allure of their own card. In addition, it seems as though older generations might have been bombarded with more invitations to apply for credit cards through mailers and promotional booths on college campuses than those in Generation Z. And, who can resist wanting to get that free incentive just to apply? But, today, getting a credit card isn't as easy, because getting approved can be a challenge.[93] So, the opportunity for a free credit card and Frisbee are probably long gone.

In addition, the financial literacy of many in Generation Z appears to be high. Whether due to discussions with their parents or classes they have taken, those in Generation Z know their financial stuff.[94] Findings from a study by TransUnion indicate that nearly half of the 13 to 17 year-olds surveyed said they were familiar with what a credit score is and how it is calculated.[95] The study also found a link between understanding how to build credit and saving money. as 91 percent of Generation Z teens familiar with credit scores are currently saving money.[96] This is considerably higher than the 74 percent of those who are unfamiliar with credit scores who are currently saving.[97]

Despite having fewer credit cards, early reports from Experian indicate that the average credit score of those in Generation Z (631) is fairly comparable to that of Millennials (634), who have had much more time to establish a credit history.[98] If Generation Z follows suit with Millennials, as they too have been saddled with extensive student loan debt, we may not see the average credit score go much higher for those in Generation Z in their early adulthood. Low credit scores could potentially impact their ability to secure loans at good rates, as they get older, if they can get them at all.

Buying assets

Despite their feelings about debt, many in Generation Z do not seem to be hesitant about buying major assets they see as essential for having a good life. Nearly 80 percent equate homeownership with the American Dream.[99] It makes sense then that findings from our Generation Z Goes to College Study revealed that nearly two-thirds are concerned about finding affordable and accessible housing.[100] This likely stems from growing up during a recession and burst of the housing bubble where they saw the struggles of many families, possibly including their own, in trying to keep their homes. The post-Recession era has seen a tightening of financial regulations that have since made it difficult for some prospective homebuyers to secure a mortgage. But, that is not stopping those in Generation Z from wanting to buy their own homes. Many aim to do so by the time they are 28 years-old, which according to the National Association of Realtors, is earlier than 31, the median age of other first-time homebuyers.[101]

“ The good life would be being 'able to buy a house in a good neighborhood.' ”
- Member of Generation Z

But, as those in Generation Z hit the housing market to make their dreams come true, some Millennials may also be on the lookout to purchase a home. Younger Millennials came of age during the burst of the housing bubble, making access to home loans incredibly difficult. Rebounding from the Recession and housing market crash, we have a more stabilized housing market and lower unemployment rates,[102] creating an ideal opportunity for homeownership. The influx of those in Generation Z entering the housing market over the next decade coupled with Millennials now ready to make a home purchase may lead to a market with more buyers than sellers.

In addition to purchasing a home, the other large asset those in Generation Z are interested in acquiring is a vehicle. A study by Autotrader found that 92 percent plan to own their own cars.[103] Unlike Millennials, though, those in Generation Z are not as big of fans of ride sharing, co-ownership of cars, pay-as-you-go vehicles, or public transportation as alternatives to owning their own vehicles.[104] Having a car gives them a sense of freedom and convenience.[105] Many are drawn to hybrid and energy efficient vehicles, but not necessarily for the reasons we might think. Forty-three percent say an advantage to having an environmentally friendly vehicle is to save money on gas, whereas only 30 percent pointed out that having one helps prevent global warming.[106] This aligns with the findings from our Generation Z Goes to College Study that although many are concerned about climate change, far more are concerned about money.[107]

Investing

It might seem a little early to think about Generation Z and investing given that most are still young and may not have the financial capital to do so. But, because of their socially conscious approach to life,[108] we can anticipate that their investments will focus on companies that are ethical and sustainable.

Aside from the types of companies they may invest in, there are a few key trends that could shape the investing behavior of Generation Z. First, like banking and shopping, many in this generation are very comfortable engaging in financial transactions in the digital world. But the traditional broker-investor relationship is likely not going to work for them. We may find that those in Generation Z would rather bypass a third party and take control of their own investing directly with do-it-yourself broker apps like Robinhood. With this platform, individuals can engage in free stock trading, giving them both the freedom to control their investing while ensuring their money is going into an investment and not to fees.[109] This shift will not just affect brokers but financial advisers as well. Those at Charles Schwab believe that financial advisers will become more like life coaches for this generation because those in Generation Z trust computer models more than human beings when investing.[110]

Philanthropy

It seems hard to imagine the financially prudent members of Generation Z donating money to charitable causes. While they might not donate their own money, many are excited and eager to raise money for causes they care about, earning them the name of "philanthro-teens."[111] But, fundraising isn't just for teens; more than 60 percent of Generation Z college seniors indicated having engaged in raising money for an issue or cause while in college.[112] Having a bake sale may be a tried and true fundraiser, but platforms like GoFundMe and Kickstarter allow individuals to gain wide reach in soliciting donations from their social networks, family, and friends to help fund an issue or cause.

Conclusion

With 143 billion dollars in purchasing power,[113] Generation Z will likely continue to make a major impact on retail, financial institutions, the service industry, investment firms, the housing market, and the economy. So, how Generation Z views and uses money is important for the rest of us waiting to see what they do with those billions. Whether they are investing, saving, or spending, the financial behaviors of Generation Z will have ripple effects and impacts across industries for years to come.

Notes

1 The Center for Generational Kinetics. (2017). *The state of Gen Z 2017: Meet the throwback generation.* Retrieved from http://3pur2814p18t46fuop22hvvu.wpengine. netdna-cdn.com/wp-content/uploads/2017/04/The-State-of-Gen-Z-2017-White-Paper-c-2017-The-Center-for-Generational-Kinetics.pdf
2 Kroeger, T., Cooke, T., & Gould, E. (2016). *The class of 2016: The labor market is still far from ideal for young graduates.* Retrieved from www.epi.org/publication/class-of-2016/
3 Kurtzleben, D. (2013, October 23). CHARTS: *Just how fast has college tuition grown? U.S. news & world report.* Retrieved from www.usnews.com/news/articles/2013/10/23// charts-just-how-fast-has-college-tuition-grown
4 Seemiller, C. & Grace, M. (2016). *Generation Z goes to college.* San Francisco: Jossey-Bass.
5 College Board. (2015). *Highlights from trends in student aid.* Retrieved from http://trends. collegeboard.org/student-aid/highlights
6 Sallie Mae. (2017). *How America pays for college.* Retrieved from www.salliemae.com/ assets/Research/HAP/HowAmericaPaysforCollege2017.pdf

7 Federal Reserve Bank of New York. (2017). *Quarterly report on household debt and credit.* Retrieved from www.newyorkfed.org/medialibrary/interactives/householdcredit/data/pdf/HHDC_2016Q4.pdf

8 Hossler, D., Ziskin, M. B., Gross, J. P. K., Kim, S., & Cekic, O. (2009). Student aid and its role in encouraging persistence. In J. C. Smart (Ed.), *Higher education: Handbook of theory and research* (Vol. 24, pp. 389–425). New York: Springer.

9 Carnevale, A. P., Smith, N., Melton, M., & Price, E. W. (2015). *Learning while earning: The new normal.* Georgetown University. Retrieved from https://cew.georgetown.edu/wp-content/uploads/Working-Learners-Report.pdf

10 Sallie Mae. (2017).

11 Johnson, J., Rochkind, J., Ott, A. N., & DuPont, S. (2009). *With their whole lives ahead of them: Myths and realities about why so many students fail to finish college* (A Public Agenda Report). New York, NY: Public Agenda.

12 Sallie Mae. (2017).

13 Seemiller, C. & Grace, M. (2014). *Generation Z goes to college study.* Unpublished raw data.

14 Seemiller, C. & Grace, M. (2016).

15 Sallie Mae. (2017).

16 Sallie Mae. (2017).

17 Robb, A. (2015). *92 percent of college students prefer reading print books to e-readers.* Retrieved from https://newrepublic.com/article/120765/naomi-barons-words-onscreen-fate-reading-digital-world

18 National Association of College Stores. (2017). *Highlights from student watch attitudes & behaviors toward course materials 2016–2017 report.* Retrieved from www.nacs.org/research/studentwatchfindings.aspx

19 Selingo, J. (2017). *Why universities are phasing out luxury dorms.* Retrieved from www.theatlantic.com/education/archive/2017/08/why-universities-are-phasing-out-luxury-dorms/537492/

20 Seemiller, C. & Grace, M. (2017). *Generation Z stories study.* Unpublished raw data.

21 Seemiller, C. & Grace, M. (2017).

22 The Center for Generational Kinetics. (2017).

23 Maciag, M. (2017). *What America's "Baby Bust" means for public policy.* Retrieved from www.governing.com/topics/health-human-services/gov-baby-bust-birth-rates-policy-states.html

24 The Center for Generational Kinetics. (2017).

25 The Center for Generational Kinetics. (2017).

26 The Center for Generational Kinetics. (2017).

27 The Center for Generational Kinetics. (2017).

28 Adams, J. T. (1931). *The epic of America.* Boston, MA: Little, Brown, and Company, p. 404.

29 Adams, J. T. (1931).

30 Howe, N. (2014a). *Generations in pursuit of the American Dream.* Retrieved from www.forbes.com/sites/neilhowe/2014/07/16/part-1-generations-in-pursuit-of-the-american-dream/#4f6b609f5db0

31 Bridgeworks. (2015). *The evolution of the American Dream.* Retrieved from www.generations.com/2015/09/21/the-evolution-of-the-american-dream/

32 Fishman, R., Ekowo, M., & Ezeugo, E. (2017). *The American Dream: Findings by generation.* Retrieved from www.newamerica.org/in-depth/varying-degrees/beliefs-about-american-dream-generation/

33 Howe, N. (2014a).

34 Fishman, R., Ekowo, M., & Ezeugo, E. (2017).

35 Bridgeworks. (2015).

36 Fishman, R., Ekowo, M., & Ezeugo, E. (2017).

37 Fishman, R., Ekowo, M., & Ezeugo, E. (2017).

38 Bridgeworks. (2015).

39 Nguyen, K. & Moriarty, R. (2015). *Are Millennials redefining the American Dream?* Retrieved from www.huffingtonpost.com/krystina-nguyen/are-millennials-redefinin_b_8805056.html

40 Bridgeworks. (2015).

41 History.com Staff. (2010d). *The 1950s.* Retrieved from www.history.com/topics/1950s

42 Steele Flippin, C. (2017). *Generation Z in the workplace.* n.p.: Author.

43 The Center for Generational Kenetics & Dorsey, J. (2016). *iGen's political & civic outlook.* Retrieved from http://genhq.com/igen/

44 Vision Critical. (2016). *The everything guide to Generation Z.* Retrieved from www.visioncritical.com/wp-content/uploads/2016/10/GenZ_Final.pdf

45 Vision Critical. (2016).

46 Vision Critical. (2016).

47 Better Homes and Gardens. (2014). *Move over Millennials, Better Homes and Gardens Real Estate reveals homebuying dreams of Gen Z teens.* Retrieved from www.prnewswire.com/news-releases/move-over-millennials-better-homes-and-gardens-real-estate-reveals-homebuying-dreams-of-gen-z-teens-274452691.html

48 The Center for Generational Kinetics. (2017).

49 JWT Intelligence. (2012). *Gen Z: Digital in their DNA.* Retrieved from www.jwtintelligence.com/wp-content/uploads/2012/04/F_INTERNAL_Gen_Z_0418122.pdf

50 TD Ameritrade. (2014). *Generation Z and money survey 2014.* Retrieved from https://s1.q4cdn.com/959385532/files/doc_downloads/research/Gen-Z-and-Money-2014-Research-Report.pdf

51 Better Homes and Gardens. (2014).

52 Better Homes and Gardens. (2014).

53 Seemiller, C. & Grace, M. (2014).

54 Seemiller, C. & Grace, M. (2017).

55 Seemiller, C. & Grace, M. (2016).

56 Arthurrson, D. (2016). *How Millennials are defining the sharing economy.* Retrieved from www.entrepreneur.com/article/275802

57 Stillman, D. & Stillman, J. (2017). *Gen Z @ work: How the next generation is transforming the workplace.* New York: HarperCollins.

58 Wang, Y. (2016). *An Emerson College student rented his dorm room on Airbnb: Now he's in trouble.* Retrieved from www.washingtonpost.com/news/morning-mix/wp/2016/02/03/an-emerson-college-student-successfully-rented-his-dorm-room-on-airbnb-and-hes-not-the-only-one/?utm_term=.dcdb808436b9

59 Seemiller, C. & Grace, M. (2014).

60 History.com Staff. (n.d.a). *Bank run.* Retrieved from www.history.com/topics/bank-run

61 History.com Staff. (n.d.a).

62 FDIC. (1998). *A brief history of deposit insurance in the United States.* Retrieved from www.fdic.gov/bank/historical/brief/brhist.pdf

63 PBS.org. (2010). *The true cost of the bank bailout.* Retrieved from www.pbs.org/wnet/need-to-know/economy/the-true-cost-of-the-bank-bailout/3309/

64 Edelman. (2012). *2012 Edelman trust barometer: U.S. financial services and banking industries.* Retrieved from www.slideshare.net/EdelmanInsights/2012-edelman-trust-barometer-us-financial-services-and-banking-industries

65 Norman, J. (2016). *Americans' confidence in institutions stays low.* Retrieved from http://news.gallup.com/poll/192581/americans-confidence-institutions-stays-low.aspx

66 Altitude. (2017). *Designing for Gen Z.* Retrieved from www.altitudeinc.com/through-the-eyes-of-gen-z/

67 Raddon. (2017). *Generation Z: The kids are all right: How high schoolers perceiver financial needs and opportunities.* Retrieved from www.raddon.com/sites/default/files/genz-executive-summary.pdf

68 Raddon. (2017).

69 Raddon. (2017).

70 Raddon. (2017).

71 Anatole, E. (2013). *Generation Z: Rebels with a cause.* Retrieved from www.forbes.com/sites/onmarketing/2013/05/28/generation-z-rebels-with-a-cause/#48208d2669c2

72 Transunion. (2017). *Generation Z's financial report card.* Retrieved from www.transunion.com/docs/TUC_GenZReport_FINAL_06.22.17_US[2].pdf

73 The Center for Generational Kinetics. (2017).

74 The Center for Generational Kinetics. (2017).

75 Sallie Mae. (2017).

76 Melton, M. (2017). *Gen Z shows little loyalty to loyalty programs.* Retrieved from https://retail.emarketer.com/article/gen-z-shows-little-loyalty-loyalty-programs/597915b8ebd40003acdf2dc7

77 American Express. (2017). *How Gen Z expectations are reshaping brand experiences.* Retrieved from http://about.americanexpress.com/news/docs/Amex-Forrester-Gen-Z-Research.pdf

78 American Express. (2017).

79 Piper Jaffray. (2018). *Taking stock with teens.* Retrieved from www.piperjaffray.com/3col.aspx?id=4986

80 Piper Jaffray. (2018).

81 Vision Critical. (2016).

82 Piper Jaffray. (2018).

83 Piper Jaffray. (2015). *Taking stock with teens.* Retrieved from www.piperjaffray.com/private/pdf/TSWT_Infographic_Sp15.pdf

84 IBM. (2017). *Uniquely Generation Z.* Retrieved from www-01.ibm.com/common/ssi/cgi-bin/ssialias?htmlfid=GBE03799USEN&

85 American Express. (2017).

86 American Express. (2017).

87 The Center for Generational Kinetics. (2017).

88 Sallie Mae. (2017).

89 Cilluffo, A. (2017). *5 facts about student loans.* Retrieved from www.pewresearch.org/fact-tank/2017/08/24/5-facts-about-student-loans/

90 Vision Critical. (2016).

91 Transunion. (2017).

92 Experian Information Solutions, Inc. (2016). *2016 state of credit.* Retrieved from www.experian.com/live-credit-smart/state-of-credit-2016.html

93 McGuire, V. (2016). *Getting my first credit card: What every student should know.* Retrieved from www.nerdwallet.com/blog/credit-cards/my-first-credit-card/

94 Better Homes and Gardens. (2014).

95 Transunion. (2017).

96 Transunion. (2017).

97 Transunion. (2017).

98 Experian Information Solutions, Inc. (2016).

99 Better Homes and Gardens. (2014).

100 Seemiller, C. & Grace, M. (2016).

101 Better Homes and Gardens. (2014).

102 Bureau of Labor Statistics. (2017). *Labor force statistics from the current population survey.* Retrieved from https://data.bls.gov/timeseries/LNS14000000

103 Autotrader. (2016). *What's driving Gen Z?* Retrieved from https://coxautoinc.app.box.com/v/autotrader-kbb-gen-z-research/file/56691606014

104 Autotrader. (2016).

105 Autotrader. (2016).

106 Autotrader. (2016).

107 Seemiller, C. & Grace, M. (2016).

108 Seemiller, C. & Grace, M. (2016).

109 Constine, J. (2014). *Robinhood raises $13M to democratize stock market with zero-commission trading app.* Retrieved from https://techcrunch.com/2014/09/23/robinhood-stock-app/

110 Randall, D. (2016). *Marketers are already targeting Generation Z.* Retrieved from http://time.com/money/4348414/generation-z-marketing/

111 Tiller, C. (2011). Philanthro-teens: The next generation changing the world. *Media Planet, 2* (USA Today). Retrieved from http://doc.mediaplanet.com/all_projects/6574.pdf

112 Higher Education Research Institute. (2017). *College Senior Survey.* Data prepared by Higher Education Research Institute.

113 Barkley. (2018). *The power of Gen Z influence.* Retrieved from www.millennialmarketing.com/research-paper/the-power-of-gen-z-influence/#download-popup

Relationships

8 Family

· ·

With Generation Z coming of age in such a fast-paced and information-overloaded society, many must feel like they are pulled in a million directions. How do they make authentic friendships? Is it safe for them to go to school? How should they prepare themselves for getting a job? Will they always be buried in debt? Will they find "the one?" In the midst of all of this chaos swirling around them, one thing that grounds them is family. Having close relationships with their parents and family members is essential for many in Generation Z,[1] and it is evident that their experience growing up with their families will vastly shape how they partner and parent.

Parenting trends

As children, we're convinced our parents know nothing about our issues and our lives. How could they understand how we connect with our friends? Or what's even cool? While parents of Generation Z may not fully understand the ins and outs of being a teen or young adult today, their influence in shaping their children's perspectives and behaviors is paramount.[2]

Consider how family trends and values have evolved over the last century. The G.I. Generation was raised in a time directly after the Industrial Revolution, in which the protection, safety, and development of children was a great focus.[3] The G.I. Generation was the first to experience required elementary education and after-school programs,[4] and organizations like the Boy Scouts and Girl Scouts were created to keep children busy with personal development activities.[5] While there was much more focus on child development as the G.I. Generation grew up, they also experienced times of struggle and uncertainty. Growing up and coming of age during the Great Depression and wartime inspired the G.I. Generation to find balance as parents as they wanted to provide security and comfort for their Baby Boomer children, while also passing down the grit and resilience they needed during their own childhoods.[6]

The Silent Generation was raised under the notion that "children should be seen and not heard," giving way to the name, Traditionalists, which stems from their rule-following nature and conformity with expectations.[7] Growing up during the rebuilding years after the Great Depression and World War II, this generation also learned that hard work and sacrifice lead to success.[8] One thing the Silent Generation may have passed down to their children, who are mostly Generation X, is the value of hard work. As adults and parents, however, many in Generation X have found that work-life balance is critical.[9] Rather than working around the clock, Gen Xers know where to draw boundaries so they can spend quality time with loved ones.[10]

Baby Boomers grew up in a time of stability and prosperity with most having G.I. Generation parents able to provide new luxuries and life experiences for their children.[11] This is something Baby Boomers adopted as they became parents themselves, primarily to Millennials. Baby Boomers became the highly involved, "helicopter" parents who seemed to hover over their children.[12] While helicopter parenting can still happen with adult Millennials, a new phenomenon, the "boomerang," is becoming prevalent with this Baby Boomer parent–Millennial child duo. To "boomerang" is to return home to live with your parents after college.[13] Interestingly, Boomers didn't grow up being encouraged to return to their parents' nest. The mindset of the G.I. Generation was to grow old and retire peacefully away from their adult Boomer children.[14] In fact, according to the U.S. Census Bureau, when Boomers were young adults (18 to 34 years-old), 26 percent reported living with their parents.[15] In 2016, the number of 18 to 34 year-olds living at home was at 31 percent.[16] While this age range includes some older members of Generation Z, it primarily consists of Millennials.

Millennials have started becoming parents and growing families of their own. It seems as though they've adopted a similarly involved parenting style as their Baby Boomer parents. In a 2015 Pew study of Millennials who reported having children, 61 percent agreed that parents could never be too involved in their child's education, whereas only 51 percent of Baby Boomers agreed.[17] Further, 68 percent of Millennial parents identify as overprotective with only 54 percent of Boomers identifying similarly.[18] So, while many Baby Boomers may have been helicopter parents, their Millennial kids might hover so closely that they end up charting their children's course entirely.

In nearly every aspect of people's lives, the perspectives and behaviors of those in older generations have shaped the way those who are younger see and navigate the world. Given the strong influence that parents have on their children, it's no surprise that parenting practices passed down through the generations can affect how people parent their own children.

The new normal is nuclear no more

The term "nuclear family" was first included in the dictionary in 1947 to describe the traditional family makeup of two parents of the opposite sex and their children.[19] While the notion of the nuclear family was around prior to 1947, the term was made mainstream just prior to the 1950s during a time when the post–World War II society provided more security to raise families.[20] Aside from the typical makeup of the family, the nuclear family unit also emphasized very specific gender roles. It was common for the father to be the sole financial provider and the mother to raise the children and manage the household. Shows like *Leave It To Beaver* modeled the ideals of the nuclear family. However, families today have more diverse arrangements[21] and look less like the Cleavers and more like those found on *Modern Family* or *The Fosters*.

Single parents, multigenerational households, and same-sex couple parenting

In 2014, The Pew Research Center found that only 62 percent of children under the age of 18 lived with two married parents, far less than the 87 percent who did in 1960.[22] Between 1960 and 2014, there has also been an increase in single-parent households as well as households with cohabiting non-married parents.[23] Notably, single-parent households of children living with their mothers have steadily increased since 1960 and, by 2017, 22 percent of households with children were comprised of single mothers.[24]

Along with an increase in single-parent households and cohabiting non-married parents, multigenerational households are becoming more common with various family members raising Generation Z kids. Multigenerational households consist of two or more generations of adults living under one roof.[25] As of 2016, 20 percent of the U.S. population lived in a multigenerational household.[26] And while there has been growth in multigenerational households across all racial and ethnic groups since 2008, these living arrangements have become more common among non-White families.[27]

There has also been an increase in kids being parented by same-sex couples. As of 2013, nearly one in five households with same-sex couples were raising children under the age of 18.[28] Among same-sex couples, 27 percent of those with two females have children under 18 in their homes as do 11 percent of those with two males.[29]

Growth in interracial and interethnic families

Today, a large number of children are growing up in interracial and/or interethnic households. A study by the Pew Research Center found that, in 2015, 10 percent of all married people in the U.S. reported having a spouse of a different race or ethnicity, which is more than triple the 3 percent in 1967 when interracial marriage, specifically, became legal across the U.S.[30] This increase aligns with the mindset of the 39 percent of adults in a 2017 Pew study who indicated that marrying a person from a different race is good for society.[31] This is up 15 points from just seven years earlier.[32] With more interracial and interethnic couples today, there are also more multiracial and multiethnic children being born. In 2000, during the earlier part of the Generation Z birth year range, one in seven babies born were of a multiracial or multiethnic background.[33] Increasing more than 50 percent since 2000, multiracial children, in particular, have become the fastest growing identity group among American youth.[34]

In addition to interracial and interethnic families with biological children, some parents are adopting children of a race or ethnicity other than their own. While this is not a new trend, it is a growing one. In 1999, 29 percent of Millennial-adopted kindergarteners had a different race or ethnicity than their adoptive mother.[35] The number spiked to 44 percent in 2011 when the oldest in Generation Z were starting kindergarten. And, in looking at trends of immigrant adoptions, rates nearly tripled between 1994 and 2004,[36] years which primarily span the earlier part of the Generation Z birth range. These rates then began a rapid decline from 2009 to 2015, ending considerably lower than the rate in 1994.[37]

Shifting social and gender norms

Gender norms are also evolving from those that were present in the traditional nuclear family. For example, consider the rise of women as a family's breadwinner. In 2013, 40 percent of homes with children under 18 years-old had mothers who served as the exclusive or main income source for the family, up from only 11 percent in 1960.[38] While the majority of households with female breadwinners in 2013 were single-parent homes, 37 percent were those comprised of married women who earned more than their husbands.[39] The number of stay-at-home fathers is also increasing and has almost doubled since the late 1980s.[40] Despite the fluctuating job market having influenced this increase, more than one in five stay-at-home dads are choosing to stay home.[41] Although there are still inequities in pay for women and negative perceptions regarding stay-at-home fathers, there is a growing societal acceptance of evolving gender roles.[42]

Generation Z has not only grown up seeing family structures and norms evolving, they have been the products of these changing dynamics. As a diverse and accepting group, we can anticipate they will continue to challenge and change the notion of family life.

X raising Z

Although not all Generation Z children are parented by Generation X, it is likely that most are. Gen Xers were between 15 and 30 years old when kids in 1995 were born and between 30 and 45 when kids in 2010 were born. While it's important to recognize that some Baby Boomers and Millennials also are the parents of Generation Z children, Gen Xers who were in their young adulthood during the birth range of Generation Z would likely comprise a large share of their parents.

Baby's first post

As those in Generation X were some of the initial users of the desktop computer, they are some of the first to have children born in the digital era. For many in Generation Z, their digital footprint was already making imprints long before they were born. For example, using social media to post a birth announcement photo or share milestones and updates through pregnancy has become common and almost expected. A 2010 study by the Internet security company, AVG, found that 23 percent of children had their sonograms posted online before they were even born, and by two years-old, 92 percent had some form of an online identity resulting from their parents and family members sharing online.[43]

In addition to parents sharing family photos and exciting news about their kids on social media, some are going even further and engaging in sharenting, which is "online sharing about parenting."[44] Sharenting may involve blogging about personal parenting issues, posting YouTube videos of embarrassing behavior of their children,[45] or even crowdsourcing ideas to address disciplinary issues.[46]

While sharing about family life online can be exciting and helpful for some parents, there is room for consideration about how sharenting practices may impact the children being shared about. Sharents may unintentionally disclose personal information about their child or provide access to their child's identifiable data (i.e. name, age, photo) or location.[47] In addition, sharents ultimately create a permanent digital footprint without their child's consent.[48] Drawn to high levels of online privacy, it would make sense that members of Generation Z would not be fans of sharenting.

Family first

Generation X grew up in a time of high divorce rates and increasing numbers of dual-parent employed households,[49] which meant many spent less time together as a family during their childhoods. Generation X parents have taken their own experiences as latchkey kids and set a new precedent for spending time with their children. A study of the daily activities of more than 60,000 mothers and 53,000 fathers in 11 Western countries found that the time parents spent caring for their children has doubled for mothers and more than tripled for fathers since 1965.[50] In 1965, mothers reported spending 54 minutes per day caring for their children, but, by 2017, that number increased to 104 minutes.[51] And the rate for fathers went from 16 minutes in 1965 to 59 minutes in 2017.[52] The increase in parenting time appears to be making a difference for individual parent-child relationships. Father-son generational duo, David and Jonah Stillman, share that two-thirds of Gen Xers feel like they are closer to their Generation Z children than their parents were with them.[53]

Even though parents are spending more time with their Generation Z children, according to a 2015 Pew study, nearly half of parents of school-age kids wish they were more engaged with their children's education, specifically.[54] As there are only so many hours in the day outside of work, it can be challenging for parents to carve out even more time to spend with their children, especially helping with homework or going to school-sponsored events. It's not surprising then that a study by Ernst & Young found that one in four Generation X employees have difficulty in balancing their work, family, and personal responsibilities.[55] This work-life balance challenge likely points to why more than 70 percent of Generation X employees value the ability to work flexibly, a number higher than that of Baby Boomers and Millennials.[56] In addition to flexible schedules and remote work, some Gen Xers may be dedicating more time to their families by working for themselves. With a growth in the gig economy and self-employment, parents of Generation Z may find that being able to create their own schedules around the school play or soccer game is the only way to parent.

Co-pilot parenting is the new helicopter parenting

Gen Xers' desire to be more present in their children's lives does not look like the highly involved helicopter parenting style made popular by Baby Boomers. Recognizing learning can happen through failure,[57] Generation X parents are taking more of a hands-off approach to parenting, giving their Generation Z children more space and independence.[58]

For those in Generation Z, rather than seeing their parents hovering and monitoring their every move, many believe their parents are more like co-pilots, invited by them for the ride.[59] In fact, 89 percent of those in Generation Z rank their parents as the biggest influence on their values,[60] and 88 percent report being extremely close with their parents.[61] For more than half, the perspectives of their parents and family members matter in their decision-making.[62] It seems that there is some reciprocity here in that parents often include their Generation Z kids in family decision-making as well, especially in regard to financial purchases. According to a study by Ernst & Young, 93 percent of parents reported that their Generation Z children have an influence when they are making a purchase.[63] Similarly, in a study by IBM, more than 60 percent of members of Generation Z shared that they influence their family's spending in the area of clothes and shoes, electronic goods, dining out, food and beverages, travel, household goods, and furniture.[64] While some members of Generation Z may have to physically set the table for family dinner to earn an allowance, many are also given a figurative seat at the table by their parents in regard to financial decision-making.

❝ Whenever I am struggling to find motivation to get through the day, I remind myself that I am working hard in school right now. One day my hard will pay off and I will be able to reap the rewards of my diligence in school. ❞

— Member of Generation Z

Passing down preparation, pragmatism, and independence

Counter to the optimistic, "participation-trophy" philosophy used in raising Millennials, those in Generation X don't believe people should be rewarded just for trying.[65] These Gen Xer parents are teaching their Generation Z children to prepare for an uncertain future through personal and professional skill development, to think strategically about their plans, and to understand the consequences of their actions.[66] It's not surprising then that more than half of Generation Z teens have been encouraged by their parents to gain professional experience early in their lives to prepare for the future.[67]

> *I would also like my children to be healthy and have them be motivated to reach for their dreams. My reasoning behind this 'good life' is because this was how I grew up.*
> *- Member of Generation Z*

In addition, Generation X parents are helping their kids develop skills to handle difficult situations today. Having witnessed the negative impacts of helicopter parenting, those in Generation X are providing more space for their Generation Z children to develop a sense of independence and self-reliance.[68]

From Millennials to Alphas: Sibling relationships

Brothers and sisters are often the first peers children interact with and thus play a highly influential role in shaping the perspectives and behaviors of their siblings.[69,70] While it is likely most members of Generation Z will have siblings within their same generational cohort, some may have brothers or sisters from a different generation. Because older siblings often serve as role models, mentors, and teachers for younger siblings,[71] we may see a blending of generational characteristics in which the younger sibling exhibits traits of the older sibling's generation. Some members of Generation Z may have older siblings who are Millennials and thus end up taking on some of their characteristics. On the other hand, some members of Generation Z may be serving as older siblings to Generation Alpha (born after 2010) and pass down some Generation Z-like perspectives and behaviors to them.

Generation Z's perspective on family

From much of the research already discussed, it's pretty clear that many members of Generation Z place a high value on their relationships with their parents and family members. Findings from our Generation Z Stories Study further illuminate the importance of family as nearly half described a "good life" being one that included family.[72] In addition, a study by the Collage Group found that family was the second most important characteristic of an ideal life for those in Generation Z, with 65 percent ranking family among the five most important characteristics.[73]

As most members of Generation Z are still among the youth population, a majority have not entered a phase of life where they are starting their own

Table 8.1 Generation Z's Views on Family and Good Life[74]

"I think a good life would be achieved if I had a happy and healthy family life, if I had kids and raised them to be kind and loving." *– Member of Generation Z*	*"A good life is one where I have a family and provide for them and not have to worry about making ends meet or keeping food on the table."* *– Member of Generation Z*	*"A good life would be . . . having a family who works towards loving one another and others through developing spiritually, mentally, physically, and emotionally."* *– Member of Generation Z*

families. But given what we know about their perspectives and characteristics, along with their upbringing, we can begin to develop some ideas about Generation Z and family life.

Finances before fiancé and family

We may be able to glean insight into this generation's future by looking at the increasing age in which American adults are getting married and starting families. The median age of a first marriage in the United States has been consistently increasing since 1960[75] when it was 22 years-old for men and 20 years-old for women.[76] By 1990, numbers jumped to 26 years-old for men and 23 years-old for women.[77] In 2017, that number increased even more to 29 years-old for men and 27 years-old for women.[78]

For many, getting married later in life is not just happenstance but rather due to the shifting economic and educational circumstances facing today's young adults. A study by the Pew Research Center found that more than 40 percent of unmarried American adults indicated the primary reason for being unmarried is due to lacking financial security.[79] In addition, a study by TD Ameritrade found that, for Millennials, the desire to pay off student loan debt heavily influences the timing of when to get married and have children – with the desire to put off these life events until after chipping away at some debt.[80] Millennials are also starting families later in life, with the average age of Millennial women becoming moms at 26.[81]

While few in Generation Z are likely married or parents yet themselves, many do have goals to one day have families of their own.[82] In a study of Generation Z by the Varkey Foundation, when thinking about their future, nearly half deemed family as the most important factor.[83] And, more than 70 percent of Generation Z college seniors reported raising a family as very important or essential.[84] Many in Generation Z, though, are facing

> ❝ *A good life would include a loving family, a stable job, and happiness. I want to make sure I am able to provide for my family by having a stable job that pays the bills.* ❞
> *– Member of Generation Z*

high student loan debt, like their Millennial counterparts, and have a fear of not finding a job with a comfortable salary.[85] Thus, it makes sense that 71 percent believe it has become harder for them to afford to have a family than it was for their parents at their age.[86] It's entirely plausible then that this generation will continue the trend of getting married and having children at an older age when they are more financially sound.

Conclusion

It is apparent that those in Generation Z value close familial relationships, whether with the families they grew up with or future spouses/partners and children. We may see Generation Z parent like pragmatic and independent co-pilot Gen Xers or chart their own course. No matter what, family is certainly an essential component of what many in Generation Z believe is a "good life."[87]

❝ To me, the 'good life' is getting married, loving my wife all my life, working as an equal partner with her to raise our children, and growing old with her. It does not matter to me if we live in a mansion or a bamboo hut, just so long as we work every day to make our situation (and the situation of our children and neighbors) better. If I develop solid relationships with my children, that is also a big part of the 'good life' for me. ❞
– Member of Generation Z

Notes

1 Seemiller, C. & Grace, M. (2017). *Generation Z stories study*. Unpublished raw data.
2 Varkey Foundation. (2017). *Generation Z: Global Citizenship Survey*. Retrieved from www.varkeyfoundation.org/what-we-do/policy-research/generation-z-global-citizenship-survey/
3 Library of Congress. (n.d.). *Children's lives at the turn of the twentieth century*. Retrieved from www.loc.gov/tachers/classroommaterials/primarysources/childrens-lives/pdf/teacher_guide.pdf
4 Watson, S. (2008). *How public schools work*. Retrieved from https://people.howstuffworks.com/public-schools.htm
5 Library of Congress. (n.d.).
6 Howe, N. (2014b). *The G.I. Generation and the "Triumph of the Squares."* Retrieved from www.forbes.com/sites/neilhowe/2014/07/30/the-g-i-generation-and-the-triumph-of-the-squares-part-2-of-7/#14b57a629c8e
7 Kane, S. (2017b). *Common characteristics of the Silent Generation*. Retrieved from www.thebalance.com/workplace-characteristics-silent-generation-2164692
8 Kane, S. (2017b).
9 Ernst & Young. (2015). *Global generations: A global study on work-life challenges across generations*. Retrieved from www.ey.com/us/en/about-us/our-people-and-culture/ey-study-highlights-work-life-is-harder-worldwide

10 Ernst & Young. (2015).

11 Encyclopedia of Aging. (2002). *Baby Boomers*. Retrieved from www.encyclopedia. com/social-sciences-and-law/sociology-and-social-reform/sociology-general-terms-and-concepts/baby-boom

12 Somers, P. & Settle, J. (2010). The helicopter parent: Research toward a typology. *College and University: The Journal of the American Association of Collegiate Registrars*, 86(1), 18–27.

13 Parker, K. (2012). *Who are the boomerang kids?* Retrieved from www.pewsocialtrends. org/2012/03/15/who-are-the-boomerang-kids/

14 Howe, N. (2014b).

15 United States Census Bureau. (2017c). *1975 and 2016 current population survey annual social and economic supplement*. Retrieved from www.census.gov/content/dam/Census/ library/publications/2017/demo/p20-579.pdf

16 United States Census Bureau. (2017c).

17 Pew Research Center. (2015d). *Parenting in America*. Retrieved from www.pewsocial trends.org/files/2015/12/2015-12-17_parenting-in-america_FINAL.pdf

18 Pew Research Center. (2015d).

19 BeBusinessEd.com. (2017). *History of nuclear families*. Retrieved from https:// bebusinessed.com/history/history-nuclear-families/

20 BeBusinessEd.com. (2017).

21 Cohen, P. (2014). *Family diversity is the new normal for America's children*. Retrieved from https://familyinequality.files.wordpress.com/2014/09/family-diversity-new-normal.pdf

22 Pew Research Center. (2015d).

23 Pew Research Center. (2015d).

24 United States Census Bureau. (2017a). *Historical living arrangements of children*. Retrieved from www.census.gov/data/tables/time-series/demo/families/children.html

25 Cohn, D. & Passel, J. S. (2018). *A record 64 million Americans live in multigenerational households*. Retrieved from www.pewresearch.org/fact-tank/2018/04/05/a-record-64-million-americans-live-in-multigenerational-households/

26 Cohn, D. & Passel, J. S. (2018).

27 Cohn, D. & Passel, J. S. (2018).

28 Gates, G. J. (2013). *LGBT parenting in United States*. Retrieved from williamsinstitute. law.ucla.edu/wp-content/uploads/LGBT-Parenting.pdf

29 Gates, G. J. (2013).

30 Livingston, G. & Brown, A. (2015). *Intermarriage in the U.S. 50 years after Loving v. Virginia*. Retrieved from www.pewsocialtrends.org/2017/05/18/intermarriage-in-the-u-s-50-years-after-loving-v-virginia/

31 Livingston, G. & Brown, A. (2015).

32 Livingston, G. & Brown, A. (2015).

33 Livingston, G. (2017). *The rise of multiracial and multiethnic babies in the U.S.* Retrieved from www.pewresearch.org/fact-tank/2017/06/06/the-rise-of-multiracial-and-multiethnic-babies-in-the-u-s/

34 Sparks & Honey. (2014). *Meet Generation Z: Forget everything you learned about Millenni-als*. Retrieved from www.slideshare.net/sparksandhoney/generation-z-final-june-17

35 Zill, N. (2017). *The changing face of adoption in the United States*. Retrieved from https:// ifstudies.org/blog/the-changing-face-of-adoption-in-the-united-states

36 Jones, J. & Placek, P. (2017). *Adoption by the numbers*. Retrieved from http://www.adoption council.org/files/large/249e5e967173624

37 Jones, J. & Placek, P. (2017).

38 Wang, W., Parker, K., & Taylor, P. (2013). *Breadwinner moms*. Retrieved from www.pewsocialtrends.org/2013/05/29/breadwinner-moms/

39 Wang, W., Parker, K., & Taylor, P. (2013).

40 Livingston, G. (2014). *Growing number of dads home with the kids*. Retrieved from www.pewsocialtrends.org/2014/06/05/growing-number-of-dads-home-with-the-kids/

41 Livingston, G. (2014).

42 Wang, W., Parker, K., & Taylor, P. (2013).

43 Business Wire. (2010). *Digital birth: Welcome to the online world*. Retrieved from www.businesswire.com/news/home/20101006006722/en/Digital-Birth-Online-World

44 Steinberg, S. B. (2017). Sharenting: Children's privacy in the age of social media. *Emory Law Journal, 66*. Retrieved from https://scholarship.law.ufl.edu/facultypub/779/, para. 1.

45 Stadtmiller, M. (2017). *Kids don't have parents anymore: They have "sharents."* Retrieved from www.thedailybeast.com/kids-dont-have-parents-anymorethey-have-sharents

46 Steinberg, S. B. (2017).

47 Steinberg, S. B. (2017).

48 Steinberg, S. B. (2017).

49 Greenwood, J. & Guner, N. (2009). Marriage and divorce since World War II: Analyzing the role of technological progress on the formation of households. *NBER Macroeconomics Annual, 23*, 231–276.

50 First for Women. (2017). *Parents today spend twice as much time with their kids than parents 50 years ago*. Retrieved from www.firstforwomen.com/posts/parents-spend-time-with-kids-147849

51 First for Women. (2017).

52 First for Women. (2017).

53 Stillman, D. & Stillman, J. (2017). *Gen Z @ work: How the next generation is transforming the workplace*. New York: HarperCollins.

54 Parker, K., Horowitz, J. M., & Rohal, M. (2015). *Parenting in America: Outlook, worries, aspirations are strongly linked to financial situation*. Retrieved from www.pewsocialtrends.org/2015/12/17/parenting-in-america/

55 Ernst & Young. (2015).

56 Ernst & Young. (2015).

57 Stillman, D. & Stillman, J. (2017).

58 Sparks & Honey. (2014).

59 Seemiller, C. & Grace, M. (2016). *Generation Z goes to college*. San Francisco: Jossey-Bass.

60 Varkey Foundation. (2017).

61 Ologie. (2017). *We are Generation Z*. Retrieved from https://ologie.com/gen-z/#

62 Seemiller, C. & Grace, M. (2016).

63 Mackman, M. (2015). *Rise of Gen Z: New challenges for retailers*. Retrieved from www.ey.com/gl/en/industries/consumer-products/ey-rise-of-gen-znew-challenge-for-retailers

64 Cheug, J., Glass, S., McCarty, D., & Wong, C. K. (2016). *Uniquely Generation Z: What brands should know about today's youngest consumers*. Retrieved from www-01.ibm.com/common/ssi/cgi-bin/ssialias?htmlfid=GBE03799USEN&

65 Stillman, D. & Stillman, J. (2017).

66 Altitude. (2017). *Designing Gen Z: 4 insights for powerful generational design*. Retrieved from www.altitudeinc.com/designing-for-gen-z/

67 Schawbel, D. (2014). *The high school careers study*. Retrieved from http://millennialbranding.com/2014/high-school-careers-study/

68 Sparks & Honey. (2014).

69 Howe, N. & Recchia, H. (2014). *Sibling relations and their impact on children's development*. Retrieved from www.child-encyclopedia.com/peer-relations/according-experts/sibling-relations-and-their-impact-childrens-development

70 Ciciora, P. (2010). *Siblings play formative, influential role as "agents of socialization."* Retrieved from https://news.illinois.edu/view/6367/205739

71 Ciciora, P. (2010).

72 Seemiller, C. & Grace, M. (2017).

73 Collage Group. (2016). *Quick chart: What Gen-Z & Millennials really want in life.* Retrieved from www.collagegroup.com/2016/09/19/gen-z-millennials-values/

74 Seemiller, C. & Grace, M. (2017).

75 United States Census Bureau. (2017b). *Historical marital status.* Retrieved from www.census.gov/data/tables/time-series/demo/families/marital.html

76 United States Census Bureau. (2017b).

77 United States Census Bureau. (2017b).

78 United States Census Bureau. (2017b).

79 Parker, K. & Stepler, R. (2017). *As U.S. marriage rate hovers at 50%, education gap in marital status widens.* Retrieved from www.pewresearch.org/fact-tank/2017/09/14/as-u-s-marriage-rate-hovers-at-50-education-gap-in-marital-status-widens/

80 TD Ameritrade. (2017). *Young money survey: Attitudes toward money, education and working life.* Retrieved from https://s1.q4cdn.com/959385532/files/doc_downloads/research/2017/Young-Money-Survey-Findings.pdf

81 Holmes, S. (2017). *Millennials are rejecting helicopter parenting: Here's why that matters for marketers.* Retrieved from www.adweek.com/brand-marketing/millennials-are-rejecting-helicopter-parenting-heres-why-that-matters-for-marketers/#/

82 Seemiller, C. & Grace, M. (2017).

83 Varkey Foundation. (2017).

84 Higher Education Research Institute. (2017). *College Senior Survey.* Data prepared by Higher Education Research Institute.

85 Seemiller, C. & Grace, M. (2017).

86 Fishman, R., Ekowo, M., & Ezeugo, E. (2017). *The American Dream: Findings by generation.* Retrieved from www.newamerica.org/in-depth/varying-degrees/beliefs-about-american-dream-generation/

87 Seemiller, C. & Grace, M. (2017).

9 Friends and peers

Making friends is a critical aspect of growing up. Not only do friends serve as support systems and social companions, but peers can help shape one's self-identity as well as influence behaviors. Today, however, making and keeping friends can be quite different than it was for older generations when they were young. While those in Generation Z can and do still develop friendships at school, work, and through their extracurricular involvement, technology and social media, without a doubt, plays a large role for this generation in developing and maintaining friendships.

> **❝** Life is all about relationships, and it is so important to constantly foster those relationships. I wake up every day excited to spend time with my boyfriend and other new friends I have made in college. Spending time with these people makes me feel loved and encouraged. **❞**
> – Member of Generation Z

World Wide Web of friends

Think about *The Sandlot* gang playing baseball together until the sun went down. Or Kevin Arnold, Paul Pfiefer, and Winnie Cooper of *The Wonder Years*. For prior generations, some may have had a faraway pen pal or a friend they stayed in touch with from summer camp, but for most, making friends likely started with the kids in their neighborhood or at school. The world of Generation Z is much bigger than those places, as today, friendships can be made and sustained online. With technology available to overcome distance, the social network of Generation Z extends beyond local and even national boundaries. Their connections are so global that one in four members of Generation Z would have to travel by plane to spend time in person with most of their friends from social media.[1]

Diverse social circles

While there may be an inclination for people to develop friendships with those of similar social identities, for many in this generation, doing so is not really important. As Generation Z is a diverse group of young people, it's not surprising that they expect their friend groups to be as diverse as they are. In our Generation Z Goes to College Study, we found that half of respondents indicated that a shared cultural background is not important at all in making new friends, and an additional 30 percent indicated it only being slightly important.[2] It's not to say that those in Generation Z do not value each person's background, but rather, that having similarity in backgrounds is not a critical factor in developing new friendships. Whether having a diverse social circle is intentional or emerges organically, many in Generation Z are surrounded with people who are different from them.

For example, consider sexual orientation. A half-century ago, young people may not have known or knew they knew someone who identified as LGBTQ. Then, a few decades ago, perhaps there were one or two "out" kids in school. Today, the likelihood of having a friend who identifies as LGBTQ is actually more common. According to a study by the J. Walter Thompson Innovation Group, members of Generation Z see sexual orientation and gender as more fluid than even their open-minded Millennial counterparts,[3] and a much higher percentage actually identify as LGBTQ.[4] It makes sense then that more than half of those in Generation Z know someone who utilizes gender-neutral pronouns (i.e. they, them, or ze).[5]

Aside from diversity of identity, many in Generation Z also value diversity of viewpoints. Eighty-two percent of Generation Z college seniors rated themselves above average or in the highest 10 percent of their peers in their tolerance for others with different beliefs.[6] While they can't all be in the top 10 percent, their own perception of their openness is a hallmark characteristic of this generation, which easily translates to having friends with a diverse array of perspectives. Take, for example, religion. A study by the Varkey Foundation found that two-thirds of those in Generation Z have a friend who is of a different religion than their own.[7]

> **❝ My generation is pretty open and culturally diverse and accepting; we need to spread that mentality around the globe. ❞**
> *- Member of Generation Z*

Online influencers as "friends"

For Generation Z, their peers serve as a great source of influence on their lives, both in terms of support as well as for offering recommendations and advice. Second only to their parents, Generation Z's values are heavily influenced by their friends.[8] For example, having friends talk about a product is the number one aspect that makes a product "cool"[9] in the eyes of Generation Z. In their own way, this generation has provided a resurgence of the value of the word-of-mouth recommendation. But the influence of their peers is no longer reserved for the social circles young people encounter at school or in their extracurricular activities; it also occurs in their online communities and social groups comprised of people they may not even know. For instance, members of Generation Z might follow a well-known video blogger on YouTube or a social media personality on Instagram, taking their thoughts and opinions to heart. Those in Generation Z may feel connected to online influencers, consider them "friends," and listen to their suggestions and recommendations, even if they don't have that one-on-one relationship with them.

Making friends

Although many in Generation Z might not feel that having a shared cultural background or a similarity in beliefs is important for their friendships, being able to connect with others who have a similar foundation of values is simply critical. In our Generation Z Goes to College Study, we found that having friends with similar values is considerably more important for this generation than having the same hobbies or belonging to the same groups or organizations.[10] In addition, physical appearance was not a factor for the majority, and, not surprisingly, proximity was not critical given their global networks.[11] But, 70 percent indicated that shared values were important or very important in making new friends.[12] Beyond sharing values, 78 percent of those in Generation Z say their friends play an influential role in actually shaping their values.[13] Members of Generation Z are not just looking to find friends with similar values; they hope to associate with people who will enhance their values as well. Highly motivated by relationships and their passion to make a difference,[14] their desire to connect with like-minded peers is understandable. If they want to change the world positively, having a team of friends with shared values is an important asset to have.

Social self-confidence

The art of making friends hasn't changed much with each passing generation. Whether it is asking the new neighbor kid to play, having sleepovers with middle school best friends, chatting in the locker room with teammates, or even grabbing coffee with a study partner, making friends requires confidence and social skills. But, only about half of Generation Z college seniors report having higher than average social self-confidence.[15] This number is considerably lower than the 64 percent who report having higher than average intellectual self-confidence.[16] It appears that while they might be confident intellectually, they are simply less confident socially. And, when it comes to making friends, lacking social confidence might translate to being a bit apprehensive about making that first move.

Friendmaking in the digital world

School and extracurricular activities have been a way for young people of all generations to meet peers and develop friendships. Digital technology not only allows people to connect more often and in more ways, it also allows users to connect with people who they might not have otherwise met. In a Pew Research Center study of 13 to 17 year-old teens, more than half reported having made two or more friends online, with the most popular ways of doing so through social media and online gaming.[17] Of teens who have met a friend online, 64 percent did so through a social media site and 57 percent of boys, specifically, had done so while playing video games.[18]

❝ Every person has a story or experiences and every day there's at least someone out there to find and get to know. Equally, there's someone out there that may get to know you. ❞

– Member of Generation Z

Despite their burgeoning online friendships, only one in five Generation Z teens has actually met their virtual friends in person.[19] Not many may turn online friends into real-life friends, however, many turn real-life friends into online friends. One of the first things teens share when they meet someone new is their social media username.[20]

"Friends" and followers: The online peer community

While most might not be making their best friends virtually, building and maintaining their online peer community is paramount for many in Generation Z. For some, this community may be comprised of thousands of "friends" or followers. In the online world, however, it can be more about the number of "friends" rather than the depth of these friendships that's most important. In a study conducted by Google, 53 percent of Generation Z teens reported that the number of followers and subscribers on their social channels is important to them.[21] Having a large following on social media may give Generation Z the feeling that they have a substantial community of support from friends and like-minded peers. Vandita Pendse, a member of Generation Z and writer for AdWeek, highlights that some social media platforms, like Instagram, can be a place to share daily life but also a source for receiving validation.[22] Having more followers, connections, likes, and comments may lead to a heightened sense of public support but not necessarily to the development of deep and meaningful friendships.

Maintaining friendships

Relationships are very important for Generation Z – so much so that, as we found in our Generation Z Goes to College Study, the top two motivators for this generation are relationship-oriented.[23] In addition, we found in our 2017 Generation Z Stories Study that the most reported reason for what gets them excited about getting up each day involves relationships with others.[24]

> 66 *Seeing my friends gets me excited about getting up every day; knowing that they will be there is always refreshing.* 99
> – Member of Generation Z

In addition to fostering motivation, relationships for them are also fundamental to their happiness. A study by the Varkey Foundation found that more than 90 percent of members of Generation Z ranked having a good relationship with their friends as an important factor in their overall happiness.[25]

Hanging with friends "IRL"

While Generation Z is often associated with high rates of social media use and connecting with friends via technology, they are still spending a considerable amount of time with their friends in person. A study by the Pew Research Center found that 95 percent of teens (ages 13 to 17) reported spending time in person with their friends outside of school at least occasionally, and 25 percent daily.[26] Aside from school, the place where teens spend the most time with their friends is at someone's house.[27] Spending time face-to-face isn't just limited to Generation Z teenagers. In a study of college seniors, more than half shared that they spend between 6 and 15 hours a week in person with their friends.[28]

Text messages and group chats

While social media provides a way to keep up with peers, many in Generation Z actually use texting to communicate with their friends. According to a study by the Pew Research Center, nearly 90 percent of Generation Z teens reported that they communicate with their peers via text message, and more than half of them text their friends every day.[29] This isn't surprising in that nearly half of Generation Z teens note that texting is their first platform of choice to reach their closest friends.[30] While both teen boys and girls text their friends, the rate for doing so is considerably higher for girls.[31] For boys, 22 percent actually chat with their friends during social gaming.[32]

Along with texting individuals, members of Generation Z use group text messaging as a way to connect with multiple friends and peers at once. Engaging in group texts appears to be a practice used far more frequently by younger people. A study by Statista found that nearly half of young adults (under 34) use group chats at least once a day, with 30 percent using group chats multiple times a day.[33] That number decreases to 18 percent for 35 to 54 year-old users and 7 percent for those over 55.[34] Apps such as GroupMe and WhatsApp are free to use and allow for multiple people to engage in a group text thread, and even

> **‘‘** *It's so easy to get in touch with people [via text] and have a large group conversation which you can't do through a phone call.* **’’**
> – Member of Generation Z

SMS programs and iMessage platforms built into phones can make group messaging easy.

The use of group texts is not solely reserved for when people are separated by distance. People can use text to carry on a private conversation they don't want everyone who is present to hear. An example might be a sidebar between three individuals who are chatting exclusively while other people in the room are present. Or people might be having a conversation via group text that excludes someone who is in the room because they are discussing something they either don't want that person to hear or are texting about that person. Some argue that group texting might foster digital cliques, in which select groups of people gossip and say mean things about others in a group chat.[35] Think of how the notorious Plastics from *Mean Girls*[36] would have been with the ability to group text.

And, even when not intentional, managing multiple conversations on text can result in accidentally sending out a message to the wrong group, possibly resulting in embarrassment for the sender and hurt feelings for someone on the receiving end.[37] But, group texts aren't always exclusive or a haven for sharing hurtful words. They also offer the ability to loop those not present into a group conversation.

Spending time "together" online

When those in Generation Z are not hanging out with their friends in person, they are finding other ways to connect that help them feel like they are together in real life. Group video messaging apps, such as Houseparty and Fam, allow multiple users to engage in a mobile-based video chat similar to FaceTime or Skype. Participating in video chats has become known as "live chilling."[38] Apps that facilitate live chilling sessions for multiple users are rapidly growing and becoming popular among Generation Z teens and young adults. For example, Houseparty reached a million daily users within 7 months of launching, and Fam was downloaded a million times within 12 days of its debut.[39] Now, Facebook, Snapchat, and others have developed their versions of video chatting.[40] It appears that the popularity for young people to engage in live chilling on a video app comes from the opportunity to casually connect without the worry of the interaction being captured on recorded video or documented on social media. Sima Sistani, co-founder of Houseparty, likens live video chatting with the post-selfie era because there isn't the pressure of online permanence.[41]

Even with some live features and video chat functions, social media platforms are still widely used in a semi-asynchronous mode in which users communicate via posts, comments, and text chats. While it might not simulate the in-person connection that video chatting provides, for Generation Z, social media is still a primary means of connecting with friends and peers. Seventy-two percent of Generation Z teens spend time online with their friends through social media, with one in five doing so daily.[42] Similarly, more than half of Generation Z college seniors in 2017 indicated spending between 3 and 10 hours on social media each week.[43] Beyond interaction, Generation Z views social media as a way to gain information about, feel connected to, and support their friends.[44] When they might not be able to hang out in person, it appears that those in Generation Z are finding other ways through technology to spend quality time with friends.

Foes, fallouts, and feeling alone

It seems as though the Internet and technology have opened up numerous opportunities for information sharing, connection, and communication. However, the digital world is not simply a place to post happy Snapchat filtered photos; it also serves as a space where toxic and even harmful experiences for young people can occur, including cyberbullying, friendship fallouts, and loneliness.

Cyberbullying

Cyberbullying has become a prominent issue for many in Generation Z. A study by the Cyberbullying Research Center found that a third of Generation Z middle and high school students have experienced cyberbullying at some point in their lives.[45] The most prominent forms involved posting "mean or hurtful comments about someone online" or spreading "rumors online."[46] While not as prominent, yet still highly concerning, nearly 13 percent indicated being called mean names or having comments posted about them online that are sexual in nature, 12 percent received threats through social media or text to hurt them, 11 percent posted a "mean or hurtful picture," 10 percent "pretended to be me," and 7 percent actually "created a mean or hurtful web page about me." And these statistics were just referencing the 30 days prior to the survey.[47] As previous generations could escape the school bully when they went home, the same can't be said for Generation Z when bullies and peer cruelty can follow young people home. And only 11.5 percent of Generation Z teens report being cyberbullies themselves,[48] meaning that either there are some really busy cyberbullies tormenting several individuals at once or some teens may be engaging in this behavior without realizing what it even is.

Unfriending

Whether it be from drifting apart or from a full-on fight, some friendships end and never reach the forever part of being BFFs. For those in older generations when they were young, the end to a friendship might simply involve avoiding the ex-friend in real-life settings. For those in Generation Z, though, posts, images, and even chats with former friends are often embedded deeply into their social media accounts, allowing these ex-friends to remain a part of their online community and thus, making it difficult to avoid them. It's not surprising then that more than half of Generation Z teens have unfriended or unfollowed an ex-friend on social media.[49] Some feel the need to cut ties even further as 45 percent have blocked a former friend on social media, and 42 percent have deleted a photo with a former friend from social media.[50] While those in Generation Z may not be able to control whether or not they see an ex-friend at school or in other social settings, they can control who they interact with on social media.

Feeling alone . . . even online

While missing an event, experience, or even conversation can result in feeling left out, it is the deeper sense of loneliness and isolation plaguing this generation that is of grave concern. In a study of 20,000 adults in the U.S., Cigna found that 48 percent of Generation Z young adults (ages 18 to 22) report experiencing loneliness, which was higher than any other generation included in the study.[51] Further, more than 60 percent of Generation Z young adults reported feeling shy, isolated from others, alone, that no one really knew them, and that there were people around them, but not really with them.[52] Although 75 percent report feeling outgoing and friendly, they still report the lowest levels compared to other generations of feeling they have people who understand them, feeling "in tune" with people around them, and that they have people to turn to and talk to.[53] As older generations in the Cigna study reported lower levels of loneliness, this may be something that Generation Z grows out of as they age. But that does not negate the prominence of those in Generation Z who report loneliness at this stage in their lives.

Even with access to and prominent use of social media, many young people still report feeling lonely. This may be due in part to how they use social media. Rather than using it for connection, many in Generation Z are using social media to fill spare time and find entertaining content.[54] Only 42 percent report that their primary use of social media is to stay in touch with what their friends are doing.[55] Social media and technology can facilitate some aspects of social connection but cannot serve as a complete substitute for quality time spent together in face-to-face settings. This is evidenced in findings from the Cigna study in that those who have more frequent in-person interactions have much lower rates of loneliness.[56] Even though Generation Z may feel comfortable finding friends and maintaining friendships online, engaging in more face-to-face interaction might help combat their feelings of loneliness.

Conclusion

Regardless of generation, friendships are important for young people. But, in this digital era, Generation Z is facing interesting opportunities and challenges never present when older generations were teens and young adults. While their heads seem to be buried in their smartphones, it might not be all about watching silly videos or playing games. Many in Generation Z also use digital technology to reach out to their diverse global networks, perhaps video chatting with their best friend across the country, coordinating a road trip in a group chat, or writing the perfect Instagram caption about an adventure with their friends.

Notes

1 Sparks & Honey. (2014). *Meet Generation Z: Forget everything you learned about Millennials*. Retrieved from www.slideshare.net/sparksandhoney/generation-z-final-june-17

2 Seemiller, C. & Grace, M. (2016). *Generation Z goes to college*. San Francisco: Jossey-Bass.

3 Tsjeng, Z. (2016). *Teens these days are queer AF, new study says*. Retrieved from https://broadly.vice.com/en_us/article/kb4dvz/teens-these-days-are-queer-af-new-study-says

4 Tsjeng, Z. (2016).

5 Tsjeng, Z. (2016).

6 Higher Education Research Institute. (2017). *College Senior Survey*. Data prepared by Higher Education Research Institute.

7 Varkey Foundation. (2017). *Generation Z: Global Citizenship Survey*. Retrieved from www.varkeyfoundation.org/what-we-do/policy-research/generation-z-global-citizenship-survey/

8 Varkey Foundation. (2017).

9 Google.com. (2017a). *Generation Z: New insights into the mobile-first mindset of teens*. Retrieved from http://storage.googleapis.com/think/docs/GenZ_Insights_All_teens.pdf

10 Seemiller, C. & Grace, M. (2016).

11 Seemiller, C. & Grace, M. (2016).

12 Seemiller, C. & Grace, M. (2016).

13 Varkey Foundation. (2017).

14 Seemiller, C. & Grace, M. (2016).

15 Higher Education Research Institute. (2017).

16 Higher Education Research Institute. (2017).

17 Lenhart, A., Smith, A., Anderson, M., Duggan, M., & Perrin, A. (2015). *Teens, technology, and friendships*. Retrieved from www.pewinternet.org/2015/08/06/teens-technology-and-friendships/

18 Lenhart, A., Smith, A., Anderson, M., Duggan, M., & Perrin, A. (2015).

19 Statista. (2015). *Share of teenagers in the United States who have met online friends in person of March 2015, by age and gender*. Retrieved from www.statista.com/statistics/453893/us-teens-meeting-online-friends-irl-age-gender/

20 Lenhart, A., Smith, A., Anderson, M., Duggan, M., & Perrin, A. (2015).

21 Google.com. (2017a).

22 Pendse, V. (2017). *Instagram and Snapchat: The tale of the Gen Z tape*. Retrieved from www.adweek.com/digital/vandita-pendse-blend-guest-post-instagram-vs-snapchat/

23 Seemiller, C. & Grace, M. (2016).

24 Seemiller, C. & Grace, M. (2017). *Generation Z stories study*. Unpublished raw data.

25 Varkey Foundation. (2017).

26 Lenhart, A., Smith, A., Anderson, M., Duggan, M., & Perrin, A. (2015).

27 Lenhart, A., Smith, A., Anderson, M., Duggan, M., & Perrin, A. (2015).

28 Higher Education Research Institute. (2017).

29 Lenhart, A., Smith, A., Anderson, M., Duggan, M., & Perrin, A. (2015).

30 Lenhart, A., Smith, A., Anderson, M., Duggan, M., & Perrin, A. (2015).

31 Lenhart, A., Smith, A., Anderson, M., Duggan, M., & Perrin, A. (2015).

32 Lenhart, A., Smith, A., Anderson, M., Duggan, M., & Perrin, A. (2015).

33 Statista. (2017a). *Frequency of using group chat function of text messaging (SMS) or online messaging applications according to adults in the United States as of December 2017, by age group.* Retrieved from www.statista.com/statistics/800650/group-chat-functions-age-use-text-online-messaging-apps/

34 Statista. (2017a).

35 Goodman, C. & Alderman, R. (2016). *Are group chats the new digital cliques?* Retrieved from https://raisingteensblog.com/group-chats-new-digital-cliques/

36 IMDB. (2004). *Mean girls.* Retrieved from www.imdb.com/title/tt0377092/?ref_=fn_al_tt_1

37 Smith, M. E. & Tang, J. C. (2015). *"They're blowing up my phone": Group messaging practices among adolescents.* Retrieved from https://pdfs.semanticscholar.org/06f8/10047de0ed b8100e00e6054d4c6fc2ce9c44.pdf

38 Mims, C. (2017). *For Generation Z, "Live Chilling" replaces hanging out in person.* Retrieved from www.wsj.com/articles/for-generation-z-live-chilling-replaces-hanging-out-in-person-1487519134

39 Mims, C. (2017).

40 Wagner, K. (2018). *Snapchat is rolling out group video chats like Messenger and Houseparty.* Retrieved from www.recode.net/2018/4/3/17191044/snapchat-group-video-messaging-chat

41 Mims, C. (2017).

42 Lenhart, A., Smith, A., Anderson, M., Duggan, M., & Perrin, A. (2015).

43 Higher Education Research Institute. (2017).

44 Lenhart, A., Smith, A., Anderson, M., Duggan, M., & Perrin, A. (2015).

45 Cyberbullying Research Center. (2016). *2016 cyberbullying data: Cyberbullying victimization.* Retrieved from https://cyberbullying.org/2016-cyberbullying-data

46 Cyberbullying Research Center. (2016).

47 Cyberbullying Research Center. (2016).

48 Cyberbullying Research Center. (2016).

49 Lenhart, A., Smith, A., Anderson, M., Duggan, M., & Perrin, A. (2015).

50 Lenhart, A., Smith, A., Anderson, M., Duggan, M., & Perrin, A. (2015).

51 Cigna. (2018). *Cigna U.S. loneliness index: Survey of 20,000 Americans examining behaviors driving loneliness in the United States.* Retrieved from www.multivu.com/players/English/8294451-cigna-us-loneliness-survey/

52 Cigna. (2018).

53 Cigna. (2018).

54 Beer, C. (2018b). *Reasons for using social media by generation.* Retrieved from https://blog.globalwebindex.com/chart-of-the-day/reasons-for-social-media/?utm_campaign=Chart%20of%20the%20Day&utm_source=hs_email&utm_medium=email&utm_content=62891161&_hsenc=p2ANqtz-9rMvnWS1WTKiuL2yuExeJZztXpH_iu 55QnDWc8Y22MeulyFRoL2ubxmyNglgSCU_aheqgFprt2dMKsESr1k-PmGvma-A&_hsmi=62891161

55 Beer, C. (2018b).

56 Cigna. (2018).

10 Romance

· ·

Dating and romance have certainly changed over the last century. While members of each generation have managed to find love and even get married, the road to romance during various generational eras is in some ways unique. We moved from the formality of the gentleman caller in the early 1900s to spending years exchanging love letters during World War II.[1] During the 1930s and 1940s, courtship moved from doing public things in private spaces, like talking in the parlor of the house, to doing private things in public spaces, like kissing at the drive-in theater.[2] By the 1950s, teen girls were wearing their boyfriend's letter jacket at school, and the 60s and 70s saw the sexual revolution and free love.[3] The AIDS crisis during the 1980s, though, brought a scare to everyone, especially the LGBTQ community.[4] In the 1990s, while some Gen Xers were making mix tapes for their crushes, others were sifting through personal ads in the newspaper to find the perfect match. And like the generations that came before them, historical and contemporary events and context have shaped how Generation Z approaches romance.

Sliding into the DMs: How Generation Z starts relationships

Swipe left. Swipe right. Left. Left. Left. Right. It's a Match! Like many aspects of modern life, the landscape for romance has changed dramatically as technology has emerged. Between Match.com, eHarmony, OKCupid, Tinder, Grindr, Hinge, and Bumble, there are various online dating options available. You can open up your phone and swipe your way towards finding that perfect someone, making romance more accessible than ever. But just because there are more opportunities to connect with eligible singles does not mean that dating has magically become easier for young people. More than 60 percent of Generation Z teens have never actually been in a relationship or romantically involved with someone.[5] And, compared to Baby Boomers and Gen Xers when they were in high school, the number of those in Generation Z who date is much lower.[6] Whether they simply don't go on dates or spend their social time in groups, dating is just not on the radar for many of them. But, when they do date, how do they find their partners?

Social media: Digital vetting

For many, social media plays a role in the dating lives of those in Generation Z. A national study by the Center for Generational Kinetics found that more than a quarter of members of Generation Z believe social media affects dating prospects.[7] This may be because social media offers opportunities to meet people they wouldn't otherwise. For one, seeing shared connections and mutual friends online can help Generation Z meet and vet potential dating partners. If a love interest on social media is connected through a close friend, it is easy to view that person's profile as well as get the scoop on that person directly from the friend. And, since peers are highly influential in Generation Z's decision-making,[8] having insight from a close friend may signal to Generation Z whether pursuing that love interest is a good idea. While social media has made it easy to sort through friends' connections online to look for a match, being fixed up on a blind date with a friend of a friend is nothing new. Regardless of generation, trusting your inner circle to connect you with potential dating partners appears to be a tried-and-true formula for romance.

Although 55 percent of Generation Z teens say flirting in-person is their preferred way to show interest,[9] half will friend their crush on social media, while more than 45 percent will like, comment, or share content with their crush to show interest.[10] But, in some cases, these behaviors are unwanted and inappropriate. More than a third of Generation Z teen girls have blocked or unfriended someone because of an unwanted advance or inappropriate flirting through social media.[11]

Online dating: Swipe left . . . swipe right

The stigma of online dating is fading as more people gravitate towards the swipe-friendly culture for finding romance. Nearly 60 percent of adults in America think online dating is a great way to meet people, a rate that has risen from 44 percent in 2005.[12] As of 2016, 15 percent of American adults had used some type of online dating site or app.[13] The rate is even higher for younger adults (ages 18 to 24) with more than a quarter having used one.[14] But, it appears that these sites and apps are being used more for casual dating than finding "the one." Of dating app users, more than 60 percent report using them to find other people with shared interests or hobbies, whereas only 42 percent use them to find a long-term relationship or marriage.[15] This holds true even with young people. In a study by the mobile gaming company, Pocket Gems, Millennial and Generation Z survey respondents indicated that the least likely place to meet their significant other was online.[16] But, this may not be true for all in Generation Z. Online dating sites can be a great place for LGBTQ young people to connect with each other. Because users don't need to come out to be on these sites, they can serve as a safe space to meet others for friendship and dating.

Like any social media platform, online dating allows for users to carefully craft the information and photos they share. What you see in online dating is not always what you get. A study by eHarmony found that more than 50 percent of online daters lie in their profile and most do so about their age, height, weight, job, or income.[17] And while there is the ability to provide misleading information, many in Generation Z don't necessarily want to share a lot of details at all. In a study by the Center for Generational Kinetics, more than half of those in Generation Z indicated being concerned about personal privacy when using online dating platforms.[18]

In-person

Even with the growing acceptance and use of online dating platforms, young people are still more likely to meet their significant other in an in-person environment. Research from Pocket Gems also found that 45 percent of Millennials and members of Generation Z were more likely to meet their significant other at school.[19] Further, the Pew Research Center reported that fewer than 10 percent of Generation Z teens have met a romantic partner in an online setting,[20] which likely stems from the desire of many of them to connect face-to-face.[21] While social media and online dating platforms provide a way to meet new people, these platforms may not be the place where Generation Z is going to find their love interests at least not at this stage in life.

#BAE: Generation Z in a relationship

While they might not be frequenting the digital world to find a dating partner, technology and social media do play a significant role for those in Generation Z who are already in romantic relationships.[22] For 65 percent of Generation Z teen boys and 52 percent of Generation Z teen girls, social media platforms help them feel a greater sense of connection to what is happening in their significant others' lives.[23]

Dating digitally

Social media also serves as an important platform for communication between dating partners. Those in Generation Z may not be staying up late on phone calls with their crush or significant other, but they are very likely staying up late texting, Snapchatting, and FaceTiming.

Similar to staying in touch with friends who may live thousands of miles away, technology and social media have also created more opportunity to manage long-distance relationships. A couple may not be able to fly or drive to spend time together but they might hold a Skype or FaceTime date instead. Video chatting certainly does not replace the quality time spent together in person, but technology does provide a way for couples to connect in a more personal way online. In our Generation Z Goes to College Study, many who identified being in long-distance relationships expressed the positive impact of technology in providing new opportunities to overcome the challenge of distance.[24]

Beyond using technology to communicate with each other, many in Generation Z find it socially acceptable to use technology while hanging out in person with their significant others. More than any other generation, those in Generation Z feel it is acceptable to use their smartphones while on a date, meeting their significant other's parents, and even during their own wedding ceremony.[25] Whether or not they send a selfie on Snapchat as they walk down the aisle on their wedding day, technology is such an integral part of Generation Z's world, and it shows up in various ways in their romantic lives.

Modern-day PDA

Social media is also a space for modern-day public displays of affection. As a way to express their feelings and share information about their dating lives, some in Generation Z showcase their romantic relationships online. Whether through posts, uploaded pictures, or a display of relationship status, putting out the details of dating to their social networks can validate that relationship for them.

> *It is a way to express with the world my romantic relationship in itself but not our problems or negative things of that sort.*
> – Member of Generation Z

For some, posting details about their relationship online is a way to show they are taken. For others, though, social media is a way to express affection and appreciation for their significant other. Hashtag trends like #ManCrushMonday and #WomanCrushWednesday are ways in which users dedicate social media posts to their significant other or crush. However, social media PDA also has its downside as users may feel social pressure to publicly display their relationship when they would prefer not to. Not posting about a significant other on Valentine's Day, their birthday, or during the holidays may cause friction within a relationship or even lead others to question the strength of that relationship.

Similar to digital PDA, promposals also offer a way for those in Generation Z to publicly highlight their interest in someone. A promposal is the "the eyebrow-raising high-school ritual wherein students go to elaborate, terribly public lengths to ask each other to prom."[26] Whether it is inviting a date over the loudspeaker at a football game or posting a billboard with "Will you go to prom with me?" the ask must be over-the-top creative. While promposals, in some fashion, have likely been around long before social media was available to capture them, they have become more commonplace with today's young people. Simply being asked to a school dance might not just be boring; it might actually be a letdown.

Healthy relationships

While reminiscing on first relationships and first loves can elicit fond memories, for some, those teen years are also filled with heartache and heartbreak – especially in high school where relationships can feel amplified and intense.[27] As it's always the hope that young people are in healthy and productive relationships, that isn't always the case. In a report by Concept Systems, Inc., the perspective of many high school teens is that if you can get through tough relationship issues, then the relationship is "meant to be."[28] Teens in the study did recognize, however, that having little relationship experience makes it difficult to see if they are in a bad or abusive relationship. According to the Centers for Disease Control and Prevention, of high schoolers who had dated in the past year, nearly 10 percent had experienced at least one episode of physical abuse and nearly 11 percent had experienced unwanted sexual behavior.[29] These numbers might be even higher if teens were better able to discern abuse.

But, those in Generation Z don't just have to be on the lookout for physical or sexual abuse; with technology today, issues of emotional abuse are ever-present. Being able to peek into the lives of significant others through technology presents potential relationship issues such as jealousy, violation of trust, and temptation to cheat. One in four of those in Generation Z with dating experience feel like technology has had a negative impact on their relationship and led them to become jealous or question their relationship.[30] This may be caused by something such as their partner liking someone else's photo or seeing a Snapchat where their partner is hanging out with someone else.

> *Technology gets in the way of relationships. It's too easy to become consumed with wanting to know what your significant other is doing all the time and actually being able to find out is a little excessive.*
> *– Member of Generation Z*

The ability to engage in digital surveillance can contribute to toxic, unhealthy, and possibly even abusive relationships. Researchers, in an article in the *Journal of Adolescence*, use the term "digital dating abuse" to describe "using digital media to monitor, control, threaten, harass, pressure, or coerce a dating partner."[31] These researchers found the most common form of digital dating abuse among Generation Z teens involves monitoring and controlling, which includes pressuring to respond to texts, monitoring whereabouts and activities, sending numerous messages to the point of making their partner uncomfortable, looking at private information without permission, and monitoring who their partner can talk to and spend time with.[32] One initiative that aims to help young people identify abusive behavior in relationships is #ThatsNotLove.[33] The campaign empowers teens and young adults to educate their peers on signs of relationship abuse.

Table 10.1 Impact of Technology and Social Media on Romantic Relationships[34]

"Technology is what is keeping my relationship with my girlfriend alive. I get to see her face every night, and it really makes the gap feel smaller."	"It helps me see what my romantic partner is doing & what they're up to when we're not together. There are times when it plays the 'bad guy' because jealousy can be brought on in certain situations when it comes to social media and technology."
"Technology aids in my romantic relationship. It allows us to contact each other even when we aren't near each other, and it allows us to continue to develop our relationship without the necessity of being physically together."	"Technology gets in the way of relationships. It's too easy to become consumed with wanting to know what your significant other is doing all the time and actually being able to find out is a little excessive."
"It plays an important role in keeping touch, however the physical and emotional part of a relationship is just as important."	"I think social media oftentimes destroys romantic relationships. There's often a 'he said, she said' factor that takes place on social media that creates problems that are intensified on the Internet."

It's complicated: Ending relationships

Ending a relationship is not often a positive experience, and technology does not make breaking up any easier. Generation Z's value of in-person communication carries over into the uncomfortable experience of ending a relationship. Most of those in Generation Z agree that utilizing technology by texting, calling, sending a message, or changing their status to "single" on social media are not the most appropriate ways to end a romantic relationship; nearly 80 percent of Generation Z teens, in particular, instead believe an in-person conversation is most acceptable.[35] In line with their belief that breaking up should be done face-to-face, only 22 percent of those in Generation Z have ended a relationship in an online or digital setting.[36] While technology has the ability to make most aspects of our lives easier and more efficient, the same can't be said for those in Generation Z when ending a relationship. These young people recognize that tough and truly emotional things need to be done face-to-face.

Permanent memory book

Social media can also be a reminder of past memories with a significant other after a relationship ends. Where older generations may have physically packed their mementos in a box after a breakup or burned pictures or love letters, for those in Generation Z, prom pictures and photos with their high school sweetheart may continue to live online through social media far after a relationship ends. Packing away these digital memories for Generation Z includes blocking, unfriending, or unfollowing an ex as well as deleting photos of memories shared together. Nearly half of Generation Z teen girls who have dated someone have unfriended an ex or deleted a photo or tag with their ex.[37] But, sometimes, deleting a photo just isn't an option. Generation Z teen, Gabi Dunn, wasn't going to let her great prom photos be ruined after her breakup. Dunn's tweets went viral after she shared the photos with an image of Ryan Reynolds photoshopped over her ex's face.[38]

While Generation Z users can mostly control the content they share, some aspects of social media are more permanent. Posts and comments that users are tagged in are harder to eliminate, as those users may not have control over the content. What were previously intended to be cute digital public displays of affection can come back as unwelcome reminders of a previous relationship.

"Hanging out" and hooking up

Rather than having one dating partner, some in Generation Z engage in "hanging out," which involves spending time with a romantic interest without officially dating or being in a monogamous relationship. Consider the rise in the popularity of the term "Netflix and Chill," which refers to hanging out with someone in a relaxed setting with the likelihood of a sexual encounter.[39] "Hanging out" keeps relationships open and casual but can be a bit different than "hooking up," which often involves a singular physical or sexual encounter with someone without the intention of seeing each other again. The underlying philosophy of the hook-up is in not "catching feelings" or becoming emotionally attached. While friends with benefits might also be an option for some, the notion is that keeping feelings out of the physical relationship is key.

Dr. Lisa Wade explored the hook-up culture on college campuses and found that 14 percent of Generation Z college students in her study were "enthusiasts" who enjoyed casual sexual relationships, and 34 percent were "abstainers" who avoided the casual sex hook-up culture.[40] Wade's research also found that 45 percent of students in her study were "dabblers," who were not necessarily opposed to casual sex, but not necessarily enthusiasts or regular participants.[41] Even if technology and online dating may promote a casual, hook-up culture, Generation Z is actually having less sex than older generations when they were young.[42] The hook-up culture that has become associated with teens and young adults today is not necessarily a myth but is also not likely as rampant as it may appear to be.

> ❝ [Technology] is how I meet all the guys I know and none of them just want a relationship. ❞
> – Member of Generation Z

Conclusion

> **❝** *In my eyes, a 'good life' is being happily in a relationship/married, having a good job, and a good overall income, and doing what I'm passionate about every day.* **❞**
> *- Member of Generation Z*

Generation Z is still relatively young. For many, they aren't engaging in typical dating behaviors. But like those in older generations, many will eventually want that someone special to spend their lives with. And, whether they meet them at school, through a friend, or online, they too will ultimately find love.

Notes

1 Chatel, A. (2014). *How the "first date" has changed in every decade through history.* Retrieved from https://mic.com/articles/105556/why-there-s-no-need-to-sweat-the-picture-perfect-first-date-according-to-history#.e16bwAd5K

2 Burzumato, S. (2007). *A brief history of courtship and dating in America, Part 1.* Retrieved from www.boundless.org/relationships/2007/a-brief-history-of-courtship-and-dating-in-america-part-1

3 Chatel, A. (2014).

4 Khan Academy. (2018). *Emergence of the AIDS crisis.* Retrieved from www.khanacademy.org/humanities/ap-us-history/period-9/apush-1980s-america/a/emergence-of-the-aids-crisis

5 Lenhart, A., Anderson, M., & Smith, A. (2015c). *Teens, technology, and romantic relationships.* Retrieved from www.pewinternet.org/2015/10/01/teens-technology-and-romantic-relationships/

6 Twenge, J. M. (2017). *iGen: Why today's super-connected kids are growing up less rebellious, more tolerant, less happy – and completely unprepared for adulthood – and what that means for the rest of us.* New York: Atria Books.

7 Center for Generational Kinetics & Dorsey, J. (2016). *iGen Tech Disruption: 2016 national study on technology and the generation after Millennials.* Retrieved from http://genhq.com/wp-content/uploads/2016/01/iGen-Gen-Z-Tech-Disruption-Research-White-Paper-c-2016-Center-for-Generational-Kinetics.pdf

8 Varkey Foundation. (2017). *Generation Z: Global Citizenship Survey.* Retrieved from www.varkeyfoundation.org/what-we-do/policy-research/generation-z-global-citizenship-survey/

9 Pew Research Center. (2015f). *Teen voices: Dating in the digital age.* Retrieved from www.pewinternet.org/online-romance/

10 Pew Research Center. (2015f).

11 Anderson, M. (2015a). *Digital romance: How teen boys and girls differ.* Retrieved from www.pewresearch.org/fact-tank/2015/10/13/digital-romance-how-teen-boys-and-girls-differ/

12 Smith, A. & Anderson, M. (2016). *5 facts about online dating.* Retrieved from www.pewresearch.org/fact-tank/2016/02/29/5-facts-about-online-dating/

13 Smith, A. (2016). *15% of American adults have used online dating sites or mobile dating apps*. Retrieved from www.pewinternet.org/2016/02/11/15-percent-of-american-adults-have-used-online-dating-sites-or-mobile-dating-apps/

14 Smith, A. (2016).

15 Statista. (2017f). *Why do or did you use online dating sites or apps?* Retrieved from www.statista.com/statistics/709926/reasons-for-using-online-dating-site-and-app-in-us/

16 Volkman, E. (2016). *How Millennials and Gen Z use mobile*. Retrieved from https://tech.co/millennials-gen-z-use-mobile-infographic-2016-04

17 Thottam, I. (2018). *Online dating statistics you should know*. Retrieved from www.eharmony.com/online-dating-statistics/

18 Center for Generational Kinetics & Dorsey, J. (2016).

19 Volkman, E. (2016).

20 Lenhart, A., Anderson, M., & Smith, A. (2015c).

21 Seemiller, C. & Grace, M. (2016). *Generation Z goes to college*. San Francisco: Jossey-Bass.

22 Seemiller, C. & Grace, M. (2016).

23 Anderson, M. (2015a).

24 Seemiller, C. & Grace, M. (2016).

25 Center for Generational Kinetics & Dorsey, J. (2016).

26 Dewey, C. (2014). *A short history of the "promposal."* Retrieved from www.washingtonpost.com/news/arts-and-entertainment/wp/2014/04/21/a-short-history-of-the-promposal/?noredirect=on&utm_term=.bb85881170f2, para. 2.

27 Concept Systems, Inc. (2014). *Teen dating relationships: Understanding and comparing youth and adult conceptualizations, final report*. Retrieved from www.ncjrs.gov/pdffiles1/nij/grants/248464.pdf

28 Concept Systems, Inc. (2014), p. 38.

29 Centers for Disease Control and Prevention. (2016b). *Youth risk behavior surveillance: United States, 2015*. Retrieved from www.cdc.gov/mmwr/volumes/65/ss/pdfs/ss6506.pdf

30 Lenhart, A., Anderson, M., & Smith, A. (2015b). *Chapter 4: Social media and romantic relationships*. Retrieved from www.pewinternet.org/2015/10/01/social-media-and-romantic-relationships/#many-teens-view-social-media-and-text-messaging-as-a-space-for-connection-emotional-support-and-occasional-jealousy-in-the-context-of-their-relationships-although-most-say-social

31 Reed, L. A., Tolman, R. M., & Ward, L. M. (2017). Gender matters: Experiences and consequences of digital dating abuse victimization in adolescent dating relationships. *Journal of Adolescence, 59*, 79–89, p. 79.

32 Reed, L. A., Tolman, R. M., & Ward, L. M. (2017).

33 Wallace, K. (2016). *#ThatsNotLove: Helping teens spot signs of relationship abuse*. Retrieved from www.cnn.com/2016/02/24/health/teen-dating-abuse-thatsnotlove-one-love-foundation/index.html

34 Seemiller, C. & Grace, M. (2014). *Generation Z goes to college study*. Unpublished raw data.

35 Lenhart, A., Anderson, M., & Smith, A. (2015a). *Chapter 5: After the relationship, technology, and breakups*. Retrieved from www.pewinternet.org/2015/10/01/after-the-relationship-technology-and-breakups/

36 Northeastern University. (2014). *Innovation survey*. Retrieved from www.northeastern.edu/news/2014/11/innovation-imperative-meet-generation-z/

37 Anderson, M. (2015a).

38 Reinstein, J. (2017). *This teen photoshopped Ryan Reynolds over her ex in prom photos and Reynolds was here for it.* Retrieved from www.buzzfeed.com/juliareinstein/dont-mess-with-gabi?utm_term=.pajjyP8XD4#.dc5d1Jo4KL

39 Dictionary.com. (n.d.b). *Netflix and chill.* Retrieved from www.dictionary.com/e/slang/netflix-and-chill/

40 Wade, L. (2016). *Sex on campus isn't what you think: What 101 student journals taught me.* Retrieved from www.theguardian.com/us-news/2016/aug/23/sex-on-campus-hookup-culture-student-journals

41 Wade, L. (2016).

42 Centers for Disease Control and Prevention. (2016b).

Mind, body, and spirit

··

11 Physical well-being

A desire for a healthy life seems to take more center stage as one gets older and experiences declining health.[1] But, many young people also have health and wellness on their minds. Forty-four percent of those in Generation Z believe health is one of the most important aspects of an ideal life.[2] But, what health issues might be facing this generation and how well do they take care of themselves?

" A good life is one in which I am happy. To me, this means balance in my life and having my physical, spiritual, mental, and emotional needs filled satisfactorily. "
- Member of Generation Z

Illnesses and diseases

Thinking back to the 1930s, those in the G.I. Generation worried about diseases like polio, diphtheria, and smallpox, all which have been eradicated or reduced substantially through mass immunization protocol.[3] Even more recent diseases have been eliminated from the childhood roster of illnesses. For example, in 1995, the start of the Generation Z cohort, a vaccine for Chickenpox was licensed in the U.S. for use.[4] What was once a childhood rite of passage has now become history shared through stories from generational elders.

While many old diseases are being contained, diseases that were

" I have a lot of worry about my health. A lot of it is probably anxiety and all in my head, but recently I have started getting more and more worried about whether or not I'm healthy. Every little thing that happens to my body, every mark, every bump, every itch, every pain, I immediately wonder if it can be life threatening or serious or if it will kill me. I really worry about that most. "
- Member of Generation Z

relatively unheard of even 15 years ago are also being eradicated. For example, 2008 Nobel Prize winner, Harald zur Hausen, found a link between cervical cancer and the human papillomavirus.[5] But, with the vaccine only available starting in 2006 and available for use on individuals up to 26 years-old, Generation Z will be the first generation where all members will have had access to the vaccine.[6] Although those in Generation Z may not worry about some of the diseases of the early twentieth century, other illnesses like bird flu, Ebola, swine flu, mad cow disease, H1N1, SARS, and Zika were not even on the minds of older generations when they were younger.

Despite the emergence of new illnesses, many of those in Generation Z see themselves as being in good health, or at least not in bad health. Nearly half of Generation Z college seniors surveyed rated their current physical health above average or in the highest 10 percent compared to their peers, and 39 percent indicated their health as average.[7] Those numbers point to a fairly healthy generation, at least in terms of their self-perception. On the one hand, perhaps a large majority of them are actually healthy, especially given their age and access to medical technology and advances in medicine that weren't always in existence. Take, for example, penicillin, which was not available for nearly the first half of the twentieth century,[8] making a bacterial infection that was once deadly into a day home from school today.

And with life expectancy rates having increased around 25 years in the last century,[9] it might seem to those in Generation Z that nearly everyone gets to live into their 80s and 90s. But, being healthy is more than just being free from illness at the moment. Behaviors like diet, exercise, and sleep contribute to a healthy or unhealthy lifestyle. While most of those in Generation Z may see themselves as healthy today, they may be engaging in unhealthy actions that could later catch up to them.

Healthy eating and sustainable foods

While many in the G.I. Generation grew up with meat and potatoes, the palettes of their Generation Z great-grandchildren appear to be quite different. Technomic, a foodservice research and consulting group, released a report indicating the top ten food trends for Generation Z included "hyperlocal sourcing, chef-driven fast-casual, natural ingredients/clean menus, environmental sustainability, locally sourced produce, locally sourced meat and seafood, food waste reduction, meal kits, simplicity/back to basics, and nutrition."[10] These were hardly the food concepts trending in early the twentieth century.

❝ [I want] to be able to purchase enough food and not have to eat low quality foodstuff such as Ramen Noodles or fast food. ❞
– Member of Generation Z

Those in Generation Z have a great focus on consuming nutritious and healthy food. Forty-five percent watch what they eat,[11] 67 percent look at nutritional content, and 60 percent look at ingredients on food labels.[12] Technomic also found that 25 percent of college students limit gluten; 25 percent follow a special diet like being a vegan, vegetarian, or flexitarian; and 39 percent avoid or limit animal products.[13]

Not only do they want to consume healthy food, they are aware of the dangers of mass food production. In our Generation Z Goes to College Study, 30 percent of those surveyed indicated caring about healthy and safe food,[14] and nearly 46 percent were concerned about factory farming/unhealthy food production.[15] Their thoughts on the issue may inspire them to create ways to grow and produce foods that are healthy and safe.

According to the Aramark Dining Styles fall 2016 aggregate report, 45 percent of Generation Z

*** I am extremely passionate about personal health and I don't approve of all the unnatural ingredients in the food industry. I also do not like the fact that most people are oblivious to what they are consuming. ***
– Member of Generation Z

*** I am very concerned about the methods of food manufacturing and have a great amount of concern about the dangers of processed foods, which seem to be a large factor [in] increasing detrimental health effects. ***
– Member of Generation Z

college students indicated wanting healthy food options on campus.[16] And, they are willing to pay for it. Nearly one-third said they would pay a premium for organic food and more than half for fresh food.[17] In addition, 57 percent of those in Generation Z are willing to pay more for sustainable food compared to 43 percent of the general population.[18] Overall, many in Generation Z want healthy, specialty, and sustainable foods, and despite their moderate views on spending money, they are willing to pay for them.

Getting that kick: Soda, coffee, and energy drinks

While no living generation has known a time when soda did not exist, it appears there is more attention today about the dangers of soda consumption than ever before – cavities, weight gain, elevated blood pressure, kidney damage, and the list goes on.[19] Perhaps that is why a lower percentage of Generation Z teens drink a lot of soda compared to Millennials when they were in high school. A study from the Centers for Disease Control and Prevention found that, in 2007, more than 19 percent of high school students drank two or more sodas a day, whereas, in 2015, that number had decreased to 13 percent.[20] Not only do fewer teens drink a lot of soda, there are far more teens today that are not drinking soda at all. In 2007, just less than 19 percent reported not drinking soda at all. By 2015, that number increased to just more than 26 percent.[21]

Despite the decrease in soda consumption, researchers found that caffeine intake with children and adolescents did not change between 1999 and 2010.[22] An increase in drinking coffee and energy drinks has made up for the decrease in soda in the caffeine consumption habits of young people.[23] This might not be surprising in that some of those in Generation Z have been drinking kid-sized mocha lattes from coffee establishments since they were toddlers. Consider that, in 1995, the first-year of the Generation Z's birth, Starbucks had 667 stores. By 2013, when those born in 1995 turned 18, the number of Starbucks stores soared to nearly 20,000.[24] And, with non-fat and sugar-free options available, health-conscious members of Generation Z can still partake in their coffee consumption without feeling like they are making an unhealthy choice.

Since the late 1990s, energy drinks have also become more popular.[25] While Jolt may have been all the rage for Generation X teens in the 1980s, it pales in comparison to the array of energy drinks Generation Z has grown up on such as Monster, Red Bull, and Rockstar. But, not all young people are downing these drinks; researchers have found that those in Generation Z who consume energy drinks are also more likely to consume other sugar-sweetened beverages and smoke.[26] So, it appears that the members of Generation Z who seek a healthy lifestyle aren't necessarily the ones who are consuming energy drinks.

Calories and portion sizes

Those in the G.I. Generation were the first youth to be introduced to fast food with White Castle in 1921 and Kentucky Fried Chicken in 1930.[27] They then grew up to experience with the invention of TV dinners in the early 1950s.[28] And while Salisbury steak on a foil plate made for an easy dinner preparation, it also might have been the start of the obesity epidemic.[29] In 1963, Weight Watchers was created by a housewife with the purpose of bringing together women to provide support for each other to lose weight.[30] And, many still count their points today. Whether it is Weight Watchers, the grapefruit diet,[31] or SlimFast,[32] dieting to lose weight has been a common practice for many generations.

> ❝ I am concerned about unhealthy food production because of the obesity epidemic in the U.S. and the frightening fact the healthy food (fruits, vegetables, etc.) are more expensive and less available than the fried and processed foods. ❞
> – Member of Generation Z

But, with a generation so focused on consuming healthy food and a million diets to choose from to lose weight, why are obesity rates of youth so high and continue to rise? In 1999, the obesity rate was 10.6 percent but increased to 13.9 percent by 2015.[33] Research points to a diet high in calories, fat, and sugar along with portion sizes and consumption of fast food and snack foods as contributing factors to childhood obesity.[34] And, this generation's lower level of physical activity is certainly making it difficult for them to burn off extra calories.[35]

Sedentary lifestyles and getting to 10,000 steps

Like most trends, fitness fads come and go with each generation. Whether it was Hula Hoops in the 1950s, Jazzercise in the 1970s, aerobics in the 1980s, Tae Bo in the 1990s, or Cross Fit today, each generation has had some type of focus on exercise.[36] But over the past 30 to 40 years, the volume and intensity of physical activity with youth, in particular, has been on the decline.[37] According to the Centers for Disease Control and Prevention, 14.3 percent of high school students in 2015 had not participated in at least 60 minutes of physical activity within the last week.[38] That trend seems to continue with Generation Z college students. The American College Health Association reported that nearly 21 percent of college students surveyed had not logged even 30 minutes of moderate physical activity in the week just before the survey.[39] This aligns with findings from the 2017 College Senior Survey in that 9 percent of Generation Z seniors indicated logging zero hours of weekly exercise, with another 55 percent only indicating having been active five or less hours a week.[40]

There may be two reasons for the high rates of physical inactivity. First, starting in the early 2000s, there has been a decrease in time spent on physical education in schools.[41] Not only are kids exercising less, they are also spending less time learning various sports and games that might lure them toward physical activity outside of school. For example, a child who never learned how to play soccer in a physical education class might have little to no interest in joining a recreational soccer team. One research study found that a prominent aversion to physical activity for this generation is the fear of incompetence.[42] So, not only might there simply be less opportunities for them to learn a sport or activity, their concern that others might not think they were skilled enough could lead to decreased voluntary participation.

Another potential reason for these rates is that youth in Generation Z have more sedentary lifestyles than previous generations.[43] This may be due to time spent on their devices, where they can stream an entire season of a TV show in one weekend or stay up all night engaging in online gaming. The United States Report Card on Physical Activity for Children and Youth measures a number of categories of healthy lifestyles across various age groups. In the category of sedentary behaviors, which measures screen time use, just around 31 percent of 12 to 19 year-olds studied met the screen time guidelines of 2 hours or less per day, yielding an overall D–grade in 2016.[44] This is down from a D grade in the 2014 report.[45]

One way young people are enhancing their physical activity is through the use of fitness trackers. These devices have been found to be effective in increasing daily "steps."[46] Oral Roberts University has capitalized on this technology as a way to encourage physical fitness, requiring all first-year students to wear a fitness tracker.[47] Based on the amount of activity, students are awarded aerobic points that are automatically fed into the campus learning management system grade book.[48] However, critics point out that, with young people, fitness trackers can encourage eating disorders and over-exercising[49] as well as can elicit feelings of pressure and guilt.[50] Despite these concerns, a greater number of younger adults than older adults are wearing fitness trackers,[51] reflecting the notion that young people find them useful in working toward their fitness goals.

Lack of sleep

While those in Generation Z might be more sedentary, that doesn't seem to translate to getting a lot of sleep. A study by the Varkey Foundation found that only 18 percent of those in Generation Z feel they get enough sleep, rest, and relaxation.[52] Another study found that only about 27 percent of high school students get eight or more hours of sleep at night,[53] a decline from 2007 when just more than 31 percent indicated sleeping at least 8 hours a night.[54] Why might they be sleeping less? It could be related to the time they spend on their personal devices. Researchers have found that teens who use their devices three or more hours each day were considerably more likely to get less sleep.[55]

It's not just Generation Z high school students who aren't getting a lot of sleep. College-aged Generation Z students are also lacking sleep as only 24 percent sleep at least 8 hours a night.[56] But, sleep patterns of those in Generation Z are not universal across cultures. In a study of more than 4,000 Generation Z college students in six different countries, researchers found that Chinese students get the most sleep at an average of 7.5 hours a night, whereas U.S. students get the least sleep with 6.8 hours a night.[57] The lack of sleep for this generation may be related to staying up late to hang out with friends or cram for an exam like their older generational counterparts did, but may also be a result of staying up late using their devices trying not to miss a beat.

Future of medicine

Generation Z is growing up in a time of rapid advancements in medicine. The future of healthcare could include more widespread use of robots who assist surgeons in the operating room, stress monitoring bracelets, new therapies derived from research on the bacteria in the body, interception protocol that stops diseases from progressing, personal DNA mapping included in health records, healthcare startups that revolutionize innovative medicine, and the use of precision medicine to eradicate diseases like cancer.[58] And with personalized medicine emerging, Generation Z may live nearly their whole lives only knowing healthcare marked by "the tailoring of medical treatment to the individual characteristics, needs and preferences of each patient."[59]

But, who is going to pay for these advanced treatments? The concept of health insurance as we know it today actually emerged in the 1930s when the G.I. Generation was coming into adulthood, meaning that every living generation today has known a world in which health insurance existed in some form.[60] The debate over insurance – who would get it, who would offer it, who would pay for it, and how it would work – continues today. But, there doesn't seem to be that debate with many in this generation. Nearly three-quarters of Generation Z college seniors agreed or strongly agreed that a "national health plan is needed to cover everybody's medical costs."[61]

Conclusion

It appears that many in Generation Z care deeply about their health and wellness and see it as "a complex, holistic balancing act" of their physical, emotional, social, and mental well-being.[62] However, this is a generation that is more sedentary, less fit, more obese, and lacking in sleep than previous generations. While there might be medical tech-

> ❝ At the end of my journey, I want to have lived a happy life . . . One that includes family, friends, and overall mental and physical wellness. ❞
> – Member of Generation Z

nology and advancements, it is still critical to help these young people engage in healthy behaviors so they can live long and healthy lives.

Notes

1 Collage Group. (2016). *Quick chart: What Gen Z & Millennials really want in life*. Retrieved from www.collagegroup.com/2016/09/19/gen-z-millennials-values/
2 Collage Group. (2016).
3 Hayes, J. (1986). *Deadly diseases of past reduced to bad memories*. Retrieved from http://articles.chicagotribune.com/1986-11-16/health/8603260778_1_polio-rheumatic-fever-yellow-fever
4 Centers for Disease Control and Prevention. (2016a). *Varicella*. Retrieved from www.cdc.gov/vaccines/pubs/pinkbook/varicella.html
5 Nobelprize.org. (2017). *Harald zur Hausen: Biographical*. Retrieved from www.nobelprize.org/nobel_prizes/medicine/laureates/2008/hausen-bio.html
6 Brookes, L. (2016). *The HPV vaccine: Then and now*. Retrieved from www.medscape.com/viewarticle/866591
7 Higher Education Research Institute. (2017). *College Senior Survey*. Data prepared by Higher Education Research Institute.

8 Rothman, L. (2016). *This is what happened to the first American treated with penicillin.* Retrieved from http://time.com/4250235/penicillin-1942-history/

9 Schanzenbach, Nunn, & Bauer. (2016). *The changing landscape of American life expectancy.* Retrieved from www.brookings.edu/wp-content/uploads/2016/07/Full-Paper-2.pdf

10 Aramark. (2017). *Higher ed trends.* Philadelphia, PA: Aramark, p. 14.

11 Sensis and Think Now Research. (2016). *We are Gen Z report.* Retrieved from www.wearegenzreport.com/

12 Vision Critical. (2016). *The everything guide to Generation Z.* Retrieved from www.vision-critical.com/wp-content/uploads/2016/10/GenZ_Final.pdf

13 Aramark. (2017).

14 Seemiller, C. & Grace, M. (2014). *Generation Z goes to college study.* Unpublished raw data.

15 Seemiller, C. & Grace, M. (2014).

16 Aramark. (2017).

17 Aramark. (2017).

18 Aramark. (2017).

19 Boyles, S. (2011). *Sodas and your health: Risks debated.* Retrieved from www.webmd.com/diet/features/sodas-and-your-health-risks-debated#2

20 Centers for Disease Control and Prevention. (2016b). *Youth risk behavior surveillance: United States, 2015.* Retrieved from www.cdc.gov/mmwr/volumes/65/ss/pdfs/ss6506.pdf

21 Centers for Disease Control and Prevention. (2016b).

22 Branum, A. M., Rossen, L. M., & Schoendorf, K. C. (2014). Trends in caffeine intake among U.S. children and adolescents. *Pediatrics, 133*(3), 386–393.

23 Branum, A. M., Rossen, L. M., & Schoendorf, K. C. (2014).

24 Starbucks.com. (2018). *Starbucks company timeline.* Retrieved from www.starbucks.com/about-us/company-information/starbucks-company-timeline

25 Heckman, M. A., Sherry, K., & Gonzales de Mejia, E. (2010). Energy drinks: An assessment of their market size, consumer demographics, ingredient profile, functionality, and regulations in the United States. *Comprehensive Reviews in Food Science and Food Safety, 9,* 303–317.

26 Larson, N., DeWolfe, J., Story, M., & Neumark-Sztainer, D. (2014). Adolescent consumption of sports and energy drinks: Linkages to higher physical activity, unhealthy beverage patterns, cigarette smoking, and screen media use. *Journal of Nutritional Educational Behavior, 46*(3), 181–187.

27 Aronica, M. (2014). *Where your favorite fast-food chains began.* Retrieved from www.usatoday.com/story/travel/destinations/2014/05/31/fast-food-chains-origins/9729901/

28 Farhi, P. (2005). *The man who gave America a taste of the future.* Retrieved from www.washingtonpost.com/wp-dyn/content/article/2005/07/21/AR2005072102249.html

29 Farhi, P. (2005).

30 Weight Watchers. (2017). *History and philosophy.* Retrieved from www.weightwatchers.com/about/his/history.aspx

31 Davis, S. (2017). *The grapefruit diet.* Retrieved from www.webmd.com/diet/a-z/grapefruit-diet

32 Rotchford, L. (2014). *Diets through history: The good, the bad and the scary.* Retrieved from www.cnn.com/2013/02/08/health/diets-through-history/index.html

33 Centers for Disease Control and Prevention. (2016b).

34 Sahoo, K., Sahoo, B., Choudhury, A. K., Sofi, N. Y., Kuman, R., & Bhadaria, A. S. (2015). Childhood obesity: Causes and consequences. *Journal of Family Medicine and Primary Care, 4*(2), 187–192.

35 Sparks & Honey. (2014). *Meet Generation Z: Forget everything you learned about Millennials*. Retrieved from www.slideshare.net/sparksandhoney/generation-z-final-june-17

36 Gibson, C. (2016). *The evolution of exercise in 10 iconic fitness trends*. Retrieved from www.washingtonpost.com/sf/style/2016/07/05/the-evolution-of-exercise-in-10-iconic-fitness-trends/?utm_term=.4aae6710081e

37 Institute of Medicine, Food and Nutrition Board. (2013). *Educating the student body*. H. W. Kohl, III & H. D. Cook (Eds.). Washington, DC: The National Academies Press.

38 Centers for Disease Control and Prevention. (2016b).

39 American College Health Association. (2017). *National College Health Assessment II: Spring 2017 reference group executive summary*. Retrieved from www.acha-ncha.org/docs/NCHA-II_SPRING_2017_REFERENCE_GROUP_EXECUTIVE_SUMMARY.pdf

40 Higher Education Research Institute. (2017).

41 Institute of Medicine. (2013). *Educating the student body: Taking physical activity and physical education to school*. Retrieved from www.nationalacademies.org/hmd/~/media/Files/Report%20Files/2013/Educating-the-Student-Body/EducatingTheStudentBody_rb.pdf

42 Biber, D. D., Czech, D. R., Harris, B. S., & Melton, B. F. (2013). Attraction to physical activity of generation Z: A mixed methodological approach. *Open Journal of Preventive Medicine, 3*(3), 310–319.

43 Sparks & Honey. (2014).

44 National Physical Activity Plan. (2016). *The 2016 United States report card on physical activity for children and youth*. Retrieved from www.physicalactivityplan.org/reportcard/2016FINAL_USReportCard.pdf

45 National Physical Activity Plan. (2016).

46 Poirier, J., Bennett, W. L., Jerome, G. J., Shah, N. G., Lazo, M., Yeh, H. C., . . . Cobb, N. (2016). Effectiveness of an activity tracker – and Internet-based adaptive walking program for adults: A randomized controlled trial. *Journal of Medical Internet Research, 18*(2). Retrieved from www.jmir.org/2016/2/e34/

47 Oral Roberts University. (2016). *Oral Roberts University integrates wearable technology with physical fitness curriculum for incoming students*. Retrieved from www.oru.edu/news/oru_news/20160104_fitbit_tracking.php

48 Oral Roberts University. (2016).

49 Ali, A. (2016). *Oral Roberts University criticised for making new students wear "grade-issuing" Fitbit trackers*. Retrieved from www.independent.co.uk/student/news/oral-roberts-university-criticised-for-making-new-students-wear-grade-issuing-fitbit-trackers-a6989821.html

50 Kerner, C. & Goodyear, V. A. (2017). The motivational impact of wearable healthy lifestyle technologies: A self-determination perspective on Fitbits with adolescents. *American Journal of Health Education, 48*(5), 287–297.

51 Pai, A. (2015). *Forrester: 35 percent of Millennials will buy a fitness wearable in the next year*. Retrieved from www.mobihealthnews.com/47134/forrester-35-percent-of-millennials-will-buy-a-fitness-wearable-in-the-next-year

52 Varkey Foundation. (2017). *Generation Z: Global Citizenship Survey*. Retrieved from www.varkeyfoundation.org/what-we-do/policy-research/generation-z-global-citizenship-survey/

53 Centers for Disease Control and Prevention. (2016b).

54 Centers for Disease Control and Prevention. (2016b).

55 Twenge, J. M. (2017). *iGen: Why today's super-connected kids are growing up less rebellious, more tolerant, less happy – and completely unprepared for adulthood – and what that means for the rest of us*. New York: Atria Books.

56 Sodexo. (2017). *The Sodexo international university lifestyle survey*. Retrieved from www.sodexo.com/home/media/publications/studies-and-reports/international-university-lifesty.html

57 Sodexo. (2017).

58 Peterson, S. (2015). *7 ways health care could be different for Generation Z*. Retrieved from www.jnj.com/health-and-wellness/7-ways-health-care-could-be-different-for-generation-z

59 Hamburg, M. A. (2013). *Paving the way for personalized medicine*. Retrieved from www.fda.gov/downloads/scienceresearch/specialtopics/personalizedmedicine/ucm372421.pdf, p. 2.

60 Morrisey, M. A. (2013). *Health insurance* (2nd ed.). Chicago, IL: Health Administration Press.

61 Higher Education Research Institute. (2017).

62 The Hartman Group. (2016). *New kids on the block: A first look at Gen Z*. Retrieved from www.forbes.com/sites/thehartmangroup/2016/03/31/new-kids-on-the-block-a-first-look-at-gen-z/#300544c71bab, para. 12.

12 Mental health

∙∙∙

Mental health encompasses our "emotional, psychological, and social well-being" and affects how we "think, feel, and act."[1] While issues related to mental health affect all age groups, they are on the rise with Generation Z youth and college students.[2,3] It's not surprising then that nearly 18 percent of Generation Z college seniors surveyed rated their emotional health as below average or lower.[4]

A worried generation

The world today is different than it was even a decade ago, let alone a century ago. There seems to be much more for a young person to be worried about. As kids, many in Generation Z missed out on playing outside by themselves, walking to school alone, or hanging out at the park without an adult present. The debate over free-range parenting has emerged in the last few years with both social and legal repercussions for parents who have let their kids walk to and from school or play at the park unsupervised.[5] This tight, hand-holding behavior (for what many deem to be legitimate reasons) sends a message to kids that the world is a dangerous place and bad things are bound to happen. The naiveté that has in the past come with childhood seems to be overshadowed by this generation's exposure at a young age to the reality of what appears to be a scary world – one in which we need to constantly protect ourselves. In 2017, marketing and research firm, Ipsos, conducted a study of more than 29,000 people in 38 different countries to better

> ❝ *[I worry most about] everything. I worry too much, even about stuff I shouldn't worry about.* ❞
> *– Member of Generation Z*

understand their estimation of problems facing their countries. Overwhelming trends were found that individuals overestimate the problems and dangers, ultimately demonstrating that things are "NOT as bad as they seem!"[6]

But, with parents and adults in their lives worried about the problems and dangers of the world, it's not surprising then Generation Z is a generation of worriers. In our Generation Z Stories Study, less than 1 percent of all students indicated that they try not to worry; the remaining more than 99 percent described at least one worry in their lives.[7] We found that their most prominent worries center on three areas – fear of failure, money, and larger societal issues.[8]

Fear of failure

We found that the most prominent worry for this generation was the fear of failure or not being successful, which garnered discussion among 18 percent of the nearly 1,300 surveyed.[9] Particularly, they focused on worrying about not living up to their own expectations, disappointing others, having low self-worth, and not making a difference.[10] The fear of failure or disappointing others may stem from the notion that many in Generation Z are motivated by their relationships with others[11] and care deeply about others' perceptions.[12]

❝ I worry that I will fail. I worry that I won't be smart enough, or fast enough, or self-controlled enough, or creative enough, or driven enough, or kind enough, or generous enough. I worry that I won't like myself when I look in the mirror. ❞
- Member of Generation Z

Some participants in our study also shared their worries of making mistakes, rejection, missed opportunities, regret, and just being average.[13] These worries aren't surprising in that rates of perfectionism in college students have linearly increased between 1989 and 2016 due to young people believing that "others are more demanding of them, [they] are more demanding of others, and [they] are more demanding of themselves."[14]

❝ It's hard not to constantly think about the tens of thousands of dollars that I already owe, on top of paying day-to-day expenses once I graduate. I'm worried that I won't be able to get a job that will be able to handle all of the burdens that I already carry and impede me from accomplishing or attaining other things in life. ❞
- Member of Generation Z

Money

Money was the second most prominent worry that emerged from our study, aligning with findings from the Varkey Foundation that the most cited source of anxiety for those in Generation Z was money.[15] These young people have the weight of the world on them financially, knowing they need to pay for school and living expenses, get a job, and be able to afford to take care of themselves and their loved ones in the future. It's no surprise then that nearly one-third of college students indicate having experienced trauma or difficulty related to finances.[16]

World issues

Another prominent worry for this generation is carrying the weight of all that is happening in the world around them. Many are concerned about education, equality, the environment, and safety and security.[17] Their concerns around these issues are discussed more in other chapters of this book; however, the issue at hand is that this young generation is shouldering the burden of large-scale macro issues facing the world while trying

❝ I worry about climate change and what is going to happen in the years to come. I am feeling very sick just talking about it. I try to ignore it, what's going on with our animals, nature, our atmosphere and it is so awful that we are taking no initiative to change. I'm confused and angered by everyone for not caring!! ❞
- Member of Generation Z

to balance their school and personal lives as youth and young adults. In doing so, worrying about the world's issues may be taking a toll on their mental health.

Realism over optimism

Having an optimistic outlook can offer great benefits for both health and longevity.[18] Thus, it is promising that we found only 5 percent of Generation Z college students are not optimistic about the future.[19] But, the rest are not fully optimistic either. Sixty percent indicate being optimistic and 27 percent only slightly optimistic, while 8 percent are unsure.[20] And 62 percent shared that they prepare for the worst-case scenario.[21] There has been a substantial decline in optimism in recent years as 89 percent of Millennials identified as being optimistic when they were in college.[22] Considering the context, it might make sense that Millennials would be more optimistic. Many grew up pre-9/11, pre-Recession, and pre-housing bubble burst. Not only might the world have seemed less scary at this time, Millennials were also infused with confidence, fostering the belief that they deserved anything they wanted.[23] Therefore, it's probably hard not to be optimistic when expecting positive outcomes.

In looking back nearly a century, the G.I. Generation was facing similar contextual issues as Generation Z is today, like those around the economy and human rights. But, those young members of the G.I. Generation were still

❝ I'm reconsidering having children because I am nervous of what my children will encounter. ❞
- Member of Generation Z

optimistic about their future.[24] While not pessimistic, those in Generation Z don't seem to exude the same optimism as their cultural counterpart G.I. Generation or the adjacent Millennial Generation. And, many in Generation Z are even less optimistic about their children's future.[25] Perhaps their outlook stems from the realism infused by their Generation X parents or the overwhelming concerns about issues of the future.[26]

Happy?

A 2016 study by the market intelligence agency, Collage Group, found that 76 percent of those in Generation Z list happiness as the most important characteristic of an ideal life.[27] It makes sense then that happiness was interwoven into responses for nearly every question in our Generation Z Stories Study. They want to be happy in their lives, in their jobs, and in their relationships.[28] This focus on happiness appears to follow a trend with Millennials who also indicated happiness as the most important characteristic of an ideal life.[29]

So, while those in Generation Z believe happiness is important, the bigger question may be whether or not they are actually happy. In a global study of Generation Z youth, 68 percent indicated being happy.[30] But, interestingly, the percentage of those identifying as happy is lower with each older age group. For 15 to 16 year-olds, 69 percent report being happy, whereas 59 percent of 17 to 18 year-olds and 52 percent of 19 to 21 year-olds indicate being happy.[31]

When looking only at those from the U.S., overall happiness of Generation Z is higher at 73 percent than the global average of 68 percent.[32] But a slightly higher percentage of those in Generation Z are unhappy (10 percent) as compared to the global average of 9 percent.[33] And, in comparing Generation Z and Millennials when they were the same age, those in Generation Z appear to have lower levels of life satisfaction.[34]

❝ A good life would be . . . one with happiness and people to share that with. ❞
– Member of Generation Z

So, what actually makes those in Generation Z happy? It seems that being physically and mentally healthy as well as having good relationships with family and friends are the keys to their happiness.[35] This doesn't differ much from what researchers found in a 75-year study that tracked college students from the 1930s until recently; researchers determined that close relationships are what keep people happy throughout their lifetimes, more than any other factor.[36]

All stressed out

Considering their worries along with optimism and happiness dispositions, it's not surprising that many in Generation Z are stressed out. Whereas 30 percent do not think about problems much or feel anxious,[37] 64 percent feel stressed once a week or more.[38] Nearly 95 percent of Generation Z college seniors said that during the past year, they had occasionally or

> **A good life would be not stressing about every little detail of my life.**
> – Member of Generation Z

frequently felt overwhelmed by everything they had to get done.[39] Couple their youth stressors with worries of larger global issues, and it makes sense that teens are more stressed out than adults today.[40] And the stress levels of many in Generation Z are on the rise. Thirty-one percent say they have had an increase in stress over the last year, and 34 percent think that it will continue to increase.[41]

Given these high rates of stress, what might those in Generation Z be doing for stress relief? Many are likely not turning to drinking and drug use as we wouldn't have decreasing rates of substance use.[42,43] And, declines in exercise rates[44] also don't point to physical activity as a prominent stress reliever. A study by Sodexo of Generation Z college students, however, found that nearly a third would be interested in taking classes on mindfulness.[45]

High rates of anxiety and depression

Of all mental and emotional health issues facing this generation, anxiety appears to be one of the most prominent for both Generation Z youth and young adults. In 2015, 12 percent of boys and 18 percent of girls under the age of 17 had received mental health services for anxiety disorders.[46] And, more than one in five college students surveyed by the American College Health Association had been diagnosed or treated for anxiety,[47] an increase from around 4 percent in 2000.[48] This increase has greatly impacted college counseling centers across the U.S. In looking at data from

> **I think I worry the most about being in control. I deal with extreme anxiety issues when it comes to control and the fear of the unknown. When I do not feel that I have control of [the] future I find myself very anxious.**
> – Member of Generation Z

the 2015–2016 school year for 139 college counseling centers, of the 44 concerns that emerged among student clients, anxiety was the most prevalent.[49]

Depression is also a concern with Generation Z. In 2015, 12.5 percent of adolescents ages 12 to 17, which is around 3 million youth, had at least one "major depressive episode" in the last year.[50] This number has steadily increased, with the exception of a few slight rises and dips, since 2004 when the rate was 9 percent.[51] Depression appears to be more prominent with girls than with boys as 22 percent of girls treated for a mental health issue had a diagnosis of depression, more than twice the rate of depression with boys.[52] Depression is also prevalent among young adults. Nearly half of all college student clients are concerned with depression,[53] and, in 2017, nearly 17 percent were diagnosed,[54] up from 9 percent in 2000.[55] In addition, although not necessarily clinically diagnosed with depression, nearly two-thirds of Generation Z college seniors surveyed indicated occasionally or frequently feeling depressed during the last year.[56]

So, whether they are officially diagnosed with depression or feeling down, many in this generation seem to be struggling. And some are really struggling. Take, for example, LGBTQ youth. In addition to general teen stressors, issues like bullying, rejection from family and friends, isolation, and harassment are impacting their mental well-being, resulting in difficulty sleeping and high levels of stress.[57] It's not surprising then that 41 percent of LGBTQ youth indicated having received counseling or psychological services in the past 12 months to address struggles related to their identities.[58]

In addition to growing rates of anxiety and depression with members of Generation Z, there is also cause for grave concern around issues related to suicide. Rates have been on the rise for hospital medical professionals' diagnoses of suicidality/self-inflicted harm in young people[59] as well as actual teen and young adult suicides.[60]

Factors contributing to mental health

While there are empirical factors that contribute to stress, unhappiness, depression, anxiety, and other mental and emotional health issues that transcend generations, there are some nuances specific to Generation Z's upbringing that might also be affecting them.

Fear of missing out

One factor that may be impacting Generation Z's mental and emotional health is due to their constant connection. A study by Common Sense Media found that half of teens feel they are addicted to their cell phones and nearly three-quarters feel they need to respond immediately to texts, messages, and notifications.[61] The sheer amount of dependence on their devices and sense of urgency to connect and respond may be explained by FOMO or the "Fear of Missing Out."[62] Being disconnected from their phones for any length of time may be disconcerting and cause great anxiety for them, literally resulting in a feeling that they are missing something while offline.

Vicarious trauma

We are living in a time of a never-ending news cycle. There is no signing off on the radio at the end of each night or the playing of the national anthem on TV at midnight marking the day's end. The news is 24/7 on hundreds, if not thousands, of television, radio, print, and digital news outlets. Being able to consume information every minute of the day can make one hyper-aware of the world's problems, which can be overwhelming and lead to the feeling that many in Generation Z have of worrying about larger societal issues.[63]

In addition, being able to witness nearly any disaster, misfortune, tragedy, or scandal online, all of us are now prone to experiencing vicarious trauma,[64] a type of trauma often limited to counselors, first responders, and others in helping professions.[65] The ability for everyday people to see images, view recordings, and even tune in to live feeds of tragic events in progress can make those events feel more personal as people picture themselves or their loved ones in those situations.

Another factor related to vicarious trauma involves someone reading about or seeing images of misfortunes happening to their online "friends," making these tragedies feel much closer to home. A celebrity breakup shared over Instagram may trigger emotions in that person's followers, even though the followers have no relationship with the star. And while all of us are living in an era in which we can experience vicarious trauma, those of us in older generations didn't have to deal with it when we were Generation Z's age.

The personal fable

Although other generations likely felt the pressure to succeed weighing on them, those in Generation Z feel they have little room for failure because many of them watched as others lost jobs and homes during the Recession.[66] This intense stress for success and the ability to compare that success with others on social media may be just enough to cause distress with this young generation. In addition, they may struggle with the paradox of maintaining an external image online that may exaggerate success, happiness, and great fortune while coping behind the scenes with the realities of life. Jill Walsh, author of *Adolescents and Their Social Media Narratives: A Digital Coming of Age*, discusses the concept of impression management and the personal fable, which asserts that teens thoughtfully craft the image and content that represents their fable and post it online for all to see, comment on, like, and judge.[67] Not only might it be stressful to manage this external impression, but managing the judgment of it might also induce anxiety.

> *I worry about the way I present myself to others. I am constantly worried about other people's perceptions of me.*
>
> – Member of Generation Z

Digital reliving

Another factor that may be related to mental and emotional health issues with this generation is the notion of digital reliving. Because digital communication is often in written form (text, social media message, etc.) as opposed to oral form, it may be easier to relive a conflict over and over simply by re-reading printed content.[68] Oral communication can just vanish into thin air with no documentation to revisit, whereas having a rude text sit in an inbox or a conflict of words documented on social media could re-trigger the feelings originally associated with the incident.

Virtual support

Jean Twenge, in her book about this generation, discusses the correlation between increases in screen time and less in-person social interaction, which she says is associated with higher rates of unhappiness and depression.[69] While there may be a relationship between the two, it could also be that screen time is a proxy for underlying causes of mental health issues. And, while increased screen time might lead to depression, it might instead be that those who are depressed might use their devices more often to avoid loneliness or to seek help and support. For example, one study found that for teenagers who seek support through social media and feel they get that support, their depressed mood decreased; for those who didn't feel they got support after reaching out, their depressed mood increased.[70]

There can also be a heightened sense of rejection when using digital communication because receiving responses can be slow or intermittent.[71] If someone doesn't reply to a message right away, brains can fill with stories as to why they aren't responding.[72] A teen or young adult who was seeking support for an initial problem may then also become stressed out about why the person they reached out to is not responding.

Counseling and support services

For a generation steeped in rising mental and emotional health issues, having counseling and support services can be critical. But, in the early 2000s when many Generation Z youth were growing up, some school counselors were pulled away from counseling students[73] to instead administer standardized tests.[74] Thus, there may have been a gap in what youth needed and what was available, meaning that many older members of Generation Z may not have received adequate mental and emotional health support in their schools.

Many of these very same members of Generation Z have since come to college, likely accounting for the increase of mental and emotional health issues on college campuses.[75,76] Although fewer than 12 percent of first-year Generation Z college students indicated there was a good chance they would seek personal counseling,[77] nearly 35 percent of college seniors just 3 years later indicated occasionally or frequently having sought personal counseling.[78] According to the Center for Collegiate Mental Health 2015 annual report, utilization of counseling centers grew by 30 percent over the last 5 years while average institutional enrollment only grew by 5 percent.[79]

Not only have college counseling centers seen an increase in students seeking help, these students are having more serious issues than even just a few years prior.[80] But, policies like a limit on the number of sessions that students are allowed or associated fees can determine how a student's treatment comes to an end.[81] A student who may need ongoing appointments may find that they have maxed out their session allotment for the school year, leaving them without critical resources and support. So, if the policies permitted, rates of use might even be higher. But, some campuses are responding to the increase in need by increasing their rapid-access hours (walk-in, triage, on-call, and crisis, etc.),[82] and others are bringing counselors to the students in their residence halls, athletic facilities, or even Starbucks rather than having them go to the counseling center.[83] Ohio State University even implemented a S.M.A.R.T. Lab (Stress Management and Resiliency Training) that provides coaching, computer-mediated learning, and group activities to help students reduce stress and increase their resiliency.[84]

Conclusion

Those in Generation Z are dealing with traditional youth and young adult pressures. At the same time, many are also trying to manage the stress of carrying the world's problems on their shoulders and balancing their real and virtual lives. These young people have a lot going on. But, with support

❝ I always worry about everything all the time. I can't even be classified as human. I'm just a ball of anxiety. ❞
– Member of Generation Z

and resources, along with stress reduction techniques and mindfulness training, there may be some creative, innovative, and effective strategies for helping members of this generation manage their emotional and mental well-being.

Notes

1 U.S. Department of Health & Human Services. (n.d.). *What is mental health?* Retrieved from www.mentalhealth.gov/basics/what-is-mental-health/index.html, para. 1.
2 Substance Abuse and Mental Health Services Administration. (2016). *Key substance use and mental health indicators in the United States: Results from the 2015 national survey on drug use and health.* Retrieved from www.samhsa.gov/data/sites/default/files/NSDUH-FFR1-2015/NSDUH-FFR1-2015/NSDUH-FFR1-2015.pdf
3 Pennsylvania State University. (2016). *Center for Collegiate Mental Health 2016 annual report.* Retrieved from https://sites.psu.edu/ccmh/files/2017/01/2016-Annual-Report-FINAL_2016_01_09-1gc2hj6.pdf
4 Higher Education Research Institute. (2017). *College Senior Survey.* Data prepared by Higher Education Research Institute.

5 Ludden, J. (2015). *Kids' solo playtime unleashes "free-range" parenting debate.* Retrieved from www.npr.org/sections/health-shots/2015/02/18/384050825/kids-solo-playtime-unleashes-free-range-parenting-debate

6 Ipsos. (2017). *Perils of perception.* Retrieved from www.ipsos.com/ipsos-mori/en-uk/perils-perception-2017

7 Seemiller, C. & Grace, M. (2017). *Generation Z stories study.* Unpublished raw data.

8 Seemiller, C. & Grace, M. (2017).

9 Seemiller, C. & Grace, M. (2017).

10 Seemiller, C. & Grace, M. (2017).

11 Seemiller, C. & Grace, M. (2016). *Generation Z goes to college.* San Francisco: Jossey-Bass.

12 Sensis and Think Now Research. (2016). *We are Gen Z report.* Retrieved from www.wearegenzreport.com/

13 Seemiller, C. & Grace, M. (2017).

14 Curran, T. & Hill, A. P. (2017). Perfectionism is increasing over time: A meta-analysis of birth cohort differences from 1989 to 2016. *Psychological Bulletin.* Advance online publication. http://dx.doi.org/10.1037/bul0000138

15 Varkey Foundation. (2017). *Generation Z: Global Citizenship Survey.* Retrieved from www.varkeyfoundation.org/what-we-do/policy-research/generation-z-global-citizenship-survey/

16 American College Health Association. (2017). *National College Health Assessment II: Spring 2017 reference group executive summary.* Retrieved from www.acha-ncha.org/docs/NCHA-II_SPRING_2017_REFERENCE_GROUP_EXECUTIVE_SUMMARY.pdf

17 Seemiller, C. & Grace, M. (2017).

18 Harvard Men's Health Watch. (2008). *Optimism and your health.* Retrieved from www.health.harvard.edu/heart-health/optimism-and-your-health

19 Seemiller, C. & Grace, M. (2014). *Generation Z goes to college study.* Unpublished raw data.

20 Seemiller, C. & Grace, M. (2014).

21 Seemiller, C. & Grace, M. (2017).

22 Levine, A. & Dean, D. R. (2012). *Generation on a tightrope: A portrait of today's college student.* San Francisco: Wiley.

23 Stein, J. (2013). *Millennials: The me me me generation.* Retrieved from http://time.com/247/millennials-the-me-me-me-generation/

24 Allen, J. T. (2010). *How a different America responded to the Great Depression.* Retrieved from www.pewresearch.org/2010/12/14/how-a-different-america-responded-to-the-great-depression/

25 Vision Critical. (2016). *The everything guide to Generation Z.* Retrieved from www.visioncritical.com/wp-content/uploads/2016/10/GenZ_Final.pdf

26 Seemiller, C. & Grace, M. (2017).

27 Collage Group. (2016). *Quick chart: What Gen Z & Millennials really want in life.* Retrieved from www.collagegroup.com/2016/09/19/gen-z-millennials-values/

28 Seemiller, C. & Grace, M. (2017).

29 Collage Group. (2016).

30 Varkey Foundation. (2017).

31 Varkey Foundation. (2017).

32 Varkey Foundation. (2017).

33 Varkey Foundation. (2017).

34 Twenge, J. M. (2017). *iGen: Why today's super-connected kids are growing up less rebellious, more tolerant, less happy – and completely unprepared for adulthood – and what that means for the rest of us.* New York: Atria Books.

35 Varkey Foundation. (2017).
36 Mineo, L. (2017). *Good genes are nice, but joy is better.* Retrieved from https://news. harvard.edu/gazette/story/2017/04/over-nearly-80-years-harvard-study-has-been-showing-how-to-live-a-healthy-and-happy-life/
37 Varkey Foundation. (2017).
38 Sensis and Think Now Research. (2016).
39 Higher Education Research Institute. (2017).
40 American Psychological Association. (2014). *American Psychological Association survey shows teen stress rivals that of adults.* Retrieved from www.apa.org/news/press/releases/2014/02/teen-stress.aspx
41 American Psychological Association. (2014).
42 Substance Abuse and Mental Health Services Administration. (2016).
43 Centers for Disease Control and Prevention. (2016b). *Youth risk behavior surveillance: United States, 2015.* Retrieved from www.cdc.gov/mmwr/volumes/65/ss/pdfs/ss6506.pdf
44 Higher Education Research Institute. (2017).
45 Sodexo. (2017). *The Sodexo international university lifestyle survey.* Retrieved from www. sodexo.com/home/media/publications/studies-and-reports/international-university-lifesty.html
46 Department of Health and Human Services. (2015). *Mental health annual report 2015.* Retrieved from www.samhsa.gov/data/sites/default/files/2015_Mental_Health_Client_Level_Data_Report.pdf
47 American College Health Association. (2017).
48 American College Health Association. (2010). *National College Health Assessment: Reference group data report spring 2000.* Retrieved from www.acha-ncha.org/docs/ACHA-NCHA_Reference_Group_Report_Spring2000.pdf
49 Pennsylvania State University. (2016).
50 Substance Abuse and Mental Health Services Administration. (2016), p. 38.
51 Substance Abuse and Mental Health Services Administration. (2016).
52 Department of Health and Human Services. (2015).
53 Pennsylvania State University. (2016).
54 American College Health Association. (2017).
55 American College Health Association. (2010).
56 Higher Education Research Institute. (2017).
57 Human Rights Campaign. (2018). *LGBTQ youth report.* Retrieved from https://assets2. hrc.org/files/assets/resources/2018-YouthReport-NoVid.pdf
58 Human Rights Campaign. (2018).
59 American Academy of Pediatrics. (2017). *Children's hospitals admissions for suicidal thoughts, action double during past decade.* Retrieved from www.aappublications.org/news/2017/05/04/PASSuicide050417
60 Centers for Disease Control and Prevention. (2017). *Quick stats: Suicide rates for teens aged 15–19 years, by sex: United States, 1975–2015.* Retrieved from www.cdc.gov/mmwr/volumes/66/wr/mm6630a6.htm
61 Common Sense Media. (2016). *Dealing with devices: The parent-teen dynamic.* Retrieved from www.commonsensemedia.org/technology-addiction-concern-controversy-and-finding-balance-infographic
62 Sparks & Honey. (2014). *Meet Generation Z: Forget everything you learned about Millennials.* Retrieved from www.slideshare.net/sparksandhoney/generation-z-final-june-17
63 Seemiller, C. & Grace, M. (2017).

64 Ramsden, P. (2017). Vicarious trauma, PTSD and social media: Does watching graphic videos cause trauma? *Journal of Depression and Anxiety, 6*(3), Supplement. doi: 10.4172/2167-1044-C1-002

65 Goodtherapy.org. (n.d.). *Vicarious trauma.* Retrieved from www.goodtherapy.org/blog/psychpedia/vicarious-trauma

66 Seemiller, C. & Grace, M. (2017).

67 Walsh, J. (2017). *Adolescents and their social media narratives: A digital coming of age.* Abingdon, Oxon: Routledge.

68 Twenge, J. M. (2017).

69 Twenge, J. M. (2017).

70 Frison, E. & Eggermont, S. (2015). The impact of daily stress on adolescents' depressed mood: The role of social support seeking through Facebook. *Computers in Human Behavior, 44*, 315–325.

71 Twenge, J. M. (2017).

72 Twenge, J. M. (2017).

73 Schrobsdorff, S. (2016). The kids are not all right. *Time Magazine, 188*(19), 44–51.

74 Schrobsdorff, S. (2016).

75 Rivera, C. (2015). *What colleges are doing to address students' unprecedented levels of stress.* Retrieved from www.latimes.com/local/education/la-me-higher-learning-college-20150930-story.html

76 Clay, R. A. (2013). Mental health issues in college on the rise. *Monitor on Psychology, 44*(11), 54.

77 Eagan, K., Stolzenberg, E. B., Ramirez, J. J., Aragon, M. C., Suchard, M. R., & Hurtado, S. (2014). *The American freshman: National norms fall 2014.* Los Angeles: Higher Education Research Institute, UCLA.

78 Higher Education Research Institute. (2017).

79 Pennsylvania State University. (2016).

80 Twenge, J. M. (2017).

81 Pennsylvania State University. (2016).

82 Pennsylvania State University. (2016).

83 Korn, M. (2017). *College counselors go where the students are: Dorms and Starbucks.* Retrieved from www.wsj.com/articles/college-counselors-go-where-the-students-aredorms-and-starbucks-1499631617?mod=flipboard

84 Granello, P. (2016). *Welcome to the S.M.A.R.T. Lab.* Retrieved from https://u.osu.edu/smartlab/2016/08/29/welcome-to-the-s-m-a-r-t-lab/

13 Risky behaviors

Thinking back to nearly every teen movie over the last 50 years, it seems as though simply being a teenager means engaging in risky behavior. Scenes of drugs, smoking, drinking, and sexual promiscuity seem to take center stage. Even Sandra Dee from Grease had to have a makeover by the Pink Ladies to adopt the edginess it would take to win over Danny.[1] But, do today's Generation Z teens and young adults engage in these same kinds of risky behaviors? According to a number of research studies, for the most part, the answer is "no."

According to psychology professor, Jean Twenge, youth today are less risky than the youth of the past.[2] For example, only 3 percent of teens disagree or strongly disagree that they follow the rules at their school.[3] Their rule-following nature has likely contributed to the decline in a number of risky behaviors commonly associated with teens and young adults. For example, both weapon possession on high school campuses and juvenile crime rates have declined in the last two decades. Between 1993 and 2015, the rate of high schoolers bringing a weapon to school has linearly decreased from nearly 12 percent to just above 4 percent.[4] And, in 2015, juvenile crime rates had decreased 68 percent since 1996.[5] Taking a look at a number of traditionally risky behaviors, research points to decreases in nearly all for those in Generation Z.

❝ We are constantly told that we are greedy, selfish, lazy, and generally made out to be horrible and demonized, despite being one of the best generations to date based on statistics like college attendance, drug use, and teen pregnancy. ❞
– Member of Generation Z

Smoking

Between the invention of cigarette manufacturing machines in the late 1800s and the 1913 nationwide advertising campaign by Camel cigarettes, smoking rates dramatically increased in the early part of the twentieth century.[6] By the time many of those in the G.I. Generation were heading off to World War II, free distribution of cigarettes to troops was commonplace and ultimately led to the high prevalence of smoking with that generation.[7] As soldiers were receiving their free rations of cigarettes, women who stayed home during the war were encouraged to smoke as a way to avoid eating sweets.[8] But, by the mid-twentieth century, the scientific community was linking smoking to increased disease risks.[9] Between scientific evidence and anti-smoking efforts, rates of smoking appeared to decrease through the early 1990s, with periodic small increases and decreases at points during the 1960s and 1970s.[10]

While those in the G.I. Generation started smoking before risks were well-known, Generation Z is making choices about smoking after extensive research has shown smoking's detrimental health effects. In 1991, nearly 13 percent of high schoolers (Generation X) smoked, whereas, by 2015 (Generation Z), that number was just above 4 percent.[11] In looking specifically at twelfth graders over the last decade, smoking rates fell from 21.6 percent in 2007 to 10.5 percent in 2016.[12] The decrease in smoking rates can be attributed to the increased financial cost of smoking, the prevalence of anti-smoking ads and campaigns, and the removal of flavoring added to cigarettes.[13]

Smoking alternatives: E-cigarettes, vaping, and hookah

While smoking traditional cigarettes might not be all the rage with youth, it appears that e-cigarette use just might be. According to findings from the National Youth Tobacco Survey, more than 250 million youth in grades 6 to 12 in 2013 had never smoked a cigarette but had tried e-cigarettes.[14] While many who had tried e-cigarettes might not be regular users, clearly there was a draw to e-cigarettes over regular cigarettes. Perhaps it is the added flavoring or the lack of second-hand smoke that might make e-cigarettes more alluring. With the shortage of information about associated risks, it isn't surprising that teens think e-cigarettes just aren't as harmful. Only 19 percent of teenagers surveyed in 2015 believed there is a great risk in using e-cigarettes, whereas 73 percent of that same group believed the same to be true of smoking one pack of regular cigarettes a day.[15]

It isn't just e-cigarettes that those in Generation Z are experimenting with; vaping, in general, appears to be a growing trend. Vaping is "the act of inhaling and exhaling the aerosol, often referred to as vapor, which is produced by an e-cigarette or similar device."[16] A 2015 report by the Centers for Disease Control and Prevention indicated that nearly 45 percent of high school students had tried some form of vaping.[17] Because this is a new phenomenon, there is no consistent past data to make generational comparisons. However, a recent study from the University of Michigan found a significant decrease in vaping and hookah use, specifically, with 12th graders between 2015 and 2016.[18] Perhaps as more information becomes available on the effects of vaping, this number will continue to decrease.

Drugs

Being rule followers, the views of those in Generation Z on marijuana use are interesting. First, the number of Generation Z twelfth graders in 2015 who believed marijuana should be legal was nearly twice that of twelfth graders in the 1980s.[19] This may stem from declining rates of disapproval, falling from 83.3 percent in 2007 to 68.5 percent in 2016.[20] This decline isn't consistent with rates of disapproval for other types of drugs like cocaine and heroin, as their disapproval rates have stayed relatively constant over time.[21] The lack of disapproval of marijuana by some in Generation Z may stem from the fact that a majority of them do not see marijuana as unsafe,[22] and the number of them who believe it is a "great risk" has fallen steadily since around 2006.[23] When looking more closely, these decreases align with the legalization of marijuana that has occurred in various states over the last decade. For example, in Washington, tenth graders' belief in the harmfulness of marijuana declined 16 percent between the years just preceding legalization and the years following.[24] Perhaps the legalization of marijuana is signaling to youth that it isn't as harmful as it was once made out to be.

Generation Z's more lax opinion on the legality and risk of marijuana use hasn't necessarily translated consistently to an increased use for themselves. Research from the Youth Risk Behavior Surveillance report in 2015 indicates a decrease in the rates of those who have tried marijuana from just more than 47 percent in 1997 to just less than 39 percent in 2015.[25] And, interestingly, the legalization of marijuana has had mixed effects on teen use. Findings from the Colorado Department of Public Health found marijuana use among high school students had slightly decreased, from 22 percent prior to legalization to 21.2 percent after.[26] However, use of marijuana increased after legalization among both eighth and tenth graders in the state of Washington.[27]

> *I have a personal hatred of drugs and it contributed to ending my most serious relationship.*
> – Member of Generation Z

Other drug use rates have also significantly decreased over time for this generation.[28] From 1999 to 2015, the number of high school students who had ever used cocaine dropped from just above 9 percent down to slightly more than 5 percent, and those who had ever used methamphetamines dropped from around 9 percent to 3 percent.[29] In addition, rates of those who had ever used ecstasy decreased from just around 11 percent in 2001 to 5 percent in 2015.[30] Even rates of unauthorized use of prescription drugs have also been on the decline with Generation Z. In 2009, more than 20 percent of high school–aged Millennials had taken a prescription drug without a prescription.[31] By 2015, that number had decreased to just less than 17 percent for Generation Z high schoolers.[32]

Booze and binging

Throughout history, our society has been entrenched in regulating alcohol use and abuse through efforts such as Prohibition, changes in the legal drinking age, advocacy from organizations like Mothers Against Drunk Driving, and campaigns to reduce underage drinking, binge drinking, and driving while intoxicated. While laws, norms, and policies may have changed over time, underage drinking still occurs.

But, underage drinking for Generation Z doesn't seem to be as prominent as it may have been for those in other generations. For example, rates of 12 to 20 year-olds who reported having consumed alcohol within the past month went from nearly 29 percent in 2002 to just more than 20 percent in 2015.[33] While the decline is promising in terms of reducing underage consumption, it is still important to note that more than 20 percent of 12- to 20-year-old Generation Z youth still indicated consuming alcohol. And just about 48 percent who did drink within the last month engaged in binge drinking, which is five or more drinks in one sitting for males and four or more for females.[34]

When looking specifically at high school student drinking rates, they appear to be on the decline. From 1991 to 2015, the percentage of students who had ever drunk alcohol decreased from nearly 82 percent to just more than 63 percent.[35] The study also found a drop in the rates of current alcohol use and binge drinking.[36] Perhaps that is because there has been an increase with this age group in the disapproval of binge drinking.[37]

While more than 20 percent of underage Generation Z 12 to 20 year-olds currently drink alcohol, that statistic doesn't necessarily skyrocket for Generation Z college seniors who are of legal drinking age. Based on findings from the 2017 College Senior Survey, only slightly more than 31 percent indicated frequently (as opposed to not at all or occasionally) drinking beer and 36 percent drinking wine or liquor at some point during the last year.[38] Further, more than one-quarter of all Generation Z college seniors in the study had not consumed beer at all in the last year, and nearly 14 percent hadn't consumed wine or liquor in that same time period.[39] So, while these Generation Z college seniors may be legally allowed to drink, many are choosing not to.

Sexual activity

By the time G.I. Generation soldiers were headed to World War II, messages about refraining from illicit sex for both personal and patriotic purposes were prominent.[40] While young men might have been restricted from sexual behavior, many women in the U.S. were not engaging in abstinence. A 1939 study of college women found that 69 percent of those born after 1913 (G.I. Generation) indicated having engaged in pre-marital sex, whereas only 26 percent of those born before 1913 reported doing so.[41] By the 1950s, teens and young adults were necking, petting, and parking . . . but more so going steady and taking it slow. For example, for those who turned 15 between 1953 and 1964, only 48 percent had engaged in pre-marital sex by the time they were 20.[42] But, the 1960s and 70s ushered in the sexual revolution marked by a liberalization of both sexual attitudes and behaviors.[43] By the 1980s, though, the AIDS epidemic offered a frightening reality to having sex.[44] The 1990s and 2000s emerged as a period of "friends with benefits," where young adults engaged in sexual activity with trusted friends without the intention of a romantic relationship.[45]

The sexual behavior of those in Generation Z seems to be a mix. On the one hand, it may seem like "Netflix and Chill" is all the rage as the term is used as an innuendo for having casual sex, as discussed earlier in the book.[46] Incidentally, sexual activity with Generation Z is not as widespread as it was with older generations when they were younger. Beginning as early as 1991 (with Gen Xers) and ending in 2015 (with those in Generation Z), the rate of sexual activity declined for teens in grades 9 to 12.[47] In 1991, just more than 54 percent of high school students reported having ever had sexual intercourse.[48] That number continued to decrease over the next 14 years to just more than 41 percent in 2015.[49] During this same time span, the percentage of high schools teens who indicated having had sex with four or more partners or who were sexually active also significantly decreased.[50] So, while they may "Netflix and Chill," many of them are choosing to do so with limited sexual activity and fewer partners.

Pregnancy, protection, and contraception

While more Generation Z teens and young adults may be refraining from engaging in sexual activity, only some of those who are having sex are using protection. A 2015 study found that nearly 57 percent of sexually active high school students use condoms, which is down from the 63 percent of Millennials in 2003 who reported using condoms.[51] Perhaps these teens are using other forms of birth control, like the pill? But, that doesn't seem to be the answer either as rates of birth control pill use have stayed fairly consistent from 2003 to 2015, fluctuating between 17.4 and 18.2 percent.[52] Laura Kann, an expert from the CDC who specializes in youth risk behaviors, sheds some light on why more teens today may be having unprotected sex. First, she notes that because many young people today see AIDS as a chronic disease rather than a terrible death sentence as was the case not too long ago, they don't feel as compelled to protect themselves from it.[53] Second, Kann adds that some schools are doing less to teach teens about safe sex because school officials have had to focus on other competing health issues like bullying and the epidemic of obesity.[54] In addition, in a study of teens, specifically, researchers found a significant number who say the reason they don't use protection or birth control is that they don't want their parents to find out.[55]

Even with higher rates of unprotected sex, rates of teen pregnancy are declining. A study by the Guttmacher Institute found that teen pregnancy rates in 2013 were at the lowest in 80 years.[56] Aside from a few instances of minor increases and decreases since 1957, teen birthrates have consistently declined all the way through Generation Z's adolescent years,[57] and in 2013, abortion rates among teens were the lowest since abortion was legalized.[58]

These changes in sexual behavior are not happening inadvertently. One study found that increased access to broadband Internet can explain 7 percent of the decrease in the teen birth rate.[59] Those in Generation Z with the Internet have greater access to information about making healthy choices about sexual activity, whether searching online or connecting with peers through social media.[60] In addition, being online reduces the time teens participate in face-to-face interactions thus reducing the opportunities to engage in sexual activity.[61]

Sexual violence and consent

Aside from unprotected sex, sexual violence presents another danger for these teens and young adults when it comes to sexual activity. While non-consensual sexual misconduct is still a major issue today, there has been a decrease in the rate of reported sexual violence against 12 to 17 year-old females, in particular, since 1994.[62] This rate decrease may be attributed to the emergence of intentional educational initiatives such as Take Back the Night marches, which launched in the U.S. in the 1970s, and Sexual Assault Awareness Month in the early 1990s. In addition, the National Sexual Violence Resource Center, which started in 2000, offers many resources aimed to prevent and address issues of sexual violence. Despite any decreases in the rates of reporting for women, sexual assault is still a very concerning issue – not just for young heterosexual women but for those in the LGBTQ community as well. A study by the Human Rights Campaign found that 11 percent of 13 to 17 year-old LGBTQ youth have been "sexually attacked or raped because of their actual or assumed LGBTQ identity."[63]

Although there are resources, prevention initiatives, and programs offered to curb sexual violence, there are still many in Generation Z whose perceptions of consent do not align with what constitutes affirmative consent. For example, 11 percent of Generation Z college seniors surveyed in 2017 disagreed or strongly disagreed that "sexual activity that occurs without the presence of explicit, affirmative consent (i.e., yes means yes) is considered sexual assault."[64] The recent addition of this measurement does not allow for a comparison of responses with older generations. However, 11 percent still appears to be a high number despite programs, resources, and campaigns such as It's On Us[65] designed to educate young people on the concept of consent.

Since our spring 2017 survey was conducted, however, the #MeToo Movement emerged, launching a larger discussion about sexual harassment, assault, and misconduct. Individuals have come forward even decades after incidents to share their stories, resulting in a public outcry and ousting of celebrities, politicians, and business people who engaged in sexual misconduct. Perhaps with a far greater and pressing focus on what constitutes sexual misconduct and consent, those in Generation Z who don't agree that "yes" is required for consensual sex will think differently.

Conclusion

While there is still evidence of underage drinking, drug use, smoking, vaping, and unprotected sex with this generation, the rates of many of these behaviors continue to be on the decline. And, with so many of them having negative views of a lot of these behaviors, we can hope that those opinions translate to responsible and safe choices for themselves as well as impact their peers' decision-making for the better.

Notes

1   IMDB. (n.d.c). *Grease*. Retrieved from www.imdb.com/title/tt0077631/
2   Twenge, J. M. (2017). *iGen: Why today's super-connected kids are growing up less rebellious, more tolerant, less happy – and completely unprepared for adulthood – and what that means for the rest of us.* New York: Atria Books.
3   Geraci, J., Paulmerini, M., Cirillo, P., & McDougald, V. (2017). *What teens want from their schools: A national survey of high school student engagement.* Retrieved from https://edexcellence.net/publications/what-teens-want-from-their-schools
4   Centers for Disease Control and Prevention. (2016b). *Youth risk behavior surveillance: United States, 2015.* Retrieved from www.cdc.gov/mmwr/volumes/65/ss/pdfs/ss6506.pdf
5   U.S. Department of Justice. (2015). *Juvenile arrest rate trends.* Retrieved from www.ojjdp.gov/ojstatbb/crime/JAR_Display.asp?ID=qa05200
6   Burns, D. M., Lee, L., Shen, L. Z., Gilpin, E., Tolley, H. D., Vaughn, J., & Shanks, T. G. (1997). Cigarette smoking behavior in the United States. In D. R. Shopland, D. M. Burns, L. Garfinkel, & J. M. Samet (Eds.), *Monograph 8: Changes in cigarette-related disease risks and their implications for prevention and control* (pp. 13–112). Bethesda, MD: National Cancer Institute.
7   Burns, D. M., Lee, L., Shen, L. Z., Gilpin, E., Tolley, H. D., Vaughn, J., & Shanks, T. G. (1997).
8   Burns, D. M., Lee, L., Shen, L. Z., Gilpin, E., Tolley, H. D., Vaughn, J., & Shanks, T. G. (1997).
9   Burns, D. M., Lee, L., Shen, L. Z., Gilpin, E., Tolley, H. D., Vaughn, J., & Shanks, T. G. (1997).
10 Burns, D. M., Lee, L., Shen, L. Z., Gilpin, E., Tolley, H. D., Vaughn, J., & Shanks, T. G. (1997).
11 Centers for Disease Control and Prevention. (2016b).
12 Miech, R. A., Johnston, L. D., O'Malley, P. M., Bachman, J. G., Schulenberg, J. E., & Patrick, M. E. (2017). *Monitoring the Future national survey results on drug use, 1975–2016: Volume I, secondary school students.* Ann Arbor: Institute for Social Research, The University of Michigan.
13 Miech, R. A., Johnston, L. D., O'Malley, P. M., Bachman, J. G., Schulenberg, J. E., & Patrick, M. E. (2017).

14 Bunnell, R. E., Agaku, I. T., Arrazola, R. A., Apelberg, B. J., Caraballo, R. S., Corey, C. G. . . . King, B. A. (2015). Intentions to smoke cigarettes among never-smoking US middle and high school electronic cigarette users: National Youth Tobacco Survey, 2011–2013. *Nicotine & Tobacco Research, 17*(2), 228–235.

15 Miech, R. A., Johnston, L. D., O'Malley, P. M., Bachman, J. G., Schulenberg, J. E., & Patrick, M. E. (2017).

16 The National Center on Addiction and Substance Abuse. (2016). *What is vaping?* Retrieved from www.centeronaddiction.org/e-cigarettes/recreational-vaping/what-vaping

17 Centers for Disease Control and Prevention. (2016b).

18 Miech, R. A., Johnston, L. D., O'Malley, P. M., Bachman, J. G., Schulenberg, J. E., & Patrick, M. E. (2017).

19 Twenge, J. M. (2017).

20 Miech, R. A., Johnston, L. D., O'Malley, P. M., Bachman, J. G., Schulenberg, J. E., & Patrick, M. E. (2017).

21 Miech, R. A., Johnston, L. D., O'Malley, P. M., Bachman, J. G., Schulenberg, J. E., & Patrick, M. E. (2017).

22 Twenge, J. M. (2017).

23 Miech, R. A., Johnston, L. D., O'Malley, P. M., Bachman, J. G., Schulenberg, J. E., & Patrick, M. E. (2017).

24 Seaman, A. (2016). *Teens view on marijuana change after legalization.* Retrieved from www.scientificamerican.com/article/teens-views-on-marijuana-change-after-legalization/

25 Centers for Disease Control and Prevention. (2016b).

26 Reuters. (n.d.). *Colorado teen marijuana usage dips after legalization.* Retrieved from www.scientificamerican.com/article/colorado-s-teen-marijuana-usage-dips-after-legalization/

27 Seaman, A. (2016).

28 Centers for Disease Control and Prevention. (2016b).

29 Centers for Disease Control and Prevention. (2016b).

30 Centers for Disease Control and Prevention. (2016b).

31 Centers for Disease Control and Prevention. (2016b).

32 Centers for Disease Control and Prevention. (2016b).

33 Substance Abuse and Mental Health Services Administration. (2016). *Key substance use and mental health indicators in the United States: Results from the 2015 national survey on drug use and health.* Retrieved from www.samhsa.gov/data/sites/default/files/NSDUH-FFR1-2015/NSDUH-FFR1-2015/NSDUH-FFR1-2015.pdf

34 Substance Abuse and Mental Health Services Administration. (2016).

35 Centers for Disease Control and Prevention. (2016b).

36 Centers for Disease Control and Prevention. (2016b).

37 Miech, R. A., Johnston, L. D., O'Malley, P. M., Bachman, J. G., Schulenberg, J. E., & Patrick, M. E. (2017).

38 Higher Education Research Institute. (2017). *College Senior Survey.* Data prepared by Higher Education Research Institute.

39 Higher Education Research Institute. (2017).

40 Huber, V. (2009). A historical analysis of public school sex education in America since 1900. *Master of Education Research Theses, 21.* Retrieved from http://digitalcommons.cedarville.edu/education_theses/21

41 Huber, V. (2009).

42 Finer, L. B. (2007). *Trends in premarital sex in the United States, 1954–2003.* Retrieved from www.ncbi.nlm.nih.gov/pmc/articles/PMC1802108/

43 Robinson, I., Zess, K., Ganza, B., Katz, S., & Robinson, E. (1991). Twenty years of the sexual revolution, 1965–1985: An update. *Journal of Marriage and the Family, 53,* 216–220.

44 Huber, V. (2009).

45 Rawlins, W. K. (2009). *The compass of friendship: Narratives, identities, and dialogues.* Thousand Oaks, CA: Sage Publications.

46 Rickett, O. (2015). How *"Netflix and chill" became code for casual sex.* Retrieved from www.theguardian.com/media/shortcuts/2015/sep/29/how-netflix-and-chill-became-code-for-casual-sex

47 Centers for Disease Control and Prevention. (2016b).

48 Centers for Disease Control and Prevention. (2016b).

49 Centers for Disease Control and Prevention. (2016b).

50 Centers for Disease Control and Prevention. (2016b).

51 Centers for Disease Control and Prevention. (2016b).

52 Centers for Disease Control and Prevention. (2016b).

53 Steinmetz, K. (2013). *(No) condom culture: Why teens aren't practicing safe sex.* Retrieved from http://healthland.time.com/2013/11/12/no-condom-culture-why-teens-arent-practicing-safe-sex/

54 Steinmetz, K. (2013).

55 Power to Decide (formerly the National Campaign to Prevent Teen and Unplanned Pregnancy). (2015). *Survey says: Hide the birth control.* Washington, DC: Author.

56 Kost, K., Maddow-Zimet, I., & Arpai, A. (2013). *Pregnancies, births and abortions among adolescents and young women in the United States, 2013: National and state trends by age, race, and ethnicity.* Retrieved from www.guttmacher.org/report/us-adolescent-pregnancy-trends-2013

57 Ventura, S. J., Hamilton, B. E., & Mathews, T. J. (2014). *National and state patterns of teen births in the United States, 1940–2013.* Retrieved from www.cdc.gov/nchs/data/nvsr/nvsr63/nvsr63_04.pdf

58 Kost, K., Maddow-Zimet, I., & Arpai, A. (2013).

59 Guldi, M. & Herbst, C. M. (2016). Offline effects of online connecting: The impact of broadband diffusion on teen fertility decisions. *Journal of Population Economics, 30*(1), 169–191.

60 Guldi, M. & Herbst, C. M. (2016).

61 Guldi, M. & Herbst, C. M. (2016).

62 Planty, M., Langton, L., Krebs, C., Berzofsky, M., & Smiley-MacDonald, H. (2013). *Female victims of sexual violence, 1994–2010.* Retrieved from www.bjs.gov/content/pub/pdf/fvsv9410.pdf

63 Human Rights Campaign. (2018). *LGBTQ youth report.* Retrieved from https://assets2.hrc.org/files/assets/resources/2018-YouthReport-NoVid.pdf, p. 7.

64 Higher Education Research Institute. (2017).

65 It's on Us. (n.d.). Retrieved from www.itsonus.org/

14 Religion and spirituality

Over the last century, modernization has influenced changes to the policies and practices of specific religions. Thinking back to the 1920s and 1930s when members of the G.I. Generation were youth, most families got dressed up and spent their Sundays at church.[1] While that still happens today, some contemporary churches now have rock bands and coffee bars, which are likely not out of the playbook of the early twentieth century.

Other religions also look different today than 100 years ago. Jewish associations and facilities of the early twentieth century that helped acculturate Jewish immigrants to the U.S. have since become today's Jewish Community Centers with amenities such as sports leagues, childcare, workout facilities, and educational programs.[2,3] Muslims today are grappling with the interpretation of Islam, whether that it should be strict or more loosely based on a modern-day context.[4] And the Church of Latter-day Saints has made policy changes regarding women's participation by both lowering the minimum age for women to serve as missionaries as well as participate in more leadership opportunities.[5]

Modernization of religion isn't just about how a religion has changed over time but also about how it has influenced modern society. For example, yoga, a practice derived from the Hindu religion for spiritual means[6] is now a common workout that can be streamed online. And the lexicon of Buddhism is integrated into mainstream America today with "Zen and the art of . . .,"[7] and references to the religious and philosophical notions of "karma"[8] as a casual way for non-Buddhists to say "what goes around, comes around."

Religion and spirituality in America today, in many ways, is quite different than it was 100 years ago. How have these changing dynamics over the past century impacted Generation Z's religious identities, beliefs, and practices as they enter into young adulthood?

The religious

In 1937, Gallup began surveying people about their membership in a church, synagogue, or mosque.[9] That year, 73 percent identified as being a member.[10] By the 1980s, the rate was in the upper 60 percent range, decreasing to 54 percent in 2015, the lowest point in the years the data was collected.[11] These findings align with those from the Pew Research Center, which found that religious services attendance has decreased with each generational cohort.[12] While religiosity in the U.S. appears to be decreasing, America is still a highly religious nation. Robert Putnam and David Campbell, authors of *American Grace*, note that, "Any discussion of religion in America must begin with the incontrovertible fact that Americans are a highly religious people. One can quibble over just how religion, and religiosity, should be gauged, but, by any standard, the United States (as a whole) is a religious nation."[13]

So, is Generation Z more or less religious than previous generations? In 2015, religious attendance rates for first-year college students were at 69.5 percent for this generation.[14] While this might seem higher than the 54 percent of the general population from the Gallup poll, the Generation Z number is actually lower when comparing young adults throughout the last three generations. To delve deeper, we looked at comparative data from the CIRP Freshman Survey[15] for specific time periods, each being 20 years after the first birth year of the generational cohort. We did this to ensure that the vast majority of first-year college students surveyed that year belonged to the generational cohort born 20 years earlier. Below outlines the birth and data collection years for each of the past three generational cohorts.

- Generation X – first born in 1965; 1985 data used
- Millennial – first born in 1981; 2001 data used
- Generation Z – first born in 1995; 2015 data used

Based on the data, the number of first-year college students who frequently or occasionally attended religious services in the past year has declined with each recent successive generation.[16]

While it appears that there is still a fairly high rate of religious services attendance with first-year college students, in looking at college seniors, the data tell a different story. In spring 2017, religious services attendance was at 59.1 percent for college seniors.[17] But, in tracing that cohort back 4 years to 2014 when they were first-year students, religious services participation was at 72.7 percent.[18] Although the first-year student study and the senior study were different, albeit, from the same research agency, it appears that there could be a decline in religious service participation over the course of a Generation Z student's college career.

Table 14.1 Religious Attendance of First-Year College Students[19]

	1985 (Generation X)	2001 (Millennial)	2015 (Generation Z)
Religious Services Attendance	86.5%	83.1%	69.5%

Christianity

In looking at Generation Z's identification with Christianity, it is important to understand a bit of the historical context of this religion in the U.S. over the last hundred years. Dr. James Emery White, author of *Meet Generation Z: Understanding and Reaching the Post-Christian World*, asserts that Christianity today is a result of shifting mindsets over the last century.[20] During the 1920s, as older members of the G.I. Generation were coming of age, the fights between the conservative fundamentalists (evangelicals) and liberal modernists (mainline Protestants),[21] "were often highly pitched battles," where both groups vehemently disagreed publicly over social policy.[22] This sharpening divide helped give rise to evangelicals who wanted more influence in shaping American culture, values, and laws,[23] leading to what is known today as the Religious Right.

❝ *If religion and The Bible are all that the opposing side has to offer as their argument, then America has failed in keeping the separation of Church and State.* ❞

– Member of Generation Z

Since the 1970s, in particular, evangelicals from the Religious Right have been a significant force in influencing public policy, political elections, and mainstream culture around a number of social issues.[24] Some even partially credit the election of Carter in 1976 to evangelical support, so much so that Gallup named 1976 "the year of the evangelical."[25]

Although there is still a division between evangelicals and mainline Protestants today, identification with either group appears to be lower for younger-aged cohorts. In the 2015 Pew Religious Landscape Study, researchers surveyed more than 35,000 individuals in the U.S. While more than half of those 65 years and older identified with either mainline Protestant or evangelical, the percentage of identification decreased for each subsequent younger demographic.[26]

Not only do rates of those identifying as evangelical or mainline Protestant decrease with younger age groups, according to the Center for the Study of Global Christianity, Christian identification in general among those in the U.S. is on the decline. In 1970, nearly 91 percent of the population in the U.S. was Christian, but by 2010, that number shrank to just around 80 percent. Research from the Center predicts that number to be around 78 percent by 2020.[27]

Table 14.2 Mainline Protestant and Evangelical Identification by Age[28]

	18–29 years-old	30–49 years-old	50–64 years-old	65+ years-old
Mainline Protestant	10%	13%	16%	22%
Evangelical	20%	25%	28%	29%

Table 14.3 Christian Identification Among First-Year College Student Generational Cohorts[29]

	1985 (Generation X)	2001 (Millennial)	2015 (Generation Z)
Specific Christian Denominations	75.6%	61.8%	43.1%
Other Christian	5.7%	11.2%	20.5%
Total Christian	81.3%	73%	63.6%

Perhaps the heated polarization of religion and politics that continues today may not be a draw to Christianity, especially for younger people. Instead, many of those in Generation Z appear to want to situate themselves somewhere in the middle or not participate in Christianity at all. Findings from the CIRP Freshman Survey indicate that there has been an increase in the identification with Other Christian and a decrease in denominational affiliation for each of the last three generational cohorts when they were first-year college students. And, while some who identify with a particular denomination may simply be selecting Other Christian instead, this doesn't account for the decrease in the total number who identify as Christian in general.[30]

Catholicism

Over the last century, Catholicism went from providing a church for specific immigrant groups to a unified place of worship across ethnic lines.[31] The Catholic Church was able to find ways to unite various parishes separated by ethnic identity to focus on services and resources to benefit all Catholics.[32]

Today, Catholics makeup more than 20 percent of the U.S. population.[33] Although this is a large number overall, it is more than 3 percent lower than in 2007.[34] Similarly, the percentage of first-year college students identifying as Catholic has decreased over the last three generations. In 1985 when Generation X made up the majority of the college student population, 34.5 percent of first-year students identified as Catholic.[35] By 2001 when Millennials were on campus, that rate decreased to 30.3 percent, followed by an even larger decrease in 2015 to 24.3 percent among Generation Z college students.[36] This decline in the number of Catholic youth is consistent with research findings from the Pew Research Center in that the median age for someone who is Catholic in the U.S. is 49, which has risen since 2007 when it was 45.[37] Catholicism appears to reflect an aging and declining population in the U.S.

One reason for the decline in Catholicism by young people may have to do with the growth of interfaith households. A study by the Public Religion Research Institute (PRRI) found that twice as many of those raised in a household where only one parent is Catholic ended up being religiously unaffiliated compared to those with two Catholic parents.[38] And, given that the highest rates of interfaith marriages are with the parents of Generation Z,[39] it makes sense then that there could be a decrease in youth Catholic identification. Further, research by PRRI found that 39 percent of Catholics noted that a primary reason they left the church was due to the treatment of gays and lesbians.[40] This number was considerably higher than those reported by members of other religious groups. Perhaps younger, more progressive members don't want to belong to an institution that doesn't support the LGBTQ community.

The Church of Jesus Christ of Latter-day Saints

The Church of Jesus Christ of Latter-day Saints, more informally referred to as Mormon or LDS, dates back to the 1800s in the U.S. Yet, the first half of the twentieth century saw more than a tripling in the growth of members.[41] Today, Mormons comprise 1.6 percent of the U.S. population.[42] But, a higher number of younger people identify as Mormon. Two percent of 18 to 49 year-olds identify as Mormon, whereas only 1 percent of those 50 and older identify as Mormon.[43] In looking more precisely by generation, 1.5 percent of first-year college students in 2001 (Millennial) identified as Mormon.[44] However, by 2015 (Generation Z), that number dropped to 0.3 percent, a rate similar to the 0.2 percent in 1985 when first-year college students were predominantly Generation X.[45] As Generation X is the primary parental generation of Generation Z, it makes sense that their kids might have similar rates of religious identification.

That's how I understand, visually . . . I'm able to pay attention and understand it more, and maybe watch it again if I need to.[47]

- 16 year-old member of The Church of Jesus Christ of Latter-day Saints

But, to appeal more to youth in this generation, in 2013, the LDS church instituted a new youth curriculum, *Come Follow Me*, incorporating videos, online lessons, music, and even apps.[46] A 16-year-old member noted in an interview that the new curriculum was helping her grasp the material.

But, a change in the curriculum may not be enough. A study by Jana Reiss, religious researcher and author, found that some younger people are leaving the Mormon Church because they disagree with the church's stance on LGBTQ and women's issues and do not trust their leaders to be honest in their sharing of issues that may be controversial.[48]

Other world religions

The prominent religious affiliation in the U.S. centers on Christianity, yet nearly 6 percent of Americans actually identify with other world religions.[49] When looking at identification rates by age during the same time period (2015), there appears to be only a slight variation in participation in either direction.[50]

Table 14.4 Religious Identification by Age[51]

	18–29 years-old	30–49 years-old	50–64 years-old	65+ years-old
Muslim	2%	1%	< 1%	< 1%
Buddhist	1%	1%	1%	1%
Jewish	2%	1%	2%	3%
Hindu	1%	1%	< 1%	< 1%

Overall, these numbers may appear low when looking at the entire U.S. population. But, these religions have high rates of young members – 42 percent of Muslims, 36 percent of Hindus, and 35 percent of Buddhists are under 30 years-old.[52] These figures are considerably higher than the 14 percent of young people who make up mainline Protestant or the 11 percent who comprise evangelical Christians.[53]

While they might make up a larger share of their religious groups today, the number of youth who identify with these religions has varied over the last three generations. Data from the CIRP Freshman Survey show that some groups appear to have grown, some stayed steady, and some declined.[54]

Table 14.5 Religious Identification Among First-Year College Student Generational Cohorts[55]

	1985 (Generation X)	2001 (Millennial)	2015 (Generation Z)
Muslim	.2%	.9%	1.6%
Buddhist	.4%	1.1%	1.2%
Jewish	3.6%	2.6%	2.7%

Islam

Between 1878 and 1924, an influx of Muslim immigrants arrived in the U.S. joining the small number already present.[56] Over much of the twentieth century, the overall Muslim population in America continued to grow,[57] with recent documented growth even since 2007.[58] It's not surprising then that rates of first-year college students who identify as Muslim increased over the last three generations. In 1985, 0.2 percent identified as Muslim, but by 2001, that number grew to 0.9 percent and then to 1.6 percent in 2015.[59]

But, during this period of growth, 9/11 happened, bringing Islamophobia out in the open. Hate crimes against Muslims went from less than 2 percent of all religious bias incidents in 2000[60] to 26 percent in 2001.[61] That rate today, though, is nearly as high at around 24 percent.[62] With growing numbers of Muslim college students, more may face high levels of anti-Muslim sentiment.

While having to deal with issues of prejudice and discrimination, many Generation Z Muslims are also struggling to balance the intersectionality of their identities. There is a real concern that the strength of religious identification with many younger people may not be as strong. An imam from Duke Divinity School, Abdullah Antepli, said in an interview with the *Atlantic*, "There is an incredible difference between the students and the parents in how they're thinking about American Muslim identity. . . . The parents want to invest on the Muslim side of that hyphenated identity – they are really worried for certain aspects of that identity to be preserved," whereas most students "are negotiating and brainstorming on the American side."[63]

Buddhism

Buddhism in the U.S. dates back to the nineteenth century when Chinese immigrants settled in the U.S.[64] It later grew when a prominent Japanese Zen master who had participated in the 1893 World's Fair in Chicago returned to the U.S. to lecture on Buddhism.[65] But, by World War II, there was a slowdown in the growth of the religion due to the internment of more than 100,000 Japanese and Japanese-Americans.[66] At the same time, though, there was an increased interest from some U.S. soldiers stationed in Asia who brought Buddhism home with them after the war.[67] By the 1960s and 1970s, young Americans were traveling to Asia to learn Buddhist practices.[68] And, more recently, celebrity adoption of Buddhism has drawn more mainstream attention.[69]

The rates of those who identify as Buddhist appear consistent among age groups today.[70] But, there is a slight upward trajectory when looking at first-year college students over the past three generations,[71] highlighting the growing number of young Buddhists. In May 2017, many Generation Z young adults attended the 2641st birthday of Buddha in Sacramento, California. These youth pointed out that Buddhism has helped them see other perspectives, avoid distraction, and clear their minds.[72] Phe Bach, a teacher of meditation says, "A lot of young people find Buddhism compatible with their way of life. . . . We are very friendly to the environment; we believe compassion and wisdom go hand in hand; we all have the potential to be enlightened like him, and that's very important for young people."[73]

Judaism

During the early 1900s, a wave of immigrants, primarily from Eastern Europe, increased the population of Jews in the U.S. by 1.75 million.[74] This was followed by another influx of Jewish immigrants after World War II.[75] However, today, only 12 percent of Jews in the U.S. are immigrants, and more than two-thirds are third generation.[76] Thus, most Generation Z Jews were born in the U.S. along with their parents. Rates of Jewish identification in America have fluctuated throughout history, anywhere between 3.9 percent in 1957, 3 to 4 percent in the 1950s and 60s, and 1.2 percent to 2 percent in the 2000s.[77] Today,

1.9 percent of the U.S. population identifies as Jewish.[78] A linear decrease in identification has been found in research from four major multi-year analyses from Gallup, American National Election Studies, General Social Survey, and the American Religious Identification Survey.[79] In addition, the Pew Research Center is projecting a continued decline to 1.4 percent by 2050.[80]

Like the overall decline in the adult Jewish population, the same can be said of young adults – with one exception: The last 25 or so years. In 1966, 5.2 percent of first-year Baby Boomer college students identified as Jewish, and in 1985, 4 percent of Gen Xers did.[81] But since around 1992, those rates have had little fluctuation, being between 2.5 and 3.1 percent.[82] And, the rate for Millennials in 2001 was the same as that for Generation Z in 2015 at 2.8 percent.[83] So, while the overall population of Jewish adults is on the decline, there appears to be somewhat of a plateau effect with young adults.

In addition to looking at trends of religious identification, there are some nuances with denominational affiliation when it comes to age. According to the Pew Research Center, younger Jews are more likely to identify as having no specific denomination and have the lowest percentage of individuals of any age group who identify as conservative.[84] While these numbers reflect 18 to 29 year-olds, the stark generational differences with those over 30 clearly highlight a differentiation between young and old.

Hinduism

In the early 1900s, Hindu immigrants arrived to the U.S. facing both restrictive immigration policies and nativist sentiment by the public.[85] Often portrayed as snake charmers and magicians, they were left on the fringes of American society for much of the early twentieth century.[86] But, in 1965 with the passage of the Immigration and Naturalization Act, many more Hindus immigrated to the U.S.[87] During this era, several temples were erected, and, in the 1980s and 1990s, materials and resources were developed to support Hindu youth.[88]

While the overall number of Hindus in the U.S. is not high compared to other religions, there has been a recent increase. Between 2007 and 2015, the percentage of people in the U.S. identifying as Hindu has grown from 0.4 percent to 0.7 percent.[89] In 2015, 87 percent of Hindus in America identified as immigrants, making it likely that at least some of the growth can be attributed to immigration.[90]

It's also important to note that Hinduism today is comprised of relatively young membership. For example, 39 percent of Hindus are parents of children under 18. Aside from Mormons, this rate is higher than that of any other religion in the U.S.[91] The vast number of children born to Hindu parents not only highlights a youthful membership but could also indicate a likely continuity in the rates of Hindu identification as these youth age. In addition, a higher percentage of younger versus older adults identify as Hindu.[92] The age composition likely explains the high rate of Hindus who hold progressive stances on issues such as same-sex marriage and abortion.[93] As those in Generation Z tend to have liberal views when it comes to social issues,[94] more of this generational cohort may find a congruent home in Hinduism.

Interfaith

For those who watched the 2000s teen drama, *The O.C.*, we can harken back to Seth Cohen's unwavering commitment to the holiday, Chrismukkah, as his mother was Christian and his dad was Jewish.[95] While this fictional example doesn't capture the full experience of growing up in an interfaith household, it does present a mainstream example of more young people practicing dual religions.

According to a study by Pew, the rates of being raised in a single-faith household (including unaffiliated) have steadily decreased over the past four generational cohorts.[96] For example, 87 percent of those in the Silent Generation were raised by parents who were both of the same religion.[97] That number decreased to 81 percent for Baby Boomers, 80 percent for Gen Xers, and 73 percent for Millennials.[98] This trajectory is not surprising in that marrying someone of the same faith has become less commonplace over time. For example, 81 percent of those married before 1960 did so with a partner of the same religion.[99] But, for parents of Generation Z, those numbers are lower. Seventy percent of parents married between 1990 and 1999 shared the same religion and 65 percent of those married between 2000 and 2009 did.[100]

The unaffiliated

More people today are religiously unaffiliated than in the past.[101] Back in the 1930s and 1940s, the unaffiliated made up around 5 percent of the population, with rates rising to 8.1 percent by 1990 and then to 15 percent in 2008.[102] By 2015, the Pew Research Center had that figure at 22.8 percent.[103] With a growing number of unaffiliated overall, what do we know about Generation Z's rate of unaffiliation? To better understand, we need to look at data through lifecycle and cohort lenses.

First, in looking at a snapshot of today, we find that a higher percentage of young people are unaffiliated compared to older people. Take for example the year 2016, where only 13 percent of those 65 and older were unaffiliated compared to 17 percent of 50 to 64 year-olds, 29 percent of 30 to 49 year-olds, and 39 percent of 18 to 29 year-olds.[104] While the 2016 data may be a single snapshot in time, it is part of an ongoing trend that reflects higher rates of young people's identification as unaffiliated. For instance, in 1986, 1996, and 2006, 18 to 29 year-olds also had the highest rates of unaffiliation compared to other age groups.[105]

Second, comparing data from different cohorts of young people at the same life stage indicates an increasing trend in rates of unaffiliation during young adulthood. For example, research indicates that each entering college cohort is less religiously affiliated than the one before. In 1966, only 6.6 percent of first-year college students were religiously unaffiliated (Baby Boomer), whereas, in 1985 (Generation X), that rate was at 9.4 percent.[106] In 2001 (Millennial), the rate was 15.8 percent[107] and then jumped to nearly 30 percent by 2015 (Generation Z).[108] What we are seeing is a growing number of young people who are not affiliated with a religion. And, while some may find religion as they age, most likely won't as 66 percent of all adults who grew up without a religion are still religiously unaffiliated today.[109] Thus, with rising rates of unaffiliation in young adulthood, we will likely see higher rates of unaffiliation with older cohorts in the future. This isn't surprising in that this trend already exists. In 1986, 3 percent of those 65 and older identified as unaffiliated and rose to 5 percent in 1996, 8 percent in 2006, and 13 percent in 2016.[110] So, if a larger share of those in Generation Z are religiously unaffiliated compared to members of older generations when they were young adults, we could expect relatively high rates of unaffiliation as this generation ages.

So, why are so many people religiously unaffiliated? Perhaps breaking it down into the different types of unaffiliated, we can better understand. We have the "non-believers and questioners," the "spirituals," and the "dones."

The non-believers and questioners

The "non-believers and questioners" or what might be referred to as "nones" simply aren't religious. They may be atheists, agnostics, those who were formerly religiously affiliated, or those who were never religious at all.[111] These individuals are not rejecting religion; many are not even thinking about it at all.[112] This is likely because 85 percent of them think that believing in God is not necessary for morality, a much higher rate than the 45 percent of religiously affiliated who do.[113] As for first-year college students, the rates of "none" identification has increased over the years. In 1985, only 9.4 percent identified as "none," but that number increased to 15.8 percent in 2001.[114] The 1985 and 2001 surveys did not capture data on Atheists and Agnostics separately, so participants who identified as either of those likely selected the "none" option. By 2015, the survey had choices for "none" as well as Atheist and Agnostic. While the "none" rate was only 15.4 percent, when combined with Atheist and Agnostic rates, that number jumps to 29.6 percent.[115] Thus, between one-quarter and one-third of Generation Z first-year students do not identify with a religious affiliation.

What is also of particular interest are the rates of Atheism and Agnosticism. Researchers found that 6 percent of 18 to 29 year-olds are Atheists and 7 percent are Agnostic, higher numbers than any other age group. These findings closely align with those specifically focused on first-year college students in 2015, in which 6 percent identified as Atheist and just more than 8 percent as Agnostic.[116] Although these are different studies with different populations (with one outside of the Generation Z age range as well), the consistency in the findings is telling. It appears that a higher number of younger people are identifying as Atheists and Agnostics than older people.

The spirituals: Keepin' the faith

Another group of the unaffiliated are the "spirituals" whose beliefs may not align with a specific religion or who have a particular faith but don't want to participate in the institution of organized religion. In our Generation Z Goes to College Study, we found that only 47 percent of Generation Z college students identified as participating in an organized religion, 31 percent identified as spiritual but not participating in an organized religion, and 22 percent as not religious or spiritual.[117]

These findings may be surprising given that 69.5 percent of first-year college students in 2015 identified as participating frequently or occasionally in a religious service.[118] Of the more than 30 percent who indicated not attending any services, some likely fall into the "spirituals" category. But, even for the nearly 70 percent who did attend services, could some of them be "spiritual" rather than "religious?" Perhaps. For example, some young people who actively attend services might be more comfortable thinking of themselves as spiritual because their beliefs may not fully align with the religion's stance. And, given that those who were surveyed had recently come from high school, their parents may have required them to attend religious services, regardless if they held their family's religious beliefs. Finally, those who do attend the occasional holiday service with their family may not see that as active participation in the religion. So, while attendance at services can provide some indication of religious identification, it's important to know that many in Generation Z see themselves as spiritual while not necessarily identifying with a particular religious group.

The dones

The "dones" are actually those who once participated in organized religion but have since made an intentional decision to leave.[119] Packard and Hope in their study on why people leave the Christian church, specifically, discuss how dissatisfaction with institutional religion is driving people to live their faith outside of the church.[120] Packard and Hope note about those who leave the church,

> They're done with church. They're tired and fed up with church. They're dissatisfied with the structure, social message, and politics of the institutional church, and they've decided they and their spiritual lives are better off lived outside of organized religion. As one of our respondents put it, "I guess the church just sort of churched the church out of me."[121]

Dr. White, author of *Meet Generation Z*, sums up this same notion in sharing that those who didn't attend church used to think, "God, yes; church, no" but now instead think, "God, perhaps, Christianity and Christians, no."[122] Although these examples reflect Christianity, individuals of all faiths leave their religious institutions.

While some of the "dones" might also be in the "non-believers and questioning" or "spiritual" groups as well, the path to how they got to "done" is usually laden with some negative religious experience. A study by the Public Religion Research Institute found that 82 percent of people who left their childhood religion indicated it was because the "church or congregation became too focused on politics," and 70 percent indicated the reason being the "negative religious teachings about or treatment of gay and lesbian people."[123] Even for young adults today, 60 percent believe that places of worship that support negative views about gay and lesbian people are pushing away their young members.[124] Given that the vast majority of those in Generation Z support LGBTQ rights[125,126] and a large share hold liberal stances on many social issues,[127] these young people may ultimately leave places of worship that have more conservative views that they do.

Importance of religion

Although the vast majority of Americans identify as religious or spiritual, a study by Gallup found that only 53 percent believe that religion is "very important" in their own lives.[128] When looking specifically at Generation Z, the numbers are consistent. A 2016 study by the Varkey Foundation found that only 54 percent of 15 to 21 year-old members of Generation Z surveyed believed their faith or commitment to religion is important or very important to their overall happiness.[129] And, of the seven factors explored in the study, faith/religion was by far the lowest contributor to happiness.[130] These findings are consistent with those from the 2017 College Senior Survey in which just fewer than half of Generation Z college seniors reported believing it is very important or essential to integrate spirituality into their lives.[131]

"A good life to me is having a strong faith in my religion and having my future family be strong in that religion as well."
- Member of Generation Z

So, if religion or spirituality is generally important for just about half of those in Generation Z, is it unimportant for the rest of them? The answer would be for some – yes. Nearly one-quarter of tenth and twelfth graders, and likewise 23 percent of college seniors, indicated that religion was "not important" for them.[132,133] It appears then that about half find religion or spirituality important, a quarter finds it unimportant, and the other quarter appears to be somewhere in the middle.

On the table but off the radar

Despite their lower levels of affiliation, religion is still a topic of discussion with many members of Generation Z. In 2015, more than 80 percent of first-year college students reported having frequently or occasionally discussed religion during the past year.[134] And although 80 percent is lower than the 89 percent reported by Baby Boomers in 1971, rates for other years have never dipped below 79 percent.[135] Regardless of generational era, talking about religion seems to be commonplace for first-year college students. It also appears that conversations about religion continue as students progress through college. In 2017, 77.2 percent of college seniors reported having frequently or occasionally discussed religion during the past year.[136]

Although religion may be a topic of discussion for those in Generation Z, overall it is not necessarily the first thing on many of their minds. For example, in our Generation Z Stories Study, only 5 of 1,337 responses discussed anything related to religion as what constitutes a good life.[137] In addition, only 6 out of 1,246 Generation Z students brought up religious unity as a way their generation could make the world a better place, and 9 of 1,250 discussed religion as one of the most important issues their generation will face in the future.[138]

Religion and positivity

There are many factors that may contribute to a person's positive outlook, and, for Generation Z, religion appears to be one of them. We found in our Generation Z Goes to College Study that religious affiliation and positivity go hand-in-hand. A higher percentage of those who identified as religious also indicated having a positive outlook on three separate measurements.[139] At the same time, a lower percentage of those identifying as not religious or spiritual had a lower positive outlook on the very same measures.[140]

Does this mean that being religious makes you optimistic? Perhaps. But, these figures could simply be a correlation in that those who are more positive seek out religion. In our Generation Z Stories Study, though, we did find evidence that, for some, faith contributed to a positive outlook on life. Whether it was feeling blessed for having another day on Earth or wanting to fulfill a plan set forth by a higher power, faith motivated many of them to simply get up in the morning.[141]

> **❝** I am excited to know that whether the day turns out to be terrible or great, God has a plan for my life and all things work together for my good. **❞**
> – Member of Generation Z

Table 14.6 Religiosity and Optimism Among Generation Z College Students[142]

	Not Religious or Spiritual	Spiritual, But Not Religious	Religious
I am optimistic about my future.	47%	60%	66%
I believe good things will happen for me.	37%	50%	57%
I believe people are inherently good.	18%	21%	25%

The future of organized religion

When looking at the factors that make young people hopeful for the future, religion and faith ranked dead last among six possible factors.[143] So, what does the future hold for Generation Z and religion?

Social change

First, many in Generation Z see religion as an ideal vehicle for social change. Jim Wallis, author of *The Great Awakening*, shares a story in his book about the connection between religion and social change. After giving a talk and doing a book signing, Wallis was approached by an 8-year-old girl who said, "When you talked about that silent tsunami that is killing so many children every day because of poverty – children like me . . . I was just sitting there and started to think to myself, if I'm a Christian, I better do something about that." The following week, Wallis returned to his classroom at Harvard. He shared with his students, "If some of you want to help lead this new movement for social change, you'd better get moving because a whole new generation is coming up fast behind you!"[144] Expect to see those in Generation Z seeking out opportunities to connect their religion and their desire for social change and looking closely at how their places of worship offer opportunities to do so.

Inclusion

When asked about how their generation can make a difference, the number one factor discussed by 22 percent of those in our Generation Z Stories Study was being open-minded.[145] Additionally, 20 percent said ending discrimination, and 18 percent said loving others.[146] Inclusion is clearly of importance to Generation Z as a whole, and for those who are religious, having their places of worship embrace people who have traditionally been marginalized is essential. Jim Wallis adds that there is a critical connection between spirituality and social justice and that spirituality can serve as both a motivating factor to challenge injustice and a nourishment to sustain a long journey of combatting oppression.[147] But, if certain religions aren't inclusive of particular groups to begin with, convincing young, socially open-minded individuals to embrace religion as a means to promote social justice could appear contradictory to them.

Emerging interpretations

Dr. White, author of *Meet Generation Z*, believes that in looking at the future of Christianity, in particular, we "will be forced to examine and elucidate the doctrine of humanity in ways that confront both changing morals and new technological frontiers."[148] But, it isn't just Christians that are grappling with this issue. Many Muslims in the U.S. believe that "there is more than one way to interpret their religion and that traditional understandings of Islam need to be reinterpreted to address the issues of today."[149] As some religions, or simply the members within those religions, reinterpret their teachings, we may see those in Generation Z who have felt incongruence between their personal values and those of the religion re-engage (or engage for the first time).

Conclusion

If trends hold, we will likely see rates of Generation Z participation shift from specific Christian denominations to the growing group of Other Christian. In addition, the sheer proportion of youth present in smaller religions today might be indicative of continued growth if these young people stay religiously engaged over time. We may also see more members of Generation Z fall into the "none" category as they get older while some others may re-engage with religion. Overall, though, with many of them having socially progressive stances on a number of issues,[150] it may be challenging for them to find religious groups that align with their beliefs. And, for those who remain engaged, they might just change religion from the inside out.

Notes

1 Pew Research Center. (2011). *Global Christianity*. Washington, DC: Pew Research Center.
2 JCC Association. (2018). *History*. Retrieved from http://jcca.org/about-us/history/
3 Tucson Jewish Community Center. (2018). *About us*. Retrieved from www.tucsonjcc.org/about/
4 Pew Research Center. (2017b). *Religious beliefs and practices*. Retrieved from www.pewforum.org/2017/07/26/religious-beliefs-and-practices/
5 Christensen, D. (2017). *5 years later: How the missionary age change announcement changed the work*. Retrieved from www.deseretnews.com/article/865689875/5-years-later-How-the-missionary-age-change-announcement-changed-the-work.html
6 Hammond, H. (2007). *Yoga pioneers: How yoga came to America*. Retrieved from www.yogajournal.com/yoga-101/yogas-trip-america
7 Bielefeldt, C. (2001). *Comments on tensions in American Buddhism*. Retrieved from www.pbs.org/wnet/religionandethics/2001/07/06/july-6-2001-comments-on-tensions-in-american-buddhism/15941/
8 Olivelle, P. (n.d.). *Karma*. Retrieved from www.britannica.com/topic/karma
9 Newport, F. (2016). *Five key findings on religion in the U.S.* Retrieved from http://news.gallup.com/poll/200186/five-key-findings-religion.aspx
10 Newport, F. (2016).
11 Newport, F. (2016).
12 Pew Research Center. (2010a). *Religion among the Millennials*. Retrieved from www.pewforum.org/2010/02/17/religion-among-the-millennials/
13 Putnam, R. D. & Campbell, D. E. (2010). *American grace*. New York: Simon & Schuster, p. 7.
14 Eagan, M. K., Stolzenberg, E. B., Ramirez, J. J., Aragon, M. C., Suchard, M. R., & Rios-Aguilar, C. (2016). *The American freshman: Fifty-year trends, 1966–2015*. Los Angeles: Higher Education Research Institute, UCLA.

15 Eagan, M. K., Stolzenberg, E. B., Ramirez, J. J., Aragon, M. C., Suchard, M. R., & Rios-Aguilar, C. (2016).

16 Eagan, M. K., Stolzenberg, E. B., Ramirez, J. J., Aragon, M. C., Suchard, M. R., & Rios-Aguilar, C. (2016).

17 Higher Education Research Institute. (2017). *College Senior Survey*. Data prepared by Higher Education Research Institute.

18 Eagan, M. K., Stolzenberg, E. B., Ramirez, J. J., Aragon, M. C., Suchard, M. R., & Rios-Aguilar, C. (2016).

19 Eagan, M. K., Stolzenberg, E. B., Ramirez, J. J., Aragon, M. C., Suchard, M. R., & Rios-Aguilar, C. (2016).

20 White, J. E. (2017). *Meet Generation Z: Understanding and reaching the new post-Christian world*. Grand Rapids, MI: Baker Books.

21 Putnam, R. D. & Campbell, D. E. (2010).

22 Balmer, R. (2001). *Religion in twentieth century America*. New York: Oxford University Press, Inc., p. 29.

23 White, J. E. (2017).

24 McVicar, M. J. (2016). *The religious right in America*. Oxford Research Encyclopedias. Retrieved from http://religion.oxfordre.com/view/10.1093/acrefore/9780199340378.001.0001/acrefore-9780199340378-e-97

25 McVicar, M. J. (2016), para. 16.

26 Pew Research Center. (2015e). *Religious landscape study*. Retrieved from www.pewforum.org/religious-landscape-study/

27 Center for the Study of Global Christianity. (2013). *Christianity in its global context: 1970–2020*. Retrieved from www.gordonconwell.edu/ockenga/research/documents/2ChristianityinitsGlobalContext.pdf

28 Pew Research Center. (2015c).

29 Eagan, M. K., Stolzenberg, E. B., Ramirez, J. J., Aragon, M. C., Suchard, M. R., & Rios-Aguilar, C. (2016).

30 Eagan, M. K., Stolzenberg, E. B., Ramirez, J. J., Aragon, M. C., Suchard, M. R., & Rios-Aguilar, C. (2016).

31 Balmer, R. (2001).

32 Balmer, R. (2001).

33 Pew Research Center. (2015e).

34 Pew Research Center. (2015a). *America's changing religious landscape*. Retrieved from www.pewforum.org/2015/05/12/americas-changing-religious-landscape/

35 Eagan, M. K., Stolzenberg, E. B., Ramirez, J. J., Aragon, M. C., Suchard, M. R., & Rios-Aguilar, C. (2016).

36 Eagan, M. K., Stolzenberg, E. B., Ramirez, J. J., Aragon, M. C., Suchard, M. R., & Rios-Aguilar, C. (2016).

37 Lipka, M. (2015). *A closer look at Catholic America*. Retrieved from www.pewresearch.org/fact-tank/2015/09/14/a-closer-look-at-catholic-america/

38 Cooper, B., Cox, D., Lienesch, R., & Jones, R. P. (2016). *Exodus: Why Americans are leaving religion: And why they're unlikely to come back*. Retrieved from www.prri.org/research/prri-rns-poll-nones-atheist-leaving-religion/

39 Murphy, C. (2015). *Interfaith marriage is common in U.S., particularly among the recently wed*. Retrieved from www.pewresearch.org/fact-tank/2015/06/02/interfaith-marriage/

40 Cooper, B., Cox, D., Lienesch, R., & Jones, R. P. (2016).

41 BBC. (2009). *Mormon pioneers*. Retrieved from www.bbc.co.uk/religion/religions/mormon/history/pioneers_1.shtml

42 Pew Research Center. (2015e).

43 Pew Research Center. (2015e).

44 Eagan, M. K., Stolzenberg, E. B., Ramirez, J. J., Aragon, M. C., Suchard, M. R., & Rios-Aguilar, C. (2016).

45 Eagan, M. K., Stolzenberg, E. B., Ramirez, J. J., Aragon, M. C., Suchard, M. R., & Rios-Aguilar, C. (2016).

46 The Church of Jesus Christ of Latter-Day Saints. (2013). *Mormon leaders speaking to youth in their language: Technology.* Retrieved from www.mormonnewsroom.org/article/mormon-leaders-speaking-to-youth-in-their-language-technology

47 The Church of Jesus Christ of Latter-Day Saints. (2013), para. 9.

48 Nielsen, A. (2017). *Religion scholar studies why Millennials leave LDS church.* Retrieved from http://universe.byu.edu/2017/06/01/religion-scholar-studies-why-millennials-leave-the-lds-church/

49 Pew Research Center. (2015e).

50 Pew Research Center. (2015e).

51 Pew Research Center. (2015c).

52 Cox, D. & Jones, R. P. (2017a). *America's changing religious identity.* Retrieved from www.prri.org/research/american-religious-landscape-christian-religiously-unaffiliated/

53 Cox, D. & Jones, R. P. (2017a).

54 Eagan, M. K., Stolzenberg, E. B., Ramirez, J. J., Aragon, M. C., Suchard, M. R., & Rios-Aguilar, C. (2016).

55 Eagan, M. K., Stolzenberg, E. B., Ramirez, J. J., Aragon, M. C., Suchard, M. R., & Rios-Aguilar, C. (2016).

56 PBS. (2014). *Islam in America.* Retrieved from www.pbs.org/opb/historydetectives/feature/islam-in-america/

57 PBS. (2014).

58 Pew Research Center. (2017d). *U.S. Muslims concerned about their place in society, but continue to believe in the American Dream.* Retrieved from www.pewforum.org/2017/07/26/findings-from-pew-research-centers-2017-survey-of-us-muslims/

59 Eagan, M. K., Stolzenberg, E. B., Ramirez, J. J., Aragon, M. C., Suchard, M. R., & Rios-Aguilar, C. (2016).

60 FBI. (2000). *Hate crime statistics.* Retrieved from https://ucr.fbi.gov/hate-crime/2000

61 FBI. (2001). *Hate crime statistics.* Retrieved from https://ucr.fbi.gov/hate-crime/2001

62 FBI. (2016). *Hate crime statistics.* Retrieved from https://ucr.fbi.gov/hate-crime/2016/tables/table-1

63 Green, E. (2017). *How America is transforming Islam.* Retrieved from www.theatlantic.com/politics/archive/2017/12/muslims-assimilation-weddings/549230/, para. 14.

64 Duerr, M. (2010). *How Buddhism came to the west.* Retrieved from www.pbs.org/thebuddha/blog/2010/Mar/17/how-buddhism-came-west-maia-duerr/

65 Duerr, M. (2010).

66 Duerr, M. (2010).

67 Duerr, M. (2010).

68 Duerr, M. (2010).

69 Duerr, M. (2010).

70 Pew Research Center. (2015e).

71 Eagan, M. K., Stolzenberg, E. B., Ramirez, J. J., Aragon, M. C., Suchard, M. R., & Rios-Aguilar, C. (2016).

72 Magagnini, S. & Reese, P. (2017). *What would Buddha do? Young people find out.* Retrieved from www.sacbee.com/entertainment/living/religion/article149202434.html

73 Magagnini, S. & Reese, P. (2017), para. 15.

74 Sarna, J. D. & Golden, J. (n.d.). *The American Jewish experience in the twentieth century: Antisemitism and assimilation.* Retrieved from http://nationalhumanitiescenter.org/tserve/twenty/tkeyinfo/jewishexp.htm

75 United States Holocaust Memorial Museum. (n.d.). *United States policy toward Jewish refugees, 1941–1952.* Retrieved from www.ushmm.org/wlc/en/article.php?ModuleId=10007094

76 Pew Research Center. (2015a).

77 Pew Research Center. (2013). *A portrait of Jewish Americans.* Retrieved from https://archive.nytimes.com/www.nytimes.com/interactive/2013/10/01/us/pew-research-jewish-americans.html?ref=us

78 Pew Research Center. (2015e).

79 Pew Research Center. (2013).

80 Pew Research Center. (2015c). *Jews.* Retrieved from www.pewforum.org/2015/04/02/jews/

81 Eagan, M. K., Stolzenberg, E. B., Ramirez, J. J., Aragon, M. C., Suchard, M. R., & Rios-Aguilar, C. (2016).

82 Eagan, M. K., Stolzenberg, E. B., Ramirez, J. J., Aragon, M. C., Suchard, M. R., & Rios-Aguilar, C. (2016).

83 Eagan, M. K., Stolzenberg, E. B., Ramirez, J. J., Aragon, M. C., Suchard, M. R., & Rios-Aguilar, C. (2016).

84 Pew Research Center. (2013).

85 Lucia, A. (2017). *Hinduism in America.* Retrieved from http://religion.oxfordre.com/view/10.1093/acrefore/9780199340378.001.0001/acrefore-9780199340378-e-436

86 Lucia, A. (2017).

87 Lucia, A. (2017).

88 Lucia, A. (2017).

89 Pew Research Center. (2015a).

90 Pew Research Center. (2015e).

91 Pew Research Center. (2015e).

92 Pew Research Center. (2015e).

93 Pew Research Center. (2015e).

94 Seemiller, C. & Grace, M. (2016). *Generation Z goes to college.* San Francisco: Jossey-Bass.

95 Spielberger, D. (2017). *How the O.C.'s Chrismukkah holiday became a real holiday.* Retrieved from https://broadly.vice.com/en_us/article/vbz77x/how-the-oc-chrismukkah-real-life-holiday

96 Pew Research Center. (2016). *One-in-five U.S. adults were raised in interfaith homes.* Retrieved from www.pewforum.org/2016/10/26/one-in-five-u-s-adults-were-raised-in-interfaith-homes/

97 Pew Research Center. (2016).

98 Pew Research Center. (2016).

99 Murphy, C. (2015).

100 Murphy, C. (2015).

101 White, J. E. (2017).

102 White, J. E. (2017).

103 Pew Research Center. (2015e).

104 Cox, D. & Jones, R. P. (2017a).

105 Cox, D. & Jones, R. P. (2017a).

106 Eagan, K., Stolzenberg, E. B., Bates, A. K., Aragon, M. C., Suchard, M. R., & Rios-Aguilar, C. (2015). *The American freshman*. Los Angeles, CA: Higher Education Research Institute, UCLA.

107 Eagan, K., Stolzenberg, E. B., Bates, A. K., Aragon, M. C., Suchard, M. R., & Rios-Aguilar, C. (2015).

108 Eagan, K., Stolzenberg, E. B., Bates, A. K., Aragon, M. C., Suchard, M. R., & Rios-Aguilar, C. (2015).

109 Cooper, B., Cox, D., Lienesch, R., & Jones, R. P. (2016).

110 Cox, D. & Jones, R. P. (2017a).

111 Smith, G. A. (2017). *A growing share of Americans say it's not necessary to believe in God to be moral*. Retrieved from www.pewresearch.org/fact-tank/2017/10/16/a-growing-share-of-americans-say-its-not-necessary-to-believe-in-god-to-be-moral/

112 White, J. E. (2017).

113 Smith, G. A. (2017).

114 Eagan, M. K., Stolzenberg, E. B., Ramirez, J. J., Aragon, M. C., Suchard, M. R., & Rios-Aguilar, C. (2016).

115 Eagan, M. K., Stolzenberg, E. B., Ramirez, J. J., Aragon, M. C., Suchard, M. R., & Rios-Aguilar, C. (2016).

116 Eagan, M. K., Stolzenberg, E. B., Ramirez, J. J., Aragon, M. C., Suchard, M. R., & Rios-Aguilar, C. (2016).

117 Seemiller, C. & Grace, M. (2016).

118 Eagan, M. K., Stolzenberg, E. B., Ramirez, J. J., Aragon, M. C., Suchard, M. R., & Rios-Aguilar, C. (2016).

119 Packard, J. & Hope, A. (2015). *Church refugees: Sociologists reveal why people are done with church but not their faith*. Loveland, CO: Group Publishing.

120 Packard, J. & Hope, A. (2015).

121 Packard, J. & Hope, A. (2015), pp. 1–2.

122 White, J. E. (2017), p. 84.

123 Cooper, B., Cox, D., Lienesch, R., & Jones, R. P. (2016), Table 5.

124 Cox, D. & Jones, R. P. (2017b). *Majority of Americans oppose transgender bathroom restrictions*. Retrieved from www.prri.org/research/lgbt-transgender-bathroom-discrimination-religious-liberty/

125 Varkey Foundation. (2017). *Generation Z: Global Citizenship Survey*. Retrieved from www.varkeyfoundation.org/what-we-do/policy-research/generation-z-global-citizenship-survey/

126 Eagan, K., Stolzenberg, E. B., Ramirez, J. J., Aragon, M. C., Suchard, M. R., & Hurtado, S. (2014). *The American freshman: National norms fall 2014*. Los Angeles: Higher Education Research Institute, UCLA.

127 Seemiller, C. & Grace, M. (2016).

128 Newport, F. (2016).

129 Varkey Foundation. (2017).

130 Varkey Foundation. (2017).

131 Higher Education Research Institute. (2017).

132 Twenge, J. M. (2017).

133 Higher Education Research Institute. (2017).

134 Higher Education Research Institute. (2017).

135 Higher Education Research Institute. (2017).

136 Higher Education Research Institute. (2017).

137 Seemiller, C. & Grace, M. (2017). *Generation Z stories study*. Unpublished raw data.

138 Seemiller, C. & Grace, M. (2017).
139 Seemiller, C. & Grace, M. (2016).
140 Seemiller, C. & Grace, M. (2016).
141 Seemiller, C. & Grace, M. (2017).
142 Seemiller, C. & Grace, M. (2016).
143 Varkey Foundation. (2017).
144 Wallis, J. (2008). *The great awakening.* New York: HarperCollins, pp. 283–284.
145 Varkey Foundation. (2017).
146 Varkey Foundation. (2017).
147 Wallis, J. (2008).
148 White, J. E. (2017).
149 Sciupac, E. P. (2017). *U.S. Muslims are religiously observant, but open to multiple interpretations of Islam.* Retrieved from www.pewresearch.org/fact-tank/2017/08/28/u-s-muslims-are-religiously-observant-but-open-to-multiple-interpretations-of-islam/, para. 1.
150 Seemiller, C. & Grace, M. (2016).

Life and career preparation

15 Education

Since the early 1900s, one aspect of life that nearly everyone in the U.S. has in common is having gone to school. However, schooling has evolved greatly since the early twentieth century, and each generation's educational experience is shaped by the context of the state of the world during their upbringing. Generation Z, unlike other generations, is coming of age in a unique era where technology is abundant, government-regulated standards and accountability are ever present, and schools once open to the world are surrounded by protective fences and walls. What does all of this mean for those in Generation Z?

The K–12 experience

From Kindergarten through twelfth grade, youth can spend upwards of 13,000 hours of their lives at school,[1] not including before or after-school programs. How they spend that time is not all that different from the time those in older generations spent in school. Trading food from their lunchboxes, waiting in line in Kindergarten, playing tag at recess, learning multiplication tables, putting together a project for the science fair, going to school dances, and playing on a sports team after school seem like timeless activities. While it is likely that the last six generations have more in common than not when it comes to schooling, there are still some nuances with the Generation Z K–12 experience.

> *As a generation, we are extremely privileged to be arguably the most educated generation in history. We need to continue that trend. We need to make our children, and our children's children excited about learning; excited about gaining knowledge. We need to put our degrees, our money, and our experiences into funding after school programs, into programs for those stricken with poverty, and into scholarships and grants, so those who may not be so fortunate to afford higher education can still be educated.*
>
> – Member of Generation Z

The dynamic K–12 system

For older generations, going to school often meant walking, riding a bike, or catching the school bus to the local neighborhood school. In some cases, kids attended private schools, but a large share attended the public school down the street. Today, the options for K–12 schooling are much broader, with students and their families being able to choose from a variety of specialty schools like magnet, STEM, online, and college prep. While students can go to any number of schools for these specialties, the number of students who attended a K–12 charter school has been increasing during the childhoods of those in Generation Z. For example, in 2004, 900,000 K–12 students were enrolled in charter schools. By 2014, that number had soared to 2.7 million.[2]

Along with increasingly diverse school types, homeschooling has also offered an alternative way for kids to be educated. While homeschooling is by no means a new form of education only for those in Generation Z, homeschooling boomed in the early 2000s with the number of homeschooled students more than doubling between 1999 at 850,000 and 2012 at 1.8 million.[3]

Different types of students need different types of learning opportunities.[4] For example, the size of the school, whether it offers after-school clubs and sports, and the ability to connect with a teacher are of different importance levels depending on the type of student.[5] Thus, having a variation of school types (e.g. online, magnet, dual-enrollment) fits a generation with diverse needs[6] and a desire for customization[7] and personalization[8] in other aspects of their lives.

Growing up digital

It isn't just school offerings that are different, but there are many diverse learning modalities today. Paper and pencils along with traditional textbooks are being replaced with smartphones, tablets as well as online work modules and instructional videos.[9] There are also virtual learning platforms like Khan Academy, TED-Ed, and various educational channels on YouTube that offer students a digital dive into their education. But, these innovative tech platforms aren't the only digital resources used by those in Generation Z. These students are also using "old school" learning tools that may be familiar for those in older generations, but are now getting a tech-infused twist. For example, the infamous yellow and black printed CliffsNotes guides are still around but have gone digital. And platforms like typing.com have just made typing instruction digitized using some of the same techniques as typing teachers might have used in typing class.

Digital learning is more than just using an array of online tools and platforms. We are in an era of "Googlification" of the K–12 education system.[10] More than 30 million kids use Google apps in educational settings, like Google Docs, and more than half of the devices shipped to schools are Chromebooks, Google-powered laptops.[11]

Coding not cursive?

As the educational settings populated by Generation Z students continue to become digitized, it is critical that they learn the skills associated with effectively utilizing tech tools and platforms as well as navigating the online world. But, digital skill development may end up taking the place of developing what some may deem as more obsolete skill sets. Take, for example, teaching handwriting and cursive. Because of the focus on digitization, there has been a movement asserting that coding is the new cursive, and that teaching kids to code may be far more useful than spending time teaching obsolete cursive writing.[12] A study by Gallup found that, in 2014–2015, only 25 percent of K–12 principals indicated offering a computer science course with programming or coding. Yet, by the next year in 2015–2016, that number increased to 40 percent.[13]

But, coding is likely not taking the place of cursive, as cursive writing is absent from the 2009 common core standards, alluding to the scarce instruction of it anyway. Some states, however, have actually added cursive writing to their state educational standards because of its historical importance in being able to read documents that have been written in cursive, like the U.S. Constitution.[14] It is likely that while many in Generation Z didn't learn to code in school, they also probably didn't spend a great deal of time practicing their cursive either.

The new space race: Standardized testing

Although many Millennials and Gen Xers can remember standardized testing days at school, the number of tests at the time may have seemed somewhat manageable. But, for Generation Z, it appears that many have spent countless hours preparing and taking standardized tests throughout their entire educational experience. A study by the Council of the Great City Schools in 2015 found that in the 66 districts the council represents, students were found to have taken around 112 standardized tests from pre-K through twelfth grade.[15] It's no surprise then that 37 percent of tenth through twelfth graders agree or strongly agree that their schools focus too much on preparing students for standardized tests.[16]

> *❝ Who would have thought parents would be obsessed with how kids in China perform on proficiency tests? ❞*
> *– Grace Masback, author of The Voice of Gen Z*

Much attention to standardized testing came from the passage of the No Child Left Behind Act in 2001, which was intended to increase accountability for schools.[17] After the implementation of No Child Left Behind, nearly half of school administrators indicated redirecting time spent on physical education into math and reading,[18] and less time was spent on visual arts, dance, theater, and music.[19] Thus, many Generation Z K–12 students have spent time that was previously allocated to arts and wellness instead on test preparation and test taking.

Beyond the PTA: Parental involvement

With organizations like the Parent-Teacher Association (PTA), parents since 1897 have been encouraged to take an active role in their children's school experience.[20] Even outside of PTA, parent-teacher conferences and other activities at the school level have encouraged parental involvement. But, this involvement may have gone a bit overboard during the time Millennials were growing up, resulting in the beloved name of "helicopter parents,"[21] due to their hovering closely over their kids' decision-making, problem-solving, and independence, especially in school. With parents of Generation Z acting more like co-pilots,[22] these parents are often invited by their kids into their educational journeys to serve as consultants and mentors.[23] While Gen Xers as kids wanted their own independence, as parents of Generation Z, they relish being invited to grow up again with them and be involved in their students' educational experiences. Educational technology helps facilitate this process. For example, with the advent of Google Classrooms in 2014,[24] educators can share assignments, updates, resources, and communication on a platform that is accessible by students and parents. This oversight might have felt intrusive for Generation X kids, but as parents, these Gen Xers are fairly engaged in following along with their children's educational progress, at least online. For example, 85 percent of parents of Generation Z check to see if their kids' homework is done, but only 67 percent actually talk to their kid's teachers.[25]

Metal detectors, bullying, and school safety

Most kids in earlier generations did not have metal detectors or security guards at school. For some, school might have felt like a safe haven, or a place to go when the world felt turned upside down. But, that isn't necessarily the case for students today. Only around 80 percent of Generation Z public high school students agree or strongly agree that they feel safe at school.[26] While that number may seem high, it also indicates that one in five do not really feel that school is a safe place. Feeling unsafe is even more pronounced for transgender Generation Z students. In a study by the Human Rights Campaign, 58 percent of transgender teens reported not feeling safe using the restroom or locker room that aligns with their gender identity.[27] We found in our Generation Z Goes to College Study that the fear of school violence, more specifically, is a major concern for many.[28] Since Columbine, and, more recently, Sandy Hook and Marjory Stoneman Douglas, school might not feel like a safe place for those in Generation Z.

> *« School should be a place where people feel safe. »*
> *– Member of Generation Z*

And it isn't just school shootings that they are concerned about. Nearly 54 percent of participants from our Generation Z Goes to College Study indicated being concerned or very concerned about bullying.[29] And it seems their concerns are founded – especially when it comes to bullying of LGBTQ students. According to the Human Rights Campaign, 70 percent of LGBTQ youth report having been bullied at school because of their sexual orientation.[30]

As discussed earlier in regard to mental health, bullying has evolved from only being face-to-face to also being online, making it easy to be bullied without even coming onto school grounds. Stories are rampant in the news of kids cyberbullying other kids by sending mean texts, harassing or stalking through social media, sharing insulting and embarrassing pictures and messages virally, and posting on gossip social media sites. And this appears to be a growing trend as just more than a third of teens in 2016 were affected by cyberbullying compared to 19 percent in 2007.[31]

> ❝ As a former victim of bullying, I believe the educational system neglects this as an issue and refuses to address it. If I could I would create a program to assist teens in helping them get through their middle and high school years. ❞
> – Member of Generation Z

Higher education landscape

The first traditional-age cohort of Generation Z students started college in 2013 and graduated in 2017. Our colleges and universities are bustling with those in Generation Z right now, and they will continue to be the majority of traditional-aged college students through the class of 2032. Just as factors and changes in K–12 have shaped Generation Z students' educational experiences, there are a number of contextual factors playing a role in shaping their perspectives on higher education.

Local and living at home

There is no doubt about it – college tuition can be cost prohibitive. It's not surprising then that a study by Sallie Mae found that 98 percent of families are making choices to increase college affordability.[32] One of the ways they are saving money is by having their children go to a second- or third-choice college if it is less expensive. A study by Royall & Company, a college enrollment management firm, found that, of the 54,810 student college deposit records they analyzed, 11 percent of students ended up not attending their first-choice institution after being admitted. Of those, 40 percent indicated that forgoing their first-choice was due to price-related issues.[33] Attending a public institution, especially in-state, can be a real cost-saver in the long-term. It's no surprise then that 73 percent of families indicated saving on college costs by having their student attend college in state.[34] Not only is in-state tuition less expensive than out-of-state or private college tuition, some states are now offering opportunities for free tuition at a local community college. New York, in particular, is moving to offer a free four-year university experience for in-state students in particular income brackets.[35]

> **❝ It is absurd that we must go into debt to gain an education. ❞**
> *- Member of Generation Z*

Forty-seven percent of parents and 68 percent of students have also reduced their personal spending to afford college.[36] In addition to not eating out or spending on the extras, a big cost savings measure for this generation is to forgo residence hall or apartment living. Instead, about half indicate living at home while attending college to save money and afford college.[37] After four years of having their college-age child living in their childhood room, parents may look forward to packing boxes to send their soon-to-be graduates on their way. But, some in Generation Z don't have any intention of moving out after college. And, those who didn't live at home during college might return to their parents' house. In 2014, just more than 36 percent of 18- to 34-year-old women and nearly 43 percent of men in that same age group lived at home.[38] These are the highest numbers since the 1940s when young adult members of the G.I. Generation lived at home.[39] Although those living with their families today are primarily Millennials, the trend of living at home rent-free will likely continue with those in Generation Z as doing so provides an option for them to save money on college expenses, pay down their student loans, and save to buy their own homes, which they hope to do by the age of 28.[40]

From fifth-year seniors to third-year seniors

Another way students are trying to reduce college costs is by making the time they spend in college shorter, ultimately spending less money on tuition over time. Nearly half of the older teens surveyed in a study by Barnes & Noble had taken a course in high school for college credit.[41] A study by Sallie Mae found that more than one-quarter of students had enrolled in an accelerated program to finish coursework more quickly.[42] It isn't just dual-enrollment or accelerated programs that these students are taking advantage of, but the percentage of students earning AP credit nearly doubled between 2003 and 2013.[43] Between these options and the ability for them to test out of particular courses upon entering college, Generation Z students are able to shorten their time to graduation, and ultimately save quite a bit of money.

Unlike previous generations, for Generation Z students, using college to explore different passions and majors might be a costly journey. Sixty-one percent of those in Generation Z say that they should know their future careers before coming to college.[44] So, the days of students changing their majors several times or filling their schedules with physical education courses, interesting electives, and a minor or double major may end up lessening as many of those in Generation Z try to focus on an expedited and more cost-effective college completion path. Perhaps the notion of the fifth-year senior will be replaced by the third-year senior rushing to punch the clock to graduation.

The marketable major

Being intentional about selecting a major that serves as a pipeline to a high-paying career field could also be a way to ensure Generation Z graduates could pay down their college debt. According to branding agency, Ologie, of the top five majors sought out by prospective Generation Z college students, four can be attributed to high-paying fields: Business at 19 percent, STEM at 17 percent, computer science at 15 percent, and medicine at 15 percent.[45] And while these fields also might be their life calling, as described more in the Career Aspirations chapter, a study by Sallie Mae found that 18 percent of current college students changed their majors so they could pursue a profession that was more marketable.[46]

Community college and vocational education

Community colleges and technical schools offer excellent cost savings options for Generation Z high school graduates to attain a post-secondary education. Further, though, they provide students with training and certification opportunities in vocational and technical fields without having to get a bachelor's degree. Research by Ologie found that only 44 percent of tenth graders through second-year college students had the aspiration of going to a 4-year college.[47] A shortened career-training path may be just what many in Generation Z are looking for. It's no surprise then that researchers from Barnes & Noble College found that 39 percent of middle and high school students indicated considering going to a community college, and 22 percent were interested in attending a technical or trade school.[48]

Vocational education has been around long before Generation Z's interest was piqued. But, it has its more formal roots with the G.I. Generation, which was the first generation to experience vocational education in high school due to the passage of the 1917 Smith-Hughes Act.[49] By the 1930s when the oldest of the G.I. Generation were entering adulthood, community colleges began offering widespread post-secondary vocational training.[50] But vocational education was not limited to high schools and community colleges. Proprietary schools, or what we know today as technical schools or career colleges, got an enrollment boom after World War II when many G.I. Generation veterans used their G.I. Bills to attend these institutions.[51] Fast-forward a century after the passage of the Smith-Hughes Act and we see Generation Z looking to vocational education as a viable career option.

Rising enrollment at HBCUs

While overall college enrollment is declining nationally,[52] Historically Black Colleges and Universities (HBCUs) have actually seen a recent spike in attendance.[53] The enrollment increase is not simply due to the less expensive tuition at HBCUs, running on average, $6,000 less per year than predominantly White institutions.[54] The "cultural mood in the country" is leading African-American students to seek out schools where they feel a sense of inclusion while being encouraged to participate in a "rich history of cultural activism."[55]

MOOCs and alternative educational options

Although some Generation Z students are attending community college and others are staying in-state to save money, there are many opportunities for students to gain the education and training they need for their future occupations without attending college at all. In 2016, 58 million students enrolled in 6,850 courses at 700+ universities to take a MOOC, a massive open online course.[56] Companies like Udacity, Coursera, and edX offer free or inexpensive online courses with expert instructors on nearly any topic imaginable from coding and robotics to professional development certifications in a variety of career fields. Being able to take free or highly affordable training courses to gain skills and even earn certifications could prove to be a great educational and financial investment for young adults in Generation Z in lieu of college. With blockchain technology, which was originally designed to validate online economic transactions, students can have every educational record like credit hours, micro-credentials, and certificates appear in one verified digital space, essentially creating an easily accessible, universal educational transcript.[57]

In addition, partnerships between training institutions and companies can offer Generation Z students the latest instruction paired with access to innovative businesses for hands-on experiences, internships, and possible future career opportunities. For example, MissionU offers students the ability to attend one year of free training on business intelligence and data analytics. MissionU's corporate partners, like Uber and Spotify, get first pick of the program's graduates.[58] Upon finishing the program and getting a job with a salary of more than $50,000, graduates are expected to pay back 15 percent of their salary for 3 years.

Online for fun, but not for school

One misnomer about Generation Z is that their desire to be digitally connected means they solely want online learning. According to the College Senior Survey, 67 percent of college seniors had never taken an online course.[59] And a study by INSEAD Emerging Markets found that only 13 percent of those in Generation Z would choose an online course over an in-person one.[60] That number pales in comparison to the 21 percent of Millennials and 25 percent of those in Generation X who prefer online over in-class learning.[61] As we develop more online classes in lieu of in-person courses, it is important to remember that the online learning modality aligns more with the needs of older working professionals, whereas younger Generation Z students who prefer communicating face-to-face[62] are not the target market for online courses.

Customized learning and college a la carte

We live in a world where nearly anything can be customized. You can order a rug on Amazon and pick from 15 different colors and styles, create your own watch list on Netflix, or design your own photo book on Shutterfly. This customization effect seems to carry over into the higher education setting with those in Generation Z. Aside from having the ability, in many cases, to create their own course schedules and select electives of interest to them, Generation Z students want even more customization like being able to engage in college a la carte where they can opt out of the extras of the college experience.[63] For example, if they do not plan to access the computer lab, they could get a deduction in their fees and simply not access the lab. Although this is not prevalent on college campuses, a selected service model like this could help curb costs for students and eliminate the need for them to pay for services they don't plan to use. In addition to customizing their services, many also want to customize their degree. More than 70 percent of those in Generation Z believe that they should be able to create their own course of study or even major.[64] This is likely due to their desire for careers that integrate more than one major. For example, a counselor who wants to run a private practice would need classes in both counseling as well as business. Rather than being a double major, which could prolong graduation and lead to more loan debt, Generation Z students could craft a course plan that would capitalize on all that the institution offered, even beyond the allowable elective credits.

College spaces and places

Looking back at institutional archives, it is interesting to see the physical changes that have occurred on college campuses over the last 100 years. Many of today's colleges did not exist 100 years ago, community colleges were in their infancy,[65] and there were fewer buildings on even our oldest campuses. When those in the G.I. generation were in college, many gathered in the quad to read and hang out, ate in the communal dining hall, and lived in dormitories with community bathrooms. Today, Generation Z students hang out in high tech student unions and campus recreation centers, grab their Starbucks lattes before class, and head back to their eco-friendly residence hall rooms with private bathrooms and kitchenettes. Researchers at the University of Michigan discuss this transformation as the "college as country club" phenomenon, which proposes that institutions moved towards catering to students' desires for "consumption amenities."[66] But, findings from an analysis of more than 500 colleges by Moody's Investors Service found that universities are now moving away from "trophy buildings" as administrators are prioritizing institutional spending.[67] Thomas Carlson-Reddig, Partner at Little, an architectural firm that designs campus buildings, said of Generation Z's desire for downsizing, "Students are more open to these new living arrangements than we give them credit for. . . . If you can get the cost down, students will live in a closet."[68]

This move to more modest campus amenities aligns with spending priorities of those in Generation Z. Being fiscally conservative and concerned about accruing student loan debt, as discussed in the chapter on Money, paying a high price for a fancy residence hall with features such as soundproof music practice rooms, climbing walls, Tempur-Pedic mattresses, art galleries, and karaoke lounges[69] is not something many of these students are interested in or, more aptly, can afford. Perhaps going back to more modest communal living and dining might align better with Generation Z students, perhaps even increasing the number of them who take advantage of living on campus.

Classrooms are also likely going to need to change as this generation continues through college. For example, a class that includes small group discussion, applied learning, problem-solving activities, and a facilitative instructor rather than a traditional lecturer needs a different kind of space than the typical lecture hall or classroom. These classrooms might not have a "front" of the room[70] because the instructor floats around, and there are video screens on every wall. And, with moveable furniture, instructors could have amplified flexibility to configure the space in a way that works for the class.

Despite the inordinate amount of information available online, there is still a need for libraries on campus. We might not see students crowded around card catalogs and flocking to the stacks, but having a centralized information commons still offers a relevant and important space for student discovery and learning. Students can access books and journals not available online, work with a librarian, have a quiet space to study, and have access to computers and technology resources that some students don't personally own. But, libraries with study carrels designed for independent and self-directed Gen Xers didn't seem to work for the collaborative Millennials who enjoyed the upgrades of glass study rooms, smart technology, and large tables for group learning. But, spaces designed for Millennials don't seem to fit with what many in Generation Z want. We found in our Generation Z Goes to College Study that many Generation Z students prefer independent, quiet study spaces.[71] This isn't a move back to study carrels, as those lacked the privacy and quietness Generation Z craves. But, having moveable furniture and flexible spaces where a student could roll their chair to a corner to study independently might be quite appealing. This type of furniture also lends itself to being corralled back into a circle for group work when necessary.

Safe spaces

In addition to physical spaces on college campuses, there is a newer trend in setting up emotional spaces to provide support for students. These "safe" spaces were originally designed to serve as places where marginalized students could go to feel emotionally safe within a supportive community.[72] But, safe spaces have broadened to now serve as places where students can go to shield themselves from perspectives or opinions that they might find offensive.[73] This move has been criticized, as some say that safe spaces coddle those in Generation Z.[74] Even those in Generation Z are split in terms of their support for safe spaces. A 2017 study by LendEDU, a marketplace platform to help increase transparency of private student loans, found that 36 percent of college students believe that safe spaces are absolutely necessary, 37 percent said that safe spaces were out of touch with reality, and 25 percent indicated being indifferent.[75] Now, we don't know the demographics of those who support safe spaces and those who do not, which could be an incredibly telling piece of evidence. A common argument from students about why they don't support safe spaces is similar to that of those in older generations – students are not exposed to real-world problems and civil discourse.[76] What is interesting, though, is that Generation Z students' argument in support of safe spaces is quite novel. Because Generation Z spends a great amount of time in the digital world, unlike their generational predecessors did at their age, they are faced with more opportunities for damaging emotional interactions than physical, essentially the ability to experience emotional distress from someone's words, rather than their actions. And, while someone can do their best to avoid a potentially physically dangerous situation, it can be more difficult to protect oneself from someone's offensive words.[77] The question becomes this: How can we all work to create an environment that promotes diversity of thought, deep dialogue, productive conflict, and civil discourse while ensuring environments are free from harassment, bullying, discrimination, and marginalization?

Conclusion

As those in Generation Z continue to grow and mature into adulthood, much of what they know and believe comes from their educational experiences. While what is taught is certainly critical to their education, the structures, processes, policies, and environments surrounding how and where they learn can be significant as well.

Notes

1 Center for Public Education. (2011). *Time in school: How does the U.S. compare?* Retrieved from www.centerforpubliceducation.org/Main-Menu/Organizing-a-school/ Time-in-school-How-does-the-US-compare

2 National Center for Education Statistics. (2017). *Public charter school enrollment.* Retrieved from https://nces.ed.gov/programs/coe/indicator_cgb.asp

3 U.S. Department of Education. (2012). *Statistics about nonpublic education in the United States.* Retrieved from www2.ed.gov/about/offices/list/oii/nonpublic/statistics.html

4 Geraci, J., Paulmerini, M., Cirillo, P., & McDougald, V. (2017). *What teens want from their schools: A national survey of high school student engagement.* Retrieved from https://edexcellence.net/publications/what-teens-want-from-their-schools

5 Geraci, J., Paulmerini, M., Cirillo, P., & McDougald, V. (2017).

6 Geraci, J., Paulmerini, M., Cirillo, P., & McDougald, V. (2017).

7 EY. (2015). *What if the next big disruptor isn't a what but a who?* Retrieved from www.ey.com/Publication/vwLUAssets/EY-what-if-the-next-big-disruptor-isnt-a-what-but-a-who/$File/EY-what-if-the-next-big-disruptor-isnt-a-what-but-a-who.pdf

8 Google. (2017a). *Generation Z: New insights into the mobile-first mindset of teens.* Retrieved from http://storage.googleapis.com/think/docs/GenZ_Insights_All_teens.pdf

9 Kiefer, A. (2013). *The learning environment sweet spot: Elevating the educational paradigm.* Retrieved from www.ki.com/uploadedFiles/Docs/literaturesamples/white-papers/Learning-Sweet-Spot-White-Paper.pdf

10 Singer, N. (2017). *How Google took over the classroom.* Retrieved from www.nytimes.com/2017/05/13/technology/google-education-chromebooks-schools.htmlchromebooks-schools.html, para. 4.

11 Singer, N. (2017).

12 Wagstaff, K. (2013). *Forget cursive: Teach kids how to code.* Retrieved from http://theweek.com/articles/456355/forget-cursive-teach-kids-how-code

13 Royal, D. & Swift, A. (2016). *More K-12 computer science classes teach programming/coding.* Retrieved from http://news.gallup.com/poll/196511/computer-science-classes-teach-programming-coding.aspx

14 Heitin, L. (2016). *Why don't the common-core standards include cursive writing?* Retrieved from www.pbs.org/newshour/education/scary-clown-rumors-serious-business-schools

15 Council of the Great City Schools. (2015). *Student testing in America's great city schools: An inventory and preliminary analysis.* Retrieved from www.cgcs.org/cms/lib/DC00001581/Centricity/Domain/27/Testing%20Report.pdf

16 Geraci, J., Paulmerini, M., Cirillo, P., & McDougald, V. (2017).

17 U.S. Department of Education. (2002). *The No Child Left Behind Act of 2001.* Retrieved from www2.ed.gov/nclb/overview/intro/execsumm.pdf

18 Institute of Medicine. (2013). *Educating the student body: Taking physical activity and physical education to school.* Retrieved from www.nationalacademies.org/hmd/~/media/Files/Report%20Files/2013/Educating-the-Student-Body/EducatingTheStudentBody_rb.pdf

19 Parsad, B., Splegelman, M., & Coopersmith, J. (2012). *Arts education in public elementary and secondary schools 1999–2000 and 2009–2010.* Retrieved from http://nces.ed.gov/pubs2012/2012014.pdf

20 National PTA. (n.d.). *History.* Retrieved from www.pta.org/home/About-National-Parent-Teacher-Association/Mission-Values/National-PTA-History

21 Dictionary.com. (2018). *Helicopter parenting.* Retrieved from www.dictionary.com/browse/helicopter-parent?s=ts

22 Seemiller, C. & Grace, M. (2016). *Generation Z goes to college.* San Francisco: Jossey-Bass.

23 Seemiller, C. & Grace, M. (2016).

24 Singer, N. (2017).

25 Geraci, J., Paulmerini, M., Cirillo, P., & McDougald, V. (2017).

26 Geraci, J., Paulmerini, M., Cirillo, P., & McDougald, V. (2017).

27 Human Rights Campaign. (2018). *LGBTQ youth report.* Retrieved from https://assets2.hrc.org/files/assets/resources/2018-YouthReport-NoVid.pdf

28 Seemiller, C. & Grace, M. (2016).

29 Seemiller, C. & Grace, M. (2014). *Generation Z goes to college study.* Unpublished raw data.

30 Human Rights Campaign. (2018).

31 Twenge, J. M. (2017). *iGen: Why today's super-connected kids are growing up less rebellious, more tolerant, less happy – and completely unprepared for adulthood – and what that means for the rest of us.* New York: Atria Books.

32 Sallie Mae. (2017). *How America pays for college.* Retrieved from www.salliemae.com/assets/Research/HAP/HowAmericaPaysforCollege2017.pdf

33 EAB. (2017). *Why do students decline their dream schools?* Retrieved from www.eab.com/blogs/enrollment/2017/03/why-do-students-decline-their-dream-schools

34 Sallie Mae. (2017).

35 Jaschik, S. (2017). *New York adopts free tuition.* Retrieved from www.insidehighered.com/news/2017/04/10/new-york-state-reaches-deal-provide-free-tuition-suny-and-cuny-students

36 Sallie Mae. (2017).

37 Sallie Mae. (2017).

38 Fry, R. (2015). *Record share of young women are living with their parents, relatives.* Retrieved from www.pewresearch.org/fact-tank/2015/11/11/record-share-of-young-women-are-living-with-their-parents-relatives./

39 Fry, R. (2015).

40 Better Homes and Gardens. (2014). *Move over Millennials, Better Homes and Gardens Real Estate reveals homebuying dreams of Gen Z teens.* Retrieved from www.prnewswire.com/news-releases/move-over-millennials-better-homes-and-gardens-real-estate-reveals-homebuying-dreams-of-gen-z-teens-274452691.html

41 Barnes & Noble College. (2015). *Getting to know Gen Z: Exploring middle and high schoolers' expectations for higher education.* Retrieved from https://next.bncollege.com/wp-content/uploads/2015/10/Gen-Z-Research-Report-Final.pdf

42 Sallie Mae. (2017).

43 College Board. (2014). *10 years of advanced placement exam data show significant gains in access and success: Areas for improvement.* Retrieved from www.collegeboard.org/releases/2014/class-2013-advanced-placement-results-announced

44 Stillman, D. & Stillman, J. (2017). *Gen Z @ work: How the next generation is transforming the workplace.* New York: HarperCollins.

45 Ologie. (2016). *The Gen Z report.* Columbus, OH: Ologie.

46 Sallie Mae. (2017).

47 Ologie. (2016).

48 Barnes & Noble College. (2015).

49 Steffes, T. L. (n.d.). *Smith-Hughes Act.* Retrieved from www.britannica.com/topic/Smith-Hughes-Act.

50 Drury, R. L. (2003). Community colleges in America: A historical perspective. *Inquiry,* 8(1), 1–6. Retrieved from http://files.eric.ed.gov/fulltext/EJ876835.pdf

51 Lee, L. (1996). *Community colleges and proprietary schools.* ERIC Digest. Retrieved from https://files.eric.ed.gov/fulltext/ED400003.pdf

52 National Student Clearinghouse Research Center. *Current term enrollment estimates fall 2017.* Retrieved from https://nscresearchcenter.org/wp-content/uploads/Current TermEnrollment-Fall2017a.pdf

53 HBCU Digest. (2017). *Freshman enrollment surges at several HBCUs.* Retrieved from https://hbcudigest.com/freshman-enrollment-surges-at-several-hbcus/

54 Johnson, J. (2017). *The Black Renaissance is real: HBCUs see record growth in 2017.* Retrieved from www.theroot.com/the-black-renaissance-is-real-hbcus-see-record-growth-1819841936

55 Johnson, J. (2017), para. 15 and 16.

56 Class Central. (2016). *By the numbers: MOOCs in 2016*. Retrieved from www.class-central.com/report/mooc-stats-2016/

57 Johnson, S. (2017). *In the era of microcredentials, institutions look to blockchain to verify learning*. Retrieved from www.edsurge.com/news/2017-10-31-in-the-era-of-microcredentials-institutions-look-to-blockchain-to-verify-learning

58 Ang, K. (2017). *This inexpensive one-year "college alternative" may help you land a better job than a traditional degree*. Retrieved from https://moneyish.com/upgrade/this-inexpensive-one-year-college-alternative-may-help-you-land-a-better-job-than-a-traditional-degree/

59 Higher Education Research Institute. (2017). *College Senior Survey*. Data prepared by Higher Education Research Institute.

60 Bresman, H. & Rao, V. D. (2017). *A survey of 19 countries shows how Generations X, Y, and Z are – and aren't – different*. Retrieved from https://hbr.org/2017/08/a-survey-of-19-countries-shows-how-generations-x-y-and-z-are-and-arent-different

61 Bresman, H. & Rao, V. D. (2017).

62 Seemiller, C. & Grace, M. (2016).

63 Northeastern University. (2014). *Innovation survey*. Retrieved from www.northeastern.edu/news/2014/11/innovation-imperative-meet-generation-z/

64 Northeastern University. (2014).

65 Drury, R. L. (2003).

66 Jacob, B., McCall, B., & Stange, K. (2018). College as country club: Do colleges cater to students' preferences for consumption? *Journal of Labor Economics, 36*(2), 309–348.

67 Selingo, J. (2017). *Why universities are phasing out luxury dorms*. Retrieved from www.theatlantic.com/education/archive/2017/08/why-universities-are-phasing-out-luxury-dorms/537492/

68 Selingo, J. (2017), para. 13.

69 Hoyt, E. (2014). *15 college dorms with crazy-awesome amenities*. Retrieved from www.fastweb.com/student-life/articles/the-15-college-dorms-with-crazy-awesome-amenities

70 Rickes, P. (2017). Generations in flux: How Gen Z will continue to transform higher education space. *Planning for Higher Education Journal, 44*(4), 1–25.

71 Seemiller, C. & Grace, M. (2016).

72 Ho, K. (2017). *Tackling the term: What is a safe space?* Retrieved from http://harvardpolitics.com/harvard/what-is-a-safe-space/

73 Twenge, J. M. (2017).

74 Twenge, J. M. (2017).

75 Brown, M. (2017). *What do college students think about safe spaces?* Retrieved from https://lendedu.com/blog/college-students-think-safe-spaces/

76 Brown, M. (2017).

77 Brown, M. (2017).

16 Learning

••

Understanding educational environments as they relate to Generation Z students is critical. Yet, it is equally important to explore the complex dimensionality of Generation Z as students in both K–12 and in higher education. What they bring to educational environments and how they prefer to learn ultimately shapes their experiences and expectations.

Information literacy in the digital world

With many search engines, websites, video platforms, and social media sites available, there are nearly infinite places where Generation Z students can get information. Because of this, for them, research is less about acquiring new knowledge and more about accessing a quick answer to complete an assignment.[1] Mark Bauerlin, professor and researcher, argues that their immense focus on peer-to-peer relationships in the digital world has come at the expense of developing higher learning.[2] He asserts that this generation needs to live more outside their online social networks reading and writing about critical issues rather than inside of them engaging in online dialogue, online gaming, and following pop culture.[3] But Gabriel Fuentes, a faculty member investigating Generation Z in the field of architecture, counters that there is a vast amount of information available in this "fast-paced and flattened world," making it challenging for Generation Z to navigate when educators use status quo educational techniques.[4] For those in Generation Z to engage in effective reading and writing today, they may need educational support and strategies that were not necessary when those in older generations got information primarily from encyclopedias, library books, and teachers.

And not only do those in Generation Z have to navigate this information overload, they are also likely to come across a great deal of misinformation. With Millennials, the focus was on helping them determine the credibility of the information they retrieved before consuming it as truth. Educators have had to spend time teaching students how to determine the legitimacy of sources appropriate for school as research shifts from books to Wikipedia and online databases to social media.[5] With Generation Z, though, we have to go one step further – helping them unlearn misinformation. The time it takes to engage in unlearning might be comparable to the time it takes to help them learn. So, although the Internet is our playground, it is important for those in Generation Z to understand that not everything there is accurate, safe, and helpful.

Applied and practical learning

In 1938, Napoleon Hill wrote about the importance of applied learning in education,[6] a message that younger members of the G.I. Generation heading off to college could embrace. He said, "New leaders will become a necessity. This is especially true in the field of education. The leader in that field must, in the future, find ways and means of teaching people HOW TO APPLY the knowledge they receive in school."[7]

Fast-forward to today where the importance of applied learning also holds true with Generation Z. In our Generation Z Stories Study, we found that a higher number of Generation Z college students indicated that applied learning makes learning enjoyable for them, more than any other factor.[8] Those in Generation Z want to fill their toolboxes with real-world knowledge and skills that will help them when they enter the workforce.[9] Real-world knowledge- and skill-building are not just taking place in the classroom either. Seventy-nine percent believe that educational programs should integrate opportunities like internships that offer practical and applied learning.[10]

A study by Ologie on the catchphrases used by colleges for marketing found that Generation Z students' preferred language echoes their desire for applied learning. They didn't favor phrases like "premier institution" and "tight-knit community," but gravitated towards phrases such as "hands-on learning," "real-world experience," and "professional opportunity."[11]

It's not just Generation Z college students who want applied learning. More than three-quarters of both high school students and their teachers believe that hands-on learning is an effective teaching method, a higher number than any other pedagogy.[12] They also believe that students learn best when they have the opportunity for hands-on learning.[13]

❝ *Learning becomes especially enjoyable to me when I can connect content we learned in class to things I care about or things that are pertinent to what's happening in the world at the time.* ❞
– Member of Generation Z

In addition to experiential or project-based learning that has been around long before Generation Z was even born, one unique way that both K–12 institutions and colleges are addressing this need for applied learning is through the implementation of makerspaces on campus.[14] These spaces are often open facilities filled with tools and resources where students can create, invent, and turn their ideas into innovations.

Moving from group to self-learning

For generations, the standard classroom setup included desks in rows facing the front of the room so students could see the board and the teacher. But, the transition to peer-to-peer education and collaborative learning where students sit at tables or in pods with other students seemed to be more popular by the time Millennials were in school, fostering their collaborative and interpersonal spirit. But, only 49 percent of middle and high school students in Generation Z prefer learning that involves small group work.[15] This aligns with findings from our Generation Z Goes to College Study in which interpersonal learning was one of the least-preferred learning styles, with 25 percent indicating that it was not an effective learning method at all.[16]

> *My ideal learning environment is in a quiet area, though not as quiet as the library. I like to know there are people around me as I am studying.*
> – Member of Generation Z

While many Generation Z college students are not fans of interpersonal learning, it makes sense that their most preferred learning style is intrapersonal.[17] Our Generation Z Goes to College Study revealed that many of them like the notion of independent learning where they control the timing, pace, and environment.[18] With their self-identified characteristics of being determined, responsible, thoughtful, and self-reliant,[19] it seems to fit well that many of them enjoy working on their own. The preference of Generation Z college students for this type of self-directed learning is likely an effect of participating in independent educational activities in K–12. A study by Pew found that 94 percent of teachers of those in Generation Z indicated that it was very likely that their students go online to research information for assignments.[20] Whether they used technology for researching information, interacting with a learning app, or using Google Classroom, being able to search, surf, stream, and post content online is often single-user centric, which fosters a sense of independent learning.

> *Usually I like it quiet. I like to be around others, though.*
> – Member of Generation Z

But, Generation Z students are not looking to learn in isolated settings with no human interaction. Many of Generation Z college students are social learners[21] and like to learn next to, but not with, others. This is likely why they may not resonate as much with fully online courses. Hybrid classrooms, on the other hand, allow those in Generation Z to engage in self-directed, independent learning leading up to a handful of in-person sessions with an instructor and other learners where they can have face-to-face connection. Thus, Generation Z students might enjoy flipped classrooms where students work on assignments before coming to class.[22] In doing so, they could engage in independent learning experiences beforehand and then participate in hands-on applied learning with their peers during class time. This notion of flipped learning is not just for colleges, though. Researchers at the Thomas B. Fordham Institute suggest flipped learning for high schools as well.[23]

Learning in an era of curated identities

Generation Z is the first generation to grow up in an entirely digital era, where their identities were already commented on, shaped by, and "liked" online by the time their eager Generation X parents could post their baby pictures. It makes sense then that those in Generation Z are cautious and private when online,[24] wanting to take control of how others see them – essentially managing their reputation and personal brand. This desire for reputation management could come into play in the classroom when Generation Z students are asked to raise their hands to answer a question or share a comment. Some may feel intimidated or nervous to speak up in front of the class for fear of being wrong. Maintaining a reputation for silence might seem more positive to them than running the risk of not being seen as smart by their peers and even the instructor. By wanting to be sure of their thoughts, ideas, and responses before sharing them with others, those in Generation Z might feel compelled to come to class prepared to participate.

> ❝ I don't enjoy speaking my thoughts. I like to think everything through first and organize my thoughts and present when I know I am on the right track. ❞
> – Member of Generation Z

On the other hand, however, this fear of being vulnerable might affect their self-esteem and propensity to take risks in their learning. Given that they are less physically risky and are fearful of emotional distress,[25] it would not be surprising for them to also be less apt to take academic risks in front of others. Because of this, a flipped classroom where they can complete assignments ahead of time might give Generation Z students the opportunity to become more knowledgeable and confident about class content before being asked to participate in discussions and activities during class. Enhanced confidence could result in more class engagement and/or less dislike of group learning because they are not intimidated or nervous to suggest a wrong answer in front of others.

> ❝ My ideal learning environment would be in a small group [with] individual attention to the students and where I could get help from the instructor without feeling intimidated by them. ❞
> – Member of Generation Z

Show me first and then let me try

Sixty-two percent of Generation Z high school students and 66 percent of teachers believe that watching others complete a task is an effective learning method.[26] Those in Generation Z like seeing sample exemplary work, participating in practice sessions, watching demonstrations, and working through example problems with the instructor so they are clear about the expectations of an assignment and feel comfortable attempting to complete it.[27] This may seem like hand-holding, but with Generation Z's high level of responsibility,[28] many of them just likely want to make sure they are doing the assignment correctly.

> ❝ I like it when I can see an example of what I'm supposed to do. Depending on the task, this could be step-by-step instructions or simply an example of the end result. I would have someone talk me through the process while simultaneously showing me where I'm supposed to be. ❞
> – Member of Generation Z

Video-based learning

One way in which Generation Z students can capitalize on their desire for learning by watching others is through the use of video-based learning. While those in the G.I. Generation didn't necessarily have videos in their classrooms, watching films in class seems to date back several generations. Those films were often on a reel or tape that the instructor acquired to show in class. For Gen Xers and Millennials, watching educational movies or films during school often occurred on special occasions or rainy days. For Generation Z, video-based learning is not only widespread and accessible, learning and acquiring new information is one of this generation's primary uses for video-based content.[29] Generation Z students can access nearly any recording they want, either through a streaming service or a simple Internet search. And while it may seem that many of them fill their time watching silly videos, it is still quite easy for them to seek out videos for their own learning. And they do. We found that nearly 90 percent of Generation Z college students go to YouTube to learn new knowledge.[30] And, a study by Barnes & Noble found that 80 percent of Generation Z high school teens believe YouTube is a helpful learning tool.[31]

But, not every generation, even recent ones, see video-based learning as poignant as those in Generation Z do. Take cooking, for example. How we have learned to make a particular dish has evolved over time. For centuries, recipes were often passed down from generation to generation through demonstrations and oral instruction. Then, with the ability to write, recipes could be documented in a cookbook. With the advent of the Internet, there was an explosion of written recipes, where, in some cases, a simple Internet search could yield 500 ways to make the same dish. Now, with sites that allow everyday users to upload their own videos online, it is easy to actually watch someone cook nearly any recipe that exists, with the ability to rewind and pause to ensure that no steps are missed. Despite the thousands of cooking videos available online, reading a recipe (albeit from the Internet rather than a cookbook) might still seem more comfortable for older generations because following a written recipe is how many of them learned to cook. But that isn't the case for those in Generation Z who enjoy video-based learning. While their Generation X parents might prefer to read an enchilada recipe, those in Generation Z might just turn on YouTube or a Tasty video to watch someone properly roll the tortillas before baking them.

Watching a video versus reading printed material (or even a website) taps into a different learning mode, reflecting more of consumption of information rather than interpretation. And, those in the business of educational technology are leveraging that consumption approach with Generation Z students. Rather than publishing e-books, which are essentially books to be read, Pearson has recently released choose your own adventure education subscriptions, mirroring a Netflix-type approach to digitized content, putting interactive information, videos, and animation in a manner to be "consumed" and not "read."[32] Perhaps consumption feels less rigorous or overwhelming for those in Generation Z, hence their ability to binge-watch an entire season of a series in one weekend. Or maybe because of the nearly 50 percent decrease in attention spans over the last 10 years,[33] entertaining snippets that blend multimedia rather than the one-dimensional format of printed text may be more alluring to those in Generation Z.

Digital distractions or learning aids?

Growing up in a digital age with early exposure to technology has likely fostered the desire of those in Generation Z to use personal devices in college classrooms. The same students who were encouraged, and maybe even required, to use a Chromebook in high school are now bringing their own laptops to their college classrooms. There are mixed sentiments from college instructors about students using digital devices like laptops and tablets during class.[34] Research has shown two competing findings and viewpoints. On the one hand, there is a relationship between students who use digital devices in the classroom and lower test scores,[35,36] indicating that these devices might be more distracting than helpful for learning. At the K–12 level, however, a study by online study guide platform, Quizlet, found that 70 percent of Generation Z students believe that intentional use of technology during class contributes to quicker learning than using traditional methods.[37] It is likely that the intentionality of the technology integration determines how helpful or distracting technology in the classroom can be for Generation Z students.

Learning environments

Given that those in Generation Z identify as intrapersonal, yet social, learners,[38] what they look for in an ideal learning environment reflects the way they like to learn.

First, this generation looks at all spaces to be adaptable, "blurring and balancing the boundaries between working, socializing, learning, shopping, eating, discovering, and more so spaces are distinguished by etiquette, not by function."[39] Further, due to their desire for applied and experiential learning,[40] having flexible learning spaces is key. Being able to move furniture from independent seating to group discussion and then off to the side allows the space for instruction to be fluid and adaptable.

> ❝ My ideal learning environment is 'in a large space with others who are quiet and everyone has their own table or space to work and little distractions, and I will occasionally listen to music from earbuds.' ❞
> – Member of Generation Z

In addition to flexible and mixed-use space, Generation Z college students, in particular, prefer quiet learning environments where students can tune out with headphones or earbuds either listening to music or even white noise.[41] But, their social nature means that they like to be in close proximity with other students to learn, as long as those students are serious about their learning and aren't distracting.[42]

Passionate and caring educators

It is also important to acknowledge that educators play an important role for those in Generation Z. For example, Generation Z high school students prefer teachers who are genuinely excited about teaching their subject matter.[43] That excitement can help pique their curiosity and interest in particular content. In addition, a study by Ologie found that 61 percent of high school students reported that their teachers or counselors were influential in their college selection process.[44] These students look to their teachers as individuals whose opinions they trust and respect. But they don't just want subject matter experts who can share their knowledge.

> ❝ Learning is enjoyable to me when I have a teacher who is loving the subject that they are teaching, challenging me to see beyond just the information and I am learning at least one new thing each time I'm in the classroom. ❞
> – Member of Generation Z

Generation Z high school students also look to their teachers for emotional support.[45] A study by the Thomas B. Fordham Institute found that in determining archetypes for high school students that 15 percent fall into the category of Teacher Responder, placing great value on the relationships they create with their teachers.[46] These students thrive the most when they believe their teachers are invested in their personal and academic development.[47]

We found in both of our studies that college students feel much the same way. For many of them, they see their instructors as facilitators who aid in learning instead of experts who impart their wisdom to their students.[48] And, they want their instructors to be storytellers, sharing their real-life experiences and bringing the content to life. But their instructors are more than just facilitators and storytellers. Because many of them want to feel cared about by the educators in their lives, it is no surprise that they also see them as caretakers.[49]

> **❝** *My ideal learning environment is 'with an instructor who is both highly knowledgeable of the subject and deeply passionate for teaching students, and about the students themselves.'* **❞**
> *– Member of Generation Z*

Conclusion

Many in Generation Z are lifetime learners and have been facilitating their own self-education since they could swipe a tablet. But, their preferences for learning, especially intrapersonal, self-paced, and applied, go beyond simply the access they have to today's technology. How they approach learning is likely reflective of a larger educational context and characteristics specific to this cohort. So as we uncover more about who Generation Z is, the more we can make sense of and leverage the capacities of this generation in and out of school.

Notes

1 Purcell, K., Rainie, L., Heaps, A., Buchanan, J., Friedrich, L., Jacklin, A., . . . Zickuhr, K. (2012). *How teens do research in the digital world*. Retrieved from www.pewinternet. org/2012/11/01/how-teens-do-research-in-the-digital-world/

2 Fuentes, G. (2014). Pedagogy with and against the flow: Generational shifts, social media, and the Gen Z brain. In J. Stuart & M. Wilson (Eds.), *102nd ACSA annual meeting proceedings, globalizing architecture/flows and disruptions*. Miami Beach, FL: Association of Collegiate Schools of Architecture.

3 Fuentes, G. (2014).

4 Fuentes, G. (2014), p. 670.

5 Purcell, K., Rainie, L., Heaps, A., Buchanan, J., Friedrich, L., Jacklin, A., . . . Zickuhr, K. (2012).

6   Hill, N. (1938). *Think and grow rich*. Meriden, CT: The Ralston Society.

7   Hill, N. (1938), p. 115.

8   Seemiller, C. & Grace, M. (2017). *Generation Z stories study*. Unpublished raw data.

9   Northeastern University. (2014). *Innovation survey*. Retrieved from www.northeastern. edu/news/2014/11/innovation-imperative-meet-generation-z/

10 Northeastern University. (2014).

11 Ologie. (2016). *The Gen Z report*. Columbus, OH: Ologie.

12 Adobe Educate. (2016). *Gen Z in the classroom: Creating the future*. Retrieved from www. adobeeducate.com/genz/adobe-education-genz

13 Adobe Educate. (2016).

14 Rickes, P. (2017). Generations in flux: How Gen Z will continue to transform higher education space. *Planning for Higher Education Journal, 44*(4), 1–25.

15 Barnes & Noble College. (2015). *Getting to know Gen Z: Exploring middle and high schoolers' expectations for higher education*. Retrieved from https://next.bncollege.com/wp-content/ uploads/2015/10/Gen-Z-Research-Report-Final.pdf

16 Seemiller, C. & Grace, M. (2014). *Generation Z goes to college study*. Unpublished raw data.

17 Seemiller, C. & Grace, M. (2016). *Generation Z goes to college*. San Francisco: Jossey-Bass.

18 Seemiller, C. & Grace, M. (2016).

19 Seemiller, C. & Grace, M. (2016).

20 Pew Internet. (2012). *How teens do research in the digital world*. Retrieved from www. pewinternet.org/files/old-media/Files/Reports/2012/PIP_TeacherSurveyReportWith-Methodology110112.pdf

21 Seemiller, C. & Grace, M. (2016).

22 Flipped Learning Network. (2014). *What is flipped learning?* Retrieved from https:// flippedlearning.org/wp-content/uploads/2016/07/FLIP_handout_FNL_Web.pdf

23 Geraci, J., Paulmerini, M., Cirillo, P., & McDougald, V. (2017). *What teens want from their schools: A national survey of high school student engagement*. Retrieved from https:// edexcellence.net/publications/what-teens-want-from-their-schools

24 Seemiller, C. & Grace, M. (2016).

25 Brown, M. (2017). *What do college students think about safe spaces?* Retrieved from https:// lendedu.com/blog/college-students-think-safe-spaces/

26 Adobe Educate. (2016).

27 Seemiller, C. & Grace, M. (2016).

28 Seemiller, C. & Grace, M. (2016).

29 Seemiller, C. & Grace, M. (2016).

30 Seemiller, C. & Grace, M. (2014).

31 Barnes & Noble College. (2015).

32 Schrager, A. & Wang, A. X. (2017). *College textbooks are going the way of Netflix*. Retrieved from https://qz.com/1039404/end-of-textbooks/, p. 3.

33 Vidyarthyi, N. (2011). *Attention spans have dropped from 12 to 5 minutes: How social media is ruining our minds*. Retrieved from www.adweek.com/socialtimes/attention-spans-have-dropped-from-12-minutes-to-5-seconds-how-social-media-is-ruiningour-minds-infographic/87484

34 Gose, B. (2017). *A new generation of digital distraction*. Retrieved from www.chronicle. com/article/Gen-Z-Changes-the-Debate-About/241163

35 Carter, S. P., Greenberg, K., & Walker, M. (2016). *The impact of computer usage on academic performance: Evidence from a randomized trial at the United State military academy*. Retrieved from https://seii.mit.edu/wp-content/uploads/2016/05/SEII-Discussion-Paper-2016.02-Payne-Carter-Greenberg-and-Walker-2.pdf

36 Kuznekoff, J. H. & Titsworth, S. (2013). The impact of mobile phone usage on student learning. *Communication Education, 62*(3), 233–252.

37 Glotzbach, M. (2016). *Quizlet insights: Teachers say technology makes learning more fun, students say it helps them learn.* Retrieved from https://quizlet.com/blog/survey-results-student-teacher-generations

38 Seemiller, C. & Grace, M. (2016).

39 Figenholtz, J. & Broderick, A. (2017). *Future-proofing higher education: Understanding Generation Z.* Retrieved from www.bdcnetwork.com/blog/future-proofing-higher-education-understanding-generation-z

40 Seemiller, C. & Grace, M. (2016).

41 Seemiller, C. & Grace, M. (2016).

42 Seemiller, C. & Grace, M. (2016).

43 Geraci, J., Paulmerini, M., Cirillo, P., & McDougald, V. (2017).

44 Ologie. (2016).

45 Geraci, J., Paulmerini, M., Cirillo, P., & McDougald, V. (2017).

46 Geraci, J., Paulmerini, M., Cirillo, P., & McDougald, V. (2017).

47 Geraci, J., Paulmerini, M., Cirillo, P., & McDougald, V. (2017).

48 Seemiller, C. & Grace, M. (2016).

49 Seemiller, C. & Grace, M. (2017).

17 Career aspirations

Technology's rapid advancement has resulted in the creation of innovative objects, gadgets, tools, systems, and resources that have fundamentally changed how we experience the world. Keeping up with these advancements continuously challenges us to reconsider and reimagine occupations necessary for using the technology we create. So, what are those in Generation Z aspiring to for their careers and how does that align with the jobs needed for the future?

Future landscape of work

Just as switchboard operators might never have imagined a world with text messaging or cell phones, it is hard to fully conceptualize today what the occupations of tomorrow might be. But, there is data pointing to some trends that may help us better understand if not the exact jobs, then at least the skills that will be needed in the future.

> *((What I worry about most is 'that my field will be obsolete by the time I graduate.'))*
> *– Member of Generation Z*

Jobs that don't yet exist

In a study by Adobe Educate, 94 percent of middle and high school teachers who were surveyed believed that their students would have a career in the future that "we didn't even know would exist today."[1] Although it is more conceivable to imagine an 11 year-old having a job at 45 that we couldn't foresee, researchers at Duke University found that 65 percent of incoming college students will actually have a job that does not exist today.[2] This means that what Generation Z students may be studying won't relate to their future careers.

Although we might not know for sure the exact occupations that will exist in 30 years, we can predict some themes. First, jobs of the future will likely involve some form of creation. Eighty-three percent of 11 to 17 year-olds believe that they will be creating things in their future careers.[3] They might not know yet what things they will be creating or really if there will be a demand for this, but they believe the act of creating something will somehow be part of their futures. Further, they believe they can leverage technology to build things that older generations would have never conceived,[4] liken to their grandparents who likely never imagined information being stored online in a cloud rather than in a file cabinet.

In addition, it will be no surprise to see an increase in automation in many industries, as employers won't want to pay a human to do what a robot can do for free. A study by the cloud communication firm, 8X8, found that nearly 70 percent of Generation Z respondents believed that even today some of their jobs could be automated, and more believed that to be true for the future.[5] It might not be that each job will be replaced by an automated version of a human doing that job, but certain jobs might become obsolete for human employees as technology creates new ways of operation. For example, we might not have robots like Rosie from the Jetsons cleaning our future homes but instead have self-cleaning appliances.

Finally, commercial real estate firm, CBRE, points out "new jobs will require creative intelligence, social intelligence and the ability to leverage artificial intelligence."[6] What this looks like in terms of specific occupations of the near and distant future may still be unknown, but we can certainly try to prepare Generation Z in developing the skills needed to work in a rapidly advancing society where new occupations regularly emerge. And, it will be important to remember that in addition to helping this generation develop specific skills for these future occupations, they will also need to develop critical career skills, such as communication and teamwork, which have been foundational for many earlier generations as they entered the workforce.[7]

Trending fields

We might not know what jobs will be available in the future, but we do have a sense of employment trends that will be present as those in Generation Z establish their career paths. First, popular career fields center around those that involve technological advancement. Business, engineering, and computer and information sciences were the top three degree fields sought by job recruiters at colleges and universities in 2016. This held true across associate, bachelor's, and master's degrees.[8] Both engineering as well as computer and information sciences are deeply connected to advancing technology; yet, business majors are needed to run the companies that research, design, use, and sell these technologies.

Second, according to CareerCast, trending fields for Generation Z will include jobs that are high paying, high growth, and recession proof.[9] Career-Cast's top three jobs include computer and information systems manager, environmental engineers, and financial planners.[10] For example, with the continued mass creation and collection of digital information, roles like computer and information systems managers will likely see an increase in demand, paying salaries that reflect the challenge of securing private data online.

Finally, given that more occupations will continue to be automated, popular and growing fields will also likely include those that are less prone to eventual automation. Studying, preparing, and training for a job that will be obsolete in the near future looks to be a bad investment for Generation Z, especially with the high cost of earning a college degree today. In a study by design and innovation consulting firm, Altitude, most of those in Generation Z indicated they were striving for jobs in high growth fields including education, medicine, and sales.[11] Despite advances in online education, eMedicine, and online sites like Amazon that sell virtually anything, we are still likely far away from a world without actual human teachers inspiring our children to achieve their goals, doctors diagnosing and treating diseases, and salespeople convincing us of the importance of a potential purchase. Not only do these types of jobs require inquiry and complex cognitive reasoning, they all also are grounded in human connection built on relationships and trust.[12]

Technology is expanding at an unimaginable speed, changing the nature and types of jobs in the workforce. Jobs that appear in science fiction movies today, like the time re-assigner from *Source Code* or the dream extractor from *Inception*,[13] may very well come to fruition and then become obsolete within the career lifespan of Generation Z.

What Generation Z wants

As employers hire those in Generation Z, they need to be prepared for what this new generation is searching for and will bring to the workplace. Although they will be working for older cohorts who likely have their own way of doing things, understanding what makes Generation Z tick could provide supervisors insight into helping Generation Z new hires make a smooth transition into the job and ultimately leverage their talents and strengths to benefit the organization. So, what are those in Generation Z looking for in terms of their career?

> ❝ *Having a career that integrates what I am good at (my skills) and what I want to do (my passions) with what people/the world needs (purpose) and also with what I can get paid for and live off of comfortably (stability/security).* ❞
> *- Member of Generation Z*

Enjoyment and happiness

One-third of participants in our Generation Z Stories Study reported that enjoyment is the most important factor in their future career.[14] They shared their thoughts on how essential it is to find a job they like doing every day

> **❝ It is most important to me that I am happy and truly enjoy what I am doing. I do not want to be one of those people that dreads going to work every day, and is unhappy all the time. I don't even necessarily care about the money, as long as I have enough to live. I just need to be happy. ❞**
> — Member of Generation Z

and the dread they feared in not enjoying their work. It may appear a bit paradoxical in that the market may drive them to take any job they can get as they are frugal, money-conscious individuals worried about financial security.[15] However, many do draw the line in saying that they have to enjoy their work. And, although some trending fields will be high paying, many in Generation Z will also opt for other high-growth jobs like teaching that are more modest in pay if it is an occupation that would make them happy.

Making a positive impact on others and society

In our Generation Z Stories Study, we found that 26 percent said that making a difference was the most important factor in a future career,[16] not surprising in that nearly 84 percent think it is essential or very important to help others who are in difficulty.[17] Those in Generation Z want their work to truly matter to someone, somewhere. In our study, many of them shared details of work-ing in education, medicine, and other service professions, while others talked of making the world a better place through their work in socially responsible companies.

> **❝ I want to make a difference. Don't get me wrong; it would be great to get to travel, make a lot of money and become published, but none of that means anything if you don't make a difference. ❞**
> — Member of Generation Z

Not only do they want to make a difference individually, 90 percent think it is important for their careers to contribute towards social change,[18] and 93 percent say that their decision to work at a company is affected by the company's impact on society.[19]

Fulfillment, passion, and greater meaning

Not to be confused with their desire for enjoyable work, many in Generation Z believe that work should be fulfilling. Where 69 percent of those in other generations believe that jobs should have greater meaning than making money, 74 percent of those in Generation Z believe this to be true.[20] This holds true when exploring the role of passion in their careers as well. A study by Monster found that 46 percent of those in Generation Z want a job that allows them to pursue a passion versus only 32 percent across other generations who are seeking passion from their work.[21] Beyond passion, three-quarters of those in Generation Z believe work should have a greater purpose than making money.[22] In that same study, only 45 percent of Millennials, 40 percent of Gen Xers, and 33 percent of Baby Boomers felt similarly about work needing to serve a greater purpose.[23] And, when we asked participants in our Generation Z Stories Study to talk about what a good life meant to them, surprisingly, one-quarter discussed the importance of having fulfilling work.[24]

This is a generation that wants to come home at the end of the day feeling good about what they contributed to the world through their work. If the type of work that Generation Z is being hired to do does not lend itself to internal fulfillment, employers may need to find a way to connect the role to something bigger and more meaningful.

> *The most important factor in my future career is 'making sure I'm doing something I love, not just something that pays the bills.'*
> — *Member of Generation Z*

> *A good life to me includes doing something that I am passionate about and making a difference in the lives of those around me, in the most positive way.*
> — *Member of Generation Z*

Financial stability

Given their desire for meaningful and fulfilling work, one might assume that altruistic Generation Z will work for pennies as long as they can spend their 60 hours a week changing the world. Although there may be some element of truth to that, those in Generation Z are still highly concerned about financial security[25] and are seeking a stable future,[26] with 63 percent believing they must have a competitive salary.[27] What, though, is a competitive salary to Generation Z? For many, they indicate wanting high income potential.[28] But when they discuss their future income, they describe simply wanting a paycheck that helps them achieve modest financial stability and not necessarily an abundance of wealth. For example, we found

> *A life where you don't have to live paycheck after paycheck. A life that is debt free, being able to access basic human things like healthcare, not worry what you are going to eat later in the day, being able to afford things that are a necessity.*
> — *Member of Generation Z*

in our Generation Z Stories Study that just shy of 16 percent shared stories of wanting to make "just enough money." For the 9 percent who indicated wanting a good salary that is perhaps more than "just enough," nearly all also wrote some variation of "and being happy," an indicator of not sacrificing happiness for a good salary.[29] Their desire for "just enough" may help explain why achieving financial stability, while important, is not as crucial to them as it is with Millennials.[30] For example, for only 28 percent of those in Generation Z compared to 42 percent of Millennials, "money would motivate them to work harder and stay with their employer."[31]

In addition to salary, benefits are very important to those in Generation Z. Monster Worldwide, Inc., reports that 70 percent of those in Generation Z believe that health insurance is a "must have,"[32] which aligns with findings from Stillman and Stillman who found that healthcare coverage is even more important to those in Generation Z than time off.[33] Given the volatility of healthcare in the U.S. over the last decade, it is no wonder that these fiscally minded new hires would seek out jobs that would cover what could be their largest ongoing expense.

Another benefit that would appeal greatly to those in Generation Z is tuition assistance. Because the cost of tuition is the number one concern among Generation Z college students,[34] being able to enter the workforce directly from high school could be more attractive if they knew they could receive tuition assistance from their employer. According to data from Universum Global, a firm specializing in employer branding, 60 percent of high schoolers would be willing to go straight into the workforce if their employer offered to provide educational assistance.[35]

Advancement and personal growth opportunities

Another important factor for Generation Z when seeking jobs is the opportunity for growth, both in terms of advancement[36] as well as personal development on the job.[37] First, some in Generation Z are looking for opportunities for upward mobility. A study by researcher and author, Dr. Candace Steele Flippin, found that the opportunity to advance is preferred by those in Generation Z more than making more money.[38] This aligns with findings from our initial study in which nearly 75 percent of those surveyed indicated that they were motivated by the opportunity for advancement.[39] It will be important for employers if they want to retain this generation of workers to help them see a path to their futures, especially within the organization.

In regard to personal growth and development, lifelong learning is important for Generation Z. Many fear being trapped in a job with no opportunity to learn and develop new skills. Universum Global found that 36 percent of the 50,000 high school graduates they surveyed indicated being afraid that they will be stuck in their career with no opportunities for development.[40] But, it might be easier than ever to access professional and skill development opportunities through free online courses, videos, and websites. This may be alluring to employers who believe they no longer need to provide professional development because of its broad accessibility. However, if employers drive their Generation Z employees out of the office to independently retool, those employees may find that they retool themselves right into another job in another organization.

> **❝ The most important factor in my future career is 'finding a job that keeps me thinking.' ❞**
> *– Member of Generation Z*

Success

More than one-quarter of those in Generation Z are concerned that they will be unable to fulfill their ambition.[41] This underscores another factor that is important for those in Generation Z in their jobs: The ability to be successful. However, we found that although they may strive for personal success, only seven percent of participants in our Generation Z Stories Study indicated success as being the most important factor in a future career.[42]

> **❝ I do not care that much about money, I care about working hard and earning what I deserve. ❞**
> *– Member of Generation Z*

Welcoming, diverse, and inclusive workplaces

Given their open-mindedness[43] and diverse social circles,[44] those in Generation Z seek a workplace that is similarly diverse. They see the value of differences and know that diversity is what makes organizations stronger. Diversity is so important that more than three-quarters of those surveyed by Stillman and Stillman indicated that the level of diversity in a company would affect their decision to work there.[45] But, those in Generation Z know that the beauty of diversity is far more than just having a wide representation of people and identities present. It also involves ensuring that workplace environments, practices, and policies are inclusive and supportive of people of all backgrounds, perspectives, and experiences so they can contribute to their potential. Because of this, it is no surprise that they regard fairness and the absence of discrimination in the workplace as more important than money or status.[46]

Hybrid work options

In just the last decade, there has been a move for many companies to allow an option for employees to work remotely. Some may do it to avoid a long drive to work, whereas others may do it because they feel more productive when not in an office setting, need to have the flexibility to stay at home with a child, or may just want to work in their pajamas. Whatever the reason, many individuals have participated in some element of telecommuting. Studies have shown that anywhere from nearly one-quarter to just less than one-half of workers "did some or all of their work from home."[47,48] Both the trend in allowing, or even encouraging, remote work and the independent and intrapersonal nature of Generation Z[49] might be a draw for this generation to work from home. However, only 20 percent of those in Generation Z would rather telecommute than work in a traditional workspace,[50] but nearly half also want the ability to engage in remote work.[51] Their preference appears to be for a hybrid workspace rather than one that is entirely remote or entirely at the work location. So, when does Generation Z want to work from home and when do they want to be "at work?" It seems pretty clear-cut for them. They prefer to be "at work" when meeting with others but not "at work" just to sit at a desk and work on projects they could do from home.

In the workplace, more than half of those in Generation Z prefer face-to-face communication with both colleagues and supervisors.[52] Given their openness to using video-based communication platforms[53] like Skype, FaceTime, or Google Hangouts, some may find teleconferencing is an adequate version of face-to-face communication, whereas others may find that being in the same space is preferable. These findings point to what could be an ideal arrangement for Generation Z employees. They could work from home or another place of their choosing when they are doing projects and independent work and then come to the office or video in for actual meetings. But, unlike their collaborative Millennial co-workers, don't expect those in Generation Z to want to share a workspace even if they are in the office only 5 hours a week as more than two-thirds would rather have their own workspace than a shared one.[54]

While it seems like a hybrid workspace might be a good option for where Generation Z employees might want to work, but how about when they want to work? Nearly three-quarters prefer to have flexible hours[55] in which they do their work when they need to get it done. Some may prefer to get up at 6 am and just work mornings whereas others might find that working on projects happens in small bursts throughout the day with welcome interruptions to run an errand or do something fun. For those not doing shift work but engaged in project-based employment, Generation Z will likely enjoy and be more productive when they can create and monitor their own work schedules. Like Millennials, Generation Z is highly connected and may respond to a message at midnight or on a weekend. So, despite a set schedule, staying in touch throughout the day and evening might seem normal to a Generation Z employee. Even if they are not actually working at the time they are contacted, those in Generation Z might respond more quickly than their older counterparts sitting at a desk at work.

Eighty-eight percent of Generation Z college seniors believe that work-life balance is important,[56] like their Generation X parents have modeled.[57] But this balance may look a little different than for those in previous generations who saw balance as working strictly 8 am to 5 pm and then using outside time for family and leisure.[58] If Generation Z employees are most productive late at night, do not expect them to be up and working at 8 am. And, because they check their messages around the clock, they may end their official workday in the middle of the afternoon knowing they will be connected well into the night. Generation Z employees value time for both work and play, and sometimes those lines might get a bit blurred for them. However, this arrangement will likely serve both Generation Z employees and their employers well, as those in Generation Z will likely be most productive this way, enjoy their work, and potentially contribute at higher levels to the organization.

Try it before you buy it

Making a commitment to one specific career at 17 or 18 years-old is a lofty task to ask of our youth. Despite their hesitance to pay tens, if not hundreds, of thousands of dollars, to get a college degree in their field, many are also doubtful that they will be ready for the workforce after completing their college education. For instance, in the U.S., only 38 percent felt that their colleges are preparing them with the necessary skills to join the workforce.[59]

Thus it is not surprising that 62 percent of those in Generation Z are open to the idea of entering the workforce before completing a college degree.[60] What might be driving those in Generation Z to consider putting off or not attending college at all?

Where to?

Considering the high price tag for a college degree today, some students may not want to jump right into higher education if they don't know what they want to do as a career. And, college is not where they necessarily want to explore different careers. As discussed earlier in the book, there is a cost to changing majors as doing so could result in extended time to earn a degree and extra semesters of tuition. It seems logical that some Generation Z high school graduates may want to head into the workforce until they know what they want to go to college for, or even if they want to go at all.[61] For instance, Chicago Public Schools is working towards helping their high school students set post-graduation career goals so they can help ensure their students are moving toward a productive work path following high school that suits their interests, skills, and needs. High school students will now be required to have a post-high school plan in order to graduate. This may include proof of employment; an acceptance letter to college, a trade apprenticeship, or gap year program; or proof of military enlistment.[62] The idea is that if high school graduates have a goal and plan that they may be able to focus their time, money, and resources in a viable direction.

Diploma or degree?

Some Generation Z high school students may make their way straight into the workforce because their chosen field does not require a college degree.[63] We may see this more in occupations specific to technology as those fields change rapidly, and it might not be practical to spend four years getting a degree in a subject that could be obsolete by graduation. With the high cost of education and time to degree completion, it might be a hard sell to recruit a high school graduate to a tech program in college if that student has designed his or her own apps and engaged in technology development while younger. It is not that the graduate doesn't have more to learn, but that student might know enough to get in the door and receive training directly from the organization. This is supported by evidence of by employers ranking technical skills lower on the list of essential career competencies than many cognitive reasoning and team-based skills.[64]

Practice run

Some Generation Z high schoolers may know exactly what they want to do after graduation or at least have their futures narrowed to a few career fields. However, they know that it might be important before investing in a college degree to try out each field first to make sure it is a good fit.[65] This mentality may have come from the many stories of their older counterparts who earned a degree in a major they are not using or got a degree in a field they don't like. For example, consider that student teaching is reserved for seniors at many institutions; a move designed to allow these students to put what they have learned into practice. However, what do you do with the student who is six credits from college graduation and realizes through student teaching that the field of education is not a fit? Does the student finish out college just to get a degree, even if in a field that the student will never work? Or, does the student change majors and incur the time and cost of starting over? It's a tough call for a young adult to make.

The ability to explore careers in high school is nothing new as those in older generations could take shop, automotive, or home economics classes during the school day when they were teens. Although those classes may not be as prevalent anymore,[66] some schools are still offering classes for professional preparation, albeit to prepare for a whole different set of occupations. Many schools are now providing classes on accounting and psychology, professions usually tied to college degree attainment. But, taking a class and working in the field might be two different things. If it were not, those education majors who would later not enjoy student teaching would have discovered early on that they didn't want to be teachers.

One way Generation Z high school students are exploring careers is through apprenticeships, especially in high tech fields. For example, students at a Georgia high school can participate in a drone program offered in partnership with the school, a local employer, and a nearby college. Students learn about safety, laws, and technical components related to drones and even complete FAA certification required for flying drones.[67] Students who complete the program may opt to go right into the workforce in a job related to drones, enter the military, or apply to a college engineering program.

Those in Generation Z can also explore possible careers by participating in internships. Some may intern during high school or between high school and college during a gap year, or more predominantly in college. Unfortunately, many of the best internships are reserved for college juniors and seniors as a way to get practical experience before applying for jobs. More than half of employers prefer students have work experience that comes from a related internship or co-op.[68] And, knowing the value of internships, it is no surprise that they are highly popular for those in Generation Z. A study by Accenture found that more than three-quarters of those in Generation Z entering the workforce had completed an internship,[69] similar to the 70 percent found in a study of college seniors by the Higher Education Research Institute.[70]

Despite the high participation numbers, 18 percent of Generation Z college students still feel that their institution did not provide enough internship opportunities.[71] That may be because those in Generation Z are not using internships just to gain experience for a resume; they are also using them to test out various fields before fully committing to a specific career. Given that, waiting until junior or senior year in college might be too late for career exploration. Perhaps making more internships available to high school and younger college students might help those in Generation Z explore potential careers early on. Many large companies have high school–level internships as well as summer programs for youth. For example, Microsoft, Facebook, and Google offer institutes for high school students to immerse themselves in the tech industry through classes, mentoring, and exposure to current employees.[72] These programs fit well with Generation Z's interest in having opportunities to check out future fields before making the leap into a full-fledged career. But, expanding local opportunities with smaller businesses could allow more Generation Z students to participate.[73]

On my own

Some high school students aspire to work on their own freelancing after graduation,[74] which, depending on the field, does not always necessitate a college degree. Freelancing is "working on a contract basis for a variety of companies, as opposed to working as an employee for a single company."[75] Those in occupations in the arts, trades, and technology can often freelance without a degree. Certainly being a freelancing financial planner or corporate consultant would necessitate some level of education and/or experience. But, being a photographer, landscaper, or engaging in cell phone repair services could be freelanced by someone just out of high school who is self-taught in the trade. Although there are college degrees in photography, landscaping, and computer science, they are not necessary in order to work in these fields. So, depending on the career interest of Generation Z high schoolers, they may want to dabble in a potential occupation through freelancing before or even in lieu of going to college.

For those looking to be successful in the freelancing world, we might see those in Generation Z engage in apprenticeships and internships not only to test out a particular career but to develop skills in a field they are interested in venturing into on their own later. Using apprenticeships and internships as a training ground for future freelancing could give those in Generation Z an opportunity for inexpensive hands-on training for as long or short of a time that they feel they need before going it alone.

Conclusion

With the world rapidly changing, new types of jobs are emerging that would hardly have been imagined 100 years ago, let alone even 20 years ago. Those in Generation Z are uniquely positioned to blend their dreams and aspirations with emerging occupational fields to blaze the trail for what will be the future of the world of work.

Notes

1 Adobe Educate. (2016). *Gen Z in the classroom: Creating the future.* Retrieved from www. adobeeducate.com/genz/adobe-education-genz, slide 23.
2 Stillman, D. & Stillman, J. (2017). *Gen Z @ work: How the next generation is transforming the workplace.* New York: HarperCollins.
3 Adobe Educate. (2016).
4 Adobe Educate. (2016).
5 8X8, Inc. (2016). *New study finds Generation Z will bring balance to the workforce.* Retrieved from http://investors.8x8.com/releasedetail.cfm?releaseid=1004375
6 CBRE & Genesis. (2014). *Fast forward 2030.* Retrieved from www.cbre.com/Research-Reports/Future-of-Work, Key Findings number 1.
7 National Association of Colleges and Employers. (2016). *Job Outlook Survey.* Retrieved from www.naceweb.org/s11182015/employers-look-for-in-new-hires.aspx
8 National Association of Colleges and Employers. (2016).
9 Strauss, K. (2016). *10 great jobs for Gen Z in 2016 and beyond.* Retrieved from www. forbes.com/sites/karstenstrauss/2016/06/02/10-great-jobs-for-generation-z-in-2016-and-beyond/#f1d6fed14267
10 Strauss, K. (2016).
11 Altitude. (2015). *Designing for Gen Z.* Retrieved from www.altitudeinc.com/through-the-eyes-of-gen-z/
12 Fal, D. (2017). *Recruitment industry is dying: Future of work is "connecting."* Retrieved from https://medium.com/@Djoann/recruitment-industry-is-dying-future-of-work-is-about-connecting-a26e47ad8d4d
13 Minton, T. (2016). *13 coolest sci-fi movie jobs of all time.* Retrieved from http://screenrant. com/best-sci-fi-movie-jobs-all-time/
14 Seemiller, C. & Grace, M. (2017). *Generation Z stories study.* Unpublished raw data.
15 Seemiller, C. & Grace, M. (2016). *Generation Z goes to college.* San Francisco: Jossey-Bass.
16 Seemiller, C. & Grace, M. (2017).
17 Higher Education Research Institute. (2017). *College Senior Survey.* Data prepared by Higher Education Research Institute.
18 Higher Education Research Institute. (2017).

19 Stillman, D. & Stillman, J. (2017).

20 Monster Worldwide, Inc. (2016). *Move over Millennials: Gen Z is about to hit the work-force*. Retrieved from www.prnewswire.com/news-releases/move-over-millennials-gen-z-is-about-to-hit-the-workforce-300319567.html

21 Monster. (2016). *Move over Millennials: What you'll need to know for hiring as Gen Z enters the workforce*. Retrieved from www.monstersoftwaresolutions.com/docs/genz/monster_genz_report.pdf

22 Monster Worldwide, Inc. (2016).

23 Monster Worldwide, Inc. (2016).

24 Seemiller, C. & Grace, M. (2017).

25 Seemiller, C. & Grace, M. (2016).

26 Higher Education Research Institute. (2017).

27 Monster Worldwide, Inc. (2016).

28 Higher Education Research Institute. (2017).

29 Seemiller, C. & Grace, M. (2017).

30 Adecco. (2015a). *Generation Z vs. Millennials*. Retrieved from http://pages.adeccousa.com/rs/107-IXF-539/images/generation-z-vs-millennials.pdf

31 Evans, L. (2014). *What companies can expect when they hire Gen Z*. Retrieved from www.entrepreneur.com/article/237765, para. 6.

32 Monster Worldwide, Inc. (2016).

33 Stillman, D. & Stillman, J. (2017).

34 Seemiller, C. & Grace, M. (2016).

35 Bailey, A. (2017). *Generation Z: Understanding your youngest hires*. Retrieved from http://1rivet.com/pdf/1Rivet_Insight_Gen%20Z_Andrew_B_Templated.pdf

36 Adecco. (2015b). *The difference between Gen Z and Millennials*. Retrieved from www.entrepreneur.com/article/247115

37 Universum Global. (2017). *Generation Z grows up*. Retrieved from http://universumglobal.com/generation-z/

38 Steele Flippin, C. (2017). *Generation Z in the workplace*. n.p.: Author.

39 Seemiller, C. & Grace, M. (2016).

40 Universum Global. (2017).

41 Universum Global. (2017).

42 Seemiller, C. & Grace, M. (2017).

43 Seemiller, C. & Grace, M. (2016).

44 Magid Generational Strategies. (2014). *The first generation of the twenty-first century: An introduction to the pluralist generation*. Retrieved from http://magid.com/sites/default/files/pdf/MagidPluralistGenerationWhitepaper.pdf

45 Stillman, D. & Stillman, J. (2017).

46 Euromonitor International. (2011). *Make way for Generation Z: Marketing for today's teens and tweens*. Retrieved from http://oaltabo2012.files.wordpress.com/2012/03/make-way-for-generation-z1.pdf

47 Bureau of Labor Statistics. (2016). *24 percent of employed people did some or all of their work at home in 2015*. Retrieved from www.bls.gov/opub/ted/2016/24-percent-of-employed-people-did-some-or-all-of-their-work-at-home-in-2015.htm, para. 2.

48 Chokshi, N. (2017b). *Out of the office: More people are working remotely survey finds*. Retrieved from https://mobile.nytimes.com/2017/02/15/us/remote-workers-work-from-home.html

49 Seemiller, C. & Grace, M. (2016).

50 Steele Flippin, C. (2017).

51 8X8, Inc. (2016).

52 Steele Flippin, C. (2017).

53 Seemiller, C. & Grace, M. (2016).

54 Stillman, D. & Stillman, J. (2017).

55 8X8, Inc. (2016).

56 Higher Education Research Institute. (2017).

57 Regus. (2013). *Work-life balance report 2013.* Retrieved from www.google.com/search?q=Regus+Work-Life+Balance+Index&oq=Regus+Work-Life+Balance+Index&aqs=chrome..69i57.397j0j7&sourceid=chrome&ie=UTF-8

58 Seemiller, C. & Grace, M. (2017).

59 Universum Global. (2017).

60 Universum Global. (2017).

61 Beckman, K. (2016). *10 recent high school grads on why they decided not to go to college.* Retrieved from www.cosmopolitan.com/college/news/a62449/recent-high-school-grads-on-why-they-decided-not-to-go-to-college/

62 Brown, E. (2017). *Chicago won't allow high school students to graduate without a plan for the future.* Retrieved from www.washingtonpost-com.cdn.ampproject.org/c/s/; www.washingtonpost.com/amphtml/local/education/chicago-wont-allow-high-school-students-to-graduate-without-a-plan-for-the-future/2017/07/03/ac197222-5111-11e7-91eb-9611861a988f_story.html

63 Beckman, K. (2016).

64 National Association of Colleges and Employers. (2016).

65 Beckman, K. (2016).

66 Brown, T. (2012). *The death of shop class and America's skilled workforce.* Retrieved from www.forbes.com/sites/tarabrown/2012/05/30/the-death-of-shop-class-and-americas-high-skilled-workforce/#6f3d25b4541f

67 Honaker, A. (2017). *Students who complete new drone program can earn $150-hour.* Retrieved from www.miamiherald.com/news/business/article159988449.html

68 National Association of Colleges and Employers. (2016).

69 Lyons, M., LaVelle, K., & Smith, D. (2017). *Gen Z rising.* Retrieved from https://acnprod.accenture.com/t20170525T080412__w__/us-en/_acnmedia/PDF-50/Accenture-Strategy-Workforce-Gen-Z-Rising-POV.pdf#zoom=50

70 Higher Education Research Institute. (2017).

71 Adecco. (2015b).

72 Pannoni. A. (2016). *Get experience at top tech companies as a teenager.* Retrieved from www.usnews.com/high-schools/articles/2016-08-08/get-experience-at-top-tech-companies-as-a-teenager

73 Pannoni, A. (2016).

74 Beckman, K. (2016).

75 Business Dictionary. (n.d.). *Freelance.* Retrieved from www.businessdictionary.com/definition/freelance.html

18 In the workplace

••

With Generation Z's career aspirations comes the reality of entering and participating in the workforce. In some ways, getting a job and working with co-workers is not that much different than it was a hundred years ago. Experience, expertise, and networks can lead to gainful employment and a long career. However, the occupational landscape has changed today, and technology has created more opportunities for people to find jobs, get hired, and do their work. With five generations in the workplace, a thriving gig economy, and the characteristics of those in Generation Z themselves, today's workplace looks a lot different in some ways than it did a century ago.

The ideal job candidate: Is it Generation Z?

Although those in Generation Z likely have many positive characteristics to offer an employer, this generation is still competing with the experience and honed skill sets of those in older generations. So, what are employers looking for and how does Generation Z stack up to those expectations?

Complex cognitive reasoning

In a rapidly changing world, it's no surprise that employers are interested in employees who have the skills to adapt to changing work dynamics. Although there may be an exception for some very technical professions (medicine, law, and trades, for example), findings from the National Association for Colleges and Employers (NACE) study revealed that a higher percentage of employers look for skills related to complex cognitive reasoning on candidates' resumes than technical skills.[1] Complex cognitive reasoning entails looking deeply at a situation, making critical determinations, and acting upon those determinations in productive and innovative ways. In essence, this is critical thinking to solve a problem. For example, employers may not want to hire a programmer who is excellent at coding but has no ability to solve critical problems when they arise. It might be more advantageous for that employer to instead hire a programmer who may lack coding expertise but who can engage in complex cognitive reasoning and hone their coding skills upon coming into the workplace.

Technical competence will change as technology evolves, but there is timelessness to questions of inquiry. Employers know that hiring individuals who can ask and address these types of questions can serve the organization for many years to come.

In addition to critical thinking and problem-solving being the competencies deemed most essential by employers surveyed by NACE,[2] the World Economic Forum also asserts that the number one skill needed in the workforce in 2020 will be complex problem-solving with critical thinking following as number two.[3]

> **❝ I want new experiences and puzzles and to be around people that love solving them as much as I do. ❞**
> – Member of Generation Z

Will Generation Z employees be able to effectively engage in critical thinking and problem-solving at work? Having only known a world in which access to nearly unlimited information and solutions to problems are only a click away, they may rely on getting quick answers from the online world, leaving them less able to figure it out for themselves. Whether it is a YouTube instructional video, a blog or forum offering advice, or Siri who can answer any question, those in Generation Z have been able to rely on others and technology to provide them answers. Although using these tools can help them solve problems, the vast array of ways to get an answer quickly engages them in surface level learning rather than complex problem-solving. And with so many possibilities, they need to be savvy in how they sort through and find legitimate and useful information, which may be a challenge when you combine the inordinate amount of content available with their 8-second spans.[4] And, not all answers can be found with a quick online search and require deeper investigation or even the ability to come up with their own answers. Are there opportunities available for those in Generation Z to develop the ability to engage in complex cognitive reasoning now or will they be woefully unprepared to fit the demands of their future employers?

Creativity

The word "creativity" summons up childhood memories of everything from building forts to finger-painting to writing poetry to making up songs. The beauty of creativity is that it is essentially boundless. It is drawing outside the lines, thinking outside the box, or any other saying about fostering imagination. Despite the cliché of these phrases, there is some truth to them. Imagining "what could be" and pushing the boundaries of "what has been" underscores the essence of creativity and has served as the bedrock for countless advancements in our society. Who would have thought that 3-D printers could ever "print" human organs or that cars could be driverless? Someone did – someone that employers would likely want to hire. Although only 21 percent of current employers seek out "creativity" on a candidate's resume today,[5] creativity will be a more important skill in years to come. This is evidenced in the World Economic Forum's list of essential career skills of 2020 in which creativity moved up to number 3 from number 10 in 2015.[6]

Although this generation self-identifies as having the characteristic of creativity[7] and nearly 40 percent of those in Generation Z want to invent something that will change the world,[8] their desire to create may not fully translate into the ability to do it effectively. This is a generation that has experienced deep cuts in the arts in school,[9] resulting in less time and resources for formally developing their creativity. A study of Generation Z college seniors found that 45 percent believe their level of creativity is average or below average.[10]

> " *I enjoy drawing and being creative, although I feel after 2nd grade, the school system kind of killed my creativity, but I'm finding it again in this design major.* "
> – Member of Generation Z

Both students and teachers recognize the importance of developing creativity. Seventy-six percent of Generation Z students (ages 11 to 17), as well as 75 percent of their teachers, wish there was more of an emphasis on creativity in the curriculum because both believe creativity will be critical to Generation Z's future success.[11] And, more than 60 percent of college seniors believe it is very important or essential to have a job in which they can utilize creativity.[12] The move from STEM to STEAM (inclusion of arts with science, technology, engineering, and math curriculum)[13] and focus on design thinking[14] in K–12 classrooms is evidence that there is a call to develop creativity in young people so they can engage in innovation and creative thinking. With this shift, we may start to see younger members of Generation Z coming into the workforce with a greater knack for creativity, paralleling that of the G.I. Generation whose members earned more than 100 Nobel Prizes, more than any other generation.[15]

Emotional intelligence

Imagine witnessing the person ahead of you in line at the grocery store yelling at the cashier for ringing up a purchase incorrectly. We are witnesses to scenarios like this every day, and on some occasions are the ones involved in them. These behaviors never really end up being helpful or productive, and in some cases can cause harm. Instead of yelling at the cashier, that person could have easily said, "No problem. How is your day going?" What stops us from engaging in road rage, yelling at the customer service representative, or engaging in text or tweet storms with others? It is emotional intelligence, or the ability to understand and manage our own emotions.[16]

Although the concept has been around for decades, the thousands of blogs, articles, and news stories about emotional intelligence in mainstream media highlight its importance in today's world of work. It would be hard to believe that any supervisor would want their employees to insult customers, act rudely to colleagues, or become physically outraged when disagreeing with a new policy.

If emotional intelligence is critical today, it is very likely to be a focus in the future, considering that the World Economic Forum added emotional intelligence to their list of essential workplace competencies for 2020 in the number six spot after not being present in the 2015 list at all.[17] Given that emotional intelligence is growing in importance with employers, can we say that those in Generation Z are emotionally intelligent? This is a generation that has been exposed to social and emotional learning curriculum in school, having been taught how to name their emotions and find productive ways to express them. These types of programs have proven to be effective in helping children enhance their emotional and social skills, attitudes, and behaviors.[18] In addition, those in Generation Z prefer communicating face-to-face, saying that other forms of communication leave room for misinterpretation of emotion and intention.[19] They are cautious of what they say, meaning they may be less apt to speak off the cuff. Add to that their self-perceived high levels of empathy and compassion,[20] and one could only hope that they are able to put themselves in someone else's shoes before engaging in unproductive behavior like yelling at a cashier.

&& The most important issue facing my generation will be 'lack of communication. Not just verbal and vocal, but of all kinds. . . . Lack of communication leads to lack of connection with others, lack of connection leads to lack of humanity, and lack of humanity leads to short-sightedness.' &&
- Member of Generation Z

However, despite these characteristics, Generation Z is also used to short bursts of communication,[21] which may result in possibly being too direct or even blunt. This may not occur in person, but instead through digital communication as technology provides them a great platform to quickly send messages without thinking about the consequences. Their short attention spans,[22] higher stress levels than adults,[23] and the expectation of 24/7 access to nearly anything may lead to them to hitting the send button a bit too soon. With a simple Internet search, it is easy to find stories of teens sending rude and demanding messages to teachers or professional emails with typos – communication behaviors they would likely never engage in face-to-face. It's no surprise then that the Internet is filled with articles, blogs, and podcasts for teens on how to engage in professionalism both in-person and online.

A recent study by LinkedIn found that only 42 percent of employers agreed that their new hires had the emotional intelligence skills required for their position.[24] Knowing that this critical skill is largely absent from the workforce, yet sorely needed, how can older generations help Generation Z develop into emotionally intelligent young adults?

Social intelligence

In addition to emotional intelligence, social intelligence is critical in the workforce as well. Where emotional intelligence mainly focuses on understanding oneself and being able to monitor one's own behavior, social intelligence consists of understanding and working effectively with others.[25] Closely intertwined with emotional intelligence, social intelligence is ranked high by employers as a skill they hope to see in future employees. The World Economic Forum included people management as number four and coordinating with others as number five on their list of most essential workforce skills in 2020.[26] This aligns with the findings from the 2016 NACE survey that found the number one attribute employers look for on resume is the ability to work in a team.[27]

But, those in Generation Z may enter the workforce lacking the social intelligence that those in previous generations had as young adults. Despite their desire for face-to-face communication, a Pew study on teens found that only 64 percent spend time outside of school with friends at least every few days, whereas 75 percent socialize with their friends through text at least every few days, with 55 percent doing so every day.[28] Because those in Generation Z are splitting their socializing time between the face-to-face and online world, they are inherently spending less time practicing socializing in-person, contributing to what Dr. Nicholas Karadaras refers to as the erosion of socialization.[29]

> *Many people feel that our generation is unable to have an in-person human interaction because we are so caught up with social media. I somewhat agree with them, and if we don't realize how caught up we get in social media, then this issue can only get worse.*
> – Member of Generation Z

It is more than just practice; do those in Generation Z have the ability to read the emotions of others? A study from UCLA found a link between kids' reduced screen time and their effective ability to reading other people's emotions. When the kids were screen-free for five days, their ability to read others' emotions greatly improved. This generation has the capacity for social intelligence, but it may be advantageous to help them to balance their time online with socializing offline.

What will happen when employers go to hire Generation Z workers and some lack social intelligence skills? Will Generation Z's propensity for communicating through technology and preference for individual work do them a disservice in preparing to work in-person with others in the workplace? We can hope that their we-centric concerns for others[30] and their tight-knit family relationships gave them the opportunity to develop face-to-face social intelligence skills, even if used primarily with their parents and close friends. If their level of social intelligence is not what their older generation employers are looking for, Generation Z will likely need to learn social skills on the job.

Leadership development experiences

In addition to looking for candidates with particular competencies, employers are searching for specific experiences. Two of the top three most sought-after experiences employers seek include having held a leadership position and involvement in extracurricular activities.[31] While more than two-thirds of Generation Z college students held a leadership position in an organization in college, only 42 percent actually participated in leadership training.[32] Simply being in a leadership role does not necessarily mean that person has developed the skills to engage in effective leadership. But, interestingly, more than 70 percent believe their leadership ability is higher than that of their peers.[33] In reality, however, 70 percent cannot have higher skills than their peers; the math just doesn't add up. Their collective unrealistic appraisal of their actual leadership skills may prevent them from seeking out leadership development opportunities because they may believe they already excel at leadership. This could leave a gaping hole in the preparedness of future leaders.

> ❝ *I worry 'that I might need more technical skills to be a good leader, regardless of what business sector I go into.'* ❞
> – Member of Generation Z

Landing the job

Deciding on a career path or at least a job is only part of the equation. Generation Z job candidates need to also apply for and get hired on in the workforce. Although today's job search process includes some relatively timeless elements, such as networking, interviewing, and getting references, there are some considerable differences from even just a decade ago.

It's not the classifieds anymore

The days of looking through the classified section of the newspaper as the primary way to find a job have come and gone. Although some newspapers still publish want ads, the list of jobs is far less comprehensive than it once was for job seekers. Now, with a multitude of online job search platforms available, it is easy to find a list of potential jobs simply by using keywords and search criteria. Comprehensive job sites, platform integration with social media, and the ability to narrow a job search to very specific criteria makes online job searching a great option for anyone in any generation. And Generation Z is no exception, with 31 percent indicating that using online job boards is their preferred way to look for job postings, higher than any other job-seeking method they use.[34]

But, their job search isn't limited to simply looking at digital job boards. Many are also open to having prospective employers reach out to them online. Universum Global found that 83 percent of high school and first-year Generation Z college students would support the idea of an employer contacting them through social media (but not marketing to them through pop-up ads) about job opportunities.[35] This strategy must be working to some extent as employers are increasing their use of social media for recruiting.[36] But, is the platform that employers use for outreach and the platform Generation Z uses for job searching even the same? It is likely that employers are using sites like LinkedIn. Not only is it more of a professional rather than social site, 86 percent of Baby Boomers have heard of LinkedIn,[37] making it an ideal place for employers to recruit candidates. But, only 66 percent of those in Generation Z have heard of LinkedIn,[38] which could result in many of them missing out on career opportunities posted on the site.

In addition, nearly one-third Generation Z students use their college career centers to search for jobs.[39] Whether that is using an internal job posting system or actually coming into the office for assistance, those in Generation Z find value in using their career centers. However, the once popular and highly anticipated career fair on college campuses may become a thing of the past as fewer employers are participating in career fairs than ever before, and instead opting to use technology to recruit students.[40]

While many of those in Generation Z may be searching online, they also trust their connections to help them find that great job. Twenty-eight percent of those in Generation Z like to leverage their networks for job opportunities, a rate higher than the 20 percent of Millennials who do.[41]

Casting the net wide

While employers today view the job market positively for college graduates,[42] nearly a third of those in Generation Z are worried about finding a job.[43] Given their concern for financial security, it wouldn't be surprising to see many in Generation Z throw their hats in the ring for more jobs than they may be completely interested in, just to ensure they explore several opportunities and give themselves plenty of options. At the end of the day, though, they may just hold out in accepting an offer if the job ultimately does not seem as though it would be enjoyable or fulfilling.

Customizing the first impression

Consider that, for every other living generation, a resume or some variation of a paper record of experience and achievements has served as the main collateral in the job search process. While the ability to upload a resume to a job search engine is a more recent phenomena, it's just the digitization of submitting the same information in the same format, as a document. Generation Z, however, might challenge the notion of the traditional resume, whether in print or in digital format. Although not entirely widespread yet, many in Generation Z like the concept of video resumes and actually prefer them to paper ones.[44] With better recording software on smartphones today than on most high tech video equipment 10 years ago, it is easier than ever to produce high-quality video content. Just grab a selfie stick and start recording. But, who would watch one? Actually, 89 percent of employers would watch a video resume if it was sent to them.[45]

Blockchain

An interesting technological advancement that might impact job searching for Generation Z is the implementation of blockchain into digital platforms for job searching. As discussed in Chapter 15, blockchain is a type of technology designed to "record transactions between two parties efficiently and in a verifiable and permanent way . . . contracts are embedded in digital code and stored in transparent, shared databases, where they are protected from deletion, tampering, and revision."[46] For example, a platform like LinkedIn could use blockchain to verify employment information that users post on their profiles, such as start and end dates, titles, and duties. Employers would simply need to click on a candidate's LinkedIn profile to access verified information that would normally be on a resume.[47] This could eliminate the need for prospective employees to submit a self-reported resume at all – on paper or on video – and increase Generation Z users on sites like LinkedIn.

Creating careers, not seeking jobs

Generation Z exudes an amazing entrepreneurial spirit, and many see the possibilities of creating their own careers as an alternate path to working for someone else. Despite their interest and desire to craft their careers, will they actually be prepared to do so?

Entrepreneurial spirit

In several recent studies, many in Generation Z indicate an interest in working for themselves. For example, Monster Worldwide, Inc., found that just about half of those in Generation Z want to have their own businesses.[48] Compare that to the 32 percent across all generations who want to do so,[49] and you have a motivated young generation ready to be entrepreneurs. When looking at Generation Z college students, specifically, one study revealed that 42 percent want to work for themselves,[50] and another study found that 64 percent want to start a business someday.[51] Entrepreneurial drive seems to be even higher with Generation Z high school students as research has found that 72 percent want to start a business someday with 61 percent wanting to be an entrepreneur right out of college.[52] And some are already engaging in entrepreneurial initiatives as kids. A study by Rooster Money, a company that offers an online financial tracking app for youth, found that of all the ways youth bring in pocket money, selling stuff yields the highest returns at an average of $13.18 per week, higher than babysitting at $12.44 and other chores.[53]

Generation Z's version of entrepreneurship might not be trying to launch that major startup like Twitter or Instagram as their Millennial counterparts did. Jeremy Finch from Altitude, a design and innovation consulting firm, says "[Generation Z's] version of [entrepreneurship] will likely be focused on sustainable 'singles and doubles' ventures rather than Silicon Valley 'home runs.'"[54] Many will likely aim for entrepreneurial initiatives that are modest rather than striving to be on *Inc. Magazine*'s 30 Under 30 list. Finch adds, "We found that while Gen Z likes the idea of working for themselves, the majority are risk-averse, practical, and pragmatic. Their supposed entrepreneurialism is actually more of a survival mechanism than an idealist reach for status or riches."[55]

Why entrepreneurship?

There are many likely explanations as to why Generation Z may be the next major wave of entrepreneurs. Generation Z's post-Recession mentality might influence their perspectives on taking control of their own career fate. Jeremy Finch from Altitude sums up this sentiment in saying, "Entrepreneurship is seen as a way to not have to rely on anyone (or anything) else."[56] To this point, entrepreneurship may offer a sense of control with those in Generation Z who are concerned about their financial security being in someone else's hands.

> *I am most concerned with having flexibility to travel, spend time with family, or choose to live an alternative lifestyle. Owning my own business would be ideal.*
> - Member of Generation Z

In addition, we can't underestimate the influence of their Generation X parents who witnessed Baby Boomers, Steve Jobs and Bill Gates, start their own businesses out of their garages.[57] They also saw Gen Xer, Elon Musk, launch SpaceX and co-found PayPal and Tesla,[58] and Millennials like Facebook's Mark Zuckerberg launch groundbreaking companies at a young age. With Generation X parents seeing successful startups, they may encourage their Generation Z kids to take a chance on their dreams as an entrepreneur.

It is more than just the context that Generation Z is living in that shapes their entrepreneurial spirit. Being an entrepreneur aligns with their desire to make a difference as well as find enjoyable and fulfilling work.[59] Aside from the possibility of making a lot of money, Generation Z is drawn to entrepreneurship as a way to make an impact.[60] And, as nearly 40 percent plan to invent something that will change the world,[61] their inventive mentality will provide them with the intellectual stimulus to be innovative. Together, their inventiveness, desire to make a difference, and quest for fulfillment might be the perfect blend of attributes for starting and running their own businesses.

Prepared for entrepreneurship?

It is one thing to want to be an entrepreneur and another to have the skills to do it. Working for yourself and, even more so, having employees calls for more than just having technical skills for the job at hand. For example, being a self-employed fitness trainer is quite different from working at a gym. The self-employed trainer needs to be able to engage in marketing, business management, accounting, risk management, and human resources if there are employees. Without these skills, the entrepreneur will not be able to effectively run the business, which many young adults today recognize. It's no surprise then that nearly one-third of those in Generation Z believe that their college or university did not teach them adequate business skills.[62] So, what do you do with the English major who wants to startup a small editing firm? This highly trained writer may be skilled in editing but lacks any knowledge or experience in running a business. This poses the question: Should colleges and universities offer introductory business skills classes for all students regardless of major to help prepare them for the possibility of entrepreneurship?

Being unprepared for entrepreneurship may not only be associated with lacking business skills, it may also be reflective of how those in Generation Z navigate the world in general. For example, because they like quick answers,[63] they may move too rapidly through the process of starting up a sustainable business. Skipping steps that could be seen as too time-consuming, like the thoughtful development of a mission statement, doing market research on competitors, or bidding out contracts for suppliers for the best possible fit could ultimately impact the success of the business.

However, Generation Z's pragmatic approach to life gives these burgeoning entrepreneurs a dose of reality in starting and running their own businesses. According to Millennial Branding, a research and management consulting firm, 71 percent of those in Generation Z expect their first business venture to fail but view that failure as a learning opportunity.[64]

Programs like WeWork, however, are trying to prepare this generation for success as entrepreneurs at a very young age. The startup, focused on co-working spaces, has launched a private elementary school where educators will combine traditional school subjects like math and reading with entrepreneurial initiatives.[65]

Gig economy

Being an entrepreneur, though, can also be far less formal than being a traditional business owner who might run an auto repair shop, bookstore, or restaurant with their own employees. We are now living in a gig economy, otherwise known as a 1099 or on-demand economy. The gig economy is comprised of freelance workers who do not hold long-term contracts with any one employer,[66] allowing them to work a series of singular gigs, or work events for different employers, through a portable and flexible version of self-employment. Rather than being called an entrepreneur, some have referred to these workers as solopreneurs as they engage in entrepreneurial-type behavior but run their businesses alone without the intention of hiring others.[67] Like entrepreneurship, the flexibility of the gig economy offers those in Generation Z greater control over both their income and their lives.[68] It's no surprise then that 57 million people freelanced in 2017[69] alone. And, in a study by Deloitte, 18 percent of those in Generation Z have already joined the gig economy in place of full-time employment, higher than the 14 percent of Millennials who have.[70] Further, 49 percent of those in Generation Z would considering working in the gig economy over a full-time job, higher than the 43 percent of Millennials who would.[71] Good news for those in Generation Z – the gig economy doesn't appear to be a passing fad: 220 business experts from around the world see a growth in freelancing in the future.[72]

It's also important to consider that many of the popular fields for the future include jobs that could be done in a freelance economy, like being an independent financial planner or using a computer and information sciences degree to engage in work that involves repairing computers. Then, there are other occupations that are not readily freelanced today but could involve some element of freelance work in the future such as a remote healthcare specialist or freelance professor.[73] It is hard to conceive of a healthcare specialist not working for a hospital, clinic, or private practice or a full-time professor not employed at a specific college or university as these jobs have traditionally been associated with working for a larger organization. Thus, the freelance economy is more than just renting your guest room on Airbnb; it might mean taking professions that are nearly inconceivable to be done in a freelance manner and doing just that.

The side hustle

While some freelancers draw their main source of income from their independent contracting work, others engage in side hustles, which are jobs that people do in addition to their primary employment. Often, side hustles are born from hobbies that have a revenue-generating potential, either as a the sale of product or service to others. Examples of side hustles might include the third grade teacher who makes iron sculptures after work to sell on Etsy or the accountant who does plumbing on the weekends for extra cash. Watching older adults in their lives take part in the gig economy might have inspired Generation Z to consider having a side hustle at some point. According to a study by Inc., 75 percent of those in Generation Z wish they could turn a hobby into a full-time job.[74] As discussed earlier, some are already making money in the gig economy; 14 percent of 13 to 15 year-olds, 22 percent of 16 to 18 year-olds, and 28 percent of 19 to 21 year-olds have already made money online.[75] With a foot in the door in the gig economy, their side hustles now might become their livelihoods of the future.

Generation Z's career identities

Given what we know about Generation Z today, there are three specific identities that may reflect their attributes and approaches in the workplace: The curator, the influencer, and the free agent.

The curator

When we think of curators, art galleries and museums come to mind. These are places in which curators intentionally organize, craft, and display artifacts to convey a certain message or meaning to those visiting. Just as those in Generation Z want to curate their identities, especially online, they too want to curate their careers. As discussed earlier, some will do this through entrepreneurship or freelancing, precisely designing exactly what they want in a career. However, what about those who enter an organizational culture with traditional and formal structures in place? Although it may not be altogether likely that those in older generations will embrace Generation Z's desire to carefully craft their occupational experiences, perhaps Millennials who took the workforce by storm with their desire for a customized career can pave the way for this young generation to do even more of the same.

First, many in Generation Z seek flexibility and creativity within their job duties. Because of this, one option might be to offer a workplace rotation program in which employees can try out various jobs within the organization,[76] for example, doing marketing one week and sales the next. For some, that exposure might enable them to clarify a preference for either marketing or sales. For others, though, they may discover an interest in wanting to do a bit of both – not surprising in that three-quarters of those in Generation Z would prefer multiple roles within one place of employment.[77]

In addition to wanting job duties that align with their interests, those in Generation Z also approach their work from the mindset of efficiency,[78] preferring tasks being doled out to them based on their skill set. Take for example the G.I. Generation in which supervisors were able to delegate administrative tasks to free themselves up for more job-specific duties that matched their skill sets. But, innovation around technology brought those types of tasks back into supervisor workloads requiring them to engage in administrative tasks previously done by others. Because of this model of holistic work, Baby Boomer, Generation X, and Millennial supervisors have needed to do many of these tasks themselves whether they are good at them or not (from typing memos 30 years ago to checking emails today). But, Generation Z's efficiency mentality supports the notion of spreading these tasks back out, specifically to those who might be best at completing them. Instead of delegating administrative tasks to an administrative support person, though, this efficiency model might best be described as a work trade where co-workers assist each other on their assigned tasks based on their strengths.[79] For example, one employee might seek assistance from a co-worker in managing a budget in exchange for help organizing a database. Generation Z's efficiency approach might not just be a way of intentionally delegating tasks to those whose skills match best, but it might make their jobs more enjoyable and fulfilling, two factors critically important to Generation Z.

Because of their interest in potentially mixing up job duties based on various skill sets, it is no surprise that 56 percent would prefer to write their own job descriptions rather than be given an existing one.[80] It is also not surprising that they are interested in picking their own job titles.[81] Whether they select a traditional title like Customer Service Representative, Marketing Manager, or Retail Sales Consultant or a more creative title like Innovation Sherpa, Java Jedi, or Chief Storyteller,[82] curating the perfect title could be of paramount importance to a generation that cares deeply about the image they are portraying to others.

The influencer

Supervisors of Generation Z will be excited to learn that this cohort tends to follow authority[83] and prefers a workplace with a well-defined chain of command.[84] Although they aren't prone to jumping over the head of their supervisor to provide unsolicited feedback to the president or CEO, they still plan to exert their influence in the organization.

The ability for those in Generation Z to influence decisions at home as a child may have laid the groundwork for their desire to influence decisions in the workplace. Many parents of Generation Z kids welcomed and even considered their children's opinions on household decisions.[85] This type of parent-child relationship has likely contributed to the desire for those in Generation Z to have their opinions valued in the workplace and might explain their comfort in addressing authority figures. In research by Dr. Candace Steele Flippin, 61 percent of those in Generation Z want their ideas to be listened to by their supervisors.[86] But, it is more than just wanting to be heard; having the opportunity to share their opinions is paramount. These young people want understanding, caring, friendly, respectful, helpful, fair, easygoing, and patient supervisors who take the time to get to know them.[87] Having a positive and close relationship with their supervisor could open the door for them to share their opinions with someone at a higher organizational level.

The free agent

LeBron James, Moses Malone, and Shaquille O'Neal are arguably three of the greatest basketball players in history. Besides being able to sink a game-winning shot, they all have also been free agents, or professionals uncommitted to any organization for a period of time.[88] Free agency is a way of saying, "Here is what I want . . . on my terms." Not all free agents end up with their dream scenario of being fought over and getting more than what they asked for; some don't end up with anything at all. That is the risk of free agency. For those in Generation Z that have a desire to be a true free agent, we will see them in the ranks of the many Generation Z freelancers. However, some may want the perks of free agency with the security of a paycheck from a stable job. As discussed earlier, being able to select a job title and craft a job description are not just about curation; those acts are also about free agency, or the ability to exercise autonomous decision-making. For a generation that prefers independent learning,[89] autonomy seems to align well. In our Generation Z Goes to College Study, we found that many in Generation Z prefer to execute a task rather than strategize a plan, build the team, or take initiative as the traditional leader.[90] Their desire for independence and their preference for task execution may lead them to say, "give me a project and let me run with it."

This approach may appear as though they are free agents within the organization, operating as if on their own, yet instead are working for the benefit of the organization as a whole. This free agency is akin to the concept of intrapreneurship in which employees act with the same passion, drive, and innovative mindset as their employers. Intrapreneurs are able to carve out niche roles for themselves in the organization and operate at a high level of autonomy and creative decision-making, mostly because so few above them are intimately involved in their projects.[91] As entrepreneurship may be a risky endeavor, we may see more Generation Z employees striving to be intrapreneurs, exercising their free agency within an established organization with the comfort of a consistent paycheck.

Working with other generations

Generation Z is just entering the workforce, but what we know about them can be insightful as we consider their interactions with those in other generations. While there may be some in the Silent Generation and even fewer in the G.I. Generation still working, the inter-generational dynamics that will most impact those in Generation Z have to do with Baby Boomers, Gen Xers, and Millennials.

Baby Boomers

Baby Boomers created the notion of the workaholic,[92] and sometimes struggle with not seeing their younger co-workers working around the clock. Whereas Baby Boomers might work late at the office and then come home to shut off for the night, Generation Z is always on, whether at work or not. Because of Generation Z's interest in remote work, some Baby Boomers might believe that their Generation Z employees are simply not working because they are not present. So, it will be critical to create a means to allow Generation Z to thrive in terms of when and where they work best at the same time as creating an accountability system that helps Baby Boomers (and others) see that their Generation Z colleagues are doing their part.

Another major difference between Baby Boomers and those in Generation Z centers on technology. At this point, many Boomers have smartphones and are accustomed to technology in the workplace, as Millennials didn't really give them much of a choice when they entered the workforce. So, in some ways, the trail is blazed for those in Generation Z who are digitally savvy. However, where the disconnect may come in with Baby Boomers is less about whether one generation has a stronger skill set in using technology than the other but more about each generation's perspective on the purpose of technology in the workplace in general. Baby Boomers primarily see technology as a means of productivity.[93] For example, digital spreadsheets provide a better alternative to a paper logbook, and the Internet provides access to information that would have taken far longer to get before the World Wide Web. Those in Generation Z, however, see technology as a means of connectivity.[94] For example, messaging can provide a platform to connect with clients, customers, and others for ease of communication, and social media offers a space to expand professional networks, seeking advice, as well as collaborating.

In addition to their varied perspectives on the purpose of technology, their perceptions on the acceptability of its use are also quite different. The main disparity between different age groups is when it is okay to use personal devices and when it is not.[95] For example, one study found that a higher percentage of those in Generation Z, compared to other generations, believe it is acceptable to use their phone during a job interview.[96] Baby Boomers might be appalled if they saw a job candidate pull out a phone during the interview process. So, what might be acceptable in the eyes of Generation Z could be disrespectful to those in older generations.

Generation X

Gen Xers, who comprise most of the parents of those in Generation Z, are now becoming the senior members of the workforce as Boomers retire. What Gen Xer wouldn't want to work with the amazing kids they themselves raised? Both generations are pragmatic, independent, hardworking, and have a realistic sense of the world around them. Both generations also have similar views on work-life balance. Being latchkey kids whose parents worked around the clock,[97] Gen Xers took stock in what it meant to have balance between the job and home. Unlike their Boomer supervisors who were prone to working too much, those in Generation X have taken a different approach to parenting that involves ensuring they have enough time to spend with their children. This has likely helped shape Generation Z's view of the importance of work-life balance.

When dealing with my future career, what is important to me is being able to provide for myself and family. Also, if I have a family, that my career won't get in the way and that I will be able to balance both and live a happy life.
- Member of Generation Z

Generation X and Generation Z may sound like twin generations in which the children were raised to be replicas of their parents. But, there are differences between these two generations, with one being around the use of technology. Generation X is no stranger to technology, as many Gen Xers are on social media and their smartphones just like those in Generation Z. But, there is one stark difference between these two generations – communication. One thing we know about Generation Z is that they are not fans of using email but are more interested in texting.[98] This doesn't bode well for the Gen Xers who love using email for just about everything and may not see texting as an appropriate platform for the workplace. Not only might the two generations be wanting to communicate on different platforms, the style of communication differs in its formality, with texting being much more informal than email. This may result in an email from someone in Generation Z saying, "meeting today-when?" with some type of emoji next to it; not necessarily what their Generation X supervisors would prefer to receive in the workplace.

Millennials

In many ways, Generation Z will look remarkably similar to Millennials in the workplace, especially around their use of technology and interest in flexible scheduling.[99] Although they may execute it differently, both Millennials and those in Generation Z come from a perspective of efficiency – Millennials in working smarter, not harder,[100] and Generation Z in matching job duties with strong skill sets. There are two big distinctions, though, between these two generations that will likely be apparent.

First, Millennials like a collaborative workplace and might not be excited about their Generation Z co-workers' desire to work independently.[101] Millennials' group lunches, pod workspaces, and collaborative projects may not be what many in Generation Z prefer. And, being that Millennials will likely be the direct supervisors of our new Generation Z employees, they may see the independent nature of some of their Generation Z co-workers or supervisees as off-putting and isolating.

Another major difference between Millennials and Generation Z in the workplace will likely be their depth of commitment to the organization. Millennials have been known to job hop so as to advance up the career ladder quickly,[102] which could make them less likely to be loyal to the organization they work for at the time. Those in Generation Z, though, identify as loyal, which may mean they stay with their employers for an extended duration. A study by the employment and recruiting agency, Randstad, reports that more Generation Z employees intend to stay with their employers for longer durations than Millennial employees.[103] This may mean that a Generation Z employee could potentially work with various Millennial supervisors and co-workers during the tenure of their employment, accruing seniority while reporting to their less-senior supervisors.

Conclusion

Because Generation Z is just now entering the workforce, it may be many years until we can fully grapple with their impact in the workplace. Until then, it will be important to find a way to leverage what we do know about them – their entrepreneurial spirit, inventive attitude, loyal nature, and dedication to making the world a better place. Whether in our organizations or freelancing in the gig economy, Generation Z has the capacity to make a difference in their organizations . . . all from their phones at a coffee shop.

Notes

1 National Association of Colleges and Employers. (2016). *Job Outlook Survey*. Retrieved from www.naceweb.org/s11182015/employers-look-for-in-new-hires.aspx
2 National Association of Colleges and Employers. (2016).
3 World Economic Forum. (2016). *The future of jobs*. Retrieved from http://reports.weforum.org/future-of-jobs-2016/
4 Sparks & Honey. (2014). *Meet Generation Z: Forget everything you learned about Millennials*. Retrieved from www.slideshare.net/sparksandhoney/generation-z-final-june-17
5 National Association of Colleges and Employers. (2016).
6 World Economic Forum. (2016).
7 Steele Flippin, C. (2017). *Generation Z in the workplace*. n.p.: Author.
8 Gallup & Operation Hope. (2013). *The 2013 Gallup-Hope index*. Retrieved from www.operationhope.org/images/uploads/Files/2013galluphopereport.pdf
9 Parsad, B., Splegelman, M., & Coopersmith, J. (2012). *Arts education in public elementary and secondary schools 1999–2000 and 2009–2010*. Retrieved from http://nces.ed.gov/pubs2012/2012014.pdf
10 Higher Education Research Institute. (2017). *College Senior Survey*. Data prepared by Higher Education Research Institute.
11 Adobe Educate. (2016). *Gen Z in the classroom: Creating the future*. Retrieved from www.adobeeducate.com/genz/adobe-education-genz
12 Higher Education Research Institute. (2017).
13 Land, M. H. (2013). Full STEAM ahead: The benefits of integrating the arts into STEM. *Procedia Computer Science, 20*, 547–552.
14 Riddle, T. (2016). *Improving schools through design thinking*. Retrieved from www.edutopia.org/blog/improving-schools-through-design-thinking-thomas-riddle
15 Howe, N. (2014b). *The G.I. Generation and the "Triumph of the Squares."* Retrieved from www.forbes.com/sites/neilhowe/2014/07/30/the-g-i-generation-and-the-triumph-of-the-squares-part-2-of-7/#14b57a629c8e
16 Seal, C. R., Boyatzis, R. E., & Bailey, J. R. (2006). Fostering emotional and social intelligence in organizations. *Organization Management Journal, 3*(3), 190–209.
17 World Economic Forum. (2016).
18 Durlak, J. A., Weissberg, R. P., Dymnicki, A. B., Taylor, R. D., & Schellinger, K. B. (2011). The impact of enhancing students' social and emotional learning: A meta-analysis of school-based universal interventions. *Child Development, 82*(1), 405–432.
19 Seemiller, C. & Grace, M. (2016). *Generation Z goes to college*. San Francisco: Jossey-Bass.
20 Seemiller, C. & Grace, M. (2016).

21 Sparks & Honey. (2014).

22 Sparks & Honey. (2014).

23 American Psychological Association. (2014). *American Psychological Association survey shows teen stress rivals that of adults*. Retrieved from www.apa.org/news/press/releases/2014/02/teen-stress.aspx

24 Berger, G. (2016). *Data reveals the most in-demand soft skills among candidates*. Retrieved from https://business.linkedin.com/talent-solutions/blog/trends-and-research/2016/most-indemand-soft-skills

25 Seal, C. R., Boyatzis, R. E., & Bailey, J. R. (2006).

26 World Economic Forum. (2016).

27 National Association of Colleges and Employers. (2016).

28 Lenhart, A. (2015c). *Teens, technology, and friendships*. Retrieved from www.pewinternet.org/2015/08/06/teens-technology-and-friendships/

29 Kardaras, N. (2016). *Generation Z: Online and at risk?* Retrieved from www.scientificamerican.com/article/generation-z-online-and-at-risk/

30 Seemiller, C. & Grace, M. (2016).

31 National Association of Colleges and Employers. (2016).

32 Higher Education Research Institute. (2017).

33 Higher Education Research Institute. (2017).

34 Adecco. (2015a). *Generation Z vs. Millennials*. Retrieved from http://pages.adeccousa.com/rs/107-IXF-539/images/generation-z-vs-millennials.pdf

35 Universum Global. (2017). *Generation Z grows up*. Retrieved from http://universumglobal.com/generation-z/

36 National Association of Colleges and Employers. (2016).

37 Dorsey, J. (2016). *iGen tech disruption*. Retrieved from http://genhq.com/wp-content/uploads/2016/01/iGen-Gen-Z-Tech-Disruption-Research-White-Paper-c-2016-Center-for-Generational-Kinetics.pdf

38 Dorsey, J. (2016).

39 Adecco. (2015a).

40 National Association of Colleges and Employers. (2016).

41 Adecco. (2015a).

42 National Association of Colleges and Employers. (2016).

43 Adecco. (2015b). *The difference between Gen Z and Millennials*. Retrieved from www.entrepreneur.com/article/247115

44 Stillman, D. & Stillman, J. (2017). *Gen Z @ work: How the next generation is transforming the workplace*. New York: HarperCollins.

45 Stillman, D. & Stillman, J. (2017).

46 Iansiti, M. & Lakhani, K. R. (2017). *The truth about blockchain*. Retrieved from https://hbr.org/2017/01/the-truth-about-blockchain, para. 2 and 3.

47 Carmody, B. (2017). *7 ways blockchain will enable entrepreneurs in 2018*. Retrieved from www.inc.com/bill-carmody/7-ways-blockchain-will-enable-entrepreneurs-in-2018.html

48 Monster Worldwide, Inc. (2016). *Move over Millennials: Gen Z is about to hit the workforce*. Retrieved from www.prnewswire.com/news-releases/move-over-millennials-gen-z-is-about-to-hit-the-workforce-300319567.html

49 Monster Worldwide, Inc. (2016).

50 Northeastern University. (2014). *Innovation survey*. Retrieved from www.northeastern.edu/news/2014/11/innovation-imperative-meet-generation-z/

51 Millennial Branding. (2014). *Millennial Branding and Internships.com release first ever study on high school careers*. Retrieved from http://millenialbranding.com/2014/high-school-careers-study/

52 Millennial Branding. (2014).

53 Rooster Money. (2017). *The allowance report-U.S.* Retrieved from www.roostermoney.com/pocket-money-resources/allowance-report-us

54 Finch, J. (2015). *What is Generation Z, and what does it want?* Retrieved from www.fastcompany.com/3045317/what-is-generation-z-and-what-does-it-want, para. 15.

55 Finch, J. (2015), para. 13.

56 Finch, J. (2015), para. 15.

57 Stillman, D. & Stillman, J. (2017).

58 Vernon, A. (2015). *10 business leaders you didn't know were Gen Xers*. Retrieved from www.inc.com/amy-vernon/10-business-leaders-you-didn-t-know-were-gen-xers.html

59 Seemiller, C. & Grace, M. (2017). *Generation Z stories study*. Unpublished raw data.

60 Universum Global. (2017).

61 Gallup & Operation Hope. (2013).

62 Adecco. (2015b).

63 Sparks & Honey. (2014).

64 Merriman, M. (2015). *What if the next big disruptor isn't a what but a who?* Retrieved from www.ey.com/Publication/vwLUAssets/EY-what-if-the-next-big-disruptor-isnt-a-what-but-a-who/$File/EY-what-if-the-next-big-disruptor-isnt-a-what-but-a-who.pdf

65 Plagianos, I. (2017). *WeWork is launching a grade school for budding entrepreneurs*. Retrieved from www.bloomberg.com/news/articles/2017-11-06/wework-hits-education-with-an-entrepreneurial-school-for-kids

66 Torpey, E. & Hogan, A. (2016). *Working in a gig economy*. Bureau of Labor Statistics. Retrieved from www.bls.gov/careeroutlook/2016/article/what-is-the-gig-economy.htm

67 Nunberg, G. (2016). *Goodbye jobs, hello "gigs": How one word sums up a new economic reality*. Retrieved from www.npr.org/2016/01/11/460698077/goodbye-jobs-hello-gigs-nunbergs-word-of-the-year-sums-up-a-new-economic-reality

68 Steele Flippin, C. (2017).

69 Upwork & Freelancers Union. (2017). *Freelancing in America: 2017*. Retrieved from https://s3-us-west-1.amazonaws.com/adquiro-content-prod/documents/Infographic_UP-URL_2040x1180.pdf

70 Deloitte. (2018). *2018 Deloitte Millennial survey*. Retrieved from www2.deloitte.com/global/en/pages/about-deloitte/articles/millennialsurvey.html

71 Deloitte. (2018).

72 CBRE & Genesis. (2014). *Fast forward 2030*. Retrieved from www.cbre.com/Research-Reports/Future-of-Work

73 Grothaus, M. (2015). *The top jobs in 10 years might not be what you expect*. Retrieved from www.fastcompany.com/3046277/the-top-jobs-in-10-years-might-not-be-what-you-expect

74 Stillman, D. & Stillman, J. (2017).

75 IBM. (2017). *Uniquely Generation Z*. Retrieved from www-01.ibm.com/common/ssi/cgi-bin/ssialias?htmlfid=GBE03799USEN&

76 Stillman, D. & Stillman, J. (2017).

77 Stillman, D. & Stillman, J. (2017).

78 Stillman, D. & Stillman, J. (2017).

79 Stillman, D. & Stillman, J. (2017).

80 Stillman, D. & Stillman, J. (2017).

81 Stillman, D. & Stillman, J. (2017).

82 Marinova, P. (2016). *20 ridiculous job titles that make even the most boring jobs sound thrilling*. Retrieved from www.google.com/amp/amp.timeinc.net/fortune/2016/12/02/ridiculous-job-titles/%3Fsource%3Ddam

83 Euromonitor International. (2011). *Make way for generation Z: Marketing for today's teens and tweens*. Retrieved from http://oaltabo2012.files.wordpress.com/2012/03/make-way-for-generation-z1.pdf

84 Tulgan, B. (2013). *Meet Generation Z: The second generation within the giant "Millennial" cohort*. Retrieved from http://rainmakerthinking.com/assets/uploads/2013/10/Gen-Z-Whitepaper.pdf

85 Stillman, D. & Stillman, J. (2017).

86 Steele Flippin, C. (2017).

87 Steele Flippin, C. (2017).

88 Gilberg, A. (2016). *From Moses Malone to LeBron James: How past stars have fared after leaving in free agency*. Retrieved from www.nydailynews.com/sports/basketball/nba-stars-fared-leaving-free-agency-article-1.2700297

89 Seemiller, C. & Grace, M. (2016).

90 Seemiller, C. & Grace, M. (2016).

91 Krueger, A. (2015). *The rise of the intrapreneur*. Retrieved from www.fastcompany.com/3046231/the-rise-of-the-intrapreneur

92 Ryback, R. (2016). *From Baby Boomers to Generation Z*. Retrieved from www.google.com/amp/s/www.psychologytoday.com/blog/the-truisms-wellness/201602/baby-boomers-generation-z%3Famp

93 Ryback, R. (2016).

94 Ryback, R. (2016).

95 Seemiller, C. & Stover, S. (2017). Curbing digital distractions in the classroom. *Contemporary Educational Technology*, 8(3), 214–231.

96 Dorsey, J. (2016).

97 Ryback, R. (2016).

98 Seemiller, C. & Grace, M. (2016).

99 Ryback, R. (2016).

100 Ryback, R. (2016).

101 Stillman, D. & Stillman, J. (2017).

102 Adkins, A. (2016). *Millennials: The job-hopping generation*. Retrieved from www.gallup.com/businessjournal/191459/millennials-job-hopping-generation.aspx

103 Randstad. (2016). *Gen Z and Millennials collide at work*. Retrieved from http://experts.randstadusa.com/hubfs/Randstad_GenZ_Millennials_Collide_Report.pdf

Making a difference

19 Societal concerns

Some societal concerns transcend generations – like safety or access to clean water or making a living wage. But, each generation comes of age during a specific era where the issues of the day are so contextually embedded into that time period. Growing up post-Depression and entering adulthood during World War II likely fueled concerns for the G.I. Generation around the economy, employment, and eventually the war; similarly, growing up during the era of 9/11, the Recession, and housing bubble burst has likely brought certain issues to the forefront of the minds of those in Generation Z. And although it might be easy to dismiss young people as not having a great deal of awareness of the world around them, those in Generation Z might surprise you. Nearly 79 percent of Generation Z college seniors believe they have an understanding of the issues facing their communities.[1] With the 24/7 news cycle flooding their phones with updates on nearly any global matter, it makes it possible to learn a lot of information and quickly. And, from what we found in our studies, they certainly care about a lot.

Affordable, quality education

In our Generation Z Goes to College Study, 53 percent of Generation Z students indicated caring or caring a great deal about issues related to education.[2] That's not entirely surprising as they had previously been in K–12 schools and were enrolled in college when they completed the survey. So, they had and continue to have a vested interest in education. But, it is more than simply caring about their own educational experience; they expressed concern about the entire American education system. In the study, many commented on how they believe the system of education is declining and that access to quality education is limited.[3] Many of their comments were filled with a sense of exasperation in not understanding why there was not more

❝ No nation has ever fallen from becoming too well educated, but nations have succumbed to stagnancy and lack of education. ❞
– Member of Generation Z

support for quality education in the U.S. For many of them, it seems obvious that education is an investment in America's future, both for personal success and for fostering a better society for all.[4]

❝ It's hard not to constantly think about the tens of thousands of dollars that I already owe, on top of paying day-to-day expenses once I graduate. I'm worried that I won't be able to get a job that will be able to handle all of the burdens that I already carry and impede me from accomplishing or attaining other things in life. ❞
- Member of Generation Z

In addition to being concerned about the quality of education, more than 80 percent indicated being concerned about the cost of higher education.[5] So, not only do they believe that the quality of education has been declining, but now it costs more to attend college, which might be the only place they can potentially make up any learning gaps from their previous educational experience. Unlike the G.I. Generation, who returned from war able to use the newly created G.I. Bill to cover higher education costs, Generation Z is seeing tuition rising at exponential rates with little to no assistance on the forefront.[6]

Breaking down walls, not building them

In 1987, Ronald Reagan made the line "Mister Gorbachev, tear down this wall!" famous in his speech about the Berlin Wall.[7] Fast-forward 30 years later, and the talk of walls as they relate to international relations has re-emerged – this time building them.

The most evident physical wall for those in Generation Z is the anticipated border wall between the U.S. and Mexico. Although this generation only expressed moderate concern about immigration in our initial study in 2014, either expanding access to it or halting illegal immigration,[8] the border wall is not just about immigration. The wall serves as a symbol of division in a time in which hyper-divisiveness in politics and in communities is commonplace. Albeit for different reasons, 30 years after Reagan pleaded for a border wall to be torn down in Germany, the U.S. is considering constructing their own border wall with Mexico.

However, not all walls are physical barriers. Walls can also be reflections of policies that block the free movement of people, ideas, and products. Take Brexit for example, in which the United Kingdom voted by citizen referendum to leave the European Union.[9] Despite the overwhelming youth vote to stay in, those in older generations fled to the polls and pushed the withdrawal over the finish line.[10] Brexit has implications that will take years to fully understand, likely creating barriers between the UK and the rest of the EU as well as between those within the UK who were either for or against Brexit.[11] Both the U.S. border wall and Brexit are reflective of the growing sense of nationalism emerging worldwide,[12] indicating a broader acceptance of putting up barriers rather than taking them down.

In addition, an overwhelming number of those in Generation Z are witnessing walls emerging involving oppression and discrimination of certain groups of people based on race, gender, class, sexual orientation, gender identity, religion, disability, and other identities. The news is filled with talk of travel bans, sanctuary cities, trans bathroom rights, women's healthcare, police shootings, religious freedom laws, and LGBTQ rights, to name a few. It is not surprising then that we found in our Generation Z Stories Study that many in this generation are concerned about the impact the ideological walls forming between people will have on human rights and the ability to come together to solve the world's complex problems in the future.[13]

❝ Our generation will change the world by 'work[ing] to establish, maintain, and respect a globalized, multicultural community, instead of fostering nationalism and other sorts of supremacist ideologies.' ❞
– Member of Generation Z

❝ With all that is going on in the world today, there is nothing that saddens me more than seeing the diverse gap between love and hate. It saddens me not because the gap exists, but rather because there is really no in between here, as this gap dictates how we live our lives, how we treat other people and how we will raise our children to do the same thing. ❞
– Member of Generation Z

Inclusion and equality

Racial equality and racism are also major concerns for this generation. In our Generation Z Goes to College Study, nearly 68 percent indicated caring or caring a great deal about issues of racial equality.[14] Another study put that number at almost three-quarters.[15] We found that it is more than just racial equality that fuels the fire of Generation Z; 56 percent said they were concerned or very concerned about racism.[16] They believe that equality is the

❝ In this day and age, it is time to stop living in the past and it's time to start treating each other like human beings. ❞
– Member of Generation Z

right thing to do and question why racism is still an issue.[17] They aren't naïve to think that racism has been eradicated and wondering what all the fuss is about. Instead, they are stunned as to how racism is still so prominent in the U.S. after literally having hundreds of years to work towards eliminating it.

Many in Generation Z are also concerned about issues of sexism. In 2017, in an effort to cut short a speech by Senator Elizabeth Warren on the Senate floor, Senate Majority Leader, Mitch McConnell said, "She was warned. She was given an explanation. Nevertheless, she persisted."[18] This incident occurred shortly after millions of people worldwide participated in a women's march in one of 653 cities in the U.S. and 261 cities around the world.[19] The momentum from the women's marches and the incident with Senator Warren gave rise to the "she persisted" theme, meme, slogan, and even apparel. When it comes to Generation Z, expect to see more "persistence" as findings from our Generation Z Goes to College Study indicate that more than 87 percent of those surveyed reported some level of concern about sexism.[20]

Their concerns of inequality, discrimination, and oppression are present with other identity groups as well. In our Generation Z Goes to College Study, we found that more than 55 percent care or care a great deal about gay rights and another study found that nearly half see inequality based on sexual orientation as an issue.[21] In a study by the nonprofit Varkey Foundation of 20,000 members of Generation Z worldwide, 71 percent of those from the U.S. believe that same-sex couples should be able to get married,[22] and a study of first-year Generation Z college students puts that number at just short of 82 percent.[23]

In addition to their concern over oppression and discrimination of particular groups, labeling, and categorizing individuals to fit within preset identity groups is also an issue for many in this generation. This is especially apparent in regard to gender identity where binary categories can limit the fluidity of one's true self. A study by the innovation company, Barkley and FutureCast, found that 60 percent of Generation Z teens agreed that society's changing perspective about gender is "allowing more

❝ Older generations' racism, sexism, and homophobia lingers in our society, but I think my generation will be known for our inclusiveness. ❞
– Member of Generation Z

❝ We can tackle the biggest problems our society faces if we care less about how people identify and accept them to move past problems like, 'Which bathroom should they use?' or 'What clothes should they wear?' and instead focus on issues like 'How can we conserve water in said bathrooms and lower the amount of paper waste?' and 'What kind of clothes can we make that keep people warm in the cold winters?' ❞
– Member of Generation Z

people to be themselves," which is considerably higher than the 52 percent of Baby Boomers who agreed.[24] And, now if a member of Generation Z wants to get a non-binary driver's license, they can head to Washington, DC.[25] With 75 percent of Generation Z supporting transgender equality,[26] it may be no time before more transgender inclusive laws are put in place by this generation.

Many in older generations were taught that the way to get along with people with whom they were different was by tolerating or putting up with them. But, Generation Z's inclusive attitude embodies the belief that difference is to be embraced and not just tolerated. And, although they admit their generation may have taken political correctness too far[27] and some demonstrate over-sensitivity to issues,[28] their intentions come from a place that strives for inclusion for everyone. And while this generation will likely include many individual social justice activists working toward advancing civil rights, we may also expect that the collective open-mindedness of this generation might change the culture of society towards one that is more inclusive simply by their growing older and taking up a larger share of the adult population.

Getting a J.O.B.

Think back to the year 2000 when the oldest of the Millennials were heading full speed into the workforce. With their optimistic attitudes and GeoCities home pages ready to go, they were eager and excited to get a job. The Internet was in its infancy, and startups were emerging on every street corner. The world seemed to be at their fingertips. Older Millennials came pouring out of college with a strong job market and even some high school graduates went straight into the workforce. But, then 9/11 happened. Troops were sent to Iraq and Afghanistan, the Recession hit a few years later, and the housing bubble burst, creating a foreclosure industry that gave way to blockbuster television shows about home remodeling. Younger Millennials who thought they would have their pick of jobs were now moving back in with their parents to make ends meet.

Fast-forward to the present day where Generation Z is entering today's workforce. While they might be preparing to launch into adulthood in their new careers, many in this generation are worried a great deal about actually finding a job.[29] When asked about their biggest concerns, 93 percent of Generation Z students indicated being concerned to some extent about the issue of unemployment.[30] Beyond their own anxieties about getting a job, many discussed their concern for the lack of employment opportunities in general, echoing the sentiment that "everyone should have the ability to be employed."[31]

Unemployment concerns me because even a college degree can no longer guarantee a job, making me wonder if spending thousands of dollars on a degree is going to be worth it.
    - Member of Generation Z

> **"** *As a child, my family had to close our business in 2008 because we couldn't afford to keep it open. Then a few years later, my mother was laid off from her job, which left us living on food stamps for a while. All together, I worry that what happened to my parents will happen to me and the rest of my generation.* **"**
> *– Member of Generation Z*

This concern for unemployment is likely tied to watching their parents and some Millennials struggle with high unemployment rates at 10 percent during the Recession.[32] That number might not seem high compared to the unemployment rate of nearly 25 percent in 1933,[33] plaguing the parents of those in the G.I. Generation and some of the older members of the generation themselves. Tom Brokaw notes about the G.I. Generation, "They had watched their parents lose their businesses, their farms, their jobs, their hopes."[34]

While not as extreme for those in Generation Z, both generations share the commonality of growing up during a severe economic downturn, ultimately shaping their perspectives and concerns.

Affording life

Years ago, most kids would have spent their birthday cash from grandma on the latest toy or game before the money even made it out of the envelope. With Generation Z, this is an entirely different scenario. As penny-pinching savers,[35] they have stocked away tooth fairy money since age five in the event of a future recession. Given their concern about jobs, it's no surprise that nearly three-quarters are concerned about financial security in general,[36] with nearly two-thirds being concerned about being able to afford housing.[37] While some may want luxuries and wealth, financial security for many of them simply reflects a desire to have enough money to pay for food, housing, and the essentials.[38] In their minds, this notion of "enough" is reflective of the amount it would take to ensure their families never worry about having the money they need to live safe and healthy lives.[39]

> **"** *I don't care how much money I make in my future career, but I do worry about if my family will have enough money to get through the week or not. I worry about if my family will have enough money for gas or enough money to pay the bills.* **"**
> *– Member of Generation Z*

While they certainly are thinking about their own financial security, this generation also has an overwhelming concern about the economy in general. Findings from our Generation Z Goes to College Study indicate that nearly 64 percent care about issues related to the economy, and 61 percent are concerned or very concerned about poverty.[40]

A thriving and sustainable planet

In our Generation Z Goes to College Study in 2014, we asked questions related to the environment expecting that Generation Z would also have a deep concern for the environment like Millennials.[41] However, we found that only 58 percent indicated caring or caring a great deal about environmental issues, and just more than a third were concerned or very concerned about climate change.[42] In addition to our study not finding a high number with a strong interest in the environment,[43] it appears that other studies came to similar conclusions[44] or at least had mixed results.[45] For example, data from the 2014 CIRP Freshman Survey indicate that 67 percent of Generation Z first-year college students agreed somewhat or strongly that addressing global climate change should be a federal priority, with one-third disagreeing.[46] There might be a few explanations as to why the rates of environmental support were not higher for both studies. First, some of them may have viewed environmentalism as being progressive, meaning that once we move in one direction to be more environmentally friendly, there would be little reason for regression. Because of the forward trajectory of environmentalism that was evident in the Obama Administration,[47] it is not really surprising that this was not an issue on the forefront of Generation Z's minds in 2014. It may have appeared at that time that environmental progress was on autopilot.

But, with a different political party in power after the 2016 election, the administration changed direction on resource allocation for issues related to the environment, to what extent they recognize and validate the science of climate change, and the upholding and enforcement of environmental regulations.[48] It's not surprising then that in 2017, 85 percent of Generation Z students who completed the College Senior Survey strongly agreed or somewhat agreed that addressing global climate change should be a federal priority,[49] a nearly 20 point gain from just 3 years earlier. While the 2014 study population included first-year students and the 2017 population included college seniors, which are arguably different age groups, it would be unlikely that the disparity between those numbers is attributed solely to their 3-year age difference. It is more likely that the attention paid to environmental policy that occurred between the two studies is more influential in the higher 2017 findings.

The higher results in the 2017 College Senior Survey were not just isolated to that particular study. Our Generation Z Stories Study in 2017 yielded very different results from our 2014 study as well. In addition to data collection for our second study being post-election, the information we

> *I worry about climate change and what is going to happen in the years to come. I am feeling very sick just talking about it. I try to ignore it, what's going on with our animals, nature, our atmosphere, and it is so awful that we are taking no initiative to change. I'm confused and angered by everyone for not caring!!*
> – Member of Generation Z

> *I worry about the health of our planet more than anything. We have destroyed the ecosystem without thinking of the consequences, and the consequences are taking place all around. It worries me so much because the future generations may not ever be able to see the beauty that the Earth used to be.*
> – Member of Generation Z

gathered from Generation Z survey respondents was entirely narrative, allowing them to share their thoughts using their own words. This is an important distinction in that had we asked about the environment through forced choice questions, we would likely not have been able to capture the diversity and complexity of their opinions. For example, students used words like deforestation and biodiversity,[50] which likely wouldn't have been captured through a finite number of survey choices.

While 17 percent discussed climate change or global warming when sharing what they believed to be the most important issue facing their generation,[51] many also shared issues like developing renewable and clean energy, stopping pollution, recycling, reducing emissions, protecting wildlife, using fewer resources, reducing oil dependency, reducing waste, eliminating pesticides, and reusing resources.[52] So, as much as this is a generation that may get behind environmental issues to slowdown global warming, many also seem concerned about other aspects of maintaining a thriving and sustainable planet for all.

What is striking about their interest in the environment is not just their concern for their own health and well-being now but the future of the environment in general. Many shared strong feelings about ensuring the planet would be sustainable for generations to come or frustration in being left with an environment they believe has been ruined by older generations.[53]

Feeling safe and secure

Today, it is the norm to see television shows and movies portraying violent acts including rape, torture, mutilation, and graphic killings.[54] Whether children are killing children in movies like the *The Hunger Games*, or sexual assault has become not only legal but also a way of life in *The Handmaid's Tale*, violence is commonplace in mainstream media. Although ratings and parental controls can offer some form of protection for youth in what they watch, as soon as children can access streaming services, online videos, or the Internet by themselves, they can watch just about anything. What might be scarier for this generation, though, is that what they see in fictional media is often a reflection of real life. Crime shows feature episodes "stripped from the headlines," and many movies are "based on a true story," offering re-enactments of real-life scenarios. Although violence on-screen is not a new phenomenon, a 2013 report by the American Academy of Pediatrics found that the portrayal of gun violence in movies "has more than doubled since 1950," and, by 2009, the rate of depictions of gun violence in PG-13 movies was equivalent to or greater than those in R-rated movies.[55]

> *Violence that ends with the deaths of innocents - war, terrorism, school shootings, etc. [has] become so common and rampant that the next generation who grows up with these atrocities may have serious health issues.*
> *- Member of Generation Z*

While these savvy members of Generation Z might be able to separate fact from fiction in their entertainment options, they are also able to witness real-life violence through live feeds, uploaded videos, pictures, and audio recordings they can access online. One such example is the viral video filmed by the girlfriend of a Black man shot and killed by a cop during a traffic stop.[56] As of 2018, the YouTube video alone had more than 355,000 views.[57] Whether they are videos or images of war, suicide bombings, shootings, bullying, or other violent acts, the opportunity to witness real violence is available at their fingertips.

It's not surprising then that 25 percent of those surveyed in our Generation Z Goes to College Study discussed violence as their biggest social concern.[58] And, it is not just one type of violence they worry about. We found that nearly 60 percent are concerned about Internet security, 59 percent about crime, 57 percent about war, 56 percent about school shootings, and 54 percent about bullying.[59]

> *I'm afraid of violence/ crime happening to me/ around me/to people I know because it's so prevalent in society.*
> *- Member of Generation Z*

While this data was taken from the 2014 study, given the context of today, some of these numbers could be even higher. Take, for example, school shootings. After the shooting at Marjory Stoneman Douglas High School in 2018, Generation Z high school students passionately spoke out about gun restrictions and concerns for safety to the public, the media, and lawmakers. Not only did many survivors of the shooting mobilize for gun control, they rallied youth from across the nation to join together to participate in March For Our Lives, a solidarity event to advocate for legislation to end gun violence.[60] The protest brought together over a million people in more than 800 cities around the world.[61] Generation Z's overwhelming concern about gun violence has now even dubbed them the name, "Mass Shooting Generation," by *The New York Times*.[62]

Those in Generation Z see violence all around them. Whether online, in their schools, or in their communities, many have a sense of fear and anxiety for their safety and the safety of others, and that likely won't change any time soon.

Affordable and comprehensive healthcare

Although many of those in Generation Z are too young to acquire their own healthcare plans now, a study in 2016 by The Center for Generational Kinetics found that of all generations, those in Generation Z are the least likely to believe they have access to affordable, quality healthcare.[63] Even in 2014 before the renewed political attention to healthcare, we found in our Generation Z Goes to College Study that nearly half of those surveyed were concerned about access to healthcare.[64] Whether Generation Z will have less access than their older counterparts or simply believe they will, many are concerned about whether or not they will have affordable and accessible healthcare.

❝Healthcare: Um, basic human right? I think so too.❞
– Member of Generation Z

Conclusion

As soon as they were old enough to click, swipe, or tap, those in Generation Z have had news at their fingertips about every global and local crisis, giving this generation much to worry about even at a young age. This has lead them to care deeply about many issues, especially those they believe have a significant current and future impact on society. But, as the critical nature of specific societal issues ebb and flow throughout their lifetimes and their individual needs and interests change as they age, the concerns of those in Generation Z may shift in priority.

Notes

1 Higher Education Research Institute. (2017). *College Senior Survey*. Data prepared by Higher Education Research Institute.
2 Seemiller, C. & Grace, M. (2014). *Generation Z goes to college study*. Unpublished raw data.

3 Seemiller, C. & Grace, M. (2016). *Generation Z goes to college*. San Francisco: Jossey-Bass.
4 Seemiller, C. & Grace, M. (2016).
5 Seemiller, C. & Grace, M. (2016).
6 Seemiller, C. & Grace, M. (2014).
7 Fisher, M. (2017). *"Tear down this wall": How Reagan's forgotten line became a defining moment*. Retrieved from www.washingtonpost.com/news/retropolis/wp/2017/06/12/tear-down-this-wall-how-reagans-forgotten-line-became-a-defining-presidential-moment/?utm_term=.dc713009e5f7
8 Seemiller, C. & Grace, M. (2016).
9 Hunt, A. & Wheeler, B. (2017). *Brexit: All you need to know about the UK leaving the EU*. Retrieved from www.bbc.com/news/uk-politics-32810887
10 Goulard, H. (2016). *Britain's youth voted Remain*. Retrieved from www.politico.eu/article/britains-youth-voted-remain-leave-eu-brexit-referendum-stats/
11 Hunt, A. & Wheeler, B. (2017).
12 Postel-Vinay, K. (2017). *How neo-nationalism went global*. Retrieved from www.usnews.com/news/best-countries/articles/2017-03-15/a-look-at-global-neo-nationalism-after-brexit-and-donald-trumps-election
13 Seemiller, C. & Grace, M. (2017). *Generation Z stories study*. Unpublished raw data.
14 Seemiller, C. & Grace, M. (2014).
15 Barkley & FutureCast. (2017). *Getting to know Gen Z: How the Pivotal generation is different from Millennials*. Retrieved from www.barkleyus.com/genz/
16 Seemiller, C. & Grace, M. (2016).
17 Seemiller, C. & Grace, M. (2016).
18 Victor, D. (2017). *"Nevertheless, she persisted": How Senate's silencing of Warren became a meme*. Retrieved from www.nytimes.com/2017/02/08/us/politics/elizabeth-warren-republicans-facebook-twitter.html
19 Chenoweth, E. (2017). *This is what we learned by counting the women's marches*. Retrieved from www.washingtonpost.com/news/monkey-cage/wp/2017/02/07/this-is-what-we-learned-by-counting-the-womens-marches/?utm_term=.8b02006fa991
20 Barkley & FutureCast. (2017).
21 Barkley & FutureCast. (2017).
22 Varkey Foundation. (2017). *Generation Z: Global Citizenship Survey*. Retrieved from www.varkeyfoundation.org/what-we-do/policy-research/generation-z-global-citizenship-survey/
23 Eagan, K., Stolzenberg, E. B., Ramirez, J. J., Aragon, M. C., Suchard, M. R., & Hurtado, S. (2014). *The American freshman: National norms fall 2014*. Los Angeles: Higher Education Research Institute, UCLA.
24 Barkley & FutureCast. (2017), p. 17.
25 Segal, C. (2017). *D.C. will be first in nation to offer non-binary driver's licenses*. Retrieved from www.pbs.org/newshour/rundown/d-c-will-first-nation-offer-non-binary-drivers-licenses/
26 Varkey Foundation. (2017).
27 Masback, G. (2016). *The voice of Gen Z*. (n.p.): Author.
28 Seemiller, C. & Grace, M. (2017).
29 Seemiller, C. & Grace, M. (2017).
30 Seemiller, C. & Grace, M. (2016).
31 Seemiller, C. & Grace, M. (2016), p. 104.
32 U.S. Bureau of Labor Statistics. (2012). *The recession of 2007–2009*. Retrieved from www.bls.gov/spotlight/2012/recession/pdf/recession_bls_spotlight.pdf

33 United States Census Bureau. (1999). *20th century statistics*. Retrieved from www.census. gov/prod/99pubs/99statab/sec31.pdf

34 Brokaw, T. (1998). *The greatest generation*. New York: Random House Trade Paperbacks, p. xxvii.

35 Seemiller, C. & Grace, M. (2016).

36 Seemiller, C. & Grace, M. (2016).

37 Seemiller, C. & Grace, M. (2016).

38 Seemiller, C. & Grace, M. (2017).

39 Seemiller, C. & Grace, M. (2017).

40 Seemiller, C. & Grace, M. (2014).

41 Glass Packaging Institute. (2014). *The Millennials*. Retrieved from www.gpi.org/sites/ default/files/GPI-TheMillennials-11%206%2014-FINAL.pdf

42 Seemiller, C. & Grace, M. (2016).

43 Seemiller, C. & Grace, M. (2016).

44 Barkley & FutureCast. (2017).

45 Seemiller, C. & Grace, M. (2016).

46 Eagan, K., Stolzenberg, E. B., Ramirez, J. J., Aragon, M. C., Suchard, M. R., & Hurtado, S. (2014).

47 Byrd, R. (2017). *Obama's environmental legacy: A reflection*. Retrieved from www. huffingtonpost.com/entry/obamas-environmental-legacy-a-reflection_us_ 58820e1fe4b08f5134b61fc0

48 Merica, D. (2017). *Trump dramatically changes approach to climate change*. Retrieved from www.cnn.com/2017/03/27/politics/trump-climate-change-executive-order/index. html

49 Higher Education Research Institute. (2017).

50 Seemiller, C. & Grace, M. (2017).

51 Seemiller, C. & Grace, M. (2017).

52 Seemiller, C. & Grace, M. (2017).

53 Seemiller, C. & Grace, M. (2017).

54 Parents Television Council. (2013). *An examination of violence, graphic violence, and gun violence in the media*. Retrieved from http://w2.parentstv.org/main/Research/Studies/ CableViolence/vstudy_dec2013.pdf

55 Bushman, B. J., Jamieson, P. E., Weitz, I., & Romer, D. (2013). *Gun violence trends in movies*. Retrieved from http://pediatrics.aappublications.org/content/pediatrics/ early/2013/11/06/peds.2013-1600.full.pdf

56 Herreria, C. (2016). *Cop fatally shoots black man, leaves victim's girlfriend to record tragic aftermath*. Retrieved from www.huffingtonpost.com/entry/falcon-heights-shooting_us_ 577dd795e4b0c590f7e8058f

57 YouTube. (2017). *Woman films boyfriend's death after being shot by police*. Retrieved from www.youtube.com/watch?v=ymZKi8p7i8Q

58 Seemiller, C. & Grace, M. (2016).

59 Seemiller, C. & Grace, M. (2016).

60 March for Our Lives. (2018). *Mission statement*. Retrieved from www.marchforourlives. com/

61 Wilson, R. (2018). *More than a million people participated in March for Our Lives protests*. Retrieved from http://thehill.com/homenews/state-watch/380321-more-than-a-million-people-participated-in-anti-gun-violence-marches

62 Burch, A. D. S., Mazzei, P., & Healy, J. (2018). *A "Mass Shooting Generation" cries out for change*. Retrieved from www.nytimes.com/2018/02/16/us/columbine-mass-shootings.

html?mtrref=www.google.com&gwh=03EC578FB15C117044EA60AE1453A269&gwt=pay

63 The Center for Generational Kinetics. (2016). *iGen's political and civic outlook.* Retrieved from http://3pur2814p18t46fuop22hvvu.wpengine.netdna-cdn.com/wp-content/uploads/2016/02/iGen-Gen-Z-Political-Civic-Outlook-Research-White-Paper-c-2016-The-Center-for-Generational-Kinetics.pdf

64 Seemiller, C. & Grace, M. (2016).

20 Politics

• •

From "I Like Ike" to "Yes we can!" to "Make America Great Again," a lot has changed in politics since older generations began going to the polls.[1] Although mudslinging is not relegated to just more recent politics with chants of "Lock Her Up"[2] and "Love Trumps Hate,"[3] the ability to intimately witness the resounding rancor through television, radio, Internet, and now social media is bringing political heatedness to the forefront of the lives of those in Generation Z. For older generations, they have seen negative campaigning and intense political debates, but no one can argue that today's political climate is like no other in modern U.S. history. While those who are older can put this in context with other election cycles, this is not the case for young members of Generation Z who have no other experience with politics. With the prominence of political negativity today, those in Generation Z have already determined that they don't like it and are disgusted, disenchanted, and discouraged by the whole political system in general.[4]

> **❝ Our political system is in need of a redo. ❞**
> *- Member of Generation Z*

Political ideologies and Generation Z

While political ideologies may change based on age and experience, research has shown that once a political ideology is set, it is likely to stay intact over the course of one's lifetime. To test this theory, researchers from Columbia University, Yair Ghitza and Andrew Gelman, sought to uncover trends in long-term voting patterns of generational cohorts.[5] To do so, they examined political events during each generation's adolescence and young adulthood (between 14 and 24 years-old) along with presidential approval ratings at the time. What they found is that high approval ratings of the President during a generation's formative years correlated with future voting patterns along that President's party lines. Thus, a highly popular Democratic President when a generation is young aligns with that generation voting for a Democrat in future elections.[6] The opposite was also true; low approval ratings aligned with lifetime voting

Table 20.1 Generational Voting Patterns[7]

Birth Year(s)	Generation	President	Party	Approval Ratings	Lifetime Voting Patterns
1910s/1920s	G.I./Early Silent	Roosevelt	D	High	Lean Democrat
1930s	Silent	Truman	D	Mixed	Mixed
1941	Silent	Eisenhower	R	High	Lean Republican
1952	Baby Boomers	Kennedy	D	High	Lean Democrat
		Johnson	D	Mixed	
		Nixon	R	Low	
1968	Generation X	Carter	D	Low	Lean Republican
		Reagan	R	High	
		Bush I	R	Mixed	
1985	Millennial	Clinton	D	High	Lean Democrat
		Bush II	R	Mixed	

along opposite party lines.[8] And mixed ratings aligned with mixed voting patterns.[9]

With a new generational cohort coming to the voting booth, it seems as though many candidates would want to know the political ideologies of Generation Z. But, there is not yet one clear-cut answer. Actually, this generation challenges the notion of traditional ideologies, making it even more difficult to anticipate their voting behavior. In our Generation Z Goes to College Study, we found that most members of Generation Z identify as liberal or moderate on social issues and moderate or conservative on financial issues.[10] This isn't surprising given their concern for financial security balanced with their value of inclusion and progressive stances on issues related to particular identity groups. Combined, these two political leanings don't necessarily clearly point to a specific political party or even ideology. Based on various research studies, though, five possibilities have emerged, which include Democrat, Liberal, Independent, Socially Liberal-Moderate Republican, or third party.

Democrats?

Research on both adolescents and young adults indicates Generation Z may be leaning Democratic. A 2017 study by the Public Religion Research Institute found that more young people in general (15 to 24 year-olds) have a favorable opinion of the Democratic Party (57 percent) compared to the Republican Party (31 percent).[11] It appears this favorability may be correlated with their actual party identification as well. In our 2017 Generation Z Stories Study, more than 40 percent of the college students we surveyed identified as Democrats, with 30 percent identifying as Republicans, and 20 percent identifying as Independents; the remaining identified as Libertarian, Green, and Other.[12] And, a 2017 study by the NORC Center for Public Affairs Research found that 29 percent of 13 to 17 year-olds polled said they plan to be Democrats, with 23 percent indicating Republican and 24 percent noting Independent or a third party.[13] Overall, it appears that a greater share of those in Generation Z have positive views of the Democratic Party and either currently identify as Democrat or plan to in the future.

When looking at anticipated party identification, though, it's important to also consider the presidential approval ratings of those in office during Generation Z's formative years. Thus far, two presidents have served during their adolescence and young adulthood – Barack Obama and Donald Trump. With President Obama having high approval ratings when he left office,[14] and President Trump having low approval ratings during his first 18 months in office,[15] if using the same metrics utilized in determining voting patterns of older generations, it could then be anticipated that Generation Z will lean Democrat for future voting.

Liberals?

When looking specifically at data from first-year college students on political ideology, there is a clear majority who sit in the middle-of-the-road. However, 30.5 percent indicated leaning left and 23.1 percent to the right.[16] This isn't surprising in that there appears to be more Democrats within Generation Z than Republicans.[17] And with the potential rise in Independents, middle-of-the-road might be a safe political place to be. However, fast-forward 4 years. Those first-year students became seniors, the 2016 election occurred, and Generation Z voted for the first time.

A study of college seniors in 2017 found that 13.8 percent more of those in Generation Z identified as liberal and far left-leaning, 12.2 percent fewer who identified as middle-of-the-road, and 1.5 percent fewer who identified as conservative and far right-leaning compared to the first-year student student four years earlier.[18] So, it appears that as they went through college, voted for the first time, and saw a Republican elected to the White House, their political ideology moved left. Those originally in the middle-of-the-road likely contributed to the growing share of liberals. Even a small number of conservatives appear to have moved left, likely towards middle-of-the road.

The high numbers of those in Generation Z identifying as liberal, and even far left, can be telling. While liberals are often Democrats, not all Democrats are liberal. Moderate Democrats instead appeal to a base that draws from the political

Table 20.2 Political Ideologies of the 2013 First-Year Cohort at the Beginning and End of College

	Far Left	Liberal	Middle-of-the-Road	Conservative	Far Right
2013 First-Year Students[19]	2.8	27.7	46.3	21.2	1.9
2017 Seniors[20]	5.8	38.5	34.1	20.6	1

center. Thus, moderate politicians get elected because their voters tend to include both those on the far end of the political spectrum (in this case, the far left) as well as many of those in the middle, such as Independents. Although a moderate Democrat, Hillary Clinton, won the party nomination in 2016, her opponent, Bernie Sanders, was able to mobilize the progressive and highly liberal base of the Democratic Party during the primaries. Sanders, however, wasn't able to win the nomination, but liberal-leaning Generation Z did not yet have enough voters for a full youth bloc and many who were old enough to vote didn't come out.[21] But, with the high numbers who identify as liberal and their voter-age cohort continuing to grow, will Generation Z come out to support progressive candidates in the future?

Independents?

The percentage of youth, 18 to 29, identifying as Republicans has held fairly constant between the 2008, 2012, and 2016 elections, while the percentage identifying as Democrats has decreased significantly across the same time period.[22] But it doesn't appear that they are leaving the Democratic Party to become Republicans. When looking more closely, this decrease is directly correlated with the increase in youth who identify as Independents.[23] So, while young Republicans stay Republicans, it looks like many young Democrats are becoming Independents. On the one hand, it makes sense that there are a growing number of Independents within Generation Z. As many in this generation grapple with views that don't seem to fit within one specific party platform, they may find that being an Independent gives them the freedom and flexibility to vote for candidates that share their views on issues most important to them, regardless of party. While the growing trend towards being an Independent makes sense, why they are leaving one party and not the other is a bit more curious. Perhaps it is the connection of religion with the Republican Party as twice the number of evangelicals nationwide identify as Republican rather than Democrat.[24] For those young people who identify as religious, and even more so evangelical, they may find that the Republican Party more closely aligns with their conservative social views.

Socially liberal-moderate republicans?

Jeff Brauer, a political science professor from Keystone College who studies the voting behavior of Generation Z, says, "While many are not connected to the two major parties and lean independent, Generation Z's inclinations would generally fit moderate Republicans, of which there aren't many in leadership positions anymore."[25] Data from our Generation Z Goes to College Study points to this notion of the moderate Republican as well. While only 22 percent of Generation Z college students identified as socially conservative, 32 percent indicated being financially conservative, highlighting a misalignment between their social and financial perspectives.[26] This sentiment rings true with many College Republicans who may be in favor of limited government involvement

> **❝ I think there is a lot more tolerance among young people . . . I would say it's a new generation of Republican. ❞**
> - Brady Herrington, 19-year-old Republican[29]

yet are less conservative on social issues like abortion, same-sex marriage, and immigration.[27] In an interview with *The Kansas City Star*, Brady Herrington, a 19-year-old Republican college student, affirmed the balance that many College Republicans are finding between being financially conservative and socially moderate.[28]

Libertarians?

In our first book, *Generation Z Goes to College*, we shared that this generation might actually be more Libertarian than anything, as our earlier findings showed that nearly three-quarters were very concerned about possible limitations on their personal freedoms.[30] But, findings from our 2017 study don't seem to reflect these same concerns. Only five individuals out of more than 1,200 brought up being concerned about the issue of personal freedom, and those who did discussed trying to balance freedom with security or equality, not advocating for their right to their personal freedoms.[31] So, do they lean Libertarian after all? Findings from the CIRP Freshman Study indicate that the majority of first-year college students, from 2013 forward when Generation Z came to college, agree strongly or somewhat in a woman's right to choose, the legalization of marijuana, and same-sex marriage[32] – all stances related to the desire for the government to stay out of a person's individual choice. But, the majority also believe that the U.S. should have universal healthcare and that the federal government should do more to restrict handgun sales and address global warming[33] – all positions reflective of government oversight. It seems perhaps that the Libertarianism that fits best with Generation Z might be one of "don't infringe on my personal freedoms, but make sure that I am safe and healthy."

New third party?

It also appears there is a group of members of Generation Z who might not be able to find a candidate that stands for what they believe in. Perhaps this will lead to the emergence of a competitive third party in the coming future. This would align with the perspectives of a majority of African-American (66 percent), Asian American (71 percent), Latino/a (68 percent), and White (73 percent) 18 to 29 year-olds who believe we need a third political party.[34] Given Generation Z's views, this third party they are referring to may not be one that exists today. We found in our Generation Z Stories Study that only 1 percent indicated identifying with the Green party, 4 percent as Libertarians, and slightly more than 4 percent as "Other."[35]

Voter turnout

According to the Census Bureau, 61.4 percent of eligible voters in the United States voted in the 2016 presidential election, down slightly from 61.8 percent in 2012 and down considerably from 63.6 percent in 2008 when no incumbents were running for president.[36] Although 47 percent of those in Generation Z indicated having a favorable opinion of voting[37] and in 2014, more than half said they planned to vote in upcoming elections,[38] voter turnout for Generation Z in the 2016 presidential election was only at about 40 percent.[39] And, the turnout of registered Generation Z voters was lower compared to all other generations.[40]

The inevitable winner

Looking back at history, a similar tale emerges with the G.I. Generation and their coming of age in the voting booths. The turnout for the presidential election in 1940 was 62.5 percent, but that number went down in 1944 to 55.9 percent and then to 53 percent in 1948, and back up to 63 percent in 1952 when the country elected Dwight D. Eisenhower as the first Republican president since Herbert Hoover was elected in 1928.[41] But, for the G.I. Generation's first few elections, the overall voter turnout in the country was decreasing. Perhaps the decline was due to the likely inevitable win of Franklin Roosevelt for yet another term, making voting an unnecessary ritual for some. There may have been a similar sentiment in the 2016 election in which polls had Hillary Clinton winning by landslide.[42] A near-certain victory by Clinton may have signaled to youth that their vote for either party wouldn't really matter, perhaps keeping some of them home from the polls.

Table 20.3 Registered and Eligible Voters by Generation for 2016 Election

2016 U.S. Presidential Election[43]	Birth Years	Ages	% Registered to Vote	% of Registered Voters who Voted	% of Eligible Voters Who Voted
Generation Z	1995–2010	18–21	51.83%	77.37%	40.10%
Millennials	1981–1994	22–35	63.60%	81.64%	51.92%
Generation X	1965–1980	36–51	72.71%	90.91%	66.10%
Baby Boomers	1946–1964	52–70	75.69%	90.72%	68.66%
Silent (and some G.I.)	?-1945	71+	77.69%	90.21%	70.09%

Youth turnout trends

Looking at youth turnout trends for recent elections can also be informative in understanding Generation Z's voting patterns. In looking specifically at

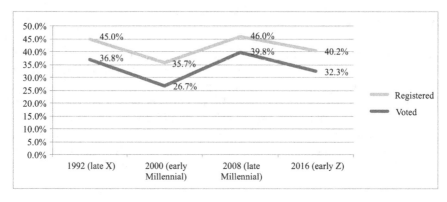

Figure 20.1

Voter Registration and Turnout Rates for 18 Year-Olds in 1992, 2000, 2008, and 2016[44,45,46,47]

18 year-olds in the past four elections (in which there was a change in the political party in power), the data tells an interesting story. In the years that Democrats won the White House (1992[48] and 2008),[49] rates of registration and turnout among 18 year-olds was higher than the years Republicans won (2000[50] and 2016).[51] Did the youth vote push the candidates to victory in 1992 and 2008? Perhaps – although both candidates won handily those years. But, it can't be left unsaid that the youth vote was crucial. In 1992, Clinton and Gore appealed to young voters by appearing on MTV,[52] and in 2008, Obama harnessed the power of social media to capitalize on Millennial engagement.[53]

It is also interesting to look at whether the 18 year-olds during each of those elections (non-incumbents) were born into the earlier part of the generation or the later part. Those who represented the second half of birth years of the generation (or late) turned out at higher rates, whereas those who represented the first half of birth years of the generation (early) turned out at lower rates (see Figure 20.1). What might this mean? If trends hold steady, perhaps we see an uptick of both registered voters and turnout with the late Z (or little Z) population.

Candidate of choice in 2016

For the 2016 election, exit polling found that the majority of 18 to 29 and 30 to 44 year-olds voted for Hilary Clinton, while the majority of 45 to 64 year-olds and 65 and older voted for Donald Trump.[54] Thus, younger voters supported Democrat, Hillary Clinton, and older voters supported Republican, Donald Trump. Being that Generation Z was the youngest voting generation and their rates are accounted for within the 18 to 29 year-old bracket, it could be argued that many members of Generation Z then voted for Clinton.

But, the difficulty in understanding Generation Z's specific voting patterns is that conventional polling data only disaggregates age by larger thresholds such as the 18 to 29 year-old range. This broad age range is impractical for truly understanding young, first-time voters. A 29 year-old voter may be voting in their third election, whereas an 18 year-old may be casting a ballot for the first time. But, Keystone College political science professor, Jeff Brauer, found a way to analyze data from 18 to 29 year-old voters to better understand how those in Generation Z might have voted in the 2016 election. In looking specifically at the state level when comparing the 2012 and 2016 elections, Professor Brauer found that in several swing states, the Democratic margin of victory of the youth vote (18 to 29 year-olds) decreased significantly, anywhere from 16 points in Florida to 21 points in Nevada.[55] Overall, between the 2012 election and 2016 election, Democratic Party identification of youth decreased from 44 percent to 37 percent.[56] He asserts that it is unlikely that the younger Millennials who voted in 2012 and became the older part of the youth cohort by the 2016 election changed their partisan leanings.[57] He believes it is more likely that these liberal Millennials at the top end of the age bracket were balanced out by the more fiscally conservative members of Generation Z, who were "able, for the first time, to express their political inclinations, especially in the economically hard-hit swing states."[58] This explanation makes sense in that, as a candidate, Trump's platform included many economic policies focused on bringing back jobs, jumpstarting the economy, and evening the playing field for the working and middle class. Despite Trump's conservative social views, which don't seem to resonate with Generation Z, the majority of those in Generation Z having moderate to conservative economic views might have been initially drawn more to his economic message. However, without actual voting data specific to this generational cohort, it's difficult to know which candidates they actually voted for. And, with such low turnout,[59] is who they voted for really representative of the views of an entire generation?

Why aren't they voting?

For the 2016 election, Generation Z's voter registration and turnout was lower than that of other generations. It's important to consider then the potential barriers to their political participation. Although there may be obstacles for any age voter, onerous voter registration requirements can certainly impact this generation.[60] Two strategies specific to increasing youth registration and turnout include automatic voter registration, which has been found to increase both youth voter registration and turnout at the polls[61] and voter pre-registration for 16 and 17 year-olds, available in 16 states, which is linked to an increased probability that youth will turn out to vote.[62]

An additional idea aimed to increase youth voting would be to lower the voting age to 16, an age in which studies have shown that individuals have the cognitive capacity for deliberative decision-making.[63] Sixteen is also an age in which teens have more stability in their lives, are often embedded in and more connected to their communities, and are studying civic engagement at school.[64] That age might then be a less tumultuous time in their lives compared to 18, which can be more unpredictable as many head to college or the workforce, potentially even living in a new community.[65] In addition, having previously voted in an election can influence the likelihood of voting in the future.[66] So, as 16 year-olds head to the polls, they establish a voting habit that may lead them to engage in more consistent voting behavior in future elections, even in times of transition and change in their lives.

Feeling overlooked and powerless

Beyond the more technical barriers to registration and voting, however, larger issues loom for this generation's political participation. First, most in Generation Z do not view political leaders as role models,[67] and fewer than 17 percent believe politicians have influenced them at all.[68] Most actually think politicians are greedy and corrupt,[69] and feel fatigued and disgusted by political partisanship. Some may simply find that no candidate is worthy of their vote.

The concerns of those in Generation Z do not just center on their view of political leaders. Many believe the political system, in general, is not responsive to the concerns of young voters – issues that include the high cost of higher education, racism, and an economy that appears to be controlled by and benefits wealthy elites.[70] Not only are their concerns left out of the political narrative, when trying to bring attention to their issues, many feel powerless and believe their opinions carry little weight with lawmakers.

While those in Generation Z care deeply about many social issues, they simply may not see a party, candidate, or even place in general for them in the current system. On the one hand, for a group that wants to change the world, politics for them might not be the venue to do so. But, on the other hand, as this generation finds issues

> **❝ I am very concerned about politics. I don't enjoy following them myself, but that's partially because of how corrupt they are. I feel as if I have no say in what's going on, democracy or not; politicians do what they do and eat up our money and do relatively little good for the people. ❞**
> *- Member of Generation Z*

> **❝ We're children. You guys are the adults. You need to take some action and play a role. Work together, come over your politics, and get something done. ❞**
> *- David Hogg, Marjory Stoneman Douglas High School Shooting Survivor[71]*

to unite around (climate change, education, gun control, etc.), we may find that their political power is far greater than anticipated.

Conclusion

With the political ideologies of Generation Z not fitting squarely into a partisan category, the time may be ripe for a shake-up in U.S. politics. While we don't know if they will reshape existing political parties or create new ones of their own, we do know that feeling disregarded and disengaged may drive this generation to either mobilize at the voting booth or simply just stay home.

Notes

1 Presidents USA. (2017). *Presidential campaign slogans.* Retrieved from www.president-susa.net/campaignslogans.html
2 Stevenson, P. W. (2016). *A brief history of the "lock her up!" chant by Trump supporters against Clinton.* Retrieved from www.washingtonpost.com/news/the-fix/wp/2016/11/22/a-brief-history-of-the-lock-her-up-chant-as-it-looks-like-trump-might-not-even-try/?utm_term=.afc2f86ef463
3 Lee, M. J. & Merica, D. (2016). *Clinton's last campaign speech: "Love trumps hate."* Retrieved from www.cnn.com/2016/11/07/politics/hillary-clinton-campaign-final-day/index.html
4 Seemiller, C. & Grace, M. (2016). *Generation Z goes to college.* San Francisco: Jossey-Bass.
5 Ghitza, Y. & Gelman, A. (2014). *The great society, Reagan's revolution, and generations of presidential voting.* Retrieved from www.stat.columbia.edu/~gelman/research/unpublished/cohort_voting_20140605.pdf
6 Ghitza, Y. & Gelman, A. (2014).
7 Ghitza, Y. & Gelman, A. (2014).
8 Ghitza, Y. & Gelman, A. (2014).
9 Ghitza, Y. & Gelman, A. (2014).
10 Seemiller, C. & Grace, M. (2016).
11 Vandermaas-Peeler, A., Cox, D., Fisch-Friedman, M., & Jones, R. P. (2018). *Diversity, division, discrimination: The state of young America.* Retrieved from www.prri.org/research/mtv-culture-and-religion/
12 Seemiller, C. & Grace, M. (2017). *Generation Z stories study.* Unpublished raw data.
13 Flaccus, G. (2017). *AP-NORC Poll: US teens disillusioned, divided by politics.* Retrieved from http://apnorc.org/news-media/Pages/AP-NORC-Poll-US-teens-disillusioned-divided-by-politics.aspx
14 Gallup. (n.d.a). *Presidential approval ratings: Barack Obama.* Retrieved from http://news.gallup.com/poll/116479/barack-obama-presidential-job-approval.aspx
15 Gallup. (n.d.b). *Presidential approval ratings: Donald Trump.* Retrieved from http://news.gallup.com/poll/203198/presidential-approval-ratings-donald-trump.aspx
16 Eagan, M. K., Stolzenberg, E. B., Ramirez, J. J., Aragon, M. C., Suchard, M. R., & Rios-Aguilar, C. (2016). *The American freshman: Fifty-year trends, 1966–2015.* Los Angeles: Higher Education Research Institute, UCLA.
17 Seemiller, C. & Grace, M. (2017).
18 Higher Education Research Institute. (2017). *College Senior Survey.* Data prepared by Higher Education Research Institute.

19 Eagan, M. K., Stolzenberg, E. B., Ramirez, J. J., Aragon, M. C., Suchard, M. R., & Rios-Aguilar, C. (2016).

20 Higher Education Research Institute. (2017).

21 United States Census Bureau. (2017d). *Voting and registration in the election of November 2016*. Retrieved from www.census.gov/data/tables/time-series/demo/voting-and-registration/p20-580.html

22 Galston, W. A. & Hendrickson, C. (2016). *How Millennials voted this election*. Retrieved from www.brookings.edu/blog/fixgov/2016/11/21/how-millennials-voted/

23 Galston, W. A. & Hendrickson, C. (2016).

24 Pew Research Center. (2015e). *Religious landscape study*. Retrieved from www.pewforum.org/religious-landscape-study/

25 Email communication between Corey Seemiller and Jeff Brauer, Keystone College, Political Science Professor, July 18, 2017.

26 Seemiller, C. & Grace, M. (2014). *Generation Z goes to college study*. Unpublished raw data.

27 Williams, M. R. (2016). *Trump's win fuels growth in the ranks of college Republicans*. Retrieved from www.kansascity.com/news/local/article117599793.html

28 Williams, M. R. (2016).

29 Williams, M. R. (2016), para. 34.

30 Seemiller, C. & Grace, M. (2016).

31 Seemiller, C. & Grace, M. (2017).

32 Eagan, M. K., Stolzenberg, E. B., Ramirez, J. J., Aragon, M. C., Suchard, M. R., & Rios-Aguilar, C. (2016).

33 Eagan, M. K., Stolzenberg, E. B., Ramirez, J. J., Aragon, M. C., Suchard, M. R., & Rios-Aguilar, C. (2016).

34 Cohen, C. J., Luttig, M. D., & Rogowski, J. C. (2016). *Understanding the Millennial vote in 2016: Findings from GenForward*. Retrieved from http://genforwardsurvey.com/assets/uploads/2016/12/Post-Election-Horse-Race-Report-__-CLEAN.pdf

35 Seemiller, C. & Grace, M. (2017).

36 United States Census Bureau. (2017d).

37 Dorsey, J. (2016). *iGen's political and civic outlook*. Retrieved from http://genhq.com/wp-content/uploads/2016/02/iGen-Gen-Z-Political-Civic-Outlook-Research-White-Paper-c-2016-The-Center-for-Generational-Kinetics.pdf

38 Eagan, K., Stolzenberg, E. B., Ramirez, J. J., Aragon, M. C., Suchard, M. R., & Hurtado, S. (2014). *The American freshman: National norms fall 2014*. Los Angeles: Higher Education Research Institute, UCLA.

39 United States Census Bureau. (2017d).

40 United States Census Bureau. (2017d).

41 The American Presidency Project. (n.d.). *Voter turnout in presidential elections: 1828–2012*. Retrieved from www.presidency.ucsb.edu/data/turnout.php

42 Reuters. (2016). *Hillary Clinton on track for electoral college landslide: Poll*. Retrieved from www.newsweek.com/hillary-clinton-track-electoral-college-landslide-510362

43 Data calculated using Table 1: Reported Voting and Registration, by Sex and Single Years of Age: November 2016 at Census.gov. (2017).

44 Census.gov. (1992).

45 Census.gov. (2002).

46 Census.gov. (2012).

47 Census.gov. (2017).

48 United States Census Bureau. (1992). *Voting and registration in the election of November 1992*. Retrieved from www2.census.gov/programs-surveys/cps/tables/p20/466/tab01.pdf

49 United States Census Bureau. (2012). *Voting and registration in the election of November 2008*. Retrieved from www.census.gov/data/tables/2008/demo/voting-and-registration/p20-562-rv.html

50 United States Census Bureau. (2002). *Voting and registration in the election of November 2000*. Retrieved from www.census.gov/data/tables/2000/demo/voting-and-registration/p20-542.html

51 United States Census Bureau. (2017d).

52 Suro, R. (1992). *The 1992 campaign: The youth vote: Democrats court youngest voters*. Retrieved from www.nytimes.com/1992/10/30/us/the-1992-campaign-the-youth-vote-democrats-court-youngest-voters.html

53 Ruggeri, A. (2008). *Young voters powered Obama's victory while shrugging off slacker image*. Retrieved from www.usnews.com/news/campaign-2008/articles/2008/11/06/young-voters-powered-obamas-victory-while-shrugging-off-slacker-image

54 CNN. (2016). *Exit polls*. Retrieved from www.cnn.com/election/results/exit-polls

55 Email communication between Corey Seemiller and Jeff Brauer, Keystone College, Political Science Professor, July 18, 2017.

56 Email communication between Corey Seemiller and Jeff Brauer, Keystone College, Political Science Professor, July 18, 2017.

57 Email communication between Corey Seemiller and Jeff Brauer, Keystone College, Political Science Professor, July 18, 2017.

58 Email communication between Corey Seemiller and Jeff Brauer, Keystone College, Political Science Professor, July 18, 2017.

59 United States Census Bureau. (2017d).

60 McElwee, S. & Rodriguez-Wollerman, C. (2017). *Democrats need to win over young voters: Here's how they can do that*. Retrieved from www.theguardian.com/commentisfree/2017/jun/19/democrats-win-young-voters-voter-turnout

61 Griffin, R., Gronke, P., Wang, T., & Kennedy, L. (2017). *Who votes with automatic voter registration?* Retrieved from www.americanprogress.org/issues/democracy/reports/2017/06/07/433677/votes-automatic-voter-registration/

62 Nonprofit Vote. (2016). *America goes to the polls 2016*. Retrieved from www.nonprofit-vote.org/documents/2017/03/america-goes-polls-2016.pdf

63 Douglas, J. (2017). In defense of lowering the voting age. *165 University of Pennsylvania Law Review Online*, 63. Retrieved from https://ssrn.com/abstract=2903669

64 Geys, B. (2006). Explaining voter turnout: A review of aggregate-level research. *Electoral Studies, 25*, 637–663.

65 Geys, B. (2006).

66 Geys, B. (2006).

67 Northeastern University. (2014). *Innovation survey*. Retrieved from www.northeastern.edu/news/2014/11/innovation-imperative-meet-generation-z/

68 VarkeyFoundation.(2017).*GenerationZ: GlobalCitizenshipSurvey*.Retrievedfromwww.varkeyfoundation.org/what-we-do/policy-research/generation-z-global-citizenship-survey/

69 Seemiller, C. & Grace, M. (2016).

70 McElwee, S. & Rodriguez-Wollerman, C. (2017).

71 Ellefson, L. (2018). *School shooting survivor to lawmakers: "You need to take some action."* Retrieved from www.cnn.com/2018/02/15/us/david-hogg-school-shooting-new-day-cnntv/index.html

21 Civic engagement and social change

Like every generation, those in Generation Z have many concerns reflective of the times in which they have grown up. But, like their G.I. Generation predecessors, this is not a generation that sits back and waits for others to address these concerns. Vikas Pota, Chief Executive from the Varkey Foundation, notes Generation Z's commitment to citizenship in saying, "In this darkening political landscape, where international institutions are under greater pressure than at any time since the end of the World War II, it is reassuring to know that, in the minds of young people, global citizenship is not dead: it could just be getting started."[1]

Take, for example, Malala Yousafzai from Pakistan who was the youngest individual ever to receive a Nobel Peace Prize.[2] She received the honor for her advocacy for girls' education after surviving a gunshot wound to the head by the Taliban.[3] And, upon learning of the death of a baby in his neighborhood who was accidentally left in a hot car, Bishop Curry, an 11-year-old boy, invented a device that could prevent the deaths of babies left in hot cars.[4] The device detects movement in the vehicle and if sensing any, blows cool air towards the baby – all while dispatching emergency assistance.[5]

But, not all members of Generation Z are going to appear on the cover of a magazine for making a life-changing contribution. This is not just because their impact might not be as monumental but also because many in this generation do not enjoy public recognition.[6] While Generation Z's contribution to the world may come with little fanfare, rest assured that many will go on to leave a lasting legacy.

Trends in Generation Z civic engagement

To gain a greater understanding of Generation Z's civic contribution, we must look at overarching trends that might affect why, how, and to what extent those in Generation Z engage with their communities. These trends include addressing issues that affect the collective community, moving toward solving problems rather than addressing symptoms, and hacking the system to create change.

Me Generation to We Generation

If Millennials were dubbed the "Me" Generation,[7] then Generation Z is the "We" generation.[8] This concern for the collective was evident in our 2014 Generation Z Goes to College Study. When asked to describe the social issues they cared about most, only one-quarter discussed me-centric issues[9] like having enough money for tuition or having difficulty finding a job. But those concerns were far fewer as the majority focused on we-centric issues like racism or the economy.[10]

Addressing symptoms to solving problems

Those in Generation Z not only recognize societal problems but also question their underlying causes, allowing them to focus their energy on providing sustainable solutions. For example, why tutor one third grader in reading when developing and instituting a literacy program could help all third graders in a community?

So, we can see a world that is cleaner, more efficient, easier, etc. We see communities and countries coming together. We see the hungry being fed, the physically and mentally disabled having all the same opportunities, and the economically disadvantaged having access to resources.
  - Member of Generation Z

Activism to hacktivism

While many in Generation Z will likely participate in activism, some may actually instead or also engage in hacktivism. Hacktivism entails infusing creativity and innovation into just about anything – seeing and doing things differently for better and faster results.[11] Logan LaPlante, a Generation Z speaker at TEDx-UniversityofNevada, points out that we all need to be prepared for his generation to hack our systems and disrupt the status quo.[12]

Everything is up for hacking . . . having a hacker mindset can change the world.
  - Logan LaPlante, Generation Z Speaker at TEDxUniversityofNevada[13]

We must be prepared for members of Generation Z to engage in activism in ways that are outside the systems and structures older generations have built. This is a generation that is going to make an impact by infusing their unique approach to traditional practices of civic engagement along with instituting entirely new ways of creating social change.

Getting informed and forming opinions

With the wide reach of the Internet and social media, along with hundreds of radio and television channels and blogs, the news is more accessible today that it was when those in older generations were youth. Even special-interest magazines like *Teen Vogue* and GQ have entered into the realm of reporting on political, economic, and social issues. Perhaps it is the sheer volume of available news or the ability to consume it in bite sizes that makes it appealing for those in Generation Z to stay up to date. But, it isn't just about the accessibility of the news, more than one-third of those in Generation Z believe it's important to be informed about current events.[14] Given what they are concerned about, it makes sense that those in Generation Z stay most informed about civil rights issues with nearly two-thirds keeping up regularly with issues related to gay rights, women's rights, and racial equality.[15]

> *Stand up for what's right and be educated about important issues that affect all of us.*
> – Member of Generation Z

Although having widespread access to and interest in the news might help keep those in Generation Z current, it also might have a large impact on the formation of their opinions. Today, it is easy to turn on a news program that aligns solely with one's specific views, feeding into the formation of a one-sided opinion. For Generation Z youth, this might even include listening to their parents' favorite radio show on the morning drive to school, essentially experiencing non-voluntary media consumption. Because there were fewer media outlets when those in older generations were young, there were simply fewer places to actually get the news. While media bias has been around long before today, it is easier than ever to consume one's choice of news based on political leanings and personal ideologies. This phenomenon is related to cyberbalkanization, which is "the segregation of the Internet into smaller groups with similar interests, to a degree that they show a narrow-minded approach to outsiders or those with contradictory views."[16]

But, there is a great desire among those in Generation Z to dismantle this type of partisanship and focus on both acceptance of diverse perspectives and unification of ideas to solve challenging issues.[17] Perhaps this will lead them to actually strive for collaboration across differences.

Changing hearts and minds

When we think about civic engagement, it's easy to associate it with actions that lead to some type of immediate result. For example, volunteering to clean up a school has immediate visible results in that there is no litter on the playground. Or, voting for a candidate has immediate implications after the election when that person takes office as the elected official. Another form of civic engagement that may have less immediate impact is that of influencing the hearts and minds of others. By educating people about particular social issues, those in Generation Z could raise awareness, ultimately contributing to a cultural shift in others' attitudes. But, this process can take time and might not immediately yield a change.

> *We can continue learning about the world and other people and respectfully spread our ideas to one another.*
> – Member of Generation Z

Beyond having conversations with others, there are many digital avenues available for sharing perspectives on particular issues. Social media, YouTube, blogs, and share buttons on news apps can provide information about an issue to both personal and global networks quickly and easily. Digital sharing is not just a happenstance process for this generation where they simply click, share, or include a hashtag in a tweet, putting forth others' opinions and ideas. Many of those in Generation Z like offer their own opinions through blogs,[18] social media, YouTube, virtual pinboards, and online forums.[19] A study of first-year Generation Z college students found that nearly 44 percent reported frequently or occasionally having publicly shared their opinion about a cause in some digitally or written format by the time they had come to college.[20] Their interest in sharing their opinions online has led to organizations like Voices of Youth to offer internships for young bloggers to help them craft messages on pertinent political topics.[21] And, youth activists on YouTube, such as Megan He, the teen who created the Greenversal channel about the environment, are garnering not only online viewers, but also recognition and awards for their work.[22] But, just because there are several means to spread their opinions doesn't mean that those in Generation Z share about anything and everything. They prefer to limit their sharing to topics they know and care about.[23]

> *I also truly believe that social media networks can serve a good purpose. My generation is very tech-savvy, we can use this to our advantage to educate people. Many teenagers are ignorant to their surroundings, I think Facebook, Twitter, Snapchat, and Instagram can all be used as outlets to reach/learn about new people, places and ideas.*
> – Member of Generation Z

While the digital world provides ample opportunity for those in Generation Z to change hearts and minds, some are still literally using paper and pencil to get the word out. For example, Postcards to Voters is an initiative that mobilizes volunteers to hand-write postcards to encourage people to vote, especially in close elections.[24] The movement has drawn in more than 20,000 volunteers, mailing more than a half a million postcards.[25] Although anyone can volunteer with the organization, many in Generation Z too young to vote are participating

> **" I can't vote, so this is a way for me to have an impact. . . . I'll initiate change and not just wait for it. "**
>
> - Piya Rao, 14-year-old volunteer with Postcards to Voters[27]

as a way to use their voice to make a difference.[26]

Even if the effort to change hearts and minds through raising awareness isn't deliberate, the mere emergence of those in Generation Z into adulthood will inadvertently change the aggregate views of the population. This is described as "intercohort" change in which those in different generations have different opinions about an issue. As one generation ages and is replaced by another, the general view of society changes toward more of the perspectives of the younger generation and less of the older one.[28] As the remaining members of the G.I. Generation and those in the Silent Generation pass away, we may find that the views of younger generations, like Generation Z, will serve as the larger societal narrative on certain issues.

Volunteerism

Volunteerism has served as a cornerstone of civic engagement in the U.S. for centuries. This facet of the U.S. piqued the interest of Alexis de Toqueville, who in the late 1820s, identified volunteerism as a unique differentiator of the American democracy.[29] This commitment to volunteerism still exists today as the U.S. has come to rely on the voluntary contributions of its residents for important community functions. Given the significance of volunteerism, it's not surprising then that participation rates for youth are quite high. To gain a better understanding of these rates, we compared the Generation Z cohort to that of Millennials when they were young adults. In doing so, we used the data from the CIRP Freshman Survey for specific time periods, each being 20 years after the first birth year of the generational cohort, similar to the analysis for data in the Spirituality chapter. We also used historical youth volunteer data from Child Trends and findings from the 2017 College Senior Survey of Generation Z students.

High rates

Both the Millennial and Generation Z first-year student cohorts indicated very high rates of volunteer participation the year before they came to college. Their rates, both in the eightieth percentile, are considerably higher than the 1985 Generation X cohort at 73.3 percent.[30] And although that rate in 1985 eventually increased through the 1990s, it did not top 80 percent until 1999.[31] By the time Millennials had reached college, 83 percent had done some type of community service in the past year.[32] That number continued to increase over the first part of the decade, reaching 88 percent by 2015 when Generation Z was in college.[33] Other research has also yielded similar findings. Using data from the

Table 21.1 Volunteerism Rates of High School Seniors

	2001 (Millennial)	2015 (Generation Z)
First-year college students who reported performing volunteer work during the past year (senior year of high school)[34]	83%	88%
Twelfth graders who reported volunteering at least once a month[35]	34.6%	38.8%

Monitoring the Future study of youth and young adults, nonprofit research center, Child Trends, found that in 2015, 38.8 percent of twelfth graders volunteered at least once a month compared to 34.6 percent in 2001 who did.[36] While both generations have high rates of participation, Generation Z's is slightly higher.

What is also interesting is that while high school senior volunteer rates are high, so too are college senior rates. In 2017, three-quarters of Generation Z college seniors reported frequently or occasionally volunteering during the past year.[37] Although the number is somewhat lower than high school participation rates at 88 percent, the decline is not surprising as college students are trying often to balance other commitments such as internships, work, extracurricular involvement, and academics.[38] While they might not have as much time to devote to volunteering, these college seniors are still committed to making a difference as nearly 46 percent believe it is essential or very important to participate in a community action program.[39]

> **❝ I think a good life or a life worth living is to change the lives of others. ❞**
> *– Member of Generation Z*

In looking at why volunteer rates are high for members of Generation Z, there are some possible explanations. First, those in Generation Z have a predisposition for helping others. According to data from the VIA Institute on Character, kindness has the second highest average of all 24 character strengths for this generation, with fairness being the fourth highest.[40] By seeing themselves as both kind and fair, it makes sense that they would want to help others access resources and opportunities that level the playing field. So, in some ways, they are just hard-wired to care about others. Second, positively impacting others is paramount to them in a variety of aspects of their lives. In our Generation Z Stories Study, we found that making a difference for others is a prominent factor in what motivates them to get up in the morning, as well as a crucial component of an ideal career and the essence of an overall good life.[41]

More than Millennials

It makes sense then that the vast majority of those in Generation Z volunteer, but it's curious as to why their rate of volunteerism is higher than that of

Table 21.2 Factors of Importance Related to Volunteerism[42]

Essential or Very Important	2001 (Millennial)	2015 (Generation Z)
Helping others who are in difficulty	61.4%	74.6%
Influencing social values	37.7%	43.9%

Millennials when they were young adults. One such possibility relates to the importance that those in Generation Z, compared to Millennials, place on different factors related to community service. For example, a considerably higher number of those in Generation Z compared to Millennials think it is essential or very important to help others who are in difficulty. Rates for Generation Z are also higher for the importance of influencing social values.[43]

Another possible explanation for Generation's Z's higher rates of service may be that some are using volunteering as a form of career preparation. Similar to the purpose of an internship, these career-minded Generation Z students, who are committed to finding a career that allows them to make a positive impact,[44] can easily find volunteer opportunities with organizations related to the industries they hope to work in.

Finally, being highly informed about social issues, organizations, and causes gives them ample opportunity to find ways to get connected with volunteer experiences that fit with their passions. And while these young people can certainly show up on site to volunteer, many opportunities can be done online without ever having to leave their rooms. For example, they can participate in a call to action or hashtag movement through social media, create a YouTube video advocating for a cause, gather signatures on a digital petition, launch an online fund campaign, or simply complete volunteer duties for an organization in the digital space.

Social change

So, not only are there higher rates of Generation Z students volunteering in high school, those who do volunteer are spending more time doing so.[45] In looking at data from the CIRP Freshman Survey, it appears that only 4.1 percent of Millennials volunteered 10 or more hours a week during their senior year of high school compared to 5.7 percent of Generation Z.[46] And, in looking closer, the rates for Generation Z volunteer participation are higher for every category except less than 1 hour and none.[47]

In addition to the reasons discussed earlier, there are two other possible explanations that could shed light on the difference in volunteer hours between the two generations. First, both generational cohorts view community service differently, and those differing views might be tied to the amount of time needed for involvement. Millennials tend to be service-oriented and engage in volunteer work as a way to help people but not necessarily for the purpose of addressing a political or social problem.[49] Examples might include participating in a neighborhood

Table 21.3 Weekly Average of Volunteerism Rates as Reported among First-Year College Students across Generational Cohorts[48]

How much time spent on average weekly doing community service during senior year of high school	2001 (Millennial)	2015 (Generation Z)
None	29.6%	25.6%
Less than 1 hour	23.1%	19.2%
1–2 hours	24.2%	26.7%
3–5 hours	13.8%	16.4%
6–10 hours	5.3%	6.4%
11–15 hours	1.8%	2.4%
16–20 hours	.9%	1.2%
More than 20 hours	1.4%	2.1%

beautification project or serving food at a shelter. But, a neighborhood cleanup will only address the symptom of larger underlying problems – people littering and lack of resources for community upkeep. And serving food can help those who are hungry today but doesn't address the larger issues of poverty and hunger. And while someone could spend an hour cleaning up a neighborhood or serve food for a meal, addressing the root causes would likely take a great deal more time.

Those in Generation Z, on the other hand, are more social change-oriented, preferring instead to focus on eradicating the underlying problems that necessitate service to begin with.[50] For instance, instead of delivering clean water to a community, those in Generation Z would rather help build a well. And, as 98.4 percent of Generation Z college seniors reported that they frequently or occasionally seek alternative solutions to a problem, this is a generation eager to create innovative and sustainable change.[51] But, creating change can take a lot of time. So, if those in Generation Z are engaging in more social change-oriented rather than service-oriented activities, they would likely need to spend more time volunteering.

> *A good life is one devoted to others. One where I use the talents and gifts given to me in their fullest and in creative ways that allow me to enjoy what I do and be original while creating change for peoples' lives and the systems/institutions they live through.*
> – Member of Generation Z

In addition, Generation Z's desire to create change transcends multiple aspects of their lives.[52] It would make sense then that they would connect their passions, motivations, concerns, and future career interests with volunteer opportunities. In doing so, they could immerse themselves deeply into service work, spending countless hours toward making a difference. Generation Z's holistic approach to volunteer work is vastly different from the approach of Millennials who may lean toward one-time or short-term volunteer initiatives that help others. By carving out specific time for volunteering, aside from other activities like school or work, Millennials could create separate niches and time blocks for their different life experiences, whereas those in Generation Z may simply integrate their volunteerism holistically within all aspects of their lives.

Community leadership roles

In addition to volunteerism, long-term community leadership roles have become essential to societal functioning. Scouts would likely not exist without the dedication of troop leaders, schools might have disengaged parents without PTA members, and nonprofits might not be able to raise money, plan events, or recruit support without volunteer boards. Although a study of first-year Generation Z college students found that just more than one-third believe it is essential or very important to become a community leader,[53] more than half of college seniors do.[54] So, perhaps college is a space to cultivate leadership awareness and thus increase their interest in being community leaders. But, what's interesting is that more than 70 percent of these very seniors rate their leadership ability as above average or in the highest 10 percent.[55] So, as a large majority see themselves having exceptional leadership capacity, not nearly as many appear to be drawn to community leadership roles. Perhaps helping reluctant members of Generation Z better understand the possibility these roles could offer in making long-term, sustainable impact could be what attracts them to participate.

> ❝ My generation can make the world a better place by . . . becoming leaders of communities to create impact on a larger scale. ❞
> – Member of Generation Z

Military service

Despite the passage of the Selective Service and Training Act on September 16, 1940, which led to the draft of U.S. soldiers to serve in World War II, nearly 39 percent of service members during the war were actually volunteers.[56] Many flocked to recruiting centers after the attack on Pearl Harbor in a call of duty.[57] Although the timing of the war following the Great Depression also made enlistment a great job option, it appears, though, that the main motivation was not career-related but service-related.

> ❝ As a child of a 100% disabled veteran I see what [war] does to people. Changes their mindset, attitude, and way of life. The worst wars are yet to come and I think when a lot of our people go to fight, it will completely change our country. ❞
> – Member of Generation Z

That desire to serve one's country also emerged to a lesser extent after 9/11, resulting in a rise in enlistment numbers.[58] But, that call to duty dipped so much by 2006 that the armed services missed their recruiting goals.[59] By 2009, around the time of the Recession and high unemployment, numbers rose again and exceeded recruitment quotas.[60] Although some today still enlist as a way to give back to their country, for many individuals, the military appears to be a career choice rather than solely a service choice, especially as the number one reported reason for enlistment is to gain a free college education.[61] With the availability of comprehensive medical coverage and a path for promotion, serving in the military, especially during a time of limited deployment, can offer a great career path with good benefits for our young adults. Being that many in Generation Z are career-focused and want to make a difference for others, serving in the military seems to offer an opportunity to blend their occupational aspirations with a civic call for duty. Yet, many are not supportive of a war mission, perhaps making military service a tough sell. In our 2014 Generation Z Goes to College Study, we found that 57 percent were concerned about war,[62] and another study found that 64 percent believed that the military gets involved in too many conflicts.[63] Despite the benefits of joining the military, some may find doing so challenges their personal values. Perhaps that is why only 4 percent of those in Generation Z who were surveyed by Northeastern University indicated that they planned to go into the military.[64]

Another factor to consider is that Generation Z's perspectives on issues of inclusion and equality may affect their decision to join. In one sense, the open-mindedness of those in Generation Z may align with practices like the military's elimination of Don't Ask, Don't Tell allowing gay and lesbian service members serve openly. However, they may also find that incidents of sexual misconduct in the military or a transgender service member ban are alarming and contrary to their views, perhaps resulting in some not wanting to participate in what they might see as an oppressive institution.

Having to recruit for an all-volunteer armed services has challenged military personnel to take a deeper look into our newest young adult cohort. Because of this, the Army put together the Force 2025 plan to focus on what the future of the Army will need to look like given the entry of this changing demographic.[65] The Army has since undertaken a new marketing strategy that focuses less on combat and more on solving problems and making a difference, catering specifically to this generation of potential recruits.[66] Rather than focusing on defense, war, combat, or even pride, the tagline at the end of their commercial says, "Join the team that makes a difference."[67]

Litigation

The court system has always played a role in the checks and balances of our legislative and executive branches. Consider that U.S. Supreme Court cases like *Brown v. Board of Education of Topeka*, *Roe v. Wade*, or *Obergefell v. Hodges* have spawned major societal change. Given that Generation Z is focused on creating social change, we should expect the courts to be busy with their litigation. This is evident even now as those in Generation Z find themselves challenging laws in the courts. For example, a group of youth, from 9 to 20 years-old, has filed a lawsuit against the federal government arguing that the failure to act on the issue of climate change has "endangered their rights to life, liberty, property and vital public trust resources."[68] They want the federal government to institute a plan that will reduce emissions to a level that scientists assert is necessary to protect the oceans and the entire climate system.[69] Their main argument is their age, in that they will be the ones who will have to fix irreparable damage long after the adults today have died. The legal fervor of these youth is not surprising in that 67 percent of Generation Z first-year college students said that it should be a priority for the federal government to address climate change.[70] This generation's use of the courts, however, is not limited to one lawsuit on climate change. Cases involving transgender youth[71] and immigrant children[72] are other examples that highlight that this is a generation motivated to engage with the court system both for protecting rights as well as advancing social issues.

Activism

Throughout the twentieth century, activism has ebbed and flowed. While the Baby Boomers marched in the streets protesting Vietnam, Generation X came along and was dubbed the "generation without a cause," in which they organized and participated in few activist events.[73] This trend continued as Millennials reached young adulthood. Those in the optimistic, "hope and change" generation[74] were not the ones chaining themselves to the Redwood trees to prevent deforestation. However, there were pockets of activism that emerged with some Millennials. These included the Occupy Movement where young people camped out to draw attention to the 99 percent of individuals who were not benefiting from the economy, the Dreamer movement that advocated for young immigrant children to be able to attend college, as well as Black Lives Matter, a movement that emerged in response to police violence against unarmed Black men. What about Generation Z, though?

Love is the root of our activism, and our activism makes this world a better place.
– Member of Generation Z

Marches, rallies, protests, and demonstrations

A 2014 study of first-year Generation Z college students found that fewer than 22 percent had actually participated in some type of demonstration by the time they had come to college.[75] In our Generation Z Goes to College Study that same year, we found that fewer than 6 percent said they believed there was a good chance that they would participate in one in the future.[76] But, fast-forward to 2017 and nearly every group has held a major march, rally, protest, or demonstration – women, scientists, environmentalists, Dreamers, gun control advocates, gun rights supporters, free speech activists, LGBTQ advocates, and the list goes on. And some of these marches have been big. For example, with hundreds of thousands of participants, the 2017 Women's March on Washington ranked as one of the largest marches in U.S. history.[77] With more activist events and experiences occurring in general, there are more opportunities for Generation Z participation in general. Further, though, some advocacy organizations have designed intentional opportunities to engage youth. One such example is the Youth Ambassador Program with the Women's March, which serves as a social justice collective, providing a platform for young people to engage in activism.[78]

While Generation Z youth might continue to jump into movements led by those in older generations, it appears that they are also paving the way for their own activism. For example, March for Our Lives brought together hundreds of thousands of youth (and adults) in Washington, DC and around the world to advocate for gun control.[79] In addition, in 2017, college students rallied on Capitol Hill to advocate for legislation to protect undocumented youth in the Deferred Action for Childhood Arrivals program.[80] Youth activism is happening at the local level as well. For instance, in 2018, students at Lincoln-Sudbury High School in Boston participated in a walkout to protest how their school was handling an alleged case of sexual assault.[81] Generation Z is already on the front lines advocating for their beliefs.

Walkouts and boycotts

Generation Z also uses school walkouts as a form of activism – whether to call for political action, create solidarity, or help inform and shift public opinion. For instance, in November 2017, students across the nation staged school walkouts in support of Dreamers who are part of the Deferred Action for Childhood Arrivals program.[82] And in March 2018, students all over the country staged walkouts to advocate for an end to gun violence in schools.[83] Both walkouts offered opportunities for everyday youth to advocate for causes important to them without having to attend a rally or march in Washington, DC.

Some members of Generation Z are also calling for boycotts as a way to draw attention to issues as well as prompt change. As a youth bloc, generation has a lot of spending power, and they know it. So, banding together to boycott something could have a huge effect. For example, in a Twitter post, Florida school shooting survivor, David Hogg, called for a spring break boycott to draw the attention of Florida lawmakers to pass gun control legislation. His post speaks directly to Generation Z youth as they are the likely majority of those going on a spring break trip. But, boycotts don't need to always be national news; there are many Generation Z student boycotts on college campuses around a variety of issues. For one, students at California State University-Northridge boycotted the implementation of an executive order affecting cultural studies classes across the California State University system.[84] To show solidarity against the order, Northridge students joined together to encourage people to refrain from buying anything on campus for one day.[85] While neither the spring break or executive order boycotts led to the desired outcomes, both efforts drew a great deal of attention and rallied supporters in their favor.

Challenging politicians

Many in Generation Z are also not afraid of challenging policymakers directly. Even though some aren't old enough to vote, there are many examples of fearless teens taking on legislators. For example, after the school shooting in Parkland, Florida, several survivors, along with lawmakers, appeared on a televised CNN town hall meeting. Ethan Zuckerman, a writer for *The Atlantic*, said about the event, "Politicians squirmed uncomfortably and failed to answer the blunt questions put forward by students."[86]

In the rural town of Santa Fe, Texas, where a school shooting took the lives of ten, several students, along with families and educators, met with lawmakers in a roundtable to discuss solutions.[87] They agreed on some measures, leading the governor to commit to supporting some gun-related regulations, but there were others that were points of contention.[88] While the rising activism from this incident in a small conservative Texas town was more muted than that of Parkland, Florida, Generation Z students still wanted their voice to be heard.[89]

While many Generation Z students have mobilized around gun control, some are also mobilizing around immigration issues. In an interview with NBC, Santiago Tobar Potes, a student at Columbia University, shared his story and thoughts on the Deferred Action for Childhood Arrivals program, drawing attention to the many young people who would be impacted if the program ended. He

> **❝ We are very quickly shut down by older generations, and we are not given many opportunities to voice our opinions on current issues, and when given that opportunity we are quickly dismissed or told to listen to our elders. Give us a chance. ❞**
> - Member of Generation Z

> **❝ Come out of the undocumented closet. ❞**
> - Santiago Tobar Potes, Columbia University Student[90]

urged other undocumented students to make themselves known and speak out to their representatives – a significant risk when the repercussions could result in deportation.

Even the little Zs are voicing their concerns to lawmakers. Take, for example, 10-year-old Luca Ingrassia, who testified before Congress advocating for a law that would require all airlines to carry epinephrine auto-injectors on board.[91] After having a frightening allergic reaction in flight, Luca's life was likely saved not by the airlines carrying an EpiPen but instead by a gracious passenger willing to share one. Luca later went to Washington, D.C. where he delivered a speech to lawmakers seven times.

It appears that Generation Z, either emboldened by their causes or empowered by their youth, is a generation that doesn't shy away from finding ways to amplify their voice on issues, even if it means challenging those in power.

Digital activism

While there are countless examples of young activists throughout history protesting wars, fighting for environmental rights, and advocating for equality, today's digital landscape has now made it possible for youth to engage in activism like never before. It's not surprising then that many in Generation Z are highly involved in digital activism.[92] For some, their involvement is limited to slacktivism, which includes retweeting, sharing posts, signing petitions, following activists on social media, and liking organizations and causes – all relatively easy actions to engage in.[93] Slacktivism gets its name from the word "slacker," suggesting that engaging in these digital behaviors takes very little effort.[94]

For others in Generation Z, though, their digital activism may fall more in line with clicktivism, which is using social media and online platforms to promote social causes.[95] Clicktivism is more than just forwarding a petition or retweeting a message; it involves educating others and raising awareness in an effort to create social change.[96] While clicktivism can include a variety of action-oriented online activities such as facilitating boycotts, organizing protests, and crowdfunding,[97] clicktivism also contributes to the hashtag movements we see today. For example, the #MeToo movement drew attention to the prevalence of sexual assault and harassment, bringing many out of the shadows to share their stories. The movement gained so much traction that many high-profile individuals ended up facing serious repercussions for inappropriate sexual behavior that occurred even decades ago. #MeToo paved the way for the subsequent #TimesUp movement, the "solution-based, action-oriented next step in the #MeToo movement . . .[designed] to create concrete change, leading to safety and equity in the workplace."[98] Other hashtag movements like #BlackLivesMatter, #IceBucketChallenge, #Ferguson, and #LoveWins have also been powerful contributors to advancing social justice causes.[99] Although it wasn't Generation Z that started these particular movements, it appears that young people have pulled from older adults' hashtag playbook with the #NeverAgain movement after the Parkland school shooting.[100] For Generation Z, the digital world is more than just a place to keep up with friends, get the news, post pictures, and watch funny videos; it is a critical space for planning, promoting, and engaging in activism to create real social change.

Raising and spending money

Money can play a huge role in civic engagement and help organizations advance social change. For example, money can help organizations purchase supplies for community improvement, offset operational costs of a nonprofit agency, or fund a political campaign of a candidate who supports particular initiatives.

Donating and fundraising

Being such a social changed-minded generation, it would be easy to expect that Generation Z is full of many donors, each of them giving their last penny for a good cause. However, the financially conservative and perhaps thrifty nature of Generation Z[101] means that as much as they feel passionately for a cause, they likely won't donate their own money towards it. It makes sense then that 87 percent of college seniors reported not having donated any money to political causes during the past year.[102]

Although they might be tight with their own checkbooks, they are drawn to philanthropy in terms of raising money from others, even having been referred to as Philanthro-teens,[103] as discussed in the Money chapter. For example, before coming to college, nearly 57 percent had frequently or occasionally helped in raising money for a campaign or cause[104] as did 62 percent of Generation Z college seniors during the past year.[105]

With platforms like GoFundMe and Kickstarter, those in Generation Z can raise money for nearly any issue in a short time. Remember, many of these were the kids who setup their own digital fundraising portals and sent out social media messaging to raise money for every "a-thon" they participated in at school. Thus, many in Generation Z appear to be comfortable in this space and can easily leverage the digital world to raise money for issues they care about.

Conscious consumerism

Philanthropy, though, is not the only form of monetary civic engagement. By spending money on businesses that align with their values, Generation Z can use their wallets as their voice for social change. A national study by Fuse, a brand marketing firm targeted at members of Generation Z and Millennials, found that 85 percent of members of Generation Z believe that companies should be obligated to solve social problems.[106] Because of their commitment to both equality and environmentalism, it isn't surprising then that 23 percent had boycotted an activity or company in the last 12 months.[107] This conscious consumerism, though, isn't solely about not supporting businesses that don't align with their beliefs but also about using their spending power as an act of support. For example, a Nielsen study found that 72 percent of those in Generation Z would pay more for sustainable offerings, higher than the 51 percent of Baby Boomers who would.[108] And, with this generation having 143 billion dollars in purchasing power,[109] we can only imagine the influence this generation can wield simply through their spending choices.

❝ We must use our money to speak for us. ❞
– Member of Generation Z

Social innovation

It's important to recognize that Generation Z is growing up during a time in which our economy has shifted from one of service to one of knowledge. Stanford professors, Walter Powell and Kaisa Snellman, note that "The key component of a knowledge economy is a greater reliance on intellectual capabilities than on physical inputs or natural resources."[110] This means the economy demands ideas, creativity, and knowledge to build our future. It takes more than just assembling a smartphone; the idea had to have been conceived of first. As discussed in the career aspirations chapter, as automation grows, this is a generation that will be called upon for their intellect over their physical labor to address complex issues. While those in Generation Z will contribute physical inputs in some capacities, there will likely be a rising demand for their creative and critical thinking.

❝ Generation Z will 'invent new things, solve old problems.' ❞
– Member of Generation Z

Every generation has developed transformational social innovations that have made an impact on the world. For example, the G.I. Generation "made breakthroughs in medicine and other sciences. They gave the world new art and literature. They came to understand the need for civil rights legislation. They gave America Medicare."[111] Nearly a century later, Generation Z carries the torch in discovery, innovation, and creation of new technology, science, art, and policy as a way to positively contribute to the world. Those in Generation Z will likely combine their social change mindset, social justice values, and social responsibility commitment as they try to solve complex issues through innovation. And two vehicles they appear to be drawn to in doing so are invention and social entrepreneurship.

Invention

In the 1930s, those in the G.I. Generation were in their adolescence or young adulthood. Inventions such as the Polaroid camera, helicopter, jet engine, photocopier, FM radio frequency, and electron microscope were just emerging.[112] Many of these initial inventions by older generations paved the way for future development and innovation. Today, cameras are in phones, radio can be accessed by satellite, and the Osprey is a hybrid helicopter and airplane. In addition to enhancing or building on the ideas of existing inventions, ideas that could not even be conceptualized in the early 1900s, like streaming television, personalized medicine, and nanotechnology, will be the inventions that Generation Z and future generations will build upon.

Although there have always been inventors among each generational cohort, 40 percent of those in Generation Z plan to change the world through the development of an invention.[113] It may seem that the aspirational hopes and dreams of this generation make it easy for so many of them to believe they will invent something of great value to society, especially as it has yet to happen for most of them. But, youth inventors today are emerging all over the world, already making an impact with their innovations. Generation Z young people are creating technology, devices, apps, and hacks for just about everything from reducing disease transmission to purifying water.[114] And, for many, their goal is simply to create low-cost, high-quality solutions to problems so that anyone can have access to their inventions. For example, 11 high school students from Australia re-created a lifesaving malaria drug when they learned of the price increase from the manufacturer from $13.50 to $750 per tablet.[115]

It's also easier than ever for those in Generation Z to obtain the resources and support they need to launch an idea from concept to product. Although a handful of young people may pitch their ideas on the TV show, *Shark Tank*, the availability of camps, programs, and events that help youth get their ideas off the ground are far more likely spaces for them to develop and market their inventions. For instance, Project Paradigm is a STEM challenge for integrating kindness, creativity, and collaboration to make a difference.[116] In 2016, the winners, Scott and Emma Bothell, created an oven mitt that converts to a fire blanket.[117] Further, Biznovator offers workshops, camps, and an academy to train youth to be the next generation of social innovators, entrepreneurs, and global leaders to make a difference in the world.[118]

In addition, schools, universities, organizations, and businesses[119] are holding hackathons that bring people together for marathon problem-solving sessions, particularly with the goal of developing technology to address a specific problem.[120] Winners may receive prizes, recognition, or even startup money to launch their invention. Hackathons have become so widespread that organizations like Major League Hacking have attempted to consolidate information about global hacking events onto one master calendar on their website.[121] And, while many hackathons are open to individuals of all ages, organizations around the world are hosting hackathon events specifically for youth.[122]

Not all spaces for invention need to be formal training programs or major events, though. The concept of a makerspace is becoming more common in schools and communities. These spaces provide places to gather with others to share ideas, resources, and tools to work on projects, prototype ideas, and develop new technologies.[123] And for any invention, seed money may not be as much of an issue as in the past. GoFundMe and Kickstarter platforms can also be used to bring in venture capital right from one's own social networks.

Social entrepreneurship

As discussed in the Career Aspirations chapter, many in Generation Z are interested in working for themselves. Some could end up as freelancers, whereas others might run their own businesses with employees. Given their interest in making a difference, it wouldn't be surprising to find Generation Z infuse their entrepreneurial endeavors with their desire for social change to ultimately engage in social entrepreneurship. A social entrepreneur is "a person who pursues an innovative idea with the potential to solve a community problem. . . . The main goal of a social entrepreneur is not to earn a profit, but to implement widespread improvements in society."[124] Social entrepreneurs' shareholders are the populations for which they serve rather than the people who have purchased shares in the company. For example, two Generation Z social entrepreneurs, Jared J. Makheja and Sejal Makheja, founded The Elevator Project. They created the organization to "enable individuals to climb out of poverty by providing apprenticeship programs, vocational training, and a mentor program."[125]

Rachel Zietz, another Generation Z social entrepreneur, turned her concern for needing safer and more durable rugby equipment into a profit-bearing enterprise.[126] Many in Generation Z are already off and running with their entrepreneurial initiatives. But, we can expect to see many more solving the world's issues through their keen business sense.

> ❝ I want to be able to have the influence to help others reach their potential (Probably through my own entrepreneurship) and to help communities bring themselves to fruition. ❞
> - Member of Generation Z

Conclusion

Those in Generation Z want to make a difference in their communities and the world. However, we may find that Generation Z will create social change by hacking the very system[127] that created our problems in the first place. For example, instead of trying to pass a law that curbs emissions, those in Generation Z might develop a solar stick that plugs into the dashboard of a car allowing it to run entirely on clean energy. Or, instead of volunteering at a children's hospital, these Generation Z innovators might be in their bedrooms or a makerspace developing the cure these kids need in order to be healthy. As

Generation Z grows older, their inventive minds, entrepreneurial spirit, and social justice mentality may inspire us all to make the world a better place.

Notes

1 Pota, V. (2017). *Generation Z: Global Citizenship Survey*. Retrieved from www.slideshare. net/luismolina787/global-young-people-report, p. 20.

2 Biography.com. (2017). *Malala Yousafzai*. Retrieved from www.biography.com/people/malala-yousafzai-21362253

3 Biography.com. (2017).

4 Fulling, J. (2017). *11-year-old's invention could prevent hot car deaths*. Retrieved from www.usatoday.com/story/news/humankind/2017/07/18/11-year-olds-invention-could-prevent-hot-car-deaths/476057001/

5 Fulling, J. (2017).

6 Seemiller, C. & Grace, M. (2016). *Generation Z goes to college*. San Francisco: Jossey-Bass.

7 Stein, J. (2013). *Millennials: The me me me generation*. Retrieved from http://time.com/247/millennials-the-me-me-me-generation/

8 Seemiller, C. & Grace, M. (2016).

9 Seemiller, C. & Grace, M. (2016).

10 Seemiller, C. & Grace, M. (2016).

11 LaPlante, L. (2013). *TEDxUniversityofNevada: Hackschooling makes me happy*. Retrieved from www.youtube.com/watch?v=h11u3vtcpaY

12 LaPlante, L. (2013).

13 LaPlante, L. (2013).

14 Seemiller, C. & Grace, M. (2016).

15 Seemiller, C. & Grace, M. (2016).

16 Techopedia. (n.d.a). *Cyberbalkanization*. Retrieved from www.techopedia.com/definition/28087/cyberbalkanization, para 1.

17 Seemiller, C. & Grace, M. (2017). *Generation Z stories study*. Unpublished raw data.

18 Eagan, K., Stolzenberg, E. B., Ramirez, J. J., Aragon, M. C., Suchard, M. R., & Hurtado, S. (2014). *The American freshman: National norms fall 2014*. Los Angeles: Higher Education Research Institute, UCLA.

19 Seemiller, C. & Grace, M. (2014). *Generation Z goes to college study*. Unpublished raw data.

20 Eagan, K., Stolzenberg, E. B., Ramirez, J. J., Aragon, M. C., Suchard, M. R., & Hurtado, S. (2014).

21 Voices of Youth. (2017). *VOY blogging internship*. Retrieved from www.voicesofyouth.org/en/sections/content/pages/voy-blogging-internship

22 Stateside Staff. (2017). *EPA honors Ann Arbor high school student for her YouTube channel*. Retrieved from http://michiganradio.org/post/epa-honors-ann-arbor-high-school-student-her-youtube-channel

23 Seemiller, C. & Grace, M. (2016).

24 Walker, M. (2018). *Teenagers are helping flip seats in 2018 elections with postcards to voters*. Retrieved from www.teenvogue.com/story/teenagers-are-helping-flip-seats-in-2018-elections-with-postcards-to-voters, para. 11.

25 Walker, M. (2018).

26 Walker, M. (2018).

27 Walker, M. (2018).

28 Putnam, R. D. (2000). *Bowling alone*. New York: Simon & Schuster.

29 New Dictionary of the History of Ideas. (2005). *Volunteerism, U.S.* Retrieved from www.encyclopedia.com/social-sciences-and-law/political-science-and-government/ military-affairs-nonnaval/us-volunteerism

30 Eagan, M. K., Stolzenberg, E. B., Ramirez, J. J., Aragon, M. C., Suchard, M. R., & Rios-Aguilar, C. (2016). *The American freshman: Fifty-year trends, 1966–2015.* Los Angeles: Higher Education Research Institute, UCLA.

31 Eagan, M. K., Stolzenberg, E. B., Ramirez, J. J., Aragon, M. C., Suchard, M. R., & Rios-Aguilar, C. (2016).

32 Eagan, M. K., Stolzenberg, E. B., Ramirez, J. J., Aragon, M. C., Suchard, M. R., & Rios-Aguilar, C. (2016).

33 Eagan, M. K., Stolzenberg, E. B., Ramirez, J. J., Aragon, M. C., Suchard, M. R., & Rios-Aguilar, C. (2016).

34 Eagan, M. K., Stolzenberg, E. B., Ramirez, J. J., Aragon, M. C., Suchard, M. R., & Rios-Aguilar, C. (2016).

35 Child Trends. (2015).

36 Child Trends. (2015). *Volunteering.* Retrieved from www.childtrends.org/wp-content/ uploads/2015/12/20_Volunteering.pdf

37 Higher Education Research Institute. (2017). *College Senior Survey.* Data prepared by Higher Education Research Institute.

38 Higher Education Research Institute. (2017).

39 Higher Education Research Institute. (2017).

40 VIA Institute on Character. (2018g). *The VIA Survey of character strengths: United States Gen Z.* Data prepared by The VIA Institute on Character.

41 Seemiller, C. & Grace, M. (2017).

42 Eagan, M. K., Stolzenberg, E. B., Ramirez, J. J., Aragon, M. C., Suchard, M. R., & Rios-Aguilar, C. (2016).

43 Eagan, M. K., Stolzenberg, E. B., Ramirez, J. J., Aragon, M. C., Suchard, M. R., & Rios-Aguilar, C. (2016).

44 Seemiller, C. & Grace, M. (2017).

45 Eagan, M. K., Stolzenberg, E. B., Ramirez, J. J., Aragon, M. C., Suchard, M. R., & Rios-Aguilar, C. (2016).

46 Eagan, M. K., Stolzenberg, E. B., Ramirez, J. J., Aragon, M. C., Suchard, M. R., & Rios-Aguilar, C. (2016).

47 Eagan, M. K., Stolzenberg, E. B., Ramirez, J. J., Aragon, M. C., Suchard, M. R., & Rios-Aguilar, C. (2016).

48 Eagan, M. K., Stolzenberg, E. B., Ramirez, J. J., Aragon, M. C., Suchard, M. R., & Rios-Aguilar, C. (2016).

49 Lopez, M. H., Levine, P., Both, D., Kiesa, A., Kirby, E., & Marcelo, K. (2006). *The 2006 civic and political health of the nation.* Retrieved from http://docplayer.net/12159697-The-2006-civic-and-political-health-of-the-nation-a-detailed-look-at-how-youth-partici- pate-in-politics-and-communities.html

50 Seemiller, C. & Grace, M. (2016).

51 Higher Education Research Institute. (2017).

52 Eagan, M. K., Stolzenberg, E. B., Ramirez, J. J., Aragon, M. C., Suchard, M. R., & Rios-Aguilar, C. (2016).

53 Eagan, K., Stolzenberg, E. B., Ramirez, J. J., Aragon, M. C., Suchard, M. R., & Hurtado, S. (2014).

54 Higher Education Research Institute. (2017).

55 Higher Education Research Institute. (2017).

56 The National World War II Museum. (n.d.d). *Research starters: U.S. military by the numbers.* Retrieved from www.nationalww2museum.org/students-teachers/student-resources/research-starters/research-starters-us-military-numbers

57 Sisk, R. (2012). *9/11 still resonates for some recruits.* Retrieved from www.military.com/daily-news/2012/09/11/911-still-resonates-for-some-recruits.html

58 Sisk, R. (2012).

59 Sisk, R. (2012).

60 Sisk, R. (2012).

61 U.S. Military.com. (n.d.). *Important reasons why people enlist in the military.* Retrieved from www.usmilitary.com/276133/important-reasons-people-enlist-military/

62 Seemiller, C. & Grace, M. (2014).

63 Northeastern University. (2014). *Innovation survey.* Retrieved from www.northeastern.edu/news/2014/11/innovation-imperative-meet-generation-z/

64 Northeastern University. (2014).

65 Cronk, T. M. (2015). *Force 2025 focuses on upcoming "Generation Z."* Retrieved from www.army.mil/article/144295/force_2025_focuses_on_upcoming_generation_z

66 Neely, A. (2016). *The data-driven evolution of U.S. Army marketing tactics.* Retrieved from www.dmnews.com/customer-experience/the-data-driven-evolution-of-us-army-marketing-tactics/article/520982/

67 GoArmy.com. (2018). *U.S. Army commercial: "Narrative 2."* Retrieved from www.youtube.com/watch?v=ovYhA26jK4Q

68 Dunlap, T. (2017). *These 21 kids are suing the federal government over climate change: "Everything is at stake."* Retrieved from http://people.com/human-interest/these-21-kids-are-suing-the-federal-government-over-climate-change-everything-is-at-stake/, para. 3.

69 Dunlap, T. (2017).

70 Eagan, K., Stolzenberg, E. B., Ramirez, J. J., Aragon, M. C., Suchard, M. R., & Hurtado, S. (2014).

71 Stout, D. (2014). *Transgender teen awarded $75,000 in school restroom lawsuit.* Retrieved from http://time.com/3615599/transgender-student-restroom-lawsuit-maine/

72 Chabria, A. (2017). *Immigrant kids can't be detained without their day in court, 9th Circuit rules.* Retrieved from www.sacbee.com/news/local/article159835739.html

73 McCollum, J. (2015). *5 forgotten protests of Generation X.* Retrieved from www.jenx67.com/2015/07/5-forgotten-protests-of-generation-x.html, para. 18.

74 Kessler, J. (2012). *Generation Y: Ready to stand up and be counted.* Retrieved from www.forbes.com/sites/onmarketing/2012/10/24/generation-y-ready-to-stand-up-and-be-counted/#9b5c1c047218, para. 1.

75 Eagan, K., Stolzenberg, E. B., Ramirez, J. J., Aragon, M. C., Suchard, M. R., & Hurtado, S. (2014).

76 Seemiller, C. & Grace, M. (2016).

77 Amatulli, J. & Saltos, G. L. (2018). *These are the biggest marches in U.S. history.* Retrieved from www.huffingtonpost.com/entry/biggest-marches-in-us-history_us_5abdb65e4b008c9e5f527f1

78 Women's March Network. (n.d.). *Youth initiative.* Retrieved from www.womensmarch.com/youth-initiative/

79 Sanchez, R. (2018). *Student marchers call Washington's inaction on gun violence unacceptable.* Retrieved from www.cnn.com/2018/03/24/us/march-for-our-lives/index.html

80 Guadalupe, P. (2017). *Students stage walkouts, rally in Congress to demand Dream Act.* Retrieved from www.nbcnews.com/news/latino/students-stage-walkouts-rally-congress-demand-dream-act-n819346

81 Khatami, E. (2018). *Hundreds of students stage walkout against high school's handling of sexual assault case*. Retrieved from https://thinkprogress.org/boston-area-high-school-students-protest-sexual-assault-case-f5c2fd01f824/

82 Guadalupe, P. (2017).

83 Grinberg, E. & Yan, H. (2018). *A generation raised on gun violence sends a loud message to adults: Enough*. Retrieved from www.cnn.com/2018/03/14/us/national-school-walkout-gun-violence-protests/index.html

84 Garcia, A. (2017). *Students boycott executive order 1100 by not purchasing anything on campus*. Retrieved from https://sundial.csun.edu/2017/10/students-boycott-executive-order-1100-by-not-purchasing-anything-on-campus/

85 Garcia, A. (2017).

86 Zuckerman, E. (2018). *A bright red flag for democracy*. Retrieved from www.theatlantic.com/politics/archive/2018/03/a-bright-red-flag-for-democracy/554777/, para. 9.

87 Swaby, A. (2018). *After Santa Fe massacre, Texas shooting survivors give lawmakers policy solutions*. Retrieved from www.texastribune.org/2018/05/24/after-santa-fe-massacre-texas-shooting-survivors-give-lawmakers-policy/

88 Swaby, A. (2018).

89 Swaby, A. (2018).

90 Pratt-Kielley, E. (2017). *Columbia student and DACA recipient says, "we have to get our voices out."* Retrieved from www.nbcnews.com/news/latino/columbia-student-daca-recipient-says-we-have-get-our-voices-n809551

91 Murphy, B., Jr. (2018). *A 10 year old American Airlines passenger nearly died: Now he's lobbying Congress for change*. Retrieved from https://flipboard.com/@flipboard/-a-10-year-old-american-airlines-passeng/f-fc60171334%2Finc.com

92 Barkley & FutureCast. (2017). *Getting to know Gen Z: How the Pivotal generation is different from Millennials*. Retrieved from www.barkleyus.com/genz/

93 Butler, M. (2011). *Clicktivism, slacktivism, or "real" activism? Cultural codes of American activism in the Internet era* (Unpublished master's thesis). Retrieved from https://scholar.colorado.edu/cgi/viewcontent.cgi?article=1011&context=comm_gradetds

94 Techopedia. (n.d.a). *Slacktivism*. Retrieved from www.techopedia.com/definition/28252/slacktivism

95 Clicktivist. (n.d.). *What is clicktivism?* Retrieved from www.clicktivist.org/what-is-clicktivism/

96 Clicktivist. (n.d.).

97 Clicktivist. (n.d.).

98 Langone, A. (2018). *#MeToo and Time's Up founders explain the difference between the 2 movements: And how they're alike*. Retrieved from http://time.com/5189945/whats-the-difference-between-the-metoo-and-times-up-movements/, para. 21.

99 Sichynsky, T. (2016). *These 10 Twitter hashtags changed the way we talk about social issues*. Retrieved from www.washingtonpost.com/news/the-switch/wp/2016/03/21/these-are-the-10-most-influential-hashtags-in-honor-of-twitters-birthday/?utm_term=.74fc8f639605

100 Gottlieb, J. (2018). *The March for our lives movement is further proof that it's time for the old to follow the young*. Retrieved from https://qz.com/1227378/americas-national-school-walkout-is-further-proof-that-its-time-for-the-old-to-follow-the-young/

101 Seemiller, C. & Grace, M. (2016).

102 Higher Education Research Institute. (2017).

103 Tiller, C. (2011). Philanthro-teens: The next generation changing the world. *Media Planet, 2* (USA Today). Retrieved from http://doc.mediaplanet.com/all_projects/6574.pdf

104 Eagan, K., Stolzenberg, E. B., Ramirez, J. J., Aragon, M. C., Suchard, M. R., & Hurtado, S. (2014).

105 Higher Education Research Institute. (2017).

106 Fuse. (2015). *Your future consumer's views on social activism and cause marketing and how it differs from what Millennials think.* Retrieved from www.fusemarketing.com/thought-leadership/future-consumers-views-social-activism-cause-marketing-differs-millennials-think/

107 Fuse. (2015).

108 Nielsen. (2015d). *The sustainability imperative.* Retrieved from www.nielsen.com/content/dam/corporate/us/en/reports-downloads/2015-reports/global-sustainability-report-oct-2015.pdf

109 Barkley. (2018). *The power of Gen Z influence.* Retrieved from www.millennialmarketing.com/research-paper/the-power-of-gen-z-influence/#download-popup

110 Powell, W. W. & Snellman, K. (2004). The knowledge economy. *Annual Review of Sociology, 30,* 199–220.

111 Brokaw, T. (1998). *The greatest generation.* New York: Random House Trade Paperbacks, p. xxvii.

112 ThoughtCo. (n.d.). *20th century timeline: 1900–1999.* Retrieved from www.thoughtco.com/20th-century-timeline-1992486

113 Gallup & Operation Hope. (2013). *The 2013 Gallup-Hope index.* Retrieved from www.operationhope.org/images/uploads/Files/2013galluphopereport.pdf

114 Weller, C. (2016). *The 10 most inspiring inventors under 18.* Retrieved from www.businessinsider.com/the-greatest-inventors-under-18-2016-5/#kylie-simonds-designed-a-backpack-that-lets-kids-feel-stylish-while-they-undergo-chemotherapy-1

115 Davey, M. (2016). *Australian students recreate Martin Shkreli price-hike drug in school lab.* Retrieved from www.theguardian.com/science/2016/dec/01/australian-students-recreate-martin-shkreli-price-hike-drug-in-school-lab

116 Project Paradigm. (n.d.). *The paradigm challenge.* Retrieved from www.projectparadigm.org/

117 Skild. (2016). *The paradigm challenge.* Retrieved from http://blog.skild.com/blog/2016/09/23/winners-announced-in-first-annual-paradigm-challenge

118 Biznovator. (n.d.). *About us.* Retrieved from www.biznovator.com/about-us

119 Major League Hacking. (2017). *Upcoming hackathons.* Retrieved from https://mlh.io/seasons/na-2017/events

120 Major League Hacking. (2017).

121 Major League Hacking. (2017).

122 EdSurge. (2015). *A guide to hosting youth hackathons.* Retrieved from www.edsurge.com/news/2015-06-24-a-guide-to-hosting-youth-hackathons

123 Educause. (2013). *7 things you should know about makerspaces.* Retrieved from https://net.educause.edu/ir/library/pdf/eli7095.pdf

124 Investopedia. (n.d.). *Social entrepreneur.* Retrieved from www.investopedia.com/terms/s/social-entrepreneur.asp, para. 1, 2.

125 The Elevator Project. (n.d.). *Mission statement.* Retrieved from www.theelevatorproject.org/about-us

126 Shandrow, K. L. (2016). *11 successful kid entrepreneurs keeping their eyes on the prize.* Retrieved from www.entrepreneur.com/slideshow/273222#8

127 Wolf & Wilhelmine. (2015). *Generation Z.* Retrieved from http://democracy.thenext-generation.org/presentations/Hackemer-preview.pdf

22 The future and legacy of Generation Z

• •

Jim Wallis, author of *The Great Awakening*, says, "Each new generation has a chance to alter two basic definitions of reality in our world – what is acceptable and what is possible."[1] It appears that Generation Z is not willing to sit back and accept the world as it is but will strive to conquer the challenges ahead to create a more inclusive, equitable, and sustainable future for all.

What lies ahead

For some in Generation Z, the future seems to have brighter days ahead. Results from the Varkey Foundation indicate that 20 percent of those in Generation Z believe the U.S. is becoming better,[2] and a study by the NORC Center for Public Affairs Research found that more than half believe the country's best days are still ahead.[3] But, for others, it is clear that the future seems bleaker. The study by the Varkey Foundation also uncovered that 40 percent believe the U.S. is becoming worse,[4] and Stillman and Stillman found that 44 percent don't like the future they see coming.[5]

While there are some in Generation Z who have a hopeful outlook on the future, it appears that there is a bit more sentiment of concern with this generation. It's hard not to imagine doom and gloom with the number of dystopian TV shows and movies like *The Handmaid's Tale*, *Hunger Games*, and *Black Mirror* streaming on our devices. And although we all have reason to feel concern, the lack of hopefulness appears to be taking more of a toll on Generation Z. A study by Universum Global found that those in Generation Z are far less hopeful about the future than Millennials,[6] which makes sense in that many young people are worried, stressed, and anxious about nearly everything.[7] To learn more about their thoughts on the future, we asked respondents in our 2017 Generation Z Stories Study, "What will be the most important issues your generation will face in 30 years?" While many shared examples of specific societal issues, there were three themes about how they feel about the future in general that emerged in their responses. These include having to address issues from today that are still unresolved in 30 years, having to reverse course on issues they believe we are moving backward on today, and needing to cleanup a mess left by older generations.[8]

First, our study uncovered that some in Generation Z believe that the issues of tomorrow are essentially the same as issues of today.[9] Comments like "issues from the past have resurfaced in new forms in the present" and "the biggest issues will only be replications of the issues we face today" appeared to be a theme.[10] Some described this phenomenon around specific issues as well, such as highlighting the impact that kicking the can down the road on climate change today will present issues for future generations tomorrow.[11]

> *The most important issues I see for my generation to overcome are all ones that have been laid out by the generations before us.*
>
> — Member of Generation Z

Not only are many in Generation Z concerned about having to address unresolved present-day issues in the future, some in our study identified being worried about regressive social change.[12] These individuals expressed concern that society is moving backward, ultimately requiring their generation to reinstate progress that was once made but has since been reversed.[13] They discussed gaps between privileged and marginalized groups growing, more "environmental disaster and backward social changes" in regard to caring for the Earth, and increases in prejudice and discrimination.[14]

> *I worry that marginalized communities will be further marginalized and that society may continue to regress back to racism, sexism, homophobia, transphobia, classism, ableism, etc.*
>
> — Member of Generation Z

Whether having unresolved issues to deal with or having to reverse what some perceive to be a regression, many in our study also shared their thoughts about feeling burdened by the mess left by older generations.[15] They used language like "pushed aside," "ignored," "destroying without thinking about our generation," and "didn't take precautions" when referring to how older generations have handled certain issues.[16] Some noted that decision-makers who are much older are not making it a priority to address issues that might be more problematic well after they are no longer alive to experience them.[17] They describe it essentially as an issue of negligence by older generations. Others in Generation Z expressed concern that their elders today are knowingly causing problems that they have no incentive to halt.[18] This is less about being negligent and more about being destructive, such as exploiting the Earth's natural resources for profit. Although discontent with older generations may not be unique to Generation Z, their

> *I think our generation worries about the environment, because we are living the outcomes of our parents' mistakes.*
>
> — Member of Generation Z

concern for being handed problems that emerged even before they were born can certainly affect this generation's outlook on the future.

Some in Generation Z, when asked about the most important issues facing their generation in 30 years, simply indicated that either there are "too many to count" or considered that everything will be an issue with comments like, "What won't be?"[19] While it may sound as though their pessimistic and unappreciative views of the contributions of older generations are naïve and disrespectful, it is important to remember two things. First, history is not on their side; their lack of context and experience drop them right in the middle of a story being told. And, it is easy to look back and judge the beginning, especially after not having been a part of it. Second, although many older people are highly invested in the sustainability and longevity of society long after they have passed away, their investment is just simply different from those whose longer life spans give them more of a stake in the game. So, while many members of Generation Z may seem critical of what older generations have left them, it can be valuable to embrace that critique as a way to empower Generation Z youth to improve upon the many amazing contributions already in place.

Issues of the future

From our Generation Z Stories Study, the three issues that this generation appears to be most concerned about in the future are related to the environment, human rights, and technology.[20] Of these, both the environment and human rights are not solely issues of the future, but also major concerns of the present as discussed earlier in the book.[21]

Saving the planet and the people on it

Whether concerns revolved around the impact of the Dust Bowl in the 1930s,[22] DDT as an insecticide in the 1960s,[23] or the Exxon Valdez oil spill[24] and the depletion of the ozone layer in the 1980s,[25] throughout history, people have worried about the future of our environment. Today is no exception. Findings from our Generation Z Stories Study indicate that 38 percent believe that, in 30 years, of all issues facing their generation, those related to the environment will be the most pressing.[26] Stillman and Stillman found similar results in their study as global warming/pollution ranked among the top three things that those in Generation Z would like to change for a better future.[27] As discussed earlier in the book, environmental issues are already a concern for this generation. And from what it appears, many don't see these concerns subsiding with time.

Of all the possible future environmental issues those in Generation Z shared in our study, two emerged most prominently. First, many expressed concern about sustainability and resource depletion, believing that we are simply going to run out of viable food, water, land, and clean air.[28] They made references to using up the little we have now for immediate gratification rather than focusing

> **❝ The earth is being depleted of its resources and habitats are being destroyed and no one really seems to care. ❞**
> *- Member of Generation Z*

> **❝ I think climate change will be regarded as the most pressing issue facing my generation. A rather large percentage of people making decisions about the world today won't be around in the next 30/40 years to see the long-range effects of their work. ❞**
> *- Member of Generation Z*

on a long-term strategy for developing and using renewable resources.[29] Bottom line: They believe we will run out of what we need, and that those who have used or are using most of the resources will be long gone when that happens.[30] Many also worry that it has become acceptable to extract resources and exploit the Earth to increase one's own personal wealth, even if it means poisoning the air, polluting the water, and killing important habitats.[31]

Second, others discussed climate change posing a serious threat to their generation, with some making reference to not even surviving 30 more years if we don't address issues of global warming immediately.[32] With higher temperatures, more droughts and heat waves, and rising sea levels,[33] they fear that that climate change will be a "bigger problem," and that "nothing will challenge us more."[34] But, many point out that politicians who don't believe in climate change science are making decisions now that will have irreversible effects in the future. They use words like "don't believe," "ignore the issue," and "deny it" when describing how they think today's decision-makers are addressing climate change.

Human rights

Over the last century, even in times of peace and national prosperity, prejudice, oppression, and discrimination have been part of the fabric of the U.S. The dark side of the Roaring 20s saw nativist anti-immigration laws, religious oppression,[35] and a resurgence of the Ku Klux Klan.[36] By the 1930s, it seemed the focus was on recovering from the Depression and ushering in the New Deal with new laws around minimum wage, work hour limitations, child labor, Social Security, and unemployment insurance.[37] During this time period, most also favored taking care of America's poorest and most vulnerable by offering free medical care.[38] Although it appears there was positive support to address issues of poverty, anti-immigration sentiments during the recovery from the Depression were still strong. Gallup polling in 1936 and 1937 found that two out of three survey respondents indicated that "'aliens on relief' should be sent back to their 'own countries.'"[39] In addition, despite the glimmer of hope that was offered for racial equality when Franklin Roosevelt took office, many New Deal programs excluded or marginalized African-Americans.[40] The KKK was still active, and racism was rampant.[41] As we know from the history books, much was to come throughout the rest of the century around addressing issues of human and civil rights.

Progress has arguably been made both legally (i.e. civil rights laws, Americans with Disabilities Act, etc.) and culturally (more support for the equitable treatment of individuals, for example, same-sex marriage,[42] and the acknowledgment of racism).[43] But, as discussed earlier in the book, this is

> *There are prejudices and social ideals of decades or even a century ago that have given rise to violence, hatred, and general disrespect.*
> *- Member of Generation Z*

> *I want us to make sure that we learn that America will be at its greatest when it finally learns that we are better as a nation united by our differences than divided by our hatred.*
> *- Member of Generation Z*

a generation still highly concerned about human rights. And many don't believe that these issues will go away in the future. More than 17 percent of qualitative responses included concerns that the world in 30 years might continue to harbor discrimination and oppression; some expressed a fear that it could be even worse than it is today.[44] Despite some expressions of hope for peace in 30 years,[45] nearly every comment about human rights in our Generation Z Stories Study focused on a concern or worry and, in some cases, a true exasperation that we as a society might not be able to advance our hearts, minds, and policies to ensure an inclusive world for all.[46] The concerns appear to cluster into two main areas – prejudice and ignorance as well as inequality.

While some in Generation Z believe that progress is being made in terms of acceptance, others feel prejudice and ignorance are festering and growing.[47] In 30 years, many worry that rather than being more open-minded, people may end up being less so.[48] This move towards more close-mindedness aligns with the research conducted by Yale psychologist, Jennifer Richeson, who found that a substantial number of White people feel threatened at the idea of becoming a minority when racial demographics in the country ultimately shift.[49] Richeson points out feeling threatened can then result in more negative attitudes toward minorities.[50] This phenomenon may also help in explaining nativism. Some Americans feel immigrants will take their jobs, be an economic drain on society, or will not assimilate into America like past immigrants have,[51] which can result in immigrants experiencing prejudice and discrimination. Some Generation Z respondents in our study expressed concern that if prejudice isn't addressed, biased attitudes could manifest into discriminatory, hateful, and even violent behaviors towards others.[52]

> **❝ I think that the prejudices and inhumane views of others that humans are building, if not addressed sooner rather than later, will gradually turn into more severe forms of violence and acts of hate. ❞**
> — Member of Generation Z

> **❝ Equality is a great thing, but while trying to create equality we are also creating a world where nothing is ok anymore. Anything can be taken offensively, and anyone can start a riot about anything. ❞**
> — Member of Generation Z

> **❝ We will be working toward repairing the environment, economy, education system, and racial and social atmosphere so that we and our children don't have to face the same injustices as many people had to in the past. ❞**
> — Member of Generation Z

While the vast majority of Generation Z students in our study discussed prejudice and discrimination against underrepresented populations, a small handful brought up the growing prejudice against those with conservative views.[53] The main concern along these lines involved political correctness having gone too far.[54] In discussing this issue, they used words like "too soft," "being offended by everything," "overly sensitive," and "not every place is going to be a safe place."[55]

In addition to prejudice and ignorance, many in our study shared concerns about having to grapple with issues of inequality in 30 years.[56] Some noted this more generally, while others were quick to point out specific marginalized groups that they believe will continue to be oppressed in the future.[57] The most discussed issue of inequality was related to racism, followed by sexism, and poverty and income inequality.[58] Although gay rights, transgender rights, religious oppression and differences, and ableism were included, there were far fewer references to these specific issues than those around race, gender, and class.[59]

Other issues around human rights that were discussed include concerns around whose story gets told, particular groups having a lack of access to resources, fundamental changes to the allocation of social services, bullying, police brutality, and discriminatory laws and policies.[60] And while these reflect issues of today, many in our study believe they will also be issues in 30 years.[61]

Technology

Each generation has had to think about how technology will advance in their lifetimes, perhaps eliciting a simultaneous sense of optimism and trepidation.

For example, the Century of Progress exposition at the 1933–1934 World's Fair in Chicago was "packed with exhibits predicting technological advances."[62] Some viewed new technology as a "path to a better society,"[63] paving the way for the formation of a new group called the "technocrats" who believed that science and technology would solve the world's problems.[64] But, some during that time feared that rapid advancement would lead to technological unemployment where humans would lose jobs to superefficient machines that could work better and faster.[65] While technology has offered each generation a more modernized approach to life, it makes sense that this advancement can be unnerving as new and unique ethical dilemmas emerge. Our study, in particular, uncovered that more than 14 percent of qualitative responses related to their biggest concerns of the future centered on society grappling with some serious issues related to technology.[66] The issues they identified include an over-dependence on technology, ethical problems emerging from scientific and technological advancements, a reduction in interpersonal interaction and connection, and the replacement of humans with technology.[67]

First, some in Generation Z believe that, in 30 years, society will have become overly dependent on technology.[68] This sentiment is reminiscent of the fears in 1999 when the world was counting down to Y2K, or the year 2000. The shift to the new Millennium was exciting, but there was also angst and fear among many as they hunkered down with food rations and prepared for a technological disaster where computers would crash due to the inability to read a new four-digit year.[69] As we know, everything went smoothly, and, by New Year's morning, people were back to their normal routines. The fear of Y2K is an early reflection of our dependence on technology at the turn of this century. It's been nearly two decades since Y2K, and it appears we may be even more dependent on technology than ever before. Cars are computer-programmed, money has become almost an entirely digital currency transferred through direct deposit and debit purchases, and smartphones have become a necessity for day-to-day communication. Even food at the grocery store is scanned and inventoried electronically. Imagine the U.S. without any computer technology for one day. Then, fast-forward 30 years and then imagine how even more dependent society will have become on technology. The sentiment of many in Generation Z is that we are already overly dependent, and there is a fear that this dependence will grow with time.[70] This reliance on, or what some referred to as an addiction to, technology would cause people to have to constantly learn new skills and platforms just to keep up.[71] Failure to do so would leave people behind. In addition, technology would serve as a substitute for the possession of both

> ❝ While my generation is increasingly headed toward a world that is more technology-oriented and innovative, I fear that technology will advance too far and we will . . . become too dependent on certain inventions and services. ❞
> – Member of Generation Z

knowledge and skills. For example, artificial intelligence would provide information and answers that would no longer need to be derived from human beings.[72] And, because technology could aid in so many activities, people then wouldn't know how to do everyday things that technology could do for them.[73]

Another concern related to technology that is on the minds of those in Generation Z involves the ethics of what technology will allow us to actually do versus what we should do.[74] In 1997, the movie *Gattaca* offered a glimpse into a dystopian future that called attention to the ethics behind technology.[75] The film centers on a hierarchy based on genetic makeup, where individuals who were born genetically modified rather than naturally are afforded more opportunities like better and higher-paying jobs.[76] The ethical issue presented in this movie shifted the concept of discrimination from factors like race, gender, and religion to the actual DNA makeup of one's body.[77] While that movie seemed like true science fiction at the time, today we can clone animals[78] and even engage in human genetic engineering.[79] With scientists getting closer to mastering the technology of biological engineering, it makes sense that some in Generation Z would have some concerns.

> *Is the technology we are developing ethical and responsible, and if it is, how is it positively affecting our culture and environment?*
> – Member of Generation Z

In addition, many in Generation Z discussed that technology is making it harder, not easier, to engage and interact with others.[80] Being that this is the same generation that indicated that communicating in-person is preferred over other forms of communication,[81] many of them point out that the replacement of human interaction with technology is a critical issue that needs to be addressed.

> *Technology is an issue! I am afraid that no one will go out for lunch and talk like normal people anymore. Instead, they will just FaceTime or Skype while they eat take-out at home.*
> – Member of Generation Z

And, some believe they are just as guilty as others when it comes to using their personal devices instead of engaging in face-to-face communication. In fact, comments related to "missing life," loss of "interpersonal connectivity," and "low communication skills" are real fears many in Generation Z have about the repercussions of the overuse of technology, now and in the future.[82]

In addition, some in Generation Z believe that technology sometimes gets in the way of authentic and meaningful interaction with others, even during a moment when there is an opportunity to connect.[83] Sherry Turkle, MIT professor and author of *Reclaiming Conversation*, asserts that devices, like smartphones, provide a comfort or crutch that ensures we won't ever experience boredom.[84] She says, "Actually allowing yourself a moment of boredom is crucial to human interaction and it's crucial to your brain as well. When you're bored, your brain isn't bored at all – it's replenishing itself, and it needs that down time."[85] One respondent in our study even equated the advancement of technology with less activity in the human brain.[86]

While they know that filling those milliseconds of perceived boredom with checking messages, likes, posts, and shares, or even being on their devices in the middle of an in-person interaction can be detrimental, they still acknowledge doing it, and recognize the problems doing so can create down the road.[87]

❝ Everyone is self-absorbed and their eyes are glued to their phone screens. I am one of them too. I find myself scrolling through my Instagram feed while I am at dinner with my family. ❞
– Member of Generation Z

The final concern related to technology expressed by those in our Generation Z Stories Study involves human jobs being overtaken by technology. In the 1930s, Aldous Huxley published *Brave New World*, a futuristic picture of a society in which "humans have become slaves to machines."[88] Although most of Huxley's thoughts of the future have not really come to fruition, automation to some extent has. Over the last 80 years or so, some human jobs have become obsolete and been replaced with technology, for example, the switchboard operator. But as technology advances, so do opportunities to automate more of today's labor force. And some in Generation Z are worried about that,[89] which makes sense given their concerns about getting and keeping a good job.[90]

❝ I think the most important issues my generation will face in 30 years is the fact that technology might be taking over. Technology is great and everything, but the more advanced it gets the more humans might be out of jobs. ❞
– Member of Generation Z

Generation Z's legacy

In March 2015, MTV conducted a study of more than 1,000 kids born after the year 2000 to name their generation.[91] A whopping 544 names were suggested, with Founders ultimately being deemed the winner.[92] The name reflected this generation's role in building a new society free from the problems of the past, or essentially, founding a new world.[93] It doesn't appear that the name Founders really stuck as we don't readily see it in the media. But, the essence of what the name was intended to represent is fairly accurate. This is a generation that truly believes they can and must change the world. And for some, the name Generation Z is reflective of that legacy. In discussing the youth movement for gun control on Twitter, one member of Generation Z posted,

> **❝** *This attitude of 'if we don't do it, nobody will, and I want to be the one to' . . . seems to drive many of the people in my generation to make a difference in the world and accomplish individual greatness. I believe coming from this place of enthusiasm for greater perception, variation, and progression will allow my generation to improve the world in all ways it needs to be improved better than any generation has before.* **❞**
> — Member of Generation Z

"There's a good reason to call us Generation Z, because we will be the ones to end this violence."[94] With Z being at the end of the alphabet, it seems fitting that Generation Z sees themselves as putting an end to some of the problems facing society today.

While major social change might seem more prohibitive to older folks who are backed by years of experience and disillusionment, those in Generation Z are ready to forge ahead and address the world's issues. Participants in our Generation Z Stories Study offered many ideas for doing so, including working around the system as well as focusing on individual rather than institutional change.[95]

Working around the system

Much of the change created by past generations has been a result of either working within or against existing systems. Working within a system involves using the structures, laws, and norms related to that system to create change or make a difference. For instance, running for office is an act that uses an existing system to create change – get elected and create policies. On the other hand, working against a system involves challenging the structures, laws, and norms of that very system. An example might include divestment, which involves challenging the existing economic system by leveraging power to exact behavior from a particular company. Working within and against systems was evident with the Civil Rights Movement in which the judicial system was used to challenge discriminatory laws, and the bus boycott challenged societal norms and policies.

It doesn't appear that working within or against current systems is how many in Generation Z see their legacy in creating change.[96] In the 2017 College Senior Survey, nearly 33 percent of Generation Z college seniors indicated they believed influencing the political structure was not important.[97] And, when asked how their generation could make the world a better place, only 4 percent of the respondents in our Generation Z Stories Study discussed any of the following – holding leadership roles, voting, creating laws, lobbying politicians, or running for elected office.[98] All of those actions take place within an existing system. But, many don't seem to see themselves working against the system either. For example, 68 percent of the respondents from the College Senior Survey had not demonstrated for a cause at any time in their college careers,[99] and, we found in our study that only 1 percent discussed activism as the way their generation will change the world.[100]

While some in Generation Z have more recently become mobilized in challenging existing systems around issues of immigration and gun control, as discussed earlier in the book, they are also engaging in tactics that work right around political and legal systems to address these issues themselves. Take, for example, Justin Rivard, a high school senior from Wisconsin, who created a device in shop class that slides under a classroom door, preventing a school shooter from opening the door.[101] So much for waiting for politicians to deal with this issue . . . Justin and other members of Generation Z are finding their own solutions to the issue of school gun violence.

Individual, not institutional

Another surprising finding from our 2017 study is that many in Generation Z are more drawn to creating individual rather than institutional change.[102] The sentiment would be that if you can change the hearts and minds of people first, necessary legal and systemic changes would follow, rather than the other way around. Three major themes emerged from our study – a commitment to open-mindedness, a focus on conservation, and a determination to bring peace and love to the world.[103]

It is apparent from their concerns about human rights that many are very worried about the possibility of growing bias, prejudice, and even hatred based on differences.[104] Nearly 22 percent of those in our study discussed how being open-minded was what their generation could do to make an impact on the future.[105] They discussed how doing so could lead to a sense of unity and not division, allowing them to work toward ending discrimination and solving major global issues.[106] As a way of fostering open-mindedness, many suggested that their generation would talk to each other, embrace diversity, agree to disagree, develop their own opinions, and learn from others' viewpoints.[107] Not only are many committed to modeling this behavior, they have high hopes that doing so will empower other generations to be open-minded as well.[108]

> *Realizing the differences between us are not merely differences that separate us, but differences that bring us together.*
> – Member of Generation Z

As discussed earlier, many in Generation Z are highly concerned about the future of the planet. They worry about running out of resources, making habitats unlivable for humans and animals, and not stopping the trajectory toward climate change.[109] While there was some discussion of their generation putting environmental laws in place, the approach that many discussed reflected more of an individual rather than an institutional approach to conservation – including individually incorporating a reduce, reuse, and recycle approach.[110] First, several respondents discussed their generation decreasing pollutant use, using less water, reducing driving by instead biking, walking, or carpooling, reducing the purchases of cheap products and those with single-use plastics, buying less stuff ("live lighter lives"), using less technology, buying local to reduce transportation costs, reducing food waste, going vegetarian, and decreasing energy usage.[111] One person even suggested having fewer kids.[112] In regard to reusing, some suggested using more renewable resources and sustainable energy as well as stopping the practice of being wasteful.[113] One suggestion even included using more efficient electronics so as to not have to buy replacements so frequently.[114] Ideas for recycling included commonly known practices such as putting recyclable materials in bins, reducing littering, and cleaning up communities.[115]

> **❝ Our generation will 'create ways to keep our Earth alive and healthy for generations to come.' ❞**
> *- Member of Generation Z*

The third most prominent theme that emerged in our study focuses on loving others as a way to make the world a better place, with 18 percent of all respondents sharing some idea reflective of love.[116] Several commented about the importance of working together, helping others, focusing on the betterment of everyone rather than just themselves, being kind, being respectful, having faith in humanity, spreading positivity, and working toward peace.[117] On the one hand, it's interesting for a generation that is not necessarily overly hopeful about the future, many believe that love can conquer all. But, perhaps it isn't as surprising if you consider that hope is tied to their active role in making a difference. A study by the Varkey Foundation found that 79 percent of those in Generation Z indicated that having more peaceful values among the young generation is what makes them hopeful for the future.[118] And while those in older generations might think of this as naïve, perhaps loving each other really can make a difference.

> **❝ I feel like the root of a better future really is love. Unconditional. Not only toward those who look like us or think like us or whose priorities and orientations resemble ours. I know that answer simplifies really complex issues, and there are actions we have to take to actually make this world a better place, but they all start with love. ❞**
> *- Member of Generation Z*

Conclusion

Feelings of concern for the way things have been done might not be new for a younger generation. But, perhaps Generation Z, like their predecessors, will find ways to leave their legacy that indeed make the world a better place. Jim Wallis, author of *The Great Awakening*, says,

> And that is always how change begins: when things we have long accepted are no longer acceptable, often first to a new generation that can't understand why we have accepted those things for so long. . . . It's time to believe in change again, to dare to dream new possibilities. And the little children may lead us.[119]

" I think we are already working to make the world a better place. People in my generation are fighting for social justice, the earth, and many other wonderful things. I think if we keep going like we are, we WILL make the world better. "
— Member of Generation Z

In fact, many already are.[120]

Notes

1 Wallis, J. (2008). *The great awakening.* New York: HarperCollins, p. 286.
2 Varkey Foundation. (2017). *Generation Z: Global Citizenship Survey.* Retrieved from www.varkeyfoundation.org/what-we-do/policy-research/generation-z-global-citizenship-survey/
3 The Associated Press-NORC Center for Public Affairs Research. (2017). *American teens are politically engaged but pessimistic about country's direction.* Retrieved from www.apnorc.org/projects/Pages/HTML%20Reports/american-teens-are-politically-engaged-but-pessimistic-about-countrys-direction.aspx
4 Varkey Foundation. (2017).
5 Stillman, D. & Stillman, J. (2017). *Gen Z @ work: How the next generation is transforming the workplace.* New York: HarperCollins.
6 Universum Global. (2017). *Generation Z grows up.* Retrieved from http://universumglobal.com/generation-z/
7 Seemiller, C. & Grace, M. (2017). *Generation Z stories study.* Unpublished raw data.
8 Seemiller, C. & Grace, M. (2017).
9 Seemiller, C. & Grace, M. (2017).
10 Seemiller, C. & Grace, M. (2017).
11 Seemiller, C. & Grace, M. (2017).
12 Seemiller, C. & Grace, M. (2017).
13 Seemiller, C. & Grace, M. (2017).
14 Seemiller, C. & Grace, M. (2017).
15 Seemiller, C. & Grace, M. (2017).
16 Seemiller, C. & Grace, M. (2017).
17 Seemiller, C. & Grace, M. (2017).
18 Seemiller, C. & Grace, M. (2017).
19 Seemiller, C. & Grace, M. (2017).
20 Seemiller, C. & Grace, M. (2017).

21 Seemiller, C. & Grace, M. (2017).

22 History.com. (n.d.b). *Dust bowl*. Retrieved from www.history.com/topics/dust-bowl

23 Encyclopedia.com. (2003a). *Environmental movement*. Retrieved from www.encyclopedia. com/earth-and-environment/ecology-and-environmentalism/environmental-studies/ environmental-movement

24 Taylor, A. (2014). *The Exxon Valdez oil spill: 25 years ago today*. Retrieved from www. theatlantic.com/photo/2014/03/the-exxon-valdez-oil-spill-25-years-ago-today/100703/

25 Encyclopedia.com. (2003a).

26 Seemiller, C. & Grace, M. (2017).

27 Stillman, D. & Stillman, J. (2017).

28 Seemiller, C. & Grace, M. (2017).

29 Seemiller, C. & Grace, M. (2017).

30 Seemiller, C. & Grace, M. (2017).

31 Seemiller, C. & Grace, M. (2017).

32 Seemiller, C. & Grace, M. (2017).

33 NASA. (2018). *The consequences of climate change*. Retrieved from https://climate.nasa. gov/effects/

34 Seemiller, C. & Grace, M. (2017).

35 Bruscino, T. A. (2010). *A nation forged in war*. Knoxville, TN: The University of Tennessee Press.

36 Encyclopedia.com. (2006). *The dark side of the 1920s*. Retrieved from www. encyclopedia.com/history/encyclopedias-almanacs-transcripts-and-maps/dark-side-1920s

37 Scholastic. (2018). *The United States turns inward: The 1920s and 1930s*. Retrieved from www.scholastic.com/browse/subarticle.jsp?id=1674

38 Allen, J. T. (2010). *How a different America responded to the Great Depression*. Retrieved from www.pewresearch.org/2010/12/14/how-a-different-america-responded-to-the-great-depression/

39 Allen, J. T. (2010), para. 36.

40 Encyclopedia.com. (2002a). *Black Americans 1929–1941*. Retrieved from www. encyclopedia.com/education/news-and-education-magazines/black-americans-1929-1941

41 Encyclopedia.com. (2002a).

42 Pew Research Center. (2017a). *Changing attitudes on gay marriage*. Retrieved from www. pewforum.org/fact-sheet/changing-attitudes-on-gay-marriage/

43 Neal, S. (2017). *Views of racism as a major problem increase sharply, especially among Democrats*. Retrieved from www.pewresearch.org/fact-tank/2017/08/29/views-of-racism-as-a-major-problem-increase-sharply-especially-among-democrats/

44 Seemiller, C. & Grace, M. (2017).

45 Seemiller, C. & Grace, M. (2017).

46 Seemiller, C. & Grace, M. (2017).

47 Seemiller, C. & Grace, M. (2017).

48 Seemiller, C. & Grace, M. (2017).

49 Resnick, B. (2017). *White fear of demographic change is a powerful psychological force*. Retrieved from www.vox.com/science-and-health/2017/1/26/14340542/white-fear-trump-psychology-minority-majority

50 Resnick, B. (2017).

51 Young, J. G. (2017). Making America 1920 again? Nativism and U.S. immigration, past and present. *Journal on Migration and Human Security*. Retrieved from http://cmsny.org/ publications/jmhs-making-america-1920-again/

52 Seemiller, C. & Grace, M. (2017).

53 Seemiller, C. & Grace, M. (2017).

54 Seemiller, C. & Grace, M. (2017).

55 Seemiller, C. & Grace, M. (2017).

56 Seemiller, C. & Grace, M. (2017).

57 Seemiller, C. & Grace, M. (2017).

58 Seemiller, C. & Grace, M. (2017).

59 Seemiller, C. & Grace, M. (2017).

60 Seemiller, C. & Grace, M. (2017).

61 Seemiller, C. & Grace, M. (2017).

62 Encyclopedia.com. (2003b). *The 1930s science and technology: Overview*. Retrieved from www.encyclopedia.com/social-sciences/culture-magazines/1930s-science-and-technology-overview, para. 1.

63 Encyclopedia.com. (2003b), para. 1.

64 Encyclopedia.com. (2003b), para. 2.

65 The Economist Staff. (2011). *Race against the machine*. Retrieved from www.economist.com/blogs/freeexchange/2011/11/technological-unemployment

66 Seemiller, C. & Grace, M. (2017).

67 Seemiller, C. & Grace, M. (2017).

68 Seemiller, C. & Grace, M. (2017).

69 Rothman, L. (2014). *Remember Y2K? Here's how we prepped for the non-disaster*. Retrieved from http://time.com/3645828/y2k-look-back/

70 Seemiller, C. & Grace, M. (2017).

71 Seemiller, C. & Grace, M. (2017).

72 Seemiller, C. & Grace, M. (2017).

73 Seemiller, C. & Grace, M. (2017).

74 Centers for Genetics and Society. (n.d.). *Human genetic modification*. Retrieved from www.geneticsandsociety.org/topics/human-genetic-modification

75 IMDB. (1997). *Gattaca*. Retrieved from www.imdb.com/title/tt0119177/

76 IMDB. (1997).

77 IMDB. (1997).

78 National Human Genome Research Institute. (2017). *Cloning*. Retrieved from www.genome.gov/25020028/cloning-fact-sheet/

79 Centers for Genetics and Society. (n.d.).

80 Seemiller, C. & Grace, M. (2017).

81 Seemiller, C. & Grace, M. (2016). *Generation Z goes to college*. San Francisco: Jossey-Bass.

82 Seemiller, C. & Grace, M. (2017).

83 Seemiller, C. & Grace, M. (2017).

84 Suttie, J. (2015). *How smartphones are killing conversation*. Retrieved from https://greatergood.berkeley.edu/article/item/how_smartphones_are_killing_conversation

85 Suttie, J. (2015), para. 13.

86 Seemiller, C. & Grace, M. (2017).

87 Seemiller, C. & Grace, M. (2017).

88 Encyclopedia.com. (2003b), para. 4.

89 Seemiller, C. & Grace, M. (2017).

90 Seemiller, C. & Grace, M. (2016).

91 Sanburn, J. (2015a). *Here's what MTV is calling the generation after Millennials*. Retrieved from http://time.com/4130679/millennials-mtv-generation/

92 Sanburn, J. (2015a).

93 White, J. E. (2017). *Meet Generation Z: Understanding and reaching the new post-Christian world*. Grand Rapids, MI: Baker Books.

94 JulienJameelah. (2018). *Twitter post*. Retrieved from https://twitter.com/jameelahjulien?lang=en

95 Seemiller, C. & Grace, M. (2017).

96 Seemiller, C. & Grace, M. (2017).

97 Higher Education Research Institute. (2017). *College Senior Survey*. Data prepared by Higher Education Research Institute.

98 Seemiller, C. & Grace, M. (2017).

99 Higher Education Research Institute. (2017).

100 Seemiller, C. & Grace, M. (2017).

101 Huppert, B. (2018). *High school student invents "JustinKase" tool that could save lives during shooting*. Retrieved from www.usatoday.com/story/news/nation-now/2018/02/20/high-school-student-develops-justinkase-tool-could-save-lives-during-school-shooting/353942002/

102 Seemiller, C. & Grace, M. (2017).

103 Seemiller, C. & Grace, M. (2017).

104 Seemiller, C. & Grace, M. (2017).

105 Seemiller, C. & Grace, M. (2017).

106 Seemiller, C. & Grace, M. (2017).

107 Seemiller, C. & Grace, M. (2017).

108 Seemiller, C. & Grace, M. (2017).

109 Seemiller, C. & Grace, M. (2017).

110 Seemiller, C. & Grace, M. (2017).

111 Seemiller, C. & Grace, M. (2017).

112 Seemiller, C. & Grace, M. (2017).

113 Seemiller, C. & Grace, M. (2017).

114 Seemiller, C. & Grace, M. (2017).

115 Seemiller, C. & Grace, M. (2017).

116 Seemiller, C. & Grace, M. (2017).

117 Seemiller, C. & Grace, M. (2017).

118 Varkey Foundation. (2017).

119 Seemiller, C. & Grace, M. (2017).

120 Wallis, J. (2008), p. 284.

Additional resources

Additional resources for this book can be found at www.routledge.com/
9781138337312

Afterword: The challenge of generational research

The Afterword provides an overview of the common limitations of generational research and how we have taken steps to mitigate these limitations.

Appendix: Study methodologies

Of the hundreds of studies referenced in this book, including our own, there
are some that we draw a considerable amount of data from or make significant
inferences from. The methodologies of these particular studies are listed in the
Appendix along with references to the sources of those studies.

References

The Notes section at the end of each chapter includes all of the references
used in the chapter. A full alphabetical listing of every reference in the book,
however, can be found on the website listed above.

Website

For more information on the authors and Generation Z, go to
www.whoisgenerationz.com.

Index

••

9/11 terrorist attacks 17–18, 147, 171, 249, 253, 283; and Islamophobia 171
1099 economy *see* gig economy
2017 Women's March on Washington 285

abortion 173, 266; rates of 162
abuse: alcohol 160; child 3; emotional 127; physical 127; relationship 127; sexual 127; *see also* digital dating abuse
activism: of Baby Boomer Generation 284; of Generation X 284; of Generation Z 275, 284–288; of Millennial Generation 284; *see also* digital activism
adoption: immigrant 104
Afghanistan 253
Agnosticism: rates of 175
AIDS crisis 8, 123, 161
Airbnb 10, 88, 235, 237
Amazon 41, 43, 91, 197, 215
American Dream 6, 85; Baby Boomer Generation and 6, 85; Generation X and 85–86; Generation Z and 86, 92; G.I. Generation and 4, 20, 85; Millennial Generation and 86; Silent Generation and 85
AOL Instant Messenger 9, 61–62
Apple Music 72
Apple Pay 43, 91
Atheism: rates of 175
attention spans 230; decrease in 208
Atwood, Margaret 71
Awakening Generation 3

Baby Boomer Generation: activism of 284; and American Dream 6, 85; as counterculture 6–7; economic landscape of 7; as "helicopter" parents 7, 9, 10, 102, 106–107, 192; as hippies 6; as parents 102, 104; pop culture of 6; and religion 173, 174, 175, 178; and retirement 7; size of 5–6, 9; and social media 32; social issues influencing 6; and technology 6, 39, 41; and Vietnam War 6; and work 217; as workaholics 7, 8, 240; as "yuppies" 6–7
Baby Boomers *see* Baby Boomer Generation
Big Zs *see various Generation Z subjects*
binge drinking 160
Black Lives Matter 21, 284
Black Thursday 19
blockchain 196, 234
Boy Scouts 68, 101; as Scouts BSA 68
Brokaw, Tom 16, 22, 254
Brown v. Board of Education of Topeka 21, 283
Buddhism 166, 172
bullying 150, 161, 193, 199, 257, 302; *see also* cyberbullying

Carter, Jimmy 168
Catholicism 169–170; and LGBTQ issues 170
Centers for Disease Control and Prevention 127, 137, 139, 158
chatting 59, 61, 115, 118; *see also* Snapchat; video chatting
Christianity 168–170; evangelicals 168, 171; mainline Protestants 168, 171; Religious Right 168; *see also* Catholicism
Church of Jesus Christ of Latter-day Saints, The 170, 173; and LGBTQ issues 170; and women's issues 170
Civil Rights Act of 1964 6, 21
Civil Rights Movement 6, 306

climate change 93, 255–256, 271, 284, 298, 300, 307
Clinton, Bill 268
Clinton, Hillary 17, 22, 31, 265, 267–268
cloning 304
cloud, the 39, 88, 214
college tuition: cost of 82, 193–194; *see also* student loan debt
Columbine: shooting at 192
communication: asynchronous 56; digital 56, 60, 62, 151–152, 230; etiquette 59–60; face-to-face 60–61, 220, 231, 304; online 59; synchronous 56; visual 57–59; *see also* chatting; digital messaging; emailing; instant messaging; phone calling; texting; video chatting
complex cognitive reasoning 215, 227–228
complex problem-solving 228
computers: desktop 8, 39, 41, 63, 104; laptop 40–41, 50, 56, 190, 208; personal 8, 40; technology 303
conversations *see* communication
creativity 228–229, 238, 275, 289–290
critical thinking 227–228, 289
crowdfunding 287
cyberbalkanization 276
cyberbullying 119, 193

DanTDM 75
dating 59, 123–127, 129–130; online 123–125, 129; *see also* digital dating abuse; online dating platforms
Deferred Action for Childhood Arrivals program 19, 285–286
de Toqueville, Alexis 278
digital activism 287–288; clicktivism 287; hacktivism 275; hashtag movements 287; slacktivism 287
digital age 208
digital dating abuse 127
digital footprint 105
digital messaging 56, 62
digital reliving 151–152
Dreamer movement 284; *see also* Deferred Action for Childhood Arrivals program

economy: knowledge 289; service 289; sharing 10, 88; *see also* gig economy
Eisenhower, Dwight D. 267

electronic devices *see* computers; iPad(s); smartphone(s); tablet(s)
emailing 23, 60, 62–64
emojis 57–58, 242
emoticons 57
energy drinks 137–138
environmentalism 255–256, 299–300
environmentally friendly vehicles 93
equality 31, 147, 251, 266, 283, 287–288; gender 20, 22; racial 6, 20–22, 251–252, 276, 301; transgender 253; *see also* income inequality
Europe 18; Eastern 172
European Union 250
Evite 59

Facebook 10, 46–47, 59, 60, 118, 223, 235; *see also* Facebook Messenger; FaceTime
Facebook Messenger 62
FaceTime 61–62, 118, 125, 220
Fam 118
family: cohabiting non-married parents 103; interethnic 103–104; interracial 103–104; multigenerational households 103; nuclear 102–104; same-sex couple parents 103; single mothers 103–104; single-parent 103; stay-at-home fathers 104
feminism 22
freelancing 82, 84–85, 223–224, 237–238, 240, 243, 291; *see also* gig economy
free-range parenting 145

Gates, Bill 235
gay rights 252, 276, 302; *see also* LGBTQ rights
gender 28, 30, 73, 251–252, 302, 304; fluidity 30, 114; identity 192, 251–253; inequality 22; -neutral 30–31, 114; -neutral pronouns 30, 114; norms 104; roles 16–17, 22, 103–104; -specific 31; *see also* transgender
Generation Alpha 41, 107
Generation X: activism of 284; and AIDS 8; and American Dream 85–86; and Cold War 8; as co-piloting parents 106, 109, 192; economic landscape of 8–9; and education 8, 191, 192, 196, 198, 207; identity and characteristics 29; as

latchkey kids 105; and marriage 8–9; as parents 8, 102, 104–107; political climate of 7; pop culture of 8; and religion 169–170, 173, 174, 175; size of 7; social issues influencing 7–9; and social media 32; and technology 8, 39, 41; volunteerism 278; and work 217; and work-life balance 8–9, 105–106

Generation Y *see* Millennial Generation

Generation Z, career aspirations of 213–224; apprenticeships 222, 223–224; desire for financial stability 217–218; enjoyable employment 215–216; flextime 220; freelancing 223–224; fulfilling employment 216–217; and health insurance 218; and internships 223–224; and lifelong learning 218; and making a difference 216; personal growth opportunities 218–219; and telecommuting 219–221; trending career fields 214–215; and tuition assistance 218; work-life balance 220–221; and workplace diversity 219

Generation Z, characteristics of 29–30, 33; communication styles 60–64; diversity of 30–31; as "earbud generation" 72, 209; vs. G.I. Generation 16; identity of 31–32; and innovation 20; as "Mass Shooting Generation" 258; motivations of 32–33; as multiracial 30, 103–104; as parents 102; size of 28; social issues influencing 20–23; and technology 23, 39–51; as "throwback" generation 74; values of 32, 33; as "We" generation 275; as working students 82–83

Generation Z, and civic engagement 274–292; activism 275, 284–288; boycotts 285–286; clicktivism 287; community leadership 282; demonstrations 284–285; digital activism 287–288; fundraising 288; hackathons 290; hacktivism 275; as inventors 290; litigation 283–284; makerspace 290–291; March for Our Lives 258, 285; military service 282–283; as Philanthro-teens 288; school walkouts 285; slacktivism 287; social change oriented 281; social entrepreneurship 291; social innovation 289–291; trends 274–275; volunteerism 278–282; as "We" generation 275

Generation Z, and education 23, 148, 189–199; and college majors 195; and community college 195; and higher education 193–199; and Historically Black Colleges and Universities (HBCUs) 196; and homeschooling 190; K–12 experience 189–193; living at home as young adults 194; MOOCs (massive open online courses) 196; and "safe" spaces 198–199; and standardized testing 191–192; and tuition assistance 218; and vocational schools 195; *see also* Generation Z, and learning

Generation Z, and entertainment 67–76; and gaming 72–74; and hobbies 67–74; and movie attendance 70; and music 71–72; and popular culture 74–75; and reading 68–70; and sports 67–68; and video gaming 73–74; and video watching 70–71

Generation Z, and family 101–109, 148; marriage plans of 108–109; perspective on family 107–109

Generation Z, and friends and peers 113–121; and FOMO ("Fear of Missing Out") 150; and friends 113–119, 148; "Netflix and Chill" 129, 161; and romance 123–130

Generation Z, future of 297–305; climate change 300; environmental issues 299–300; human rights issues 300–302; individual approach 307–308; legacy of 297, 305–309; open-mindedness 307; reduce, reuse, and recycle approach 307–308; technology issues 302–305

Generation Z, and learning 203–210; applied learning 204, 206, 209–210; independent learning 205–206; intrapersonal learning 205, 209–210; lifelong learning 218; relationship with teachers 209–210; unlearning 204; video-based learning 207–208

Generation Z, mental health of 145–153; anxiety rates 149–150; depression rates 149–150, 152; and happiness 148; and harmful online experiences 118–120; impression management and the personal fable 151, 153; and loneliness 120, 152; optimism of 148; and suicide rates 150; and vicarious trauma 150–151, 153; *see also* digital reliving

Generation Z, and money 81–94; and the American Dream 85–86, 92; and banking 89; economic landscape of 19–20, 81–85; financial literacy of 86–87, 92; and Great Recession 19–20, 23, 82, 85, 89, 93; and home ownership 92–93; and investing 93–94; and money 146–147; and philanthropy 94; relationship with money 86–88; and retirement plans 84–85; and saving 89–90; spending habits of 83, 90–91; and student loan debt 82, 91, 108–109

Generation Z, physical health of 135–141; and childhood obesity 138–140; and diet 136–139; and diseases 135–136; and healthcare costs 84, 266; sedentary lifestyle of 139–140

Generation Z, and politics 262–271; 2016 election 268–271; Democrats 263–264; Independents 265; Liberals 264–265; Libertarians 266; political climate of 17–19; political ideologies 262–266; socially liberal-moderate Republicans 265–266; voting 267–268, 269–271

Generation Z, religion/spirituality of 166–180; Buddhism 172; Catholicism 169–170; Christianity 168–170, 171; Church of Jesus Christ of Latter-day Saints 170; Hinduism 173–174; Islam 171–172; Judaism 172–173; religiously unaffiliated 174–177

Generation Z, risky behaviors of 157–163; alcohol use 160; binge drinking 160; drug use 159; sexual activity 160–163; smoking 157–158

Generation Z, societal concerns of 249–258; affordable healthcare 258; climate change 255–256; economy 254–255; education system 249–250; employment/finding jobs 253–254; environmental issues 255–256; gender identity 252–253; human rights 251; immigration 19, 250; inclusion and equality 251–253; poverty 255; privacy 88; racism 251–252; safety and security 256–258; sexism 252; sexual orientation 252; societal divisions 250–251; trust for government 24; violence 257; war 17–18

Generation Z, in the workplace 227–243; creativity of 228–229; critical thinking skills of 227–228; and curator identity 238–239; emotional intelligence of 229–231; employment of 83–84; entrepreneurial spirit of 234–238; and free agent identity 239–240; and influencer identity 239; as intrapreneurs 240; and job search 232–233; leadership skills of 232; social intelligence of 231–232; and video resumes 234; working with Baby Boomers 240–241; working with Gen Xers 241–242; working with Millennnials 242

Generation Z Goes to College Study 29, 33, 45, 47, 61–62, 83, 87–88, 92–93, 114–116, 126, 137, 176, 178, 192–193, 198, 205, 240, 249, 251–252, 255, 257–258, 263, 265, 275, 283–284

Generation Z Stories Study 32, 87, 107, 117, 146, 148, 178–179, 204, 215–219, 251, 255, 263, 266, 279, 297, 299, 301, 305–306

genetic engineering 304

Germany 250; Nazi 19

GIFs 58

gig economy 84–85, 106, 227, 236–238, 243

G.I. Generation: and American Dream 6, 21, 85–86; and banks 89; death of 278; and diet 136; economic landscape of 3–4, 19–20; and education 207; education of 23; and fast food 138; vs. Generation Z 16; and GI Bill 195; and Great Depression 3–6, 18–20, 23, 68, 89, 101–102, 282; and health insurance 141; and higher education 197, 204; and immigration 18–19; and innovation 20; inventions of 289; living at home as young adults 194; and New Deal 19–20, 81, 300–301; Nobel Prizes of 229; optimism of 148; as parents 4–6, 101; political climate of 3, 17–19; and religion 180; sexual activity 160; size of 3; and smoking 157; social innovations of 289; social issues influencing 3–4,

20–23; and technology 39, 40; and trust
for government 23–24; and vocational
education 195; and voting 267; in
World War II 4–6, 17–19, 21, 23, 102,
123, 158, 160, 172, 195, 249, 274, 282
Girl Scouts 68, 101
GoFundMe 94, 288, 291
Gomez, Selena 71, 75
Google 40, 45, 67, 75, 116, 190, 223; apps
190; as verb 45
Google Classrooms 192, 205
Google Docs 190
Google Hangouts 62, 220
Google Maps 44
Gorbachev, Mikhail 250
Gore, Al 268
GQ 276
Great Depression 3–6, 18–20, 23, 68, 89,
101–102, 282; Black Thursday 19; New
Deal 19–20, 81, 300–301
Greatest Generation see G.I. Generation
Greatest Generation, The 16, 22; see also
Brokaw, Tom
Great Recession of 2008 19–20, 23, 82, 85,
89, 93; bank bailout 89
GroupMe 61, 117
Groupon 10
group text messaging 117
group video messaging 118
GrubHub 43
gun control 257, 271, 285–286, 305, 307
gun violence 257–258, 285, 307; March for
Our Lives 258, 285

Handmaid's Tale, The 71, 257, 297
"hanging out" 118, 126, 127, 129, 145
Harding, Warren 17
He, Megan 277; Greenversal channel 277
healthcare 39, 44, 140–141, 218, 258;
access to 258; affordable 258; cost of
84; employer-sponsored 84; plans 258;
providers 44; specialist 237; women's
251; see also universal healthcare
higher education 10, 23, 90, 193, 197, 203,
221; cost of 23, 250, 270; see also college
tuition
Hinduism 173–174
Historically Black Colleges and Universities
(HBCUs) 196

Hogg, David 285
"hooking up" 129
Hoover, Herbert 267
households: with cohabiting non-married
parents 103; dual-parent employed 7,
105; with female breadwinners 104;
interethnic 103; interfaith 169–170,
174; interracial 103; multigenerational
22–23, 103; same-sex 103; single-faith
174; single-mother 103; single-parent
103; white picket fence 6
Houseparty 118
housing bubble burst 92–93, 147, 249, 253
Hulu 42, 71
Hunger Games, The 28, 70, 256, 297
Huxley, Aldous 305; Brave New World 305

identity theft 88
immigration 16–19, 173, 250, 266, 286,
300, 307
Immigration and Naturalization Service 19
inclusion 9, 31, 179–180, 196, 251–253,
263, 283
income inequality 302
information literacy 203–204
Instagram 10, 28, 32, 46–47, 57, 75,
115–116, 121, 151; celebrities 75
instant messaging 61, 63
intelligence: artificial 214, 304; creative
214; emotional 229–231; social 214,
231–232
Internet 10, 23, 40, 42, 45–46, 48–49,
50, 58, 62, 71–72, 105, 119, 162, 204,
207–208, 230, 241, 253, 257, 262, 276
iPad(s) 41
Iraq 253
Islam 166, 171–172, 179; Islamophobia 171

James, LeBron 75, 239
Jennings, Jazz 75
Jobs, Steve 235
Judaism 172–173
juvenile crime rates: decrease in 157

K–12 education system: cursive writing 191;
"Googlification" of 190
Kahn Academy 190
Kardashians 6, 75
Kennedy, John F. 24

Kennedy, Robert F. 5
Kickstarter 94, 288, 291
King, Martin Luther Jr 5–6
knowledge economy 289
Ku Klux Klan 300–301

LDS Church *see* Church of Jesus Christ of
     Latter-day Saints
learning: applied 198, 204, 206, 209–210;
     collaborative 205; emotional 230;
     experiential 209; flipped 205–206;
     group 198, 206; hands-on 204, 206;
     hybrid 205; independent 205–206, 240;
     interpersonal 205; intrapersonal 205,
     209–210; lifelong 218; peer-to-peer
     education 205; self-directed 205; self-
     paced 210; social 205, 209, 230; surface
     level 228; video-based 207–208
LGBTQ community: bullying 150, 193, 251;
     online dating 124–125; and the Mormon
     Church 170; sexual assaults 162
LGBTQ rights 177, 251
LGBTQ youth 150, 162, 193; and bullying
     150, 193; sexually assaulted 162
LinkedIn 230, 233–234
Little Zs 73, 75, 287; *see also various
     Generation Z subjects*
"live chilling" 118

makerspaces 204, 290–291
Malone, Moses 239
March for Our Lives 258, 285
marijuana 159; legalization of 159, 266
Marjory Stoneman Douglas High School:
     shooting at 192, 257, 286–287
Marshall, Thurgood 21
McConnell, Mitch 252
media bias 276
Medicare 84, 289
memes 47, 57–58, 252; niche 58
MeToo movement 162, 287
Mexico 19, 250
Microsoft 41, 223
Middle East 17–18
military service 282–283
Millennial Generation: activism of 284;
     and American Dream 86; and baby bust
     84; "boomerang" effect 102; economic
     landscape 10; and education 9, 191, 192,

196, 198, 205, 207; family decisions of 10;
     identity and characteristics 29; incomes
     of 10; living at home as young adults 194;
     and marriage 9; marriage plans of 108; as
     "Me" Generation 275; optimism of 10,
     148; as parents 102, 104; as "participation
     trophy" generation 33; pop culture of 9;
     and religion 169–170, 173, 174, 175;
     size of 9; and social media 10–11, 32;
     spending habits of 10–11; and student
     loan debt 10, 109; and technology 9–10,
     39, 41; volunteerism 278–282; and voting
     268–269; and work 217–218; and work-
     life balance 220–221
Monster Worldwide Inc. 216, 218, 234
MOOCs (massive open online courses) 196
Mormon Church *see* Church of Jesus Christ
     of Latter-day Saints
MTV 8, 70, 268, 305
music 41, 44–45, 68, 71–72, 170, 191, 198,
     209: streaming 72, 76; *see also* Apple
     Music; Pandora; Spotify
Musk, Elon 235

nativism 19, 173, 300–301
Nazi Germany 19
Netflix 42, 71, 197, 208; "Netflix and Chill"
     129, 161
NeverAgain movement 287
Nobel Peace Prize 274
No Child Left Behind Act 191

Obama, Barack 17, 31, 264, 268
Obama Administration 255
Obergefell v. Hodges 283
Occupy Movement 284
on-demand economy *see* gig economy
O'Neal, Shaquille 239
online dating platforms 123–125; Bumble
     123; eHarmony 123–124, 125; Grindr
     123; Hinge 123; Match.com 123;
     OKCupid 123; Tinder 123
online influencers 114–115
online peer community 116
optimism 10, 148, 302; decline of 147–148
organized religion 176; future of 179–180

Pakistan 274
Pandora 71–72

parenting 101–107, 241; co-pilot 106, 109, 192; free-range 145; helicopter 9, 102, 106–107; same-sex couple 103; sharenting 105
parenting trends 101–107
Parent-Teacher Association (PTA) 192, 282
Parks, Rosa 6, 21
payment portals 43; Apple Pay 43, 91; PayPal 43, 91, 235; Venmo 91; Visa Checkout 91
Pearl Harbor 18–19, 21, 282
personalized medicine 140–141, 290
phone calling 63–64
political correctness 253, 302
Postcards to Voters 277–278
post-Millennial generation *see* Generation Z
poverty 3, 179, 255, 281, 291, 300, 202
privacy 47–48, 88, 198; breeches 88; functions 48; online 48, 105; personal 125; settings 32
Prohibition 4, 160
Punchbowl 59
push notifications 44–45

racial equality 6, 20–21, 251, 276, 301
racial inequality 20–22
racism 20–22, 251–252, 270, 275, 301–302
radio 5, 18–19, 39–40, 45, 72, 150, 262, 276, 289–290; car 19; golden age of 5; transistor 72
reading 41, 68–70, 83, 191, 203, 208, 236, 275; rates 68–70
Reagan, Ronald 250
Recycling 308
Reddit 48
Robinhood 93
Roe v. Wade 15, 283
Roosevelt, Franklin 21, 24, 267, 301
Roosevelt, Theodore 3
Rosie the Riveter 4, 22

Sallie Mae 82–83, 90, 193–195
same-sex marriage 9, 173, 266
Sanders, Bernie 5, 265
Sandy Hook: shooting at 192
school shootings/violence 192–193, 257, 285–287
service economy 289
sexism 252, 302

sexting 62
sexual orientation 28, 30, 114, 193, 251–252
sexual violence 162–163
sharenting 105
sharing economy 10, 88
Shark Tank 28, 290
side hustle 237–238
Silent Generation: and American Dream 85; death of 278; economic landscape of 4–5; and Great Depression 4–5; as parents 101–102; political climate of 4–5; pop culture of 5; and religion 174; size of 4; and technology 39, 40; and World War II 4–5
Siri 228
Skype 61–62, 118, 125, 220
smartphone(s) 21, 40–45, 49, 50, 57, 59, 61, 63, 72–73, 121, 126, 190, 234, 241–242, 289, 303–304
smoking 157–158, 163; rates of 157–158
Snapchat 10, 32, 46–47, 57, 59, 118–119, 125–127
social entrepreneurship 289, 291
social media 10–11, 20, 23, 32, 39, 44–47, 51, 56–58, 60, 62–63, 72, 75, 105, 113, 115–120, 124–126, 128–129, 151–152, 162, 193, 203, 232–233, 241–242, 262, 268, 276–277, 280, 287–288; and dating 124–125; and GPS 44; for job recruitment 233; messaging 63, 288; and public displays of affection 126, 129; and self-esteem 50; *see also* Facebook; Instagram; Snapchat; Spotify; Tumblr; Twitter; YouTube
Social Security 7, 82, 84, 88, 300
Spotify 10, 44, 72, 196
standardized testing 191–192
Starbucks 90, 138, 153, 197
STEM 229, 290; move to STEAM 229
student loan debt 82, 91, 108–109
suburbs 4, 6, 21, 85–86
sustainable foods 136–137

tablet(s) 40–42, 45, 56, 69, 73, 190, 208, 210, 290
Taliban 274
TED-Ed 190
teen pregnancy: rates of 161–162

Teen Vogue 276
telecommuting 219–220
television 6, 39–40, 42, 45, 70–71, 150, 253, 256, 262, 276; cable 42, 70; Golden Era of 70; network 42; streaming 42, 290
terrorism 18
texting 23, 56, 59–64, 117–118, 125, 128, 213, 242; group 117–118; see also sexting
text messaging see texting
TimesUp movement 287
transgender 68, 75, 192, 253, 284; equality 253; rights 302; service member 283
Truman, Harry 24
Trump, Donald 17, 19, 264, 268–269
Tumblr 10, 28, 48
Twitch 74
Twitter 28, 31, 46–48, 57, 75, 285, 305

Uber 10, 88, 196
United Kingdom 250–251; Brexit 250–251
United States 16–17, 22, 28, 30, 63, 68, 73–74, 108, 162, 167, 189, 221, 252, 267, 297, 300; Buddhism in 172; Catholicism in 169; Christianity in 168, 170; college counseling centers in 149; computers/tablets in 40–41, 303; disease in 135; education in 250; GDP 20; gender equality in 22; happiness in 148; healthcare in 218, 266; Hinduism in 173; immigration to 18–19, 166, 171–173; Islam in 171–172; Judaism in 172–173; loneliness in 120; marriage in 103; Mexico border wall 250–251; Mormonism in 170; population 103, 168–170, 172–173; racial inequality in 21; racism in 252; religiosity in 167; same-sex marriage in 252; sexism in 252; sexual behavior in 160; televisions in 42; volunteerism in 278
United States Report Card on Physical Activity for Children and Youth 139
universal healthcare 16, 266
U.S. Army 283; Force 2025 plan 283
U.S. Census Bureau 102, 267
U.S. Congress 19, 21, 287
U.S. Constitution 191
user-generated content 39, 45
U.S. Senate 252
U.S. Supreme Court 5, 283

vaping 158, 163
vicarious trauma 150–151
video: streaming 71, 76; see also YouTube
video-based learning 207–208
video chatting 44, 56–57, 61–62, 118, 121, 125–126
video gaming 33, 72–76, 116; Atari 73; Fortnite 72; multi-player 74; New Yahtzee with Buddies 72; Nintendo 73; PlayStation 72; Pokémon Go! 74; virtual reality 73; Words with Friends 72; Xbox 72
Voices of Youth 277
volunteerism 278–282; as career preparation 280
voting 262–265, 267–271, 276, 306; behavior 263, 265, 270; patterns 262, 264, 267, 269; see also various generational cohorts

Wallis, Jim 179, 297, 309
Walters, Barbara 75
War on Terror 17–18
Warren, Elizabeth 252
Washington, DC 6, 253, 285, 287
Waze 44
wearable technology 40, 42–43, 56
Web 2.0 10, 45–46
WhatsApp 62, 117
Wikipedia 203
Wilson, Woodrow 3, 17
women's rights 6, 22, 276
World Economic Forum 228–231
World War I 18
World War II 4–6, 18–19, 21, 23, 102, 123, 158, 160, 172, 195, 249, 274, 282; post-5, 103; D-Day 17; see also Pearl Harbor

xenophobia 18

Yelp 44
Yousafzai, Malala 274
YouTube 28–29, 42, 45, 74–75, 105, 115, 190, 207–208, 228, 257, 277, 280; see also YouTube celebrities; YouTube Red
YouTube celebrities 75–76
YouTube Red 72

Zuckerberg, Mark 10, 235

Printed in the United States
by Baker & Taylor Publisher Services